Diversity as
Strategic Opportunity

A volume in
Ethics in Practice
Robert A Giacalone and Carole L. Jurkiewicz, *Series Editors*

Ethics in Practice

Robert A Giacalone and Carole L. Jurkiewicz, *Series Editors*

Educating in Ethics Across the Professions: A Compendium of Research, Theory, Practice, and an Agenda for the Future (2022)
    Richard M. Jacobs

How to Transform Workplace Bullies into Allies (2020)
    Jacqueline A. Gilbert

Radical Thoughts on Ethical Leadership (2017)
    Carole L. Jurkiewicz and Robert A. Giacalone

Ethics and Risk Management (2015)
    Lina Svedin

Organizational Ethics and Stakeholder Well-Being in the Business Environment (2014)
    Sean Valentine

Ethics Training in Action: An Examination of Issues, Techniques, and Development (2013)
    Leslie E. Sekerka

Ethics and Crisis Management (2011)
    Lina Svedin

Toward Assessing Business Ethics Education (2010)
    Diane L. Swanson and Dann G. Fisher

Doing Well and Good: The Human Face of the New Capitalism (2009)
    Julian Friedland

Critical Theory Ethics for Business and Public Administration (2008)
    David M. Boje

Advancing Business Ethics Education (2008)
    Diane L. Swanson and Dann G. Fisher

Human Resource Management Ethics (2006)
    John R. Deckop

Positive Psychology in Business Ethics and Corporate Responsibility (2006)
    Robert A. Giacalone, Carole L. Jurkiewicz, and Craig Dunn

Diversity as Strategic Opportunity

Exploring New Paths to Good Administration

edited by

Anna Simonati
Università degli Studi di Trento

INFORMATION AGE PUBLISHING, INC.
Charlotte, NC • www.infoagepub.com

Library of Congress Cataloging-in-Publication Data

A CIP record for this book is available from the Library of Congress
http://www.loc.gov

ISBN: 979-8-88730-547-9 (Paperback)
979-8-88730-548-6 (Hardcover)
979-8-88730-549-3 (E-Book)

Copyright © 2024 Information Age Publishing Inc.

All rights reserved. No part of this publication may be reproduced, stored in a retrieval system, or transmitted, in any form or by any means, electronic, mechanical, photocopying, microfilming, recording or otherwise, without written permission from the publisher.

Printed in the United States of America

CONTENTS

Prologue ix
Jean-Michel Eymeri-Douzans

Foreword—Integrity and Diversity of Governance:
Some Food for Thought xiii
L. W. J. C. Huberts

Acknowledgements xxxvii
Anna Simonati

Introduction xxxix
Anna Simonati

SECTION I
GENDER DIVERSITY AND EMPOWERMENT

1 Gender and Leadership: Issues and Implications for Women in Tyrol, Austria 3
   Wendy Farrell

2 Leadership Development Programs for Women as a Means to Achieve Gender Equality: What Do Women Think? 23
   Marjukka Mikkonen

v

3 Reflections on Equal Democracy, Equal Opportunities, and
   Pluralism: Against the Trivialization of Gender Quotas 45
   Giovanna Iacovone

4 Muslim (Migrant) Women Wearing the Headscarf in the
   Workplaces: Does the 2021 *WABE* and *MH* Judgment of the
   EU Court of Justice Promote Equal Treatment in (Private)
   Employment and Occupation? 63
   Arianna Pitino

SECTION II
DIVERSITY, POLICIES, AND ADMINISTRATIVE ACTION

5 Advancing Social Equity in Public Services: The Role
   of Artificial Intelligence 79
   Anna Maria Chiariello and Rocco Frondizi

6 Equal Treatment and Law Relating to Right to Be Forgotten
   (RTBF): An Examination of Some Judicial Decisions
   With Special Reference to the European Union and India 95
   Jyoti Rattan and Vijay Rattan

7 Mission United—Organizationally Divided: Inter-Sectorial
   Collaboration in the Hungarian Approach to Servicing
   Ukrainian Refugees 123
   *Agnes Jenei, Réka Zsuzsánna Máthé, Maliga Reddy,
   and Strinivasan Pillay*

8 Equal Treatment and Enhancement of Diversity: The Role
   of Urban Regeneration Practices 143
   Annalisa Giusti

SECTION III
DIVERSITY AND EQUAL TREATMENT IN THE EDUCATIONAL SYSTEM

9 Diversity and Diversity Management at Austrian Universities 159
   Esther Happacher, Lamiss Khakzadeh, and Alexandra Weiss

10 Gender Matters in Gender Difference Perceptions: The Case
of University of Rome Tor Vergata 171
*Marianna Brunetti, Nathalie Colasanti, Annalisa Fabretti,
and Mariangela Zoli*

11 Inclusion and Diversities in Italian Schools Between Theory
and Practice: A Legal Analysis 195
Stefania Baroncelli

12 Digitalization and the Education System: What Prospects
for Building a Truly Inclusive System? 223
Loredana Giani

13 Students With Migrant Background: Diversity and Equal
Treatment in Italian Schools 247
Orsolya Farkas

Closing Remarks 275
Anna Simonati

About the Contributors 285

PROLOGUE

It is for me a great pleasure and a real privilege to write a friendly prologue to the present scientific volume, since its editor, Professor Anna Simonati, from the University of Trento, is not only a respected specialist in administrative law in Italy, but is also a pillar of the European Group for Public Administration (EGPA) community of scholars, and, above all, is a friend whose way of approaching life as well as academic and research activities is close to mine.

A couple of years ago, Prof. Anna Simonati, with a nice team of co-chairpersons, namely Professor Esther Happacher from the University of Innsbruck, Assistant Professor Bice Della Piana from the University of Salerno, Professor Lamiss Khakzadeh also from the University of Innsbruck, Dr. Nathalie Colasanti from Tor Vergata University in Rome, and Assistant Professor Noemi Rossi from the University of Reggio Calabria, has taken the initiative to propose the establishment of a new Permanent Study Group of EGPA, devoted to exploring the issues of growing importance related to Public Administration, Diversity and Equal Treatment. As EGPA President, it was an honour for me to propose to my fellow colleagues sitting at the EGPA Steering Committee to validate the creation of that 23rd Permanent Study Group of our learned society: PSG XXIII.

Thanks to its proactive promoters, that newly established PSG organized very rich and fruitful panels at the major annual rally of our European scholarly community, the 44th EGPA Annual Conference, held in Lisbon, Portugal, in early September 2022. It is no exaggeration to express how glad I am to see that—only one year after the event!—the present volume, which

---

Diversity as Strategic Opportunity, pages ix–xi
Copyright © 2024 by Information Age Publishing
www.infoagepub.com
All rights of reproduction in any form reserved.

collects the best papers from Lisbon panels, is ready for publication with IAP, under the insightful and appealing title *Diversity as Strategic Opportunity*, with the programmatic subtitle *Exploring New Paths to Good Administration*.

It is remarkable—but no real surprise!—that the multidisciplinary team of 24 high-level co-authors of the volume, who come from the Septentrion of Europe to its *Mezzogiorno*, and from Western to more Oriental countries, is essentially composed of female colleagues.

The chapters they offer to our reading and reflexion, are distributed into three main sections: the first one explores the fundamental but so delicate issues of "gender diversity and empowerment"; the second poses the difficult question of the articulation between "diversity, policies and administrative action"; while the third and latest focuses on the apparently more specific but so decisive issue of "diversity and equal treatment in the educational system." The architecture of the book allows the co-authors to explore a great variety of subject matters whose social and political salience is often very high, such as the diversity policies implemented at Italian or Austrian universities, the equal treatment of students with migrant origin, the rules on gender quotas and their impact in our postmodern democracies, the case law on Muslim women wearing the headscarf in the workplaces, or the role of Artificial Intelligence in fostering better social equity in public services. Thus, there is no risk for the future readers of such a book to get bored while exploring its various facets.

In her enlightening introduction and conclusion, which represent important contributions to the advancement of the state-of-the-art debates on the evolutions and contemporary reformulations of the principle of equality, from a rather low-profile general prohibition of unfair treatments and discriminations to a more ambitious and proactive vision of equality as a goal to be sought and achieved, Anna Simonati introduces and develops the dialectical, "double" nature of diversity in our contemporary world. Indeed, diversity appears as a genuine biface Janus, one face—we hope that it is the one looking at the past—being diversity as possible source for too frequent forms of explicit or more hidden discriminations, whereas the more radiant face—the one oriented towards the future of our civilization, hopefully—is diversity as a source for richness in society, and future enrichments in public law and public administration as action, practice and craft.

Therefore, the whole volume can be seen as a real contribution from distinguished members of our EGPA family to the advancement of the agenda set, under the leadership of Geert Bouckaert and Werner Jann (Eds.), by the *European Perspectives for Public Administration. The Way Forward* (Louvain, Leuven University Press, 2020), where, amongst others, the issue of how our future legal and administrative orders will have to cope in a better way with increasing diversities of all kinds, is highlighted as being of the utmost importance if public administration wants to remain properly related to our complexifying societies as the legitimate body of servants of our more and more demanding citizenries and exigent polities. Our gratitude to Professor Anna Simonati and her team for their enrichment of the collective critical thinking of the EGPA community on the future(s) of public administration on our continent!

—**Jean-Michel Eymeri-Douzans**
Exceptional Class Professor & Vice-Rector of Sciences Po Toulouse
President of the European Group for Public Administration
(EGPA/GEAP), Brussels

FOREWORD

INTEGRITY AND DIVERSITY OF GOVERNANCE

Some Food for Thought

L. W. J. C. Huberts[1]
Vrije Universiteit Amsterdam

This challenging book about *Diversity as Strategic Opportunity: Exploring New Paths to Good Administration* is interesting for a broad (academic) audience. But how does it relate to the field of study I am involved in: the quality and in particular the integrity of governance?

When Anna Simonati asked me to write a brief contribution (a 'blurb') for this book, I was a bit in doubt because—as far as I know—there is only a limited amount of reflection on the relationship between the two principles or values of good administration and good governance: integrity and diversity/inclusiveness/anti-discrimination. At the same time that doubt was accompanied by being intrigued by the topic which in the end led to this contribution.

I will first present an overview of the basics of the field of study I am involved in.[2]

Diversity as Strategic Opportunity, pages xiii–xxxv
Copyright © 2024 by Information Age Publishing
www.infoagepub.com
All rights of reproduction in any form reserved.

This starts with a brief sketch of what integrity (of governance) is about (different views), what integrity violations are about and that we have to be specific and careful when we put someone's integrity into question (danger of integritism).

After that a brief sketch of the content of diversity inclusiveness, equality and equity will follow, leaning on Anna Simonati's remarks in the starting and concluding chapters of this book and some additional search om the internet (§4).

In the next paragraph I continue my search but now more specifically on the relationship between integrity (and integrity violations) and diversity (and anti-discrimination) and the bodies of knowledge they are part of. In the last paragraph (§6), I will use the presented knowledge to reflect on the two values and their relationship. Work in progress, more essayistic then scientific, but who knows useful. I thus hope to offer some food for thought, for scholars in the two fields of study. Some is obvious it seems, with discrimination as a type of integrity violation (behavior in conflict with relevant moral norms and values). But... are politicians and civil servant that are doubtful about diversity and equality thus acting without integrity? Food for discussion...

INTEGRITY (OF GOVERNANCE)[3]

What is integrity in my view?[4] In our research we focus on the integrity of governance. Governance is nowadays a popular concept (Bevir, 2009; Fukuyama, 2016), we define it as "authoritative policy-making on collective problems and interests and implementation of these policies" (Huberts, 2014, p. 68). This idea of governance includes public as well as private organizations. Public and corporate governance do of course differ, also public and corporate integrity. Acting with integrity as a (prime) minister or top civil servant differs from acting as an integritous[5] Chief Executive Officer (CEO), a board member or employee in a company. Nevertheless, in both contexts integrity refers to the same characteristic of that behavior. But what is integrity?

In the literature on public ánd business ethics and integrity, many views or perspectives or definitions can be found, at last eight perspectives (Huberts, 2014, 2024).

A dominant perspective, Montefiore and Vines (1999, p. 9) concluded, is in line with the meanings of the Latin integras: intact, whole, harmony, with integrity as "wholeness" or completeness, as consistency and coherence of principles and values (in Dutch often summarized with 'you say what you think and you do what you say'...). Another view sees integrity as professional wholeness or responsibility (including a view with a focus on taking into account the environment): "integrity means that a professional exercises his tasks adequately, carefully and responsibly, taking into account all relevant interests" (Karssing, 2007, p. 3).

Other perspectives focus on one or more other specific values (Dobel, 2016); for example incorruptibility, honesty, impartiality, accountability (as also in many codes of conduct). A view that fits into this category relates integrity to virtues, with integrity as acting in line with virtues such as wisdom; justice; courage; and temperance (Becker & Talsma, 2016; Van Tongeren & Becker, 2009).

In other views the relationship between integrity and morals is more prominent (what is right and wrong, good or bad). The first sees integrity as open reflection on morals (Carter, 1996). Three other viewpoints see integrity more as an umbrella concept, one that combines sets of values that are relevant for the functionary being judged. Among these is the more legal view that seems attractive because of the clarity of laws and rules on what matters (Lee & Rosenbloom, 2005).

The seventh perspective argues that a broader interpretation is necessary, also because the 'law' does not always offer clear guiding principle for many aspects of actual decision making and implementation processes in government and business, with an interpretation therefore in terms of complying with the relevant moral values and norms (see, e.g., Fijnaut & Huberts, 2002; Paine, 1994; Uhr, 1999; also Integrity–Wikipedia).[6] This interpretation, of course, comes close to "a general way of acting morally" and "morality" (Brenkert, 2004, p. 5), or, as De George (1993) put it, "[a]cting with integrity is the same as acting ethically or morally" (p. 5).

The last view sees integrity as the "stuff of moral courage and even heroism" (Brenkert, 2004, p. 5), which means that it "stands for complying in an exemplary way with specific moral standards" (Van Luijk, 2004, p. 39).

Behavior and Process Versus Outcome

All interpretations of integrity focus primarily on the behavior of the participants in governance, in decision making and decision implementation. That is, it does not concern everything in politics and business; integrity concerns behavior, process, and procedure (in a broad sense). It is not about the content of the output or the societal results (outcome).

The ethics of the content of decisions, policies, goods and services should thus be distinguished from the "moral quality" of the governance process. Policy ethics and business ethics concerning the output and the outcome are very important but should be distinguished from the integrity of the involved actors.

To simplify: a government can decide to go to war (or not) or to limit immigration (or not) with or without a process of policy and decision making (and implementation) in line with the valid moral values and norms for that process.

Integrity as Moral Quality (Huberts, 2018, p. 21)

In this contribution integrity is seen as the quality of acting in accordance or harmony with relevant moral values, norms, and rules That is, of course, not an original approach. Much of the literature on integrity considers integrity to be synonymous with being moral or ethical, which is, to a certain extent, in line with the presented perspective. What is often missing then is a clarification. What, for example, is a value or norm, a moral value or norm, a relevant or valid moral value or norm?

Defining integrity in terms of the accordance with relevant moral values, norms, and rules requires understanding of what a moral value, norm, or rule is; of what is meant by ethics, morals, and morality. Despite agreement that both concern "right and wrong" or "good and evil," different interpretations of the terms abound, especially in the realm of philosophy and the study of ethics. The terms "ethical" and "moral" are almost always used as synonyms, both denoting the principle of right and wrong in conduct (Thompson, 1985), acknowledging that "ethics" is also seen as the study of such principles (Huberts, 2014, pp. 49–50).

Kaptein and Wempe (2002, pp. 40–42) distinguished six features exhibited by moral pronouncements. They concern "right and wrong" (a normative judgment that expresses approval or disapproval, evokes shame or pride), but they also appeal to the general consent; are not a matter of individual taste; apply to everyone in similar circumstances and involve the interests of others (interpersonal); and the interests at stake are "fundamental" (2002, p. 42).

Thus, not all values and norms are relevant for ethical or moral judgments. Ethics are not, for example, concerned with what is beautiful (aesthetics), what is conventional (etiquette), or what works (science and technology; e.g., 'ISO norms'–worldwide proprietary, industrial, and commercial standards developed by the International Organization for Standardization). Integrity is about "moral" norms and values, those that refer to what is right or wrong, good or bad. The features also refer to a general consent with relevance for everyone in the same circumstances. That relates to the relevant or 'valid' moral values and norms.

In sum, morality and ethics refer to what is right or wrong, good or bad. They concern values and norms that people feel rather strongly about, because serious interests are involved that affect the community of which they are a part. A value is a belief or quality that contributes to judgments about what is good; right; beautiful; or admirable. Values thus have weight in the choice of action by individuals and collectives. A norm is more specific. Norms tell us whether something is good or bad, right or wrong, beautiful or ugly. For types of behavior, they answer the question "what is the correct thing to do?" (De Graaf, 2003; Fijnaut & Huberts, 2002, pp. 10–11; Van der Wal, 2008, pp. 10–12).

Integritism: What It Is and Why It Matters

When integrity is seen as important, it is almost by definition also important that it is clear what integrity and integrity violations are about (Huberts, 2005, 2018; Maesschalck, 2019). Many things can go wrong in an organization. There are, as Caiden (1991) convincingly argued, many bureau pathologies. But not all of these 179 pathologies should be considered integrity violations. Functionaries make mistakes, even stupid mistakes, without the violation of the moral norms and values that really do matter. Yet, when this distinction becomes too blurred, an organization loses sight of what is morally important and what is not. Although never easy, this undertaking is crucial for any organization that takes ethics and integrity seriously and that wants to prevent the oversimplification and/or overgeneralization or "integritism" (Huberts, 2014, pp. 127-128). Integritism refers to the misuse of the topic, to inappropriate accusations that functionaries did not act with integrity, without good reason because of misunderstanding what integrity is about and/or possibly with an opportunistic background (trying to harm the opponent). Another type of integritism concerns integrity accusations when actually there is a conflict about the policy content and outcome. So when a mayor's integrity is questioned by a member of the local council, because of his very fundamental objections against the mayors policy proposal, the use of the i-word is unjust and damaging, an example of integritism.

INTEGRITY VIOLATIONS[7]

Different bodies of knowledge point to many types of behavior that conflict with values and norms in different contexts. Corruption is often part of that literature, with the focus on "inappropriate private interests" conflicting with the public or organizational interest. Additional interesting research often uses other concepts for immoral or inappropriate behavior (Huberts & Lasthuizen, 2020), for example, police deviance and misconduct (Punch, 1985), organizational misbehavior (Vardi & Weitz, 2004), white-collar crime

(Friedrichs, 1996), state crime (Peoples & Sutton, 2017), and administrative evil (Adams & Balfour, 2004).

This led researchers at the Vrije Universiteit Amsterdam to construct, step by step, a broad typology of 10 integrity violation categories, with the ambition to present an overview of types of unethical behavior, from the diverse literature, with relevance for almost all (public) organizational contexts. The types of violations are present in many contexts, though the concrete behavior will of course vary in different times and places.

Since its original formulation, the typology has been discussed and tested many times using available (quantitative and qualitative) data on integrity violations (with an operationalization in specific behaviors depending on the context). Lasthuizen (2008) made a first successful attempt to empirically validate the typology for standardized surveys within the field of ethics and integrity and for organizational (mis)behavior research (see also Huberts, Lasthuizen, & Peeters, 2006; Lasthuizen, Huberts, & Heres, 2011).

The typology is summarized in Table F.1 with a brief description of the types of violation.

In the typology corruption is of course included as the abuse of powers for private gain (Graycar, 2020; Jurkiewicz, 2020). Two types of corruption are distinguished: bribery and favoritism. "Private gain" is clearly an element, but the three types of favoritism point at a broad interpretation of "private," including favoring family (nepotism), friends (cronyism), or party (patronage).

Two other types involve (the appearance of) conflicting private interest by gifts and jobs or positions elsewhere. Sometimes these are combined and seen as one type (conflict of interest).

The focus on inappropriate gain is always crucial, but also limited, given the broadness of the moral standards that matter and what behavior is seen as morally wrong. This also becomes manifest in the actual integrity discussions and scandals politicians and public servants are confronted with. Nowadays, the "appropriateness of (personal) behavior" is also very present in affairs concerning integrity. These affairs involve discrimination, intimidation, and sexual abuse (the MeToo movement) in relations at work, summarized here as "indecent treatment of colleagues or citizens and customers."

The last type of violation concerns private-time (mis)behavior with consequences for someone's credibility and integrity in (public) office. This can include a lot of immoral behavior outside work, in a person's private time, for example, domestic violence, sexual intimidation, drunken driving, tax fraud, theft of family or neighbors, intimidating tweets, and so on. As Blauw (1991, p. 36) summarized in an article about police officers and their temptations, they often involve "dames, drinks, dimes, drugs, discounts, dice, and dirty tricks." In the business sector, corporations are often

TABLE F.1 Typology of Integrity Violations (Huberts & Van Montfort, 2021, pp. 8–9)

Corruption: bribery	Misuse of (public) power for private gain: asking, offering, or accepting bribes
Corruption: favoritism (nepotism, cronyism, patronage)	Misuse of authority or position to favour family (nepotism), friends (cronyism), or party (patronage)
Fraud and theft of resources	Improper private gain acquired from the organization or from colleagues and citizens, with no involvement of an external actor
Conflict of (private and public) interest through "gifts"	Interference (or potential interference) of personal interest with public or organizational interest because of gifts, services, or assets accepted or promises made
Conflict of (private and public) interest through sideline activities	Interference (or potential interference) of personal interest with public or organizational interest because of jobs or activities practiced outside the organization
Improper use of authority	Use of illegal or improper means or methods (possibly for "noble causes")
Misuse and manipulation of information	Intended or unintended abuse of (access to) information, such as cheating, violation of secrecy rules, breaching confidentiality of information, or concealing information
Waste and abuse of organizational resources	Failure to comply with organizational standards and/or improper performance or incorrect or dysfunctional internal behavior
Indecent treatment of colleagues or citizens and customers	Unacceptable treatment that includes not only discrimination (based on gender, race, or sexual orientation), intimidation, and sexual harassment but also improper behavior like bullying, nagging, and gossiping
Misconduct in private time	Misconduct in the private sphere that harms people's trust in the (public) organization

Source: Huberts and Lasthuizen (2020); Huberts & Van Montfort (2020); Lasthuizen (2008); Lasthuizen, Huberts, & Heres (2011).

more alert on this "outside work behavior," with more and stricter rules on it then in the public sector (Kaptein, 2019).

Research shows that all types of integrity violations seem relevant to take into consideration when integrity in organizations and sectors is studied (De Graaf et al., 2018).

DIVERSITY

As mentioned before, I am rather unfamiliar with the research of almost all of the authors in this book on important topics like diversity, inclusion, equality, equity. But when I want to try to relate our fields of study, integrity and diversity, at least a first impression of what I picked up concerning the diversity research seems crucial. What is diversity?

What Is Diversity

Anna Simonati's draft introductory and concluding chapters for this book helped me to answer that question. To be more precise the very first paragraphs of the of the draft book (July 2023) summarizes in my view a number of essentials.

> As is well known, the principle of equality has always been considered as one of the fundamental values of modern societies and it is declared among the basic rules of a legal system all over the world. Looking at public action as a whole, the main corollary of the principle is the duty of administration to provide equal treatment to all subjects it enters in touch with, which is normally expressed as a general prohibition of discrimination.

Thus starting point is the value of equality, of equal treatment or no discrimination.

But public policies have started a new path which in Simonati's eyes is widely shared:

> Differently than in the past, the idea, according to which equality is not based only on protection against discrimination but also on promotion of diversity as a source of richness for society. (–) The aim at inclusion primarily involves the implementation of an integrated and inter-sectional perspective. The possible causes of discrimination are numerous: sex and gender, race, age, religion, state of health, economic and social condition, and so on.

> And "a negative" approach to differences should be replaced by a "positive" one, based on sensitivity to diversity as a relevant driver of human interaction. Moreover, equal treatment corresponds to fundamental rights of individuals and to a duty of public authorities and formally private subjects pursuing a public interest."

What do I find when I move to the interpretations of diversity' on the internet, getting an impression of the diversity of definitions and interpretations of the central concepts?

There Are Different 'Wikipedia' Definitions of Diversity[8]

For (business) organizations diversity is seen as the inclusion of people of different identities (ethnicity, gender, age) in the workforce.

Integrity and Diversity of Governance • **xxi**

More interesting concerning diversity is the webpage on Diversity, equity, and inclusion–Wikipedia. To summarize:

> Diversity, equity, and inclusion (usually abbreviated DEI) refers to organizational frameworks which seek to promote "the fair treatment and full participation of all people," particularly groups "who have historically been underrepresented or subject to discrimination" on the basis of identity or disability. These three notions (diversity, equity and inclusion) together represent "three closely linked values" which organizations seek to institutionalize through DEI frameworks.

Diversity refers to the presence of variety within the organizational workforce, such as in identity (i.e., gender, culture, ethnicity, religion, disability, class etc.), age or opinion. Equity refers to concepts of fairness and justice, such as fair compensation. More specifically, equity usually also includes a focus on societal disparities and allocating resources and "decision making authority to groups that have historically been disadvantaged," and taking "into consideration a person's unique circumstances, adjusting treatment accordingly so that the end result is equal." Finally, inclusion refers to creating an organizational culture that creates an experience where "all employees feel their voices will be heard," and a sense of belonging and integration.

An interesting website with information on diversity and inclusion is that of McKinsey.[9]

Central question is "What is diversity, equity, and inclusion (DE&I)," with clear definitions. Diversity, equity, and inclusion are three closely linked values held by many organizations that are working to be supportive of different groups of individuals, including people of different races, ethnicities, religions, abilities, genders, and sexual orientations.

Diversity refers to who is represented in the workforce. Some examples of diversity in workplaces include: Gender diversity: What makes up the composition of men, women, and nonbinary people in a given population?; Age diversity: Are people in a group from mostly one generation, or is there a mix of ages?; Ethnic diversity: Do people in a group share common national or cultural traditions, or do they represent different backgrounds?; Physical ability and neurodiversity: Are the perspectives of people with disabilities, whether apparent or not, accounted for?

Equity refers to fair treatment for all people, so that the norms, practices, and policies in place ensure identity is not predictive of opportunities or workplace outcomes. Equity differs from equality in a subtle but important way. While equality assumes that all people should be treated the same, equity takes into consideration a person's unique circumstances, adjusting treatment accordingly so that the end result is equal.

Inclusion refers to how the workforce experiences the workplace and the degree to which organizations embrace all employees and enable them to make meaningful contributions. Companies that are intent on recruiting a diverse workforce must also strive to develop a sufficiently inclusive culture, such that all employees feel their voices will be heard—critical if organizations want to retain their talent and unlock the power of their diverse workforce.

McKinsey mentioned gender, age, ethnic, (dis)ability diversity. The Workable website[10] adds more in general that 'the types of diversity in a social context are theoretically infinite: they encompass every characteristic that appears with variations among a group of people (such as hair or eye color)'. But usually, we pay attention to seven types of diversity. Workable then also mentions racial diversity, religious diversity and sexual orientation.

I conclude with my impression for now, of the content of the central concepts.

Diversity on the one hand refers to a characteristic of an organization, to the presence of variety within the organizational workforce, such as in identity (i.e., gender, culture, ethnicity, religion, disability, class, sexual orientation, etc.), age or opinion. Equality/equity adds that every group should be treated equally/fairly, non-discrimination of gender, ethnicity, etc.

On the other hand, nowadays 'diversity' is also seen as a value, diversity as something good, to be cherished and promoted. Inclusiveness then refers to how the organization deals with the diversity, whether it embraces all employees and enable them to make meaningful contributions.

Integrity and Diversity: Questions and Dilemmas

Before I sketched the meaning of integrity and integrity violations and of diversity and equality (and anti-discrimination). How do these bodies of knowledge, these concepts and phenomena, relate?

Separate Worlds

In our scientific work we are often stimulated or even forced to focus, to specialize, on our own topic. My topic is quality and integrity of governance, the topic of the authors/researchers in this volume is diversity, equality, inclusion. More than I expected, these two fields are rather separated, research on and theorizing about diversity ánd integrity is scarce.

I can illustrate that with reference to my own work. In the 2014 book with an overview of integrity of governance research (what it is, what we know, what is done, and where to go) the word 'diversity' is mentioned several times but always as 'diversity of theories', diversity of approaches' etc. Diversity as a value only pops up, when research on values in the European Union is summarized (Huberts, 2014, 23; 88-89). Bossaert and Demmke

(2005) report about their research on ethical codes in the European Union. The civil servants' obligations regarding ethical behavior are remarkably similar in all 25 national public services of the enlarged EU. This similarity is evident in the ethical requirements determined by both laws and disciplinary actions. Moreover, the traditional values of national civil services (such as neutrality, respecting the rule of law, confidentiality, impartiality, and avoiding conflicts of interest) have remained unchanged for decades. More recently, Demmke and Moilanen (2011: 30) found evidence of more change and variety in values, concluding that, over time, "new values such as transparency, diversity, sustainability, and flexibility have also been added to the classical values. [Seemingly, therefore], the future will be dominated by more value conflicts and newly emerging values."

Lack of attention of integrity researchers for diversity does not count for 'anti-diversity' behavior or discrimination. As mentioned before, discrimination and intimidation are among the types of integrity violations we distinguish as 'indecent treatment of colleagues or citizens and customers'.

The reverse also seems the case: diversity researchers do not refer to integrity. A bit simple may be, but in the two draft chapters of the book send to me (introduction and concluding remarks) the word 'integrity' is missing, although diversity and equality are connected to 'good administration' and to fairness in decision-making. "(—) the legal and ethical purpose, which represents the conceptual basis of gender equality, must be carefully indicated: one should recognize that it does not lay only on the due protection of the rights of women, but also—and primarily—on the sensitivity for diversity as a source for fairness in decision-making. Such approach allows to connect the principle—and all the implementing rules—with the general interest of the entire society."

Some Connection

After the simple search presented above, I was curious what google and google scholar would bring on the relationship between integrity and diversity.

The resulting information was rather diverse. Millions of hits, as usual, but very seldom about what I hoped for.

Very often the papers, articles, books referred to, almost completely addressed either integrity or diversity with no reflection on the relation with the other concept. For example my own Public Integrity article about integrity pops up (Huberts, 2018), but in that article the word diversity comes back twice in 'diversity of moral misbehavior' and 'diversity of the phenomena under study. Thus this article about integrity ignores the relationship with diversity (as well as many others).

What did the broader search bring on information regarding both integrity and diversity, also as a value? Are both values present in important international and national codes of ethics and good governance frameworks? And how are they related?

United Nations

The United Nations and the World Bank are important concerning global frameworks for good governance and codes of ethics. The UN Anti-Corruption Convention addresses part of the types of integrity violations that were distinguished before. Nevertheless, for integrity this is an important convention with moral norms and values on acting in the public interest. Diversity is not addressed in this convention.

The same is true for the World Bank's Worldwide Government Indicators (used to estimate the quality of governments all over the world (Kaufmann, Kraay, & Mastruzzi, 2009).[11]

WGI is about Voice and Accountability, Political Stability and Absence of Violence/Terrorism, Government Effectiveness, Regulatory Quality, Rule of Law and Control of Corruption. Integrity is present (on anti-corruption), diversity is not.

The absence of diversity seems surprising given UN's core values, and the resulting involvement of the United Nations Ethics Office.[12] The office promotes an ethical organizational culture based on UN's core values of integrity, professionalism and respect for diversity, and the values outlined in the Code of Ethics for UN Personnel which include independence, loyalty, impartiality, integrity, accountability and respect for human rights. The Ethics Office assists the Secretary-General in ensuring that all staff members perform their functions consistent with the highest standards of integrity as required by the Charter of the United Nations.

Diversity is also prominent in the United Nations System Code of Conduct to prevent harassment including sexual harassment.[13] I quote:

> UN system events are guided by the highest ethical and professional standards, and all participants are expected to behave with integrity and respect towards all participants attending or involved with any UN system event.
>
> Harassment is any improper or unwelcome conduct that might reasonably be expected or be perceived to cause offence or humiliation to another person. Harassment in any form because of gender, gender identity and expression, sexual orientation, physical ability, physical appearance, ethnicity, race, national origin, political affiliation, age, religion or any other reason is prohibited at UN system events. Sexual harassment is a specific type of prohibited conduct.

Another example of UN attention for diversity and integrity concerns an ethics course of the United Nation Office on Drugs and Crime UNODC.[14]

The UNODC Module Series on Integrity and Ethics offers 14 Modules focusing on a range of core issues within these two areas. One module explicitly explores the concepts of diversity, tolerance and pluralism. The study of diversity, tolerance and pluralism is seen as a key domain within ethics education since issues such as discrimination, misrepresentation and ethnocentricity are related to fairness, justice, identity, equality, and other ethical concerns.

The module examines ways in which the acceptance of diversity may be difficult, but can be understood and accomplished by drawing on ideas and examples of ethical behavior. The Module provides a menu of options and approaches for addressing ethical challenges involving issues of race, religious belief, gender, sexual orientation, (dis)ability, political views, and a range of others. It illustrates the relevant concepts through discussing historical social systems in which tolerance and pluralism were evident, and historical role models of integrity who provided inspirational leadership in modelling diversity and acceptance in vexing situations.

Diversity in Integrity Policy

Are there other, national, examples of codes with both values are present? Not that many, although there seems to be growing attention for diversity, in particular within integrity policies and codes.

An example of that is Eaton's (2022) article on new priorities for academic integrity: equity, diversity, inclusion, decolonization and Indigenization. She argues that academic integrity networks and organizations ought to develop intentional strategies for equity, diversity and inclusion, and decolonization in terms of leadership, scholarship, and professional opportunities.

I also found Dutch universities paying attention to diversity and integrity as their core values.

The Technical University Delft (TU Delft)[15] "strives to be both a leading university and a great place to work. At the heart of this lie our core values: Diversity, Integrity, Respect, Engagement, Courage, and Trust (DIRECT)." The code of conduct sets out what is meant by the core values, including diversity and integrity:

Diversity: "We follow The Universal Declaration of Human Rights, believing that "All human beings are born free and equal in dignity and rights." Hence, the differences between humans ought not diminish our respect for each and every individual as equally worthy of our consideration. This concerns differences in socio-economic, cultural or religious background, nationality, gender, sexual orientation, age, physical appearance as well as roles and positions."

Integrity: "Integrity means being independent, responsible, honest, transparent and sincere for its own sake. Persons of integrity hold themselves to high moral and ethical standards. In order to have integrity, we need to willingly engage in self-reflective deliberation about what those standards ought to be, and how we can work together to uphold them. (-) Integrity is not a quality that can be taken for granted; it requires a continuous effort to maintain and improve."

The Erasmus University Rotterdam focuses more on the undesirable behavior that contradicts diversity.[16] Undesirable behavior is behavior that is socially and objectively regarded as inappropriate, bothersome, hurtful, threatening or unacceptable, whereby the personal integrity of another person is verbally, non-verbally, physically, digitally or otherwise compromised, including (sexual) harassment, bullying, discrimination, threats, gossip, racist behavior, aggression.

Diversity and Integrity: Mutual Influence

Another (small) body of literature about the relationship between diversity and integrity focuses not on the content of the values but on the consequences of integrity for diversity or diversity for integrity.

Does Diversity Improve Integrity?

Choi and Lee (2018) picked up recent scholarship that suggested that representative bureaucracy improves organizational integrity. They tested this argument with respect to gender, using data from Korean government agencies from 2008 to 2014. The findings suggest that an increase in female representation and diversity in public organizations leads to an improvement in the measured level of organizational integrity. However, the also fount that that incidents of sexual harassment and sexual violence in the workplace were positively, not negatively, correlated with increased female representation. This is explained, they state, by the fact that a greater female representation may empower female officials to report unfair treatment or injustice that has hitherto been unreported and tolerated.

Representative bureaucracy theory indeed is relevant to mention here. The representative bureaucracy is a form of representation that captures most or all aspects of a society's population in the governing body of the state (Krislov, 2012). When a public organization is more representative in terms of gender, ethnicity, age etc., one would expect that decision-making and implementation of policies would be more fair, less selective, discriminating. That has been confirmed by research, in particular within the police and the prominence of racial profiling (/discrimination) (Hong, 2026, 2017).

Does Integrity Improve Diversity

McCann, Sparks and Kohntopp (2017) did research on the effects of integrity of leadership on diversity in the workplace. They examined 941 responses from workers in the United States who completed the Perceived Leader Integrity Scale and the Workplace Diversity Survey. For leaders perceived as "high ethical," there was a statistically significant (p < .01) correlation with each of the five dimensions of attitude toward diversity (incl. emotional, behavioral, personal consequences). This indicated that participants who perceived their leaders as "high ethical" had positive attitudes in the five dimensions For leaders perceived as "moderate ethical" and "low ethical," there were no significant associations with diversity.

Integrity (of leaders) thus stimulates positive attitudes towards diversity. This type, of conclusion is of course in line what we hope for and expect? That diversity contributes to integrity and integrity to diversity. That always brings along the danger bot looking at possible contrary consequences.

Negative Consequences

Van der Wal acknowledges that 'dark side' of diversity, in the sense that more diversity can lead to integrity problems (2018; 2017). Increasing diversity and the resistance that this can provoke, he states, can lead new types of tensions in terms of neutrality and manners, and more complexity and layering regarding culture, loyalty, security and conceptions of what integrity is about. And: "Even seemingly liberal, tolerant societies such as ours, appear to find it difficult to deal with. Studies and policies have celebrated diversity for decades because it contributes to the effectiveness, inclusivity and performance of teams and organizations, but practice has proven to be more unruly. (Van der Wal 2018, 36).

Fascinating but also uncomfortable questions are therefore ahead. How do you lead a department where open, flamboyant transgender people as well as conservative Muslims and Christians work? How do you ensure that everyone behaves decently and openly towards each other and continues to propagate to the outside world the neutrality and professionalism that we can expect from our government?[17]

Some doubts about the consequences of more diversity for integrity also arose when research was published on reports and investigation on integrity violations in law enforcement agencies, with a connection with organized crime (Nelen & Kolthoff, 2017). The research showed that 43% of the police officials identified in the integrity violations with some relationship with organized crime have a migration background. In the cases within the police, the share of employees with a non-western background is 40%. Against the background that about 7% of the police workforce is of non-Western origin, this led to discussion. Later research on internal investigation files of integrity violations within the police, came to other conclusions (Smit et al., 2019). It appeared that such police officers were more often suspected of leaks and therefore more often subject to disciplinary investigation, but that after such an investigation they did not appear to have leaked more often.

To be continued . . .

SOME REFLECTION

This chapter or essay in the book about 'Diversity' and 'Exploring New Paths to Good Administration' presented information from two bodies of literature, one about integrity (and integrity violations), the other about diversity and equality (and ant-discrimination).

Work in progress, rather incomplete and sketchy, I admit, but may be also convincing enough for some food of thought for both fields of study.

1. There are many views on integrity and many views on diversity which makes is very important to be clear about the meaning that is central in one's approach.

    Central in this chapter is integrity as accordance with the relevant moral values and norms (and rules) and integrity violations concern behavior that violates those moral norms and values (and rules). Diversity is a characteristic of an organization, but also the value that it is good to have variety within the organizational workforce, that every group should be treated equally/fairly, with contrary to that discrimination of gender, ethnicity etc.

2. Integrity concerns the moral quality of everybody's behavior and not the ethics or moral quality of the resulting decisions and outcome (Paanakker, Masters, & Huberts, 2020).

    That starting point is important, also to be able to distinguish relevant integrity violations and to prevent that integrity accusations are misused in conflicts over societal values (social justice, equality, equity, sustainability e.g.), thus prevent integritism.

    However, the diversity issue opens up some questions that are relevant for integrity researchers (and policy developers). Is 'diversity' nowadays a value with moral connotation, is it about good and bad concerning the composition of the organization? Is a less diverse organization less integritous? I am in doubt, and for now not in favor of that connection. What does matter though, is relat-

ing integrity more to diversity research on what goes wrong or anti-diversity (=discrimination) and anti-integrity or integrity violations.
3. Partly similar questions seem relevant for diversity researchers. What are you exactly addressing? Is diversity about behavior, process, in governance or about the policy content and societal results? I guess primarily about the organization and process of governance, and not (?) about the societal outcomes? Those outcomes matter, of course, both matter, but it is important to be (more) clear on what is addressed with 'diversity'.
4. In addition I was a bit puzzled by the diversity approach concerning what is relevant in the variety within the organizational workforce. Identity is mentioned with gender, culture, ethnicity, religion, disability, class, sexual orientation, etc., as well as age or opinion.

    Equality/equity adds that every group should be treated equally/fairly, non-discrimination on all these characteristics. That is relevant for internal treatment of employees, but also in policy making ánd implementation concerning (a variety of) citizens.

    However... What diversity then really matters to focus on, in organizations? We all differ on so much, the number of characteristics we differ on is infinitive, what is important to take into account in what context? It was for example interesting to see in also the scientific contributions whether a contested topic as sexual orientation was included (or not!). And what to do with diversity of age, opinion or religion, education? Or from a farmer family or not, or living in the countryside or in populated areas, big towns or small town, etc. What diversity does matter, what is representative politics, what representative bureaucracy, what a representative private and business organization?
5. What diversity is relevant for good administration and governance? And what deserves priority, in research and policy development? Some answers might be found in the work on representative bureaucracy. I guess diversity scholars are familiar with this work? Not that I am overoptimistic about what theory and research about representative bureaucracy will learn us about diversity and integrity, but the what is done in that field of study is, of course, relevant for scholars on diversity and integrity.
6. Sexual orientation seems to be the element of diversity that brings along most disagreement and conflict. Data from the International Lesbian, Gay, Bisexual, Trans and Intersex Association are rather shocking (ILGA, 2016).) There are 193 countries in the world that are members of the United Nations and homosexuality is punishable in 64 countries (so not punishable in 129), in 47 countries, LGBTI people can receive prison sentences, in 8 countries you can

be sentenced to life imprisonment and in at least 9 countries you can even be sentenced to death. The right to sexual orientation is established in 12 countries and gender identity in 5 countries. Same-sex marriage is recognized in 33 countries, other formal partnerships are allowed in 34 countries.

Nevertheless, the United Nations System Code of Conduct signals that internationally the 'relevant moral norms and values' clearly oppose any harassment of LGBTI+ people.

7. We are diversity and integrity scholars, favoring paying more attention to these values in research and policy making. That might lead to underestimating the dark side of ethics and also of diversity. What are the negative consequences of more diversity, and how is that for the different types of diversity? We should pay more attention in our research to those unintended negative consequences and how to deal with them as an organization.

8. Integrity and in particular diversity are not yet part of the values that are important for good governance. Integrity is often present, sometimes as anti-corruption of honesty and fairness. Diversey is not very often mentioned, although it seems to be on the move towards becoming part of our good governance idea. An open question then is what characteristics are seen as relevant? Gender and ethnicity/race are high on that agenda. Should we indeed (first) focus on those?

9. Both diversity and integrity are (becoming) part of the values of good governance. Does that mean that a public or private manager or employee is acting non-integritous when he or she is against (more) diversity? I would say no or not yet, but this offers food for thought. Not every example of bad governance concerns the integrity of the involved actors.

10. Does that mean that a public or private manager or employee can act with integrity when this person supports or tolerates unequal treatment of colleagues or citizens/customers because of characteristics that are irrelevant for deciding and acting in the public interest (or collective/organizational) interest. Of course not. Discrimination or even harassment because of ethnicity, race, gender, sexual orientation (etc.) is behavior in conflict with the relevant moral norms and values.

Thus, there seems to be much agreement about the types of behavior that are in conflict with or violating integrity and diversity. This concerns types of behavior that are now in the center of everybody's attention and involvement in integrity and diversity. After MeToo the number of scandals on transgressive behavior has risen enormously. Discrimination, intimidation and harassment (also sexual) in politics, media, sports, in almost every social sector are prominent in our newspapers.

This offers, in my view, unique and important angles for cooperative efforts by diversity and integrity researchers. How to understand the growing attention, how to explain when things go wrong and what might be done to react better on reports and whistle blowers, to improve the quality of (internal) investigations and to come to methods and instrument and organizations that prevent that things go wrong, that protect integrity and diversity and prevent discrimination and intimidation.

NOTES

1. L. W. J. C. (Leo) Huberts is emeritus professor of Public Administration at the Vrije Universiteit Amsterdam (email: l.w.j.c.huberts@vu.nl). For an overview of his research, see Leo W.J.C. Huberts — Vrije Universiteit Amsterdam (vu.nl).
2. Of course, I will build in this contribution on previous, also recent publications. The sources will be clarified, but some self-plagiarism is in my view all in the game in presenting the basics of (y)our work in a new context.
3. I copy, summarize, combine and also add to the text of Huberts, 2014, 2018 ánd more in particular and most recent my chapter for Muel Kaptein's Handbook on Organizational Integrity (Huberts, 2024).
4. Please keep in mind that almost always 'my view' is referring to 'our view' (in particular of the research group at the Vrije Universiteit I was and still are a member of.
5. It's difficult to choose in English the adjective for the noun "integrity." Carter (1996), for example, used the adjective "integral;" "integer" is common in French (integre), German (integer), or Dutch (integer). Because the term "integer" seems inappropriate in English, and "integral" refers more to integrality then integrity, in English the term "integritous" is chosen.
6. Although I know not every colleague appreciates the use of Wikipedia in scientific work, I think it is a useful source for getting an idea of the presence and meaning of concepts, in literature as well as the media and public opinion.
7. Based on, copied from Huberts and Van Montfort, 2021.
8. See Diversity–Wikipedia and Diversity, equity, and inclusion–Wikipedia (acc. 1-7-2023).
9. What is diversity, equity, and inclusion (DE&I)? | McKinsey (2022).
10. See for example the website of Workable: https://resources.workable.com/hr-terms/the-types-of-diversity#h2-2.
11. Interesting data on all indicators: https://info.worldbank.org/governance/wgi/Home/Documents
12. See its website: United Nations Ethics Office. See also The United Nations Global Compact Way | UN Global Compact. The UN Global Compact Office formulated additional values, based on the three core values Integrity, Professionalism and Respect for Diversity.

13. United Nations System Code of Conduct
14. See Integrity_and_Ethics_Module_5_Ethics_Diversity_and_Pluralism.pdf (unodc.org)
15. See for the integrity policy: https://www.tudelft.nl/en/about-tu-delft/strategy/integrity-policy and for the code of conduct The Code of Conduct.
16. See 2021-03-eur-complaints-regulation-undesirable-behaviour
17. Translated from Van der Wal, 2018, pp. 35 and 36. See also Van der Wal, 2017, 220-224.

LITERATURE/REFERENCES

Adams, G.B., & Balfour, D.L. (2004). *Unmasking administrative evil* (rev. ed.). Armonk, NY: M.E. Sharpe.

Becker, M., & Talsma, J. (2016). Adding colours to the shades of grey: Enriching the integrity discourse with virtue ethics concepts. In: A. Lawton, Z. van der Wal, & L. Huberts (Eds.), *Ethics in public policy and management: A global research companion* (pp. 33–50). London, England: Routledge.

Bevir, M. (2009). *Key concepts in governance.* London, England: SAGE.

Bossert, D., & Demmke C. (2005). *Main Challenges in the Field of Ethics and Integrity in the EU Member States.* Maastricht: European Institute of Public Administration.

Brenkert, G.G. (Ed.). (2004). *Corporate integrity & accountability.* Thousand Oaks, CA: Sage.

Caiden, G.E. (1991). What really is public maladministration? *Public Administration Review, 51*(6), 486–493.

Carter, S.L. (1996). *Integrity.* New York, NY: Harper Perennial.

Choi, H., Hong, S., & Lee, J. W. (2018). Does Increasing Gender Representativeness and Diversity Improve Organizational Integrity? *Public Personnel Management 47*(1), 73–92. https://doi.org/10.1177/0091026017738539

De George, R.T. (1993). *Competing with integrity in international business.* New York, NY: Oxford University Press.

De Graaf, G. (2003). *Tractable morality. Customer discourses of bankers, veterinarians and charity workers.* Rotterdam, the Netherlands: ERIM.

De Graaf, Gjalt, Huberts, Leo, & Strüwer, Tebbine (2018): Integrity Violations and Corruption in Western Public Governance: Empirical Evidence and Reflection from the Netherlands, *Public Integrity,* 20 (2): 131-149. At http://www.tandfonline.com/doi/full/10.1080/10999922.2017.1350796

Demmke, Christoph, & Timo Moilanen (2011). *Effectiveness of Good Governance and Ethics. Evaluating Reform Outcomes in the Context of the Financial Crisis.* Study for the Polish EU Presidency to be finalised for the DG Meeting in December 2011. Maastricht: European Institute of Public Administration.

Dobel, J.P. (2016; 1990). Integrity in the public service. *Public Administration Review,* 50(3), 354–366. Available at SSRN: https://ssrn.com/abstract ½2769133

Eaton, S.E. (2022). New priorities for academic integrity: equity, diversity, inclusion, decolonization and Indigenization. *International Journal for Educational Integrity 18*(10). https://doi.org/10.1007/s40979-022-00105-0

Fijnaut, C., & Huberts, L.W.J.C. (Eds.). (2002). *Corruption, integrity and law enforcement*. Dordrecht, the Netherlands: Kluwer Law International.

Friedrichs, D.O. (1996). *Trusted Criminals. White Collar Crime in Contemporary Society*. Belmont: Wadsworth.

Fukuyama, F. (2016). Governance: What do we know, and how do we know it? *Annual Review of Political Science*, 19, 89–105.

Graycar A. (Ed.) (2020). *Handbook on corruption, ethics and integrity in public administration*. Cheltenham, UK: Edward Elgar.

Hong S. (2016). Representative bureaucracy, organizational integrity, and citizen coproduction: Does an increase in police ethnic representativeness reduce crime? *Journal of Policy Analysis and Management*, 35, 11-33.

Hong S. (2017). Does increasing ethnic representativeness reduce police misconduct? *Public Administration Review*, 77, 195-205.

Huberts, L.W.J C. (2005). *Integriteit en integritisme in bestuur en samenleving. Wie de schoen past*. [Integrity and integritism in governance and society] Oratie 23 februari 2005. Amsterdam: Vrije Universiteit.

Huberts, L., Lasthuizen, K., & Peeters, C. (2006). Measuring corruption: Exploring the iceberg. In: C. Sampford, A. Shacklock, C. Connors, & F. Galtung (Eds.), *Measuring corruption* (pp. 265– 293). Burlington, VT: Ashgate.

Huberts, L.W.J.C. (2014). *The Integrity of Governance. What It Is, What We Know, What Is Done, and Where to Go*. Basingstoke: Palgrave Macmillan.

Huberts, L.W.J.C. (2018) Integrity: What it is and Why it is Important, *Public Integrity* 20 (S1): 18-32. DOI: 10.1080/10999922.2018.1477404

Huberts, Leo, & Lasthuizen, Karin (2020). Corruption in Context: What Goes Wrong in Governance. In: Melchior Powell, Dina Wafa, & Tim A. Mau (Eds). *Corruption in a Global Context. Restoring Public Trust, Integrity, and Accountability*. (pp. 44-67). London & New York, NY: Routledge.

Huberts, L., & Van Montfort, A. (2020). Building ethical organisations: The importance of organisational integrity systems. In A. Graycar (Ed.), *Handbook on corruption, ethics and integrity in public administration*. (pp. 449-462). Cheltenham, UK: Edward Elgar.

Huberts, L., & Van Montfort, A. (2021, February 23). Ethics, corruption, and integrity of governance: what it is and what helps. In: *Oxford Research Encyclopedia of Politics*. Oxford University Press. doi: https://doi.org/10.1093/acrefore/9780190228637.013.1403

Huberts, L.W.J.C. (forthcoming, 2024). *Integrity, Integrity Violations and Integritism: What They Are and Why They Really Matter*. In: Muel Kaptein, *Research Handbook on Organizational Integrity*. Cheltenham, UK: Edward Elgar.

ILGA (International Lesbian, Gay, Bisexual, Trans and Intersex Association) (2016). *The ILGA RIWI 20267 Global Attitudes Survey on LGBTI People in Partnership with LOGO*. Available on website ILGA.

Jurkiewicz, C.L. (Ed.). (2020). *Global corruption & ethics management: Transforming theory into action*. Lanham, MD: Rowman & Littlefield.

Kaptein, M., & Wempe, J. (2002). *The balanced company: A theory of corporate integrity*. Oxford, UK: Oxford University Press.

Kaptein, Muel (2019). Prescribing Outside-Work Behavior: Moral Approaches, Principles, and Guidelines. *Employee Responsibilities and Rights Journal* 31: 165-185. Online May https://doi.org/10.1007/s10672-019-09333-y.

Karssing, E. D. (2007). *Morele competentie in organisaties* [Moral competence in organizations]. Assen, the Netherlands: Van Gorcum. (Original work published 2001)

Kaufmann, Daniel, Kraay, Aart, & Mastruzzi, Massimo (2009). *Governance Matters VIII. Aggregate and Individual Governance Indicators 1996–2008.* The World Bank (Development Research Group, Macroeconomics and Growth Team), June 2009 WPS4978.

Lasthuizen, K. (2008). *Leading to integrity: Empirical research into the effects of leadership on ethics and integrity.* Amsterdam, The Netherlands: VU University.

Lasthuizen, K., Huberts, L., & Heres, L. (2011). How to measure integrity violations. Towards a validated typology of unethical behaviour. *Public Management Review, 13*(3), 383–408.

Lawton, A., Huberts, L., & Van der Wal, Z. (2016). Towards a global ethics: Wishful thinking or a strategic necessity? In: A. Lawton, Z. van der Wal, & L. Huberts (Eds), *Ethics in public policy and management: A global research companion* (pp. 327–343). London, England: Routledge.

Lee, Y.S., & Rosenbloom, D.H. (2005). *A reasonable public servant. Constitutional foundations of administrative conduct in the United States.* Armonk, NY: M.E. Sharpe.

Maesschalck, Jeroen (2019). When Integrity and Integrity Management Are Taken Too Seriously: On Integritism and the Integrity Industry. In: Gjalt de Graaf (ed.), *It is all about integrity, stupid. Studies on, about or inspired by the works of Leo Huberts.* (pp. 67-76). The Hague: Eleven International Publishing.

McCann, Jack, Sparks, Betsy & Kohntopp, Thom (2017). Leadership Integrity and Diversity in the Workplace. *Research in Economics and Management* October 2017. DOI: 10.22158/rem.v2n5p177.

Montefiore, A., & Vines, D. (Eds.). (1999). *Integrity in the public and private domains.* London, England: Routledge.

Nelen, H., & Kolthoff, E. (2017). Schaduwen over de rechtshandhaving. Georganiseerde criminaliteit en integriteitsschendingen van functionarissen in de rechtshandhaving. [Organised crime and integrity violations of law enforcement officials] Den Haag: Boom Criminologie.

Paanakker, H., Masters, A., & Huberts, L. (Eds.) (2020). *Quality of governance: Values and violations.* Palgrave Macmillan. https://doi.org/10.1007/978-3-030-21522-4.

Paine, L.S. (1994). Managing for organizational integrity. *Harvard Business Review* 72: 106–117.

Peoples, C., & Sutton, J.E. (2017). Political corruption and state crime. In: H.N. Pontell (Ed.), *Oxford research encyclopedia of criminology and criminal justice.* New York, NY: Oxford University Press.

Punch, M. (1985). *Conduct unbecoming. The social construction of police deviance and control.* London (etc.): Tavistock.

Smit, A., Slagmolen, N., Bronkhorst, C., Goor, J. van der & Meershock, G. (2019). *Het lekken van vertrouwelijke politie-informatie. Aard, omvang en ernst van het fenomeen bij de Politie en de Koninklijke Marechaussee.* [Leaking confidential police information. Nature, extent and severity of the phenomenon in law enforcement organizations] Den Haag: Boom Criminologie.

Thompson, D.F. (1985). The possibility of administrative ethics. *Public Administration Review* 45(5), 555–561.

Uhr, J. (1999). Institutions of integrity: Balancing values and verification in democratic government. *Public Integrity* 1(1), 94–106.

Van der Wal, Z. (2008). *Value solidity. Differences, similarities and conflicts between the organizational values of government and business.* Amsterdam, the Netherlands: VU University.

Van der Wal, Zeger (2017). *The 21st Century Public Manager.* London: Palgrave.

Van der Wal, Zeger (2018). *Integriteit 2025. Integriteitskwesties aan de horizon en hun implicaties.* [Integrity 2025. Integrity issues on the horizon and their implications] Den Haag: CAOP.

Van Luijk, H. (2004). Integrity in the private, the public, and the corporate domain. In: G.G. Brenkert (Ed.), *Corporate integrity and accountability.* (pp. 38–54). Thousand Oaks, CA: Sage.

Van Tongeren, P.V., & Becker, M. (2009). Integriteit als deugd. [Integrity as virtue]. In: E. Karssing & M. Zweegers (Eds.), *Jaarboek Integriteit 2010* (pp. 58–65). Den Haag, the Netherlands: BIOS.

Van Wijk, A. van, Olfers, M., van Vugt, M., & Barends, A. (2023). *Moreel kompas. Een onderzoek naar de determinanten van integer handelen van politiemedewerkers.* [Moral compass. An investigation into the determinants of integrity by police officers] Politiewetenschap 129. Den Haag: Sdu; politie & Wetenschap. Download via Moreel kompas | Politie en Wetenschap

Vardi, Y., & Weitz, E. (2004). *Misbehavior in organizations: Theory, research, and management.* Mahwah, NJ: Lawrence Erlbaum Associates.

ACKNOWLEDGEMENTS

Putting together this book has been a challenging, inspiring, and charming intellectual journey, during which I had the opportunity to learn a lot. This makes me deeply grateful for this wonderful opportunity to Carole L. Jurkiewicz, who gave me the idea of gathering in a collected book the papers that at present correspond to the Chapters of the volume: without her scientific foresight, enthusiasm, trust, terrific and continuous support nothing would have been possible; therefore, she deserves an impossibly great measure of recognition and thanks.

I am deeply indebted to Jean-Michel Eymeri-Douzans, President of the European Group for Public Administration, who immediately accepted my request and wrote the Prologue, from which the reader may easily grasp his scientific care and human sensitivity for the topic of diversity as an opportunity for good administration. As I point out in my Introduction in this book, an EGPA Conference was the first chance for meeting for the Authors of the Chapters; I am happy and proud to belong to the IIAS and EGPA groups, which has allowed me to know and appreciate numerous amazing people. Among them, Fabienne Maron deserves my deep and sincere gratitude because of her constant, competent, and friendly cooperation.

Moreover, I want to express my deepest appreciation to all of the authors of the chapters. The work of each of them has added much thoughtful discussion, by providing exciting facets to the critical and multidisciplinary overview. However, one of them deserves special thanks: I contacted Leo Huberts (very well known and distinguished colleague, but also an old friend of mine) with the hope to get a short blurb for the book by him;

Diversity as Strategic Opportunity, pages xxxvii–xxxviii
Copyright © 2024 by Information Age Publishing
www.infoagepub.com
All rights of reproduction in any form reserved.

he was generous enough to propose me, instead, to contribute with the Foreword, which offers a deep taxonomic reflection of the issues and topics examined in the Chapters (and beyond).

I also thank from the bottom of my heart for their kindness and patience the colleagues and friends who gave me their impressions on the book before it was published: Adam Masters, Edoardo Ongaro, and Aristide Police. Their appreciation and encouragement are an honor and a privilege to me.

Last, but not least, I want to thank Information Age Publishing for accepting this edited book... and many thanks to all and each of the future readers.

— **Anna Simonati**
University of Trento

INTRODUCTION

As is well known, the principle of equality has always been considered as one of the fundamental values of modern societies and it is declared among the basic rules of a legal system all over the world. Looking at public action as a whole, the main corollary of the principle is the duty of the administration to provide equal treatment to all subjects it enters in touch with, which is normally expressed as a general prohibition of discrimination.

However, in recent times, public policies, both at the national and supranational (especially E.U.) level, have started a new path. Differently than in the past, the idea, that equality is not based only on protection against discrimination but also on the promotion of diversity as a source of richness for society, is widely shared.

The aim of inclusion primarily involves the implementation of an integrated and inter-sectional perspective. The possible causes of discrimination are numerous: sex and gender, race, age, religion, state of health, economic and social condition, and so on. Socio-economic differences often produce or aggravate other kinds of inequalities and are the origin of the multiple-discrimination phenomenon. Starting from education, but also in other fields of social life, a "negative" approach to differences should be replaced by a "positive" one, based on sensitivity to diversity as a relevant driver of human interaction. Moreover, equal treatment corresponds to the fundamental rights of individuals and a duty of public authorities and formally private subjects pursuing a public interest. Affirmative actions are often used as a tool to erase discrimination, but other instruments (for instance, in the field of participative best practices) may be suitable as well.

Diversity as Strategic Opportunity, pages xxxix–xlii
Copyright © 2024 by Information Age Publishing
www.infoagepub.com
All rights of reproduction in any form reserved.

In such a polyhedric context, a relevant issue is the increasing complication of administrative action. Currently, new kinds of competencies and duties, to be pursued in the public interest, have been added to the traditional ones, and they correspond to (legitimate) expectations by the private individuals and groups, which are the interlocutors of the institutions and aim at receiving satisfactory performances. Another source for the complexity of contemporary administrative action—which partially derives from the increasing level of capacity and expertise, required of subjects charged with public-interest-goals action—is the assignment of some tasks to formally private entities, who are often for-profit actors. Finally (but not least) the growing digitalization of administrative procedures is an issue itself: on one hand, it may signify opportunities for stronger and proper access to services and utilities by all people; on the other hand, it can lead to the possible exclusion of certain people (belonging to the most vulnerable as less digitally literate part of population), thus creating new kinds of discrimination.

These issues are progressively emerging almost everywhere, since administrative action—like many other fields of human behavior—is unstoppably globalized. Therefore, very similar problems may be grasped in different Countries, and comparing the solutions offered in some of them could be particularly useful to propose and promote new shared ways to the legislators, the policymakers and the practitioners.

This book of course is not aimed at offering final and definite answers. Moreover, it is not a systemic study of the subject.

The research is based on the idea, that, in such an era of quick and sudden transformation of administrative action, managing new phenomena and analyzing narrow fields of intervention may be a wise and strategic move. This method allows a deep comprehension of the pros and cons of different policies, under a broad multidisciplinary umbrella. Therefore, the volume represents an effort to give an overview of some of the possible methods and tools that are nowadays experimented by administration, to properly face the practical problems connected to diversity. The study has been conceived, from the beginning of its history, as a sort of "intellectual patchwork," the fruit of the collective work by a heterogeneous group of scholars and practitioners, coming from different Countries (mainly, but not solely, in Europe) and with different scientific and technical expertise (especially, public law and public management). As a starting point, they were all involved—either as cochairs or as speakers—in the meeting of the XXIII EGPA Study Group on Administration, Diversity and Equal Treatment, held in Lisbon in September 2022. That Conference was a precious chance for a first discussion on grounds of common interest, which was later followed by further engagement in the production of the thirteen papers that are contained in the book. The result is a strongly multidisciplinary study, with contributions mainly from Italy and Austria (where the Authors mostly come from), but also by Authors from Finland, Hungary, India and South Africa; moreover, some contributions offer a supranational insight, by analyzing the European Union case law, also in comparison with specific National experiences.

The various chapters are linked to each other to highlight a conceptual path. Hence, the book is divided into three sections.

The first section is dedicated to gender diversity and empowerment. Gender studies represent a very relevant part of the research on diversity since the distinction between women and men is almost always accepted—rightly or wrongly—as a basic one, a sort of starting point for all reasoning about discrimination and bias. Therefore, numerous authors decided to focus on this topic, even though the specific fields of research and methods are quite different. The section starts with two management chapters on female leadership. The first, by Wendy Farrell, examines the leadership issues for working women in Tyrol. In the second, Marjukka Mikkonen discusses the possible efficacy and effectiveness of specific leadership programs for women in Finland. The third chapter of the section, by Giovanna Iacovone, is instead dedicated to the Italian system with a legal approach; it is aimed at examining a different field of women empowerment—the political arena—considering what is perhaps the most important tool for affirmative action: gender quotas. Finally, Arianna Pitino studies the complex interaction between gender equality, freedom of religion and the right to work through the lens of a recent judgment by the Court of Justice of the European Union.

The second section of the book aims to allow the reader to grasp the great variety of sectors and means for administrative action, where the issue of diversity between people is somehow involved. The four chapters here are consistently devoted to explaining some issues emerging from various public policies, from various perspectives. First, Anna Maria Chiariello and Rocco Frondizi match their (respectively) legal and managerial expertise to face one of the most serious issues of contemporary administrative action: the search for a proper approach to artificial intelligence, especially in service providing, to avoid the pitfalls associated with their misuse. The second chapter of the second section, by Jyoti Rattan and Vijai Rattan, enlarges the analysis beyond the borders of Europe; it is devoted to the exam of case law in a very specific area—the protection of the right to be forgotten, vis-à-vis data processing, especially in social media—offering a comparison between some judgments pronounced in the Indian system and at the EU level by the Court of Justice. In the third chapter, Agnes Jenei, Réka Zsuzsánna Máthé, Maliga Reddy and Srinivasan Pillay address the issue of diversity in administration from a different perspective, which is cooperation between three atypical partners in a joint action of assistance for refugees in Hungary: the study is useful to grasp whether and how diversity of actors may help in emergency problem-solving. In the fourth and last chapter of the section, Annalisa Giusti focuses, with a legal cut, on land planning, and more precisely on urban regeneration as scope for the development of administrative inclusive best practices.

In an ideal itinerary—from sectorial to polyfunctional, and then back to particular—the third section of the book aims at investigating another field, representing a particularly fruitful ground for both researchers and practitioners: education. In the five chapters here collected, the authors study their national system, putting into light the links with the supranational European level. Esther Happacher, Lamiss Khakzadeh, and Alexandra Weiss concentrate (from a legal perspective, but—so to say—with a double methodical approach, systemic and practical) on gender diversity management at Austrian universities. Quite similarly (notwithstanding a management approach), the second chapter by Marianna Brunetti, Nathalie Colasanti, Annalisa Fabretti, and Mariangela Zoli is focused on a specific research project on the perception of gender differences in a large Italian University. The other chapters of the third section are related to Italian schools, and they examine the issue of diversity from three different points of view: Stefania Baroncelli studies the topic holistically, starting from its constitutional legal background; Loredana Giani's interest specifically lies in the effect of digitalization, while Orsolya Farkas takes into account the principles and rules on the involvement of migrant students.

The Foreword by Leo Huberts may be seen as a sort of precious "conceptual map" of the whole research. Considering his long, deep, and fundamental work on ethics and integrity in administration, the author points out the main open issues. Some of them are the object of other chapters, some are not examined in the book; hence, Leo Huberts offers important food for (further) thought. His reflections also show once more how a multidisciplinary perspective is pivotal in the field of good governance since the sensitivities are often different in the various scientific sectors, and what can be taken almost for granted in some of them may not be for other ones.

At the end of this kaleidoscopic research, some closing remarks will be expressed. The combined and comparative reading of all the chapters offers several stimulating insights, which allow us to take a step forward in the search and discover innovative paths for administrative action, looking at diversity not just as a possible source of undue bias but as a source of richness for public decision-making.

—**Anna Simonati**
University of Trento

SECTION I

GENDER DIVERSITY AND EMPOWERMENT

CHAPTER 1

GENDER AND LEADERSHIP

Issues and Implications for Women in Tyrol, Austria

Wendy Farrell
Management Center Innsbruck

ABSTRACT

Despite women's ability to successfully handle multiple responsibilities, they remain underrepresented in top-level positions within the workforce. This qualitative study investigates the barriers women face in pursuing a career in Tyrol, Austria, and examines their perceptions of these obstacles in relation to their professional growth and work–life balance. The findings reveal a disparity in gender representation, indicating a need for greater gender equality across all organizations. Results indicate that to address these issues, institutional initiatives should be implemented, such as affirmative action policies, auditing existing systems, providing on-site quality childcare, and incorporating workplace flexibility and job-sharing opportunities. Furthermore, traditional leadership values and societal perceptions must be addressed before gender equality in the workplace can truly be realized. Accordingly, institutional support structures should be adaptable to diverse needs, and society should strive to provide comprehensive institutional support, particularly for vulnerable groups like single mothers.

Diversity as Strategic Opportunity, pages 3–22
Copyright © 2024 by Information Age Publishing
www.infoagepub.com
All rights of reproduction in any form reserved.

GENDER AND LEADERSHIP TODAY

Women juggle many balls and fulfill many roles successfully. However, despite, or perhaps because of, their capability to successfully juggle so many balls, women are still not equally represented in the upper levels of the workforce (Mandel and Semyonov 2006). According to the Chamber of Commerce in Austria, 47% of the board in government-related companies are women, which is in the gender equality zone (Haager and Wieser 2022). However, they also indicated that there is not the same level of representation in the other types of companies. For example, according to Haager & Wieser (2022), in the top 200 companies, less than 25% of the board members are women. Similarly, they show that in government-related companies, only 16.7% of women are in management; in the top 200 companies, it is down to 8.9%.

This problem becomes more concerning when we look at how younger Generations perceive women as equally capable of being leaders. According to the Reykjavik index for leadership report, of 18–34-year-olds in Italy, nearly 40% of men and over 20% of women feel that women are not equally capable of leading ("The Reykjavik Index for Leadership 2020–2021" 2021). The Index also indicated that over 40% of the men and over 30% of the women in the 18—34 age group in Germany feel that women are not equally capable of leading. This affects the extent to which women can envision themselves as leaders and put themselves into positions that could lead to leadership positions. Moreover, once women become mothers, they often take themselves out of succession planning. Accordingly, this study attempts to understand what barriers women face in pursuing a career in Tyrol, Austria.

The chapter will proceed to show what is currently known about the issues facing women in the workplace, especially considering the culture and institutions in Austria and specifically in Tyrol. It will then proceed to investigate the experiences of women in Tyrol. Finally, the discussion summarizes the lessons learned and offers suggestions for future research.

THEORETICAL BACKGROUND

Research shows that regardless of the global progress toward gender equality, many issues still influence the achievement of true equality. This is especially pronounced when looking at women in leadership. Globally, women comprise 50% of the workforce but held only 32% of leadership positions in 2022 ("Women in Business 2022: Opening the Door to Diverse Talent" 2022). One potential reason for this gap could be how individuals emerge as leaders. This often corresponds to social role theory, which suggests the more masculine values of aggression and competition, which correspond to agentic traits, lead to the emergence of leaders (Badura et al. 2018). Another reason could be that "bias, from subtle to overt, is considered by many to be the primary challenge hindering women's opportunities in organizational leadership today" (Diehl et al. 2020, 250). According to Diehl et al., subtle bias is multifaceted and includes hurdles resulting from cultural gender stereotypes as well as workplace policies, procedures, and social norms that unintentionally favor males. They identified six overarching groups of barriers. The six groups were male privilege, disproportionate constraints, insufficient support, devaluation, hostility, and acquiescence.

However, beyond barriers, will women display the intention and ability to step into a leadership position? A recent study by Farrell et al. (2022) looked at 649 self-organized global virtual teams to understand if and when women will step up and take on leadership roles. According to Farrell et al., these teams were self-directed with no external political or other incentives to take on a leadership role. The authors found that peers perceived that women showed more leadership capabilities throughout the project than did their male colleagues, which was statistically significant throughout the project. Similarly, Farrell et al. found that the gap between self and peer perception was greater for men than women, which was also statistically significant throughout the project.

Another study looked at whether differences in how women are evaluated, which could support or hinder promotion, could be because of potential rater bias (Farrell, Farriss, et al. 2022). They found that women were actually harsher evaluators for both women and men, while men were more lenient on both women and men. They also found that both women and men evaluated the women better while both women and men evaluated the men lower.

So, women can and will take on leadership positions when the opportunity arises and are evaluated positively for their contributions. Thus, it must be assumed that the previously mentioned biases and social role-related constructs are the issues that must be contended with in order to ensure equality. While such biases and social role-related constructs are found globally, their manifestations and corresponding implications are country- and region-specific. Accordingly, it can be expected that in Tyrol, Austria, unique manifestations and corresponding implications will surface.

Austria

Austria is located in Central Western Europe and is ranked 23rd in the world based on real GDP per capita but 45th in the world based on Purchasing Power Parity (CIA 2022). Furthermore, according to the CIA World Factbook, the population of Austria is about 9.9 million and as of 2020,

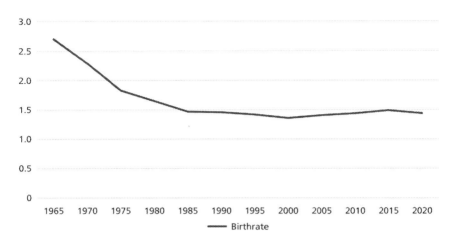

Figure 1.1 The declining birthrate in Austria (fertility rate, total [births per woman]). *Source:* World Bank DataBank, 2022

the binary statistics consider 49% of the population male and 51% of the population female.

Like many economically developed countries, Austria is experiencing a decline in birthrates (see Figure 1.1), which has led to Austria reporting a negative birth balance (deaths–births) 2020–2022 (ORF, 2023). This trend has a number of implications for the Austrian social system and is especially concerning if women must choose between family and career.

Impact of Institutions in Austria

In 2010, after recognizing that the gender gap still negatively impacted women and that having children caused a significant career slum, Federal Chancellery in Austria deliberated and created the national action plan for women's rights ("Gender Equality in the Labour Market" 2010). The plan outlined steps to be taken to alleviate the inequality. Two years later, the Austrian Federal Equal Treatment Act established the legal framework for equal treatment, especially within public service (Getz 2017). While these marked significant progress in promoting gender equality in Austria, there is still a long way to go, especially regarding the care service infrastructure and flexible workplace practices (Ziemann 2015). In 2022, the government earmarked 1 billion Euro towards childcare initiatives such as expanding childcare for toddlers and extending childcare hours of operation (Federal Chancellery of Austria 2022).

However, as the government implements these various measures, to what extent is there societal acceptance for women returning to work? As seen in Table 1.1, although women more strongly disagree, the general tendency

TABLE 1.1 Austrian Gender Equality Related Beliefs

Perception	Gender	N	Mean	Std. Deviation	Std. Error Mean
Men should have more rights to a job	M	732	2.275	1.194	0.044
	F	897	1.973	1.107	0.037
Duty towards society to have children	M	727	2.807	1.251	0.046
	F	889	2.597	1.272	0.043
Men make better business executives	M	711	2.748	0.837	0.031
	F	873	2.517	0.762	0.026
Men make better political leaders	M	711	2.889	0.895	0.034
	F	865	2.622	0.840	0.029
The university is more important for a boys	M	717	2.612	0.782	0.029
	F	875	2.379	0.654	0.022
Pre-school child suffers from working mother	M	719	3.530	0.871	0.032
	F	881	3.403	0.911	0.031

Source: EVS/WVS 2022

Note: Five-point Likert scale recoded to *strongly disagree* (1)–*strongly agree* (5). *T*-test results indicate that all differences are significant at $p < 0.01$

in Austria is that men do not have more right to a job, that a person's duty toward society is not just to have children, that men are not better executives, they are not better political leaders, and they do not have more right to go to university than women. However, a potential barrier for women can be seen in the perception that preschool children suffer if their mother returns to work. With a mean of 3.530 and 3.403, Austrians tend to agree slightly with this.

Furthermore, another potential contributor to the gender divide could be the number of women working part-time. Women are the majority of part-time employees, with 47.3% of women in Austria in part-time positions compared to only 10.7% of men, and this number is more divergent for people with children (Statistik Austria, 2022). According to the Statistik Austria, employees between the ages of 25 and 49 with children, 72.8% of women work part-time compared to 6.9 % of men.

Especially during COVID, women often felt like they had no choice when school or childcare was canceled; there were no others to care for the children. The expectation was that women would fill the gap (Collins et al., 2021).

To address some barriers, the government instituted quotas, mandating female representation on boards and at higher levels in organizations. However, while this increased female representation at higher levels, it has not yet eradicated the barriers most women face (Wroblewski, 2021).

Tyrol

Especially, the barrier to childcare services appears to be a more significant challenge in Tyrol. According to the Federal Chancellery of Austria (2022), where in other states, free childcare is available for all children or starting at 2.5 years of age, in Tyrol, the age starts at four. Furthermore, they indicate that while full-day childcare is free in other Austrian states, it is only half days in Tyrol. This means that for women who want to return to work before the child is four, and the other parent (or family member) cannot stay home with the child, greater expenses will be incurred for the luxury of working.

RESEARCH DESIGN

To shed light on how women with children perceive workplace-related barriers in Tyrol, this study takes an explanatory qualitative approach using group interviews (Frey and Fontana 1991). Two group interviews were performed, each with three participants. One group consisted of working mothers in the earlier stages of their careers, two of whom were single mothers. The second group consisted of working mothers in leadership positions. The semi-structured group interviews focused on the participants' experiences as working mothers in Tyrol. The interview guidelines incorporated the barriers addressed in the literature review.

Purposive sampling was utilized to recruit working mothers to participate in the study. The participants were sampled based on their ability to contribute to the study by being working mothers. Although the sample originated from the same employer, an educational institution in Tyrol, Austria, the focus was not on the participant's perception of their employer but rather on their experiences as working mothers in Tyrol, Austria. Accordingly, this sampling method was the most appropriate to obtain participants able to inform the study (Gill 2020). However, it should be noted that the sample consisted of women with male partners; thus, this study does not represent the experiences and constructed reality of same-sex couples.

The interviews were carried out in person and recorded. They were then transcribed using Amber Script Artificial Intelligence, which claims an 85% accuracy rate (Amberscript 2023). The scripts were then reviewed and corrections made. Once the transcripts were complete, MaxQDA was used to analyze the content. It is a computer-aided qualitative analysis tool that is considered appropriate for analyzing interviews (Kuckartz and Rädiker 2019).

The data was analyzed initially through an inductive approach using a priori codes derived from the literature. Those codes included barriers, availability of childcare, social expectations, work–life conflict, and masculine culture.

Furthermore, through coding and analyzing, the following codes emerged traditional values, maternity leave, rural deficit, child care availability, school support, unequal effort, equal pay, leadership qualities, female support, and family-friendly.

RESULTS

Traditional Values

Tyrol still preserves rather traditional values, and these values reinforced from an early age can impact what women think is possible. Some participants shared that when they grew up in smaller towns, their parents did not necessarily push them toward envisioning a career. One participant said that although she mentioned wanting to go to a gymnasium (university-bound high school) and then to university, her parents insisted she follow a more practical route to learn a trade to make money until she married. Other participants shared that they were neither encouraged nor discouraged with regard to pursuing higher education and a career.

However, once a woman has children, there is the feeling that in Tyrol, it is expected that women stay home for at least a year, and then if they do return to work, it should not be more than part-time.

On the other hand, one parent needs to be home for the children, so if the woman pursues a career [and earns more], then the man should stay home. It depends on how the couple works together as to how successful this more progressive solution can be. It all boils down to how the couple agrees to distribute the roles and that the woman does not just automatically take on the full responsibility for the children.

Another participant recently returned to work from child leave and expressed that her partner is stepping up and reducing his hours to help her with the child. Nevertheless, it is taking careful planning on their part to make it work.

There is still the feeling that role distribution is not equal, and gender stereotypes persist in this matter. One participant shared that in her past relationships with men, she felt they would express pride in "helping" her with "her job" by cooking. She expressed further the frustration that cooking and household chores should not automatically be perceived as woman's work; instead, men should take ownership of an equal portion of household chores.

It was expressed that the values associated with women and their ability to pursue a career and even be a leader must be addressed early in child rearing. Especially seeing their mother successfully pursue a career and take on a leadership position will help change the values that negatively affect women. At the same time, it is clear that the values still should respect those who do choose a more traditional path.

Stereotypes

There is the feeling that, to some extent, the traditional stereotype still exists that women belong in the kitchen and men belong at work. Moreover, even though there has been progress in this area, it was still suggested that women themselves might perpetuate some of the stereotypes with the traditional expectation that the man should open the door; the man should pay on the dates, etc. Similarly, some participants felt that stereotypes were still apparent in their private life where the woman cooks, and the man fixes. However, in one case, it was noted that the extra housework fell on her primarily because she worked part-time, so she spent more hours at home than her partner.

In the workplace, however, the women felt positive about the lack of such stereotypes within their department and noted an overall positive tone toward working mothers. One participant even recalled her male department head defending working mothers. It was clear that, for the most part, the perception was that duties and tasks were assigned based on need and competence, not gender.

Support for Single Parents

There was a perception that institutions are built around the expectation of the Mother-Father-Child family and that the institutions do not consider the existence of single parents. For example, should extra help be needed, the child's grandparents are expected to fill in the gap. This is especially true outside of the state capital of Innsbruck. It was addressed that saddling one's parents with a full-time job caring for one's children was in no way appropriate, nor should it be expected. Participants agreed that it could not be assumed that the parents are still living and that the relationship with the parents exists.

When the single parents did need help, they expressed feeling disappointed. One participant shared that during COVID, she needed to stay home with her sick daughter. She shared how the government expected her to provide proof that it was just her and her daughter and that she did not have any parents or relatives nearby who could help her. She had to take all her documentation to the city magistrate for special approval. Similarly, she would not have otherwise gotten childcare during the summer vacation.

Another participant shared that while she was ill and on medical leave, she had to fight to get any support from the government. Her son needed special attention, and she needed to have her child in childcare so she could have a few hours to herself during the day to rest and recover. However, since she was not working, the government did not want to support her. She had to fight long and hard to get minimal support for her child to attend childcare.

Work–Life Conflict

It was noted that time and priorities are the major contributors to work–life conflict. On the one hand, family is important, while on the other hand, earning a living and potentially having a career are equally as important. Especially evening appointments and networking events prove problematic for working mothers. Many meetings or events do not start until five or six in the evening, which is family time. So choosing family time means forgoing events necessary to promote and sustain one's career. In this aspect, it was perceived that this is not an issue for men. They find a way to make time for it, whereas it seems to come at a higher cost for women with children.

It was expressed that as a working mother, one permanently has a guilty conscience because when they are at home with the child, they feel guilty that they are not at the office, and when they are at the office, they feel guilty that they are not at home with the child. It was also expressed that trying to give 100% at home and 100% at work comes at the price of personal mental health, hobbies, friends, and free time. This eases a little as the children get older and become more independent. Still, one does not feel able to take full advantage of training and development opportunities, especially if travel is involved.

Childcare

Availability

All respondents shared that it is relatively well known that there is a deficit in childcare in Tyrol. Participants shared that if one is lucky enough to get their child into childcare, social expectations suggest it should be only for half a day. If the child is in the childcare for the full day, the child is perceived as the exception, and it is felt there is a negative stigma to this. It was perceived that for the child, among their peers, there was a negative connotation to them being there the full day. However, it must be said that some of the women noted that they expect that this had gotten a little better since their children were in childcare.

However, there was a consensus among the participants that there is still room to improve. There are still limited childcare opportunities that start before 7:30 or that are available past 5 pm. Beyond that, often to get the child into full day childcare, the participants shared that they must prove that they work full time. On the one hand, this supports working mothers being able to get their child into the childcare for the full day, but on the other hand, it negatively affects others. One participant shared that there was a time in her life when she had health problems and was on disability leave. As she was not working, she was denied full day childcare even though she needed it then more than ever.

Furthermore, for those participants who through choice or need, did need a care solution before the child turns three or four, there was a large expense associated with that. One participant estimated her monthly costs for child care to be around 700€.

Even more problematic is care during the school breaks. One participant who lived outside Innsbruck mentioned that during the summer, there is no facility that offers childcare throughout the summer. There is only individual care for one week at a time, which costs about 200 to 500 € per week. Similarly, it was expressed that what is offered during the summer and other breaks is "fun camp" for the kids, but the hours are generally between 8:30 am and 3 pm. The participant shared that in such cases, the drop-off location is generally somewhere inconvenient, and the week costs 300€. Overall, this was a large stress point for mothers with full-time jobs, especially single mothers with no local support. It was felt that in Tyrol, consistent with traditional values, there is an expectation that the children's grandparents will step in during school breaks and other times when help with care is needed. It was questioned whether grandparents could and should be expected to intervene in such situations. Unfortunately, this is not even an option for many women, and this was especially true for the participants who were single moms. They had a huge barrier to overcome to work full-time and ensure their children had the care they needed. The participants noted their frustration with the institutions in Tyrol being built around the Mother-Father-Child model with little thought for non-traditional situations.

The women expressed hope for company-based childcare but noted that while it would benefit those close to their employer, it might not be as helpful for people who live in the surrounding towns and commute to work.

Rural Deficit

It is perceived that there is an extreme lack of childcare in the smaller towns. It was suggested that many parents remedied this for years by enrolling their children in childcare in Innsbruck. However, more recently, regulation has been passed so that only children living in Innsbruck are allowed to be enrolled in childcare in Innsbruck.

It was expressed that there are limited facilities with limited capacity during the school year, but the situation worsens during school breaks. One parent had reached out to the mayor of her town to enquire and was told that the need did not exist. She shared during the interview that she questioned such an answer given the town's size and the number of children living there with working parents. She felt it was impossible for there not to be a need.

Still, the consensus was that while those participants who lived in Innsbruck had it hard, those living in smaller towns and areas that are more rural had it much worse.

Social Expectations

Beyond the availability of childcare, there is a social stigma about those who enroll their children in full-day care. The traditional value is that the child is best off at home with a loving mother. While this is undoubtedly true for some, this is not true or even possible in every situation. Still, there is a feeling that leaving a child in childcare all day is not socially acceptable and that mothers who do so are judged.

One participant shared that she had her first child 16 years ago, and it was clear that she would go back to work. She explained that someone who planned to send their child to childcare for full days, attracted attention. She felt other parents viewed her skeptically for having her child in full-day care. She concluded that in this respect, she believes that social constraints still exist.

Another participant shared a similar sentiment. "I was living in a small town with a real small-town environment. There, the women always stay at home and take care of the children. When I told another woman that since I was attending University and working full time, my daughter went to the babysitter before and after school. That woman looked at me so critically. I felt this from women more than men".

However, one participant who was a single mother early on shared that she did not feel judged for sending her child to full-day care. She said everyone knew her situation and, to some extent, admired that she could do so much. She said that where she did feel social pressure was when she got sick and wanted to send her child to childcare. While she felt understood from her family, her sick leave meant she was not working, so she felt she was negatively judged by the childcare facility and corresponding government institutions.

School Support

It was also discussed that there was a perception that the mothers are also expected to be teachers for their children, as the schools are not offering sufficient support for the children. One participant shared that her son has ADP. Although he can perform in a traditional school and has the mental wherewithal to do so, she has to send her child to a special school because traditional schools do not offer support for the children. Another participant confirmed this and said that although her daughter has some learning difficulties, she sent her child to the traditional school. This means that when she returns home from work, she has to spend four hours every night working with her child on schoolwork. They agreed that there is a desperate need for better support in the schools and a better understanding of the needs of the children.

Barriers to Career Development

The participants felt that having kids still impacts one's career trajectory. First and foremost, it was agreed that, especially when the children are younger, there is a limit to what can be done. For example, the participants shared that travel became problematic, especially for single mothers. Being away from the children overnight was not an option. While for women with significant others, this was less of a problem, still long distance trips with multiple overnights were perceived as problematic. This decreases the number of events such as conferences, workshops, and training one can attend. This, in turn, affects skills development and networking opportunities.

One of the participants, a single mother, shared that she was recently able to travel for a workshop. Preparing for the trip took a lot of extra effort, such as trying to prepare everything for her child's school week, ensuring that she supported her child studying prior to her trip, and in general setting up the week's logistics so nothing would go wrong in her absence. She shared that during her trip, her child had an exam, and this became an issue that she was not home to help her child prepare. Therefore, while the trip was successful, its psychological toll was large enough to affect her decision for future such opportunities.

Furthermore, there was the feeling by women at all levels that because they felt they had to invest so much in their job, there was little time left for training or networking events. The perception was that being present could have helped be considered in succession planning. This was especially true for women returning to work part-time. It was expressed that when a woman takes extended maternity leave and then returns to work part-time for ten years, by the time she is in a position to be considered for a leadership position, she is nearing retirement and thus is not considered for the position. That being said, not all women expressed the desire to pursue a career actively, and thus the choice to work part-time until their children are older is one with which they currently feel happy.

Maternity Leave

Returning from maternity leave is legally regulated, but the perception was expressed that, in practice, it works differently. That being said, the perception was also shared that it is different today than it was 15 years ago, and has improved greatly.

One of the senior-level participants explained that she took extended maternity leave, and doing so negatively impacted her position and set her career back. The other senior-level participants opted to not take the extended maternity leave and instead returned to work shortly after the end of the mother protection time. The reasons for the quick return ranged from the work's importance to wanting to retain their management position. Therefore, 15 years ago women had to decide earlier in their children's life if they wanted to choose their career.

It was believed that a woman returning from maternity leave to work part-time for 10 years is not taken into account for succession planning during that time. After that time, when she is back to working full-time, she missed the opportunities for advancement. It is perceived as common knowledge that currently one cannot have a career if they can only work part-time. However, it was suggested that job sharing could be the simple solution to this problem. It was expressed that there is a need to develop new leadership models and that it is quite possible to lead a department in pairs.

Unequal Effort

There was the feeling that women needed to expend greater effort than men. One participant shared, "As a woman, you always have different expectations that you have to fulfill because you always have to be dressed up to look great, and you have to deliver a great performance or present yourself in a great way because you are always being judged."

It was questioned if these feelings are self-imposed expectations of perfection or if societal expectations drive them. On the one hand, there was the feeling that men could prove themselves once, but women must keep proving themselves. Similarly, there is a perceived need to keep up with the other mommies who post on Instagram about how perfect they are raising their children. On the other hand, there was a feeling that women wanted to have it all and be great in everything. Thus excelling at work while being a perfect mother leads to women expending a disproportionately large amount of effort.

Some participants commented that they are trying to be better at setting boundaries and realize that not everything needs to be perfect. The day only has 24 hours.

Masculine Culture

There is a sense that even though there is not equal representation at the management level, women are taken seriously. It was explained that in Tyrol, it is possible to pursue a career as a woman and be a leader; however, then a woman should not be conspicuous or have special needs in terms of their family. The woman should be functional like a man. It was mentioned that the Scandinavian countries do a far better job of addressing the gender disparities surrounding having a career and family. For example, it was suggested that there the meetings are not scheduled at 6:00 PM but simply earlier.

The one area where the participants did perceive a masculine culture in Tyrol was with regard to the lack of networking opportunities for women (or parents) with children. Especially those with leadership positions recognize the value of networking and mourn the loss of time and the corresponding opportunity to do so. There was a sensation that men make the time for networking, meeting one another, and sharing and women need to be more cognizant of the importance of networking.

Although it was not perceived that women, especially mothers, were not invited to events and networking opportunities, it was perceived that the events were often at times that are relatively unfeasible for mothers.

Furthermore, it was suggested that perhaps a difference is that men get validation from the public stage, while women draw validation from the results of their work and this impacts the drive to network. The question remained if this indicates that women should put themselves on the public stage more, even if the source of their validation lies elsewhere.

There was still the perception that in Tyrol, a leader must work at least 60 hours, be available 24/7, be at every event, etc. This is the price for becoming an executive. Moreover, it was noted that women tend to go along with this, focusing on achieving at the expense of changing. Finally, it was perceived that companies in Tyrol still have a long way to go regarding placing families first and supporting a work–life balance.

Leadership Qualities

It was largely agreed that women are accepted and taken seriously in the educational industry. In Tyrol, however, the expectation is that gender equality is perhaps not always a given. It was expressed that in the more traditional environments, women would need to exhibit greater strength and toughness to achieve greater equality.

The participants felt that the culture in Tyrol, Austria, is still very traditional, with a male image of leadership. Men are strong; men are pragmatic; men are dominant; women are weak, emotional, and so on. They further explained that these typical leadership traits are attributed to the male gender rather than the female gender. They felt that when a man is a leader, his ability and competence are never questioned. With a woman, everything is questioned. Her looks, her competence, and her skills are all questioned. If a woman interrupts a conversation, she is bitchy. If a man interrupts a conversation, it is considered dominant. He is showing his strength and leadership skills. Still, there was hope, and it was suggested that as the world changes, it is believed that female leadership qualities, or at least those qualities ascribed to females, are more likely to be successful in the future.

One big problem was the recognition that women must support other women more. Often women who succeed are lone wolves and are sometimes forced to try to do so much that there is little time for networking and supporting one another. Therefore, in such cases, while on the one hand, these expectations are self-imposed, on the other hand, there is the sensation that societal expectations and limitations drive this.

One participant shared a previous experience going to a meeting full of heads of departments. She was in a subordinate position at the time. She noted that for her, it was rather intimidating and that she perceived a couple of the male participants exhibiting dominant behavior. She questioned if she, as a subordinate, could or should share her ideas and opinions. Although at that particular meeting, she did not have anything to share, upon reflection; she recognized that had she wanted to participate, self-confidence and toughness were what was needed to be taken seriously.

Another participant shared that women tend to be more sensitive and emotional and interact more diplomatically. They noted that conflict increases conflict, which results from the more masculine, agentic approach. They also noted, however, that when a man takes on a more communal approach, their mere stature makes this approach come across as more masculine.

Equal Pay

There is a perception that the pay gap is getting better. Especially at lower levels, there is a sensation of pay parity. It was suggested that one reason for the pay gap in Austria is that women tend to end up in lower-paying professions. However, the question remained if, at higher levels, there was gender parity.

Females Supporting Females

Overall, there was the feeling that women should support each other more. It was acknowledged that there is still more room for improvement. From jealousy and cattiness to simply being exhausted, the participants recognized that there were still barriers preventing women from truly support other women.

One of the senior-level women noticed of herself that when she felt the expectation on her to work at least 60 hours, be available 24/7, be at every event, etc., she found herself being judgmental of women not working full time. She recognized that for women to move forward, we need to overcome those feelings and try to help support those women in their careers so they can grow and become strong role models for the next generation.

She noted that exhaustion and fatigue make women stop fighting for one another, and women must work to overcome that.

Beyond self-reflection, most of the participants had not experienced queen bee superiors and felt lucky that they had largely been in environments where women did not erect barriers for other women.

Family Friendly

Participants shared the desire and need for companies in Tyrol to recognize that families are important and take steps to become more family friendly. It was expressed that this is not just in the interest of women, but also men with children and is essential given the declining birth rate. The interviews revealed that this is important not only for parents but for society as a whole.

It was suggested that companies should create a family-friendly area where employees could meet their children after school and have lunch or coffee and a snack. Use family friendliness positively and make it part of the corporate culture.

In addition, flexible work hours was another solution suggested by participants as something that companies in Tyrol could do to support work–life balance. One example of the flexibility that could benefit working parents is splitting the day and working in the office during school hours. Then after school, parents pick the children up and have time for them in the afternoon. In the evening, when things have calmed down, parents can use the time to work remotely on tasks that do not need to be completed synchronously with others. That kind of flexibility would support greater productivity and a family-friendly atmosphere.

Job sharing was discussed as a positive way to promote a family-friendly workplace. Regardless of the stage in life, whether new parent or caregiver for parents, job sharing can allow people to choose both career and family.

There are different life phases that require different levels of flexibility, and the participants express hope that some more progressive employers in Tyrol have already began moving toward such flexible worktime models.

DISCUSSION

This study aimed to understand what barriers women face in the workplace and how they perceive them as affecting their career and work–life balance. Moving forward, we must look to employers and institutions to address these issues. While, on the one hand, affirmative action policies can be problematic for companies when trying to attract qualified employees, such policies force companies to look for new ways to attract and retain qualified employees. Companies must audit their current systems and processes to see where women are underserved (Ammerman and Groysberg 2021) and identify ways to support them better. Specifically for working parents, benefits like on-site quality childcare not only help prepare children to succeed in school (Waldfogel 2002), but it can also significantly raise the employment rate of working women (Han and Waldfogel 2001). Given the critical situation in Tyrol with regard to childcare, this is one-way companies can attract and retain qualified employees. Furthermore, especially during the pandemic, services such as subsidized backup care helped employees in the USA not miss work (Modestino et al. 2021). Although the pandemic seems to be a concern of the past, companies would be remiss to think that another pandemic or other emergency will not arise, making such services indispensable.

Beyond offering benefits, structuring the workplace to be more flexible and incorporating more job-sharing opportunities can help women remain in positions that will keep them in line for succession planning or even allow them to remain in leadership positions (Watton, Stables, and Kempster 2019). The idea of job sharing was mentioned a couple of times during the interviews as an option that could help reduce work–life conflict, regardless of gender or life situation. Especially this solution is an ideal one to help unify the more traditional values in Tyrol with greater support for gender equality.

The traditional leadership values experienced by the participants are consistent with social role theory that suggests that more agentic traits, like being aggressive, lead to leader emergence (Badura et al. 2018). Traditional values are not easy to change, but as children grow up seeing their mothers working and being successful, the perception of women will begin to change. It should not be expected that every mother needs to work and send their child to full-day care, but rather the different needs of the different members of society should be respected and integrated into the institutional support structures. Furthermore, society needs to do better to support those most vulnerable. The single mothers pointed out a gap in the availability of institutional support. The prevalence of the traditional family and support structure is diminishing, and the diverse needs of all members of society need to be taken into account. It is in society's best interest to have women more present in the workplace, as doing so can positively affect GDP (Modestino et al. 2021). Accordingly, we must begin taking larger strides to ensure a level playing field.

Limitations to this study include that it was conducted in one company in the capital city of Tyrol and thus cannot be considered representative of the various regions and companies throughout Tyrol. Still, it is an indication of the areas where Tyrol still has room for improvement.

Future research should expand on these findings to quantitatively understand how women throughout Tyrol are impacted by the lack of childcare and the need for greater work–life balance.

ACKNOWLEDGMENTS

The author would like to acknowledge and thank Nadin Reinstadler. Nadin became an advocate for the research, in many cases driving it forward and helping to create the requisite atmosphere in the interviews to make them successful. Her contribution was invaluable and contributed greatly to the success of this research.

This research received no external funding.

The author declares no conflict of interest.

REFERENCES

Amberscript. 2023. "Accurate Transcripts Made for You, Not by You." Amberscript–Products. 2023. https://www.amberscript.com/en/products/transcription/.

Ammerman, Colleen, and Boris Groysberg. 2021. "How to Close the Gender Gap." *Harvard Business Review*, May 1, 2021. https://hbr.org/2021/05/how-to-close-the-gender-gap.

Badura, Katie L., Emily Grijalva, Daniel A. Newman, Thomas Taiyi Yan, and Gahyun Jeon. 2018. "Gender and Leadership Emergence: A Meta-Analysis and Explanatory Model." *Personnel Psychology* 71(3), 335–367. https://doi.org/10.1111/peps.12266.

CIA. 2022. "Austria." In *The World Factbook*. Central Intelligence Agency. https://www.cia.gov/the-world-factbook/countries/austria/.

Collins, Caitlyn, Liana Christin Landivar, Leah Ruppanner, and William J. Scarborough. 2021. "COVID-19 and the Gender Gap in Work Hours." *Gender, Work & Organization* 28 (S1): 101–12. https://doi.org/10.1111/gwao.12506.

Diehl, Amy B., Amber L. Stephenson, Leanne M. Dzubinski, and David C. Wang. 2020. "Measuring the Invisible: Development and Multi-industry Validation of the Gender Bias Scale for Women Leaders." *Human Resource Development Quarterly* 31 (3): 249–80. https://doi.org/10.1002/hrdq.21389.

EVS/WVS. 2022. "Joint EVS/WVS 2017-2022 Dataset (Joint EVS/WVS)Joint EVS/WVS 2017-2022 Dataset (Joint EVS/WVS)." GESIS. https://doi.org/10.4232/1.14023.

Farrell, Wendy, Lucia Farriss, Dhruv Pratap SINGH, Hafsa El Kamous, Lydia Karnadi, and Marc Idelson. 2022. "Expectations of Performance in Peer Evaluations: Are Females Harsher Raters?" In . Seattle, Washington.

Farrell, Wendy, Malika Richards, Hafsa El Kamous, Lydia Karnadi, Lucia Farriss, Dhruv Pratap SINGH, and Marc Idelson. 2022. "Are You as Effective a Leader as You Think? The Impact of Gender and Personality Traits." In . Seattle, Washington.

Federal Chancellery of Austria. 2022. "Child Care in Austria." 2022. https://www.bundeskanzleramt.gv.at/en/agenda/family/child-care-in-austria.html.

Frey, James H., and Andrea Fontana. 1991. "The Group Interview in Social Research." *The Social Science Journal* 28(2), 175–187. https://doi.org/10.1016/0362-3319(91)90003-M.

"Gender Equality in the Labour Market." 2010. National Action Plan. Vienna, Austria: Federal Minister for Women and Civil Service at the Federal Chancellery. https://www.bundeskanzleramt.gv.at/en/agenda/women-and-equality/gender_equality_in_the_labour_market/national_action_plan_on_gender_equality_in_the_labour_market.html#:~:text=The%20National%20Action%20Plan%20(NAP,period%20from%202010%20to%202013.

Getz, Laura. 2017. "Bundes-Gleichbehandlungsgesetz (B-GBG)–Federal Equal Treatment Act (Austria)." Text. GenPORT. March 13, 2017. https://www.genderportal.eu/resources/bundes-gleichbehandlungsgesetz-b-gbg-federal-equal-treatment-act-austria.

Gill, Sara L. 2020. "Qualitative Sampling Methods." *Journal of Human Lactation*, 36(4), 579–581. https://doi.org/10.1177/0890334420949218

Haager, Theresa, and Christina Wieser. 2022. *AK Frauen Management Report*. AK Wien. https://wien.arbeiterkammer.at/interessenvertretung/frauen/Frauen.Management.Report.html.

Han, Wenjui, and Jane Waldfogel. 2001. "Child Care Costs and Women's Employment: A Comparison of Single and Married Mothers With Pre-School-Aged Children." *Social Science Quarterly,* 82(3), 552–568. https://doi.org/10.1111/0038-4941.00042.

Kuckartz, Udo, and Stefan Rädiker. 2019. *Analyzing Qualitative Data with MAXQDA: Text, Audio, and Video*. Cham: Springer International Publishing. https://doi.org/10.1007/978-3-030-15671-8.

Mandel, Hadas, and Moshe Semyonov. 2006. "A Welfare State Paradox: State Interventions and Women's Employment Opportunities in 22 Countries." *American Journal of Sociology* 111 (6): 1910–49. https://doi.org/10.1086/499912.

Modestino, Alicia Sasser, Jamie J Ladge, Addie Swartz, and Alisa Lincoln. 2021. "Childcare Is a Business Issue." *Harvard Business Review*, 3.

ORF. 2023. "2022 weniger Babys und mehr Sterbefälle." oesterreich.ORF.at. February 20, 2023. https://oesterreich.orf.at/stories/3195509/

Statistik Austria. 2022. "Gender-Statistik." Statistik Austria. August 3, 2022. https://www.statistik.at/web_de/statistiken/menschen_und_gesellschaft/soziales/gender-statistik/index.html

"The Reykjavik Index for Leadership 2020–2021." 2021. Kantar. https://www.kantar.com/campaigns/reykjavik-index

Waldfogel, Jane. 2002. "Child Care, Women's Employment, and Child Outcomes." *Journal of Population Economics* 15 (3): 527–48. https://doi.org/10.1007/s001480100072

Watton, Emma, Sarah Stables, and Steve Kempster. 2019. "How Job Sharing Can Lead to More Women Achieving Senior Leadership Roles in Higher Education:

A UK Study." *Social Sciences,* 8(7), 209. https://doi.org/10.3390/socsci 8070209.
"Women in Business 2022: Opening the Door to Diverse Talent." 2022. EPI.564. Grant Thornton International Ltd. https://www.grantthornton.global/en/insights/women-in-business-2022/.
World Bank DataBank. 2022. "Fertility Rate, Total (Births per Woman)." Gender Statistics | DataBank. World Bank. https://databank.worldbank.org/source/gender-statistics#.
Wroblewski, Angela. 2021. "Quotas and Gender Competence: Independent or Complementary Approaches to Gender Equality?" *Frontiers in Sociology,* 6, 740462.
Ziemann, Volker. 2015. "Towards More Gender Equality in Austria." OECD Economics Department Working Papers 1273. Vol. 1273. OECD Economics Department Working Papers. Organisation for Economic Cooperation and Development (OECD). https://doi.org/10.1787/5jrp2s4pfbnp-en.

CHAPTER 2

LEADERSHIP DEVELOPMENT PROGRAMS FOR WOMEN AS A MEANS TO ACHIEVE GENDER EQUALITY

What Do Women Think?

Marjukka Mikkonen
Tampere University

ABSTRACT

The aim of this chapter is to explore women's leadership development programs as a means to tackle gender inequality in leadership positions in the context of sports. Building on a case study approach, the current body of knowledge, and 22 interviews with women with experience of such programs, this chapter describes and analyses how participants perceive leadership development programs as a means to a) support their leadership careers and b) enhance gender equality in leadership positions. The chapter shows that many women find women's leadership development programs meaningful for career advancement and developing their leadership skills. However, the programs may not be entirely beneficial for women to attain concrete career advancement. Furthermore, the study discusses networks and the reasons behind the rather tight network created in the case program. The study also shows that the program tackles mainly individual-level barriers to advancing gender equality, and its potential for fundamental changes thus remains limited.

The scarcity of women in leadership positions in sports and of gender equality in sports organizations is a global challenge acknowledged both by academia and in practice. A low number of women in sports leadership positions[1] and women's experiences of gender inequality[2] also apply in countries that are often perceived as frontrunners in gender equality, including Finland and the other Nordic countries.[3] To tackle this, many sports organizations have implemented leadership development programs that target women and aim to empower and educate them, thereby closing the gap between the number of women and men in leadership and ultimately increasing gender equality in sports leadership (e.g., the UEFA Women in Football Leadership Programme; the Alberta Women in Sport Leadership Impact Program, Canada;[4] and the Women's Sport Leadership Academy, New Zealand[5]).

Even though these programs have increased their popularity as a means to tackle gender inequality in leadership positions and to increase the number of women who occupy them, we know fairly little about them in the context of sports. Do they work, and if so, how? Do the participants find them effective? In the sports context, studies have mainly focused on the coaching setting[6] or describing the program and strategies used in it,[7] and not on administrative leaders or board members.[8]

To increase our understanding of how leadership development programs for women work, and to answer the call of Evans and Pfister (2021) and Pike et al. (2018) for more research on gender equality interventions, the aim of this research is operationalized into two research questions:

1. How do participants perceive leadership development programs as a means to support their leadership careers?
2. How do participants perceive leadership development programs as a means to enhance gender equality in leadership positions in sports.

I utilized an instrumental case study approach[9] to enable a thorough exploration of women's perceptions and experiences of women's leadership development programs (WLDPs). The case studied, a Finnish WLDP for women in sports leadership, illustrates a typical case of these programs. Therefore, it provides a great opportunity to learn about the broader phenomena, not just this particular case. The main data of this case study consist of a scoping survey and semi-structured interviews that are complemented by publicly available documentary data from the program.

This study provides an important contribution to the current body of knowledge on leadership positions and gender (in)equality by describing and analyzing one commonly used intervention for gender equality and, in particular, giving participants (i.e., women) an opportunity to voice their experiences and perceptions of these programs in relation to their leadership careers. For practitioners, this chapter provides insights into women's experiences of WLDPs and an opportunity to develop these programs further to provide even broader support for the functionality of these programs.

LEADERSHIP DEVELOPMENT PROGRAMS FOR WOMEN AND GENDER EQUALITY

Women's careers in sports leadership often differ from those of men. Women face gendered barriers and obstacles on multiple levels that impact their leadership careers.[10] On the macro level, women's leadership careers are impacted by broader sociocultural factors, such as geographical location, political climate, employment and anti-discrimination laws, institutional sexism, and stakeholder expectations that operate at a societal level. On the meso level, women are impacted by organizational-level factors, such as diversity policies, bias in decision-making, organizational culture, and power relations. Finally, at the micro level, women's leadership careers are influenced by individual-level factors, such as investment in human and social capital as well as the self-limiting behavior of women.[11]

WLDPs have seen increasing popularity across different sectors as a means to tackle gender inequality, empower women, and develop the leadership skills of women in leadership positions or those who are aiming for such positions.[12] The need for WLDPs is often justified based on the differences identified in the career paths and leadership styles of women and men, their approach to problem-solving, and their motivations as well as because of the greater tendency of men to take up space in learning settings compared to women.[13] Therefore, leadership development programs that solely target women may offer an encouraging environment for women to gain confidence, learn, and develop leadership skills. Furthermore, these programs may offer an empowering space for women in which they feel more comfortable to speak up and engage in discussions without facing male dominance.[14] WLDPs also often provide important networks and mentorship for women,[15] which are each profoundly important. Previous studies have shown that a lack of mentors for and networks of women is one barrier that excludes women from leadership positions and hinders their leadership careers.[16] Through networks, women may, for instance, hear about new job opportunities, engage in peer support, and sparring opportunities. Mentoring relationships may also have many benefits, such as enabling mentees to understanding themselves better as leaders, and they may provide insights on what to do (and what not to do) in leadership careers. Lastly, the mentor may provide direct or indirect career opportunities.[17] However, WLDPs should be designed to specifically address the realities that women face in their leadership careers and to encourage women to define themselves according to their respective leadership identity, not according to the gendered perceptions of being an "ideal leader."[18]

WLDPs have been criticized for focusing on "fixing women" and molding them to fit into both male-dominated leadership and the existing frame of an "ideal" leader that is based on masculine norms and stereotypes, rather than changing gender-inequal organizational cultures and structures.[19] Furthermore, the programs have been criticized for being detached from the existing systems and structures of organizations, including their recruitment/selection processes, and for not receiving support from senior management nor considering the systemic nature of gender inequality in leadership.[20]

As described earlier, the myriad barriers and factors impacting women's careers in sports leadership emerge across multiple levels. To have a comprehensive understanding of WLDPs, we must also look beyond the individual level to understand the possible impacts of such programs. Scrutinizing only one level may lead only to a partial understanding;[21] therefore, I will base my understanding on Kozlowski and Klein's theories of organizations as multi-level entities[22] as well as on Black et al.'s and Black and Earnest's models on leadership development program evaluations.[23] Furthermore, I have chosen an evocative enquiry approach, which means that I will explore the perceptions, viewpoints, experiences, and feedback of individuals[24] regarding WLDPs and their leadership careers.

The theories of Black et al. and Black and Earnest are based on the assumption that individuals taking part in leadership programs are motivated to learn. The outcomes of such programs may occur on three different levels, namely the individual, organizational, and community levels.[25] Most of the direct benefits and results of leadership programs may be expected to occur on the individual level. The organizational-level benefits manifest in the organizations at which the participants work as well as in the organizations with which they have interactions. Lastly, on the community level, the benefits are realized in the social and professional networks of the participants through direct interaction or as a result of the participants' organizational work.[26] These levels are adequate, since the current body of knowledge on gender inequality and leadership positions has identified that gendered barriers, as well the means to tackle them, may occur on three different and intertwined levels, namely the socio-cultural, organizational, and individual levels.[27]

METHODS

I approached the research problem with an instrumental case study approach.[28] This means that the case is used as a means to increase our understanding of the phenomena studied (in this case, women leaders' perceptions of WLDPs in relation to their leadership careers), not necessarily of the case itself. The data include survey, interview, and some secondary data (such as information on websites). The names of the program, the informants, and their organizations are pseudonymized to protect the informants' anonymity. I chose to use mixed methods because this approach will enable a thorough exploration WLDPs in sport;[29] that is, the survey provides an opportunity to analyze the overall perceptions of women, while the qualitative data provide an understanding of women's deeper perceptions and experiences of WLDPs, instead of focusing solely on specific predetermined sections and levels of leadership development.[30]

In the first phase of data gathering, I structured a quantitative, scoping survey with Microsoft Forms that targeted women who either had participated or were participating in the case WLDP at the time ($n = 79$). Besides demographic questions, the survey included Likert-scale questions and open-ended questions about the women's individual opinions on the program, its content, and its possible impact on their own leadership skills; their career development; and gender equality. I devised the survey items based on prior research and the theoretical framework of this study.

I sent the survey link along with information on the research project, a consent form, and details of the participants' rights to all the participants' e-mail addresses via the coordinator of the case program. The survey was open from 2 November to 14 November 2021, during which time I also sent two reminder emails. The response rate was 57%, with 44 recipients in total providing responses. I analyzed the quantitative data with computer-assisted statistical analysis software (IBM SPSS) by examining means and distributions.

To enrich the survey data and to gain a deeper understanding of the women's perceptions of WLDPs in relation to their leadership careers, I conducted semi-structured interviews with some of the survey informants ($n = 22$). A total of 24 respondents had initially indicated their willingness to be interviewed; after I had contacted all 24, 22 eventually agreed to be interviewed (I was unable to reconnect with two of the respondents, even after several attempts). I used the survey data and results as the basis for the interview guide. The length of the interviews varied between 60 and 90 minutes. All interviews were transcribed verbatim.

I analyzed the interview data with reflective thematic analysis.[31] I began by familiarizing myself with the data by reading and re-reading them and taking notes, after which I coded the data with computer-assisted qualitative data analysis software (Atlas.ti). I used both semantic and latent-level coding and utilized codes based on the theoretical framework as well as more open coding. I evolved the codes over multiple rounds until they had been refined into relevant themes in relation to the research question.[32] Lastly, I used secondary data (publicly available documents, plans, and archives concerning the program that were available on the internet) to complement the interview and survey data. These data were mainly used to supplement the interview and survey data to create a holistic image of the context of the program and, for instance, the themes covered in it.

EMPIRICAL ANALYSIS

The empirical analysis led into two major themes, namely the role of WLDPs in relation to leadership development and to gender (in)equality, which are discussed below. I begin by providing some background information on the case WLDP as well as demographic information on the survey respondents and interviewees.

Background Information on the Case Program

The case WLDP targets women who aim for national or international leadership positions in sports and is arranged by a service organization for organized sports in Finland. On a broader sense, the program seeks to highlight the current gender imbalance among the people who end up in decision-making positions in sports. More concretely, there are two main aims of the program, namely to strengthen leadership skills in the sports sector and to increase the number of women in leadership positions .

The program had four cohorts between 2015 and 2022.[33] Each cohort consisted of 20 participants who had been selected from their applications. One of the cohorts consisted of women in managerial leadership positions (e.g., CEO, manager), two of women in voluntary leadership positions (e.g., chairperson, board member), and one of women in both managerial and voluntary leadership positions. Each cohort lasted for a year. The curriculum included five two-day sessions, learning assignments under the themes of leadership and the sports context (personal leadership, leadership, communication, interaction and performance, strategic management and sports management, and networking), a development plan aimed at identifying one's own goals and areas for development, and mentoring and networking.

Demographic Information on the Participants

Table 2.1 provides information on the ages, educational attainment, and positions of the participants. The majority of the survey respondents were

TABLE 2.1 Demographics of the Respondents

Age (y.o.)	n	Share (%) (n = 44)	Education level	n	Share (%) (n = 44)	Voluntary position/ employment	n	Share (%) (n = 45)
26–35	13	29.5	Bachelor's degree	10	22	Employed in a sports organization	23	51.1
36–45	21	47.7	Master's degree	34	77	Voluntary position in a sports organization	18	40.0
46–55	8	18.2				No answer	2	4.4
56–65	2	4.5				Not currently involved with a sports organization	2	4.4

36–45 years old, the second largest group was 26–35 years old, and older age groups were in a minority. The share of the respondents appeared rather natural because women in leadership positions in Finnish sports tend to be younger than men.[34] Furthermore, younger generations may feel the need for leadership training, whereas older generations are already settled in their careers. All the respondents had a higher education degree, and a clear majority (77%) had a master's level degree. A little over half of the respondents (51%) were employed in a sports organization (e.g., a manager, CEO, specialist), while 40% were in a voluntary position (e.g., chair, board member).

Table 2.2 contains information about the organizations with which the respondents were involved. Most of the respondents worked for (through employment or voluntary work) a national governing body of sport or at a sports club.

TABLE 2.2 Respondents' Sports Organization

Sports organization(s) I am working at	Share (%)	n = 54
National Governing Body of Sport	37.0	20
Sports club	33.3	18
Regional sport organization or other organization for sport and physical activity (public and 3rd sector)	11.1	6
National umbrella organization (e.g., Finnish Olympic Committee, TUL)	7.4	4
Not currently working at any sports organization	5.6	3
Sport Institute	5.6	3
Total	100.0	54

Leadership Skills and Career Development

The survey mapped the respondents' perceptions of the impact of the program on their leadership skills and career development (Figure 2.1). The first two items in Figure 2.1 are more passive by their nature, whereas the third and the fourth items are more active, meaning that they require the individual to actively do something, instead of "enjoying the benefits" of being trained. The final item considers the networks gained through the program.

When considering the first two, more passive items, a clear majority of the women felt that they had benefited from the program, with 43 of the 44 respondents agreeing that the program had increased their leadership skills. In the interviews, many women mentioned that the program's content had been beneficial and that they had learned new aspects and gained new tools. Many interviewees said that the lectures, tasks, and peer discussions had led to new knowledge and concrete changes in their behaviors and mindsets. Sometimes, the changes were small, such as structuring an email in a different way, and they were sometimes more fundamental, such as new ways for the interviewees to perceive themselves as leaders. According to the interview data, reflection seems to have been a key part of the learning process. The women described how, through reflection either with peers or by themselves, they had become able to internalize the new content. It seems important that the WLDP allowed time for reflection and unstructured discussions with peers. Besides the individual-level changes in leadership skills and behavior, some women stated in their interviews that they were able to transfer these new leadership aspects and/or tools to the organizational level. Interviewee 1 described her learning process as follows:

> The increase in competence that I got from that [the communication theme covered in the program], for example, started to build up right away. I was

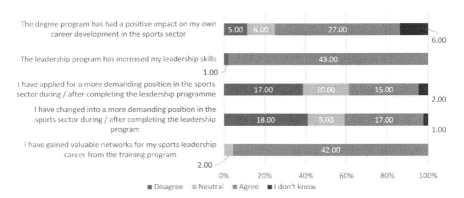

Figure 2.1 Leadership skills and career development ($n = 44$).

able to go quite far [in her learning], and it [the learning] also changed the way I worked, both on my own and in my organization. [...] It brought understanding from the perspective of communication, and it also brought new ways of working.

The new competence and leadership skills could therefore be transferred from solely an individual level to an organizational level through the participants.

Almost two-thirds of the survey respondents (61%) stated that the program had positively impacted their own career development in the sports sector. According to the interview data, most of the women highlighted the importance of peer networks and viewed the program as empowering and encouraging. They felt that these aspects were meaningful in terms of their leadership careers were. For example, Interviewee 2 said: "In my opinion, the most important thing was that it [the program] created the belief that you are capable—that you are already a sports leader—and that you can just go out and conquer the world, so to speak. So, it increased self-confidence."

These findings are similar to those of Pike et al. (2018),[35] who argued that gaining confidence is one of the main benefits that women tend to experience through WLDPs. Studies have suggested that women may behave in self-limiting ways;[36] therefore, building confidence and empowering women may be adequate tools for tackling such individual-level barriers to gender equality.

However, considering the survey data, WLDPs may not lead to concrete career-benefiting steps (such as applying for/moving into a more demanding position), compared to the more abstract-level benefits perceived, such as increasing leadership skills. It seems that the benefits of the program did not actualize in direct actions of acquiring for more demanding positions. Approximately one-third (35.5%) of the survey respondents had applied for a more demanding position during or after completing the leadership program, and on a positive note, 40% of the respondents said that they had moved into a more demanding position during or after completing the leadership program. Causal claims, naturally, cannot be made based on the data of this study; nevertheless, it seems that the ones who applied for new positions were being (s)elected. Interviewee 3 reflected the situation as follows:

> There were persons who thought that, well, they would like to be in a certain position and take certain things [forward]. These particular people had grown tremendously and gone to such places that they maybe didn't even think possible at the time. After all, those people were good at everything and somehow were given a kind of super cape; they were able to advance into positions in which they could influence and do the things they wanted, based on what they had also learned on the education side.

This quote shows how the empowerment end encouragement gained from the program resulted in behavioral changes. Interviewee 4 reflected on her own growth, stating: "I don't know if I had been able to, or had had the courage, to apply for this position, for instance [without the program]." As described earlier, many of the women found the set content of the program (e.g., communication, performance) and the tools they had learned (e.g., for understanding their leadership identity) to be meaningful in terms of their leadership careers. The leadership skills that they had acquired from the program contributed to their self-confidence as leaders. In a similar fashion, previous studies have suggested that participants often feel that they have benefited in terms of personal and professional development; however, their actual progress to senior positions depends on several different factors, such as personal motivation, family issues, the work context, and the organizational culture.[37] Therefore, the benefit of WLDPs lies more at tackling individual level barriers, thereby enhancing gender equality in leadership positions more indirectly. Based on these findings, it seems important for WLDPs to include more components that contribute to women taking action so that they are more beneficial and effective in terms of change beyond the pure individual level.

Networks

Nearly all the survey respondents (95%) felt that they had gained valuable networks from the program. The possibility to network was one of the reasons many of the women took part in the program. As Interviewee 11 put it: "[N]etworking was really interesting," and Interviewee 10 stated: "I probably had a longing for peer support." In the interviews, most of the women emphasized the meaning of the networks created in the program; for example, Interviewee 5 said:

> All the interviewees probably say that networks [were one of the most beneficial aspects of the program]. [...] There were really good lecturers [in the program]. [...] But perhaps even more fruitful was the fact that there were twenty of us women there, and when we went there [to the program venue], we saw each other in person and spent the whole weekend there in a bubble. We shared similar and common challenges and successes related to club activities, to sports leadership, and to our own activities. That was probably the best thing. [...] There were a lot of discussions about the special nature of volunteering, where it was going, how to manage and lead volunteers, and how to deal with different difficult personalities. [...] Probably the best part [of the program] was the networking opportunity, and there are still several women from the program with whom I keep in touch with and have met.

This finding supports those of previous studies by highlighting the meaning of peer networks in WLDPs.[38] The interviewees identified the opportunity to network, and the networking achieved in the program meaningful in several ways. First, it could provide new contacts and acquaintances who could be beneficial for the interviewees' leadership careers. Second, as the above quote illustrates, networking was seen as an opportunity to reflect within a group and gain peer support. Third, networking was seen as a concrete tool to enhance gender equality in sports. As one interviewee explained, since some of the women in the program already occupied powerful positions in sports, the other women could for instance learn of new job opportunities, have access to these positions, and gain tacit knowledge through their network. In a way, the women saw their networks as the equivalent of the "old boys clubs" that are often cited as among the barriers to women's inclusion and gender equality in sports leadership.[39]

The interviewees had different experiences regarding the closeness of the networks that they had formed from the program. The women who had participated in the program on-site (i.e., before the COVID-19 pandemic or when there were no assembly restrictions) seemed to be more closely connected to the network than the women who had participated in the program fully online. The women who had participated on-site elaborated on the meaning of being there in person at the venue and also the opportunity to share and discuss their experiences away from the organized activities. An interesting finding relative to that of Pike et al.'s (2018) study, is that the participants in this program seemed to have formed a closer network. This can, at least to some extent, be explained from three perspectives. First, building trust and deep connections can take time, and the case-program of this study lasted a year, compared to the one-week residency in Pike et al.'s study. Therefore, the participants in this case program had a better opportunity to develop deeper connections with each other because they had regular meetings over a longer period of time. Furthermore, between meetings, the women were able to remain in contact with each other through the different electronic communication channels that they had created and could thus build trust and a sense of belonging.

Secondly, it is easier for homogenic people to create and maintain networks.[40] The participants of this case program were rather homogeneous in terms of their social identities, such as age, education, and nationality, whereas in Pike et al.'s study, the participants were more heterogenous. Even if heterogenous networks provide more learning opportunities and lower the "fence" between different kinds of people, homogeneity has some benefits in terms of networking, since homogeneous groups tend to create and maintain networks more effortlessly.[41] When participants are more heterogenic and their (possible) similarities are at deeper levels, such as them having similar motivations or experiences, more time may be needed to identify the similarities, and thus the bonding and sharing, which are important for the success of the program, may require more time. In either case, time should be allocated for identifying similarities and common ground in order for the participants to build trust and deeper connections.[42] The greater extent of hetereogeneity and shorter period of time may also explain the scarcity of the network in Pike et al.'s study, compared to the case program in this study. However, it is notable that even though the participants in this case program were rather homogenous (e.g., somewhat of the same age, gender, educational level, nationality), their experiences varied. The women had different expectations for and needs from the program, and they worked in different kinds of positions (e.g., managers, chairs, board members, experts) and organizations (e.g., sports clubs, national associations, regional associations). Interviewee 7 described the situation as follows:

> We had different expectations for our participation. It's often [a question] of just how to deal with a really heterogeneous group. The only thing that united us was our gender and our interest in sports and exercise. Then again, considering our backgrounds, work tasks, and all these different aspects in the content [of the program] that we went through, it's really difficult for everyone to get something out of it.

As discussed above, these differences may be fruitful in terms of inclusivity, diversity, and different perspectives; however, if there is not enough common ground, it may be difficult not only to build networks but also to provide the different participants with meaningful content and opportunities to learn.

Lastly, the women in this program were physically and professionally close to each other, since they were all involved in sports in Finland. This contrasts with Pike et al.'s (2018) study, in which the participants were from different countries. Because the participants in this study were involved with a rather small common sector, namely the Finnish sports sector, the women had the explicit benefit of remaining in touch with their networks. Furthermore, they might naturally also have more interactions with each other because of the different events, such as seminars or competitions, funding opportunities, voluntary work, or other forms of cooperation.

Gender Equality

The survey also mapped out the respondents' perceptions of the impact of the WLDP on gender equality in sports. Figure 2.2 describes the respondent's opinions on the impacts of the program on three different levels.

Leadership Development Programs for Women ▪ **35**

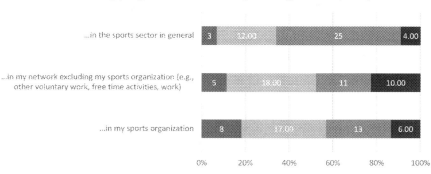

Figure 2.2 The effects of the training program on gender equality ($n = 44$).

The respondents' answers about the program's impacts on gender equality varied across three different levels. A large proportion of the women (57%) felt that the program had impacted the sports sector in general, whereas considerably fewer thought that it had impacted the networking or organizational levels. In the interviews, some of the women reasoned that the program may have had a broader impact on the sports sector, such as through media coverage. As Interviewee 12 put it: "It [the program] has brought it [gender inequality] to light." However, contradicting the survey results, many of the women who were interviewed were rather skeptical toward the program's possible impact on gender equality at the macro level. The interviewees mentioned that the positive impacts on the sports sector may have remained quite limited or not existed at all; rather, the impacts on gender equality may have occurred at the micro level, as the women gained confidence and encouragement. Interviewee 6 described this as follows:

> [T]hose who have attended this program have gained confidence and courage to pursue different sports sectors, but I don't know if this program somehow influenced it [gender equality/number of women in leadership] even more. Like, I don't know if there are more women on the board of the Olympic Committee because of [the name of the program].

When considering the impacts on gender equality in their own organizations or networks, many of the respondents were quite unsure or neutral: 41% of the respondents were neutral about the statement regarding their networks and 39% about the statement regarding their own organization. One explanation for this, based on the interviews, is that there was no specific theme allocated for content on gender equality/gender and leadership in sports. Interviewee 7 commented: "[W]e didn't have a single contact weekend during which we could have considered gender equality in sports leadership." If the participants did not learn about gender, gender equality, or how to promote gender equality in their organizations, they naturally could not take this knowledge further to their organizations or networks. The interviewees often expressed that instead of official content, their insights on gender (in)equality came from the experiences and stories that they had heard from other participants or lecturers. The shared experiences and narratives increased the participants' understanding of the status of gender inequality in Finnish sports leadership and made them aware of the possible barriers to their careers. Interviewee 8 described this as follows: "You were able to listen to the stories of the other participants, and then you realized that, okay, in that part, there could be those challenges, and so on. So I got a pretty good idea of what you sometimes have to struggle with [as being a woman in sports leadership]."

In addition to increased understanding of and interest in gender (in)equality, some of the interviewed women mentioned that through the narratives and shared experiences, they had adopted new ways of behaving in their leadership positions in a way that enhanced gender equality, thereby extending the impact of the case program to an organizational level through their changed individual behavior. One example of this was recounted by Interviewee 9, who explained how she understood that in order to have new kinds of people in leadership positions, the people in power must open the doors to them, meaning that opportunities must be given to different kinds of people, not just for the most obvious ones in the "leader pipeline." She said:

> Even though it [gender equality] was interesting before, it has maybe somehow started to interest me even more now. [...] There were good career stories [shared in the program], and we had different women tell us about their own backgrounds, how they got into their sports, and what kind of leadership positions they ended up in, so you got good examples and models. [...] [There have been examples of how] some of the glass ceilings have now been broken down, and that it is not only gray men who lead sports. [...] I think it was really important that we talked about opening doors in the program—that it doesn't matter whether it's done by women or men or whoever does it, but if you want new people—different people to join—then you have to open those doors.

Some of the interviewees criticized how the gender equality part of the program felt as if it had been "glued on top." Interviewee 1 described how she was unsure about the meaning of this part in this program. Had it been included so that the arranging organization and the sports movement would have an alibi for gender equality, or was there true will to promote gender equality through the program? She said:

> You also felt it [gender equality] was a bit like it had been glued on top. Are we [the sports community] really going to do [something] about those things [gender inequality], or are we making just making it appear [that way] so that we can say, for example, that there is now such a program, that women are now being trained? But what is the end result?

One reason for this feeling of being glued on top may be the issue discussed earlier of gender and gender equality not being covered in terms of the content of the program. If the aim of the program was to increase the number of women in leadership positions and enhance gender equality, but these themes had not been covered, it seems quite natural that some of the participants may have seen that section as being artificial. Therefore, it seems important to include content on gender and gender equality in WLDPs, which may also enable the programs to impact as far as the organizational and network levels.

Some interviewees also questioned the program's aim of solely educating women. In other words, they criticized the liberal feminist approach that is often utilized in WLDPs, which is based on the idea that women need to be educated further to be competent and to allow them fit the present (masculine) frame of a sports leader.[43] The interviewees mentioned that it would perhaps be more beneficial to train and educate people in top decision-making positions in sports (which are mostly occupied by men) about gender equality because they are the ones holding power and thus able to enact changes. Interviewee 3 said: "So, through the training, I see that this training is good for everyone, [...] and it may also be the case for associations in general, to take into account that you have certain types of people in the organization and in different roles and that there are not 99% men and so on."

Therefore, providing both a) leadership development programs for women who are in or aiming for leadership positions that are thus aimed more at tackling individual-level barriers to gender equality, such as the self-limiting behavior of women, and b) leadership development for people already in leadership positions, who therefore have better opportunities to tackle the structures and cultures that sustain inequalities, could offer a more fruitful way to enhance gender equality, instead of relying only on women's development programs,[44] which often is the case. Providing training and education for both women and men is important because people act and behave, not organizations.[45] Therefore, organizational change requires changes in the individuals constructing the organization. These collective individual changes may enable organizational change to occur.

CONCLUDING REMARKS

The aim of this chapter was to explore women's perceptions and experiences of WLDPs as a means to support their leadership careers as well to improve the state of gender equality in leadership positions in sports. The findings show that many women experienced the case WLDP as meaningful in terms of their career advancement and leadership skills. However, the programs may not be entirely beneficial for concrete career-advancing actions, such as applying for new positions, even if it seems that once participants are encouraged to apply, they tend to be chosen.

In terms of enhancing gender equality in leadership positions, WLDPs tackle in particular individual-level barriers to leadership, such as the self-limiting behaviors of women, through empowerment and encouragement and provide participants with a network of women in the same sector who can provide peer support and access to tacit knowledge.

Even if WLDPs lead to some changes beyond the pure individual level, mainly through the participants' actions, the opportunities for WLDPs to tackle the fundamental structures and cultures sustaining gender inequality in leadership positions remain limited. Therefore, WLDPs can be seen as a one means to enhance gender equality in leadership positions in sport. However, since gender inequality is a multi-level phenomenon, other means are needed to tackle and deinstitutionalize gender inequality in sports leadership.[46]

NOTES

1. Hakamäki, Turpeinen, and Lehtonen, "A Strategy to Promote Gender Equality: The Number and Status of Women in Leadership and Decision-Making Positions in Finnish Sport."
2. Mikkonen, "'We Are Going to the Right Direction... but We Are Not in Ideal World yet': Understanding Gender (in)Equality within Leadership Positions in Nordic Football Governance."
3. World Economic Forum, "Global Gender Gap Report 2022."
4. Culver et al., "The Alberta Women in Sport Leadership Project: A Social Learning Intervention for Gender Equity and Leadership Development."
5. Pike et al., "Women and Sport Leadership: A Case Study of a Development Programme."
6. e.g., Allen and Reid, "Scaffolding Women Coaches' Development: A Program to Build Coaches' Competence and Confidence"; Belding and Dodge, "Examining the Benefits of Female-to-Female Mentorship as a Result of Participation in a Female Coach Mentorship Program"; Kraft, Culver, and Din, "Exploring a Women-Only Training Program for Coach Developers"; Carson et al., "Coach Like a Woman: Learnings From a Pilot Coach Education Program."

7. e.g., Culver et al., "The Alberta Women in Sport Leadership Project: A Social Learning Intervention for Gender Equity and Leadership Development"; Kraft, Culver, and Din, "Exploring a Women-Only Training Program for Coach Developers."
8. Pike et al., "Women and Sport Leadership: A Case Study of a Development Programme." For exeptions, see Megheirkouni and Roomi, "Women's Leadership Development in Sport Settings: Factors Influencing the Transformational Learning Experience of Female Managers."
9. Stake, "Case Studies."
10. Burton, "Underrepresentation of Women in Sport Leadership: A Review of Research"; Mikkonen, "'We Are Going to the Right Direction... but We Are Not in Ideal World yet': Understanding Gender (in)Equality within Leadership Positions in Nordic Football Governance"; e.g., Alsarve, "Achieving Gender Equity: Barriers and Possibilities at Board Level in Swedish Sport"; Oakley, "Gender-Based Barriers to Senior Management Positions: Understanding the Scarcity of Female CEOs."
11. Cunningham, "Gender."
12. Kraft, Culver, and Din, "Exploring a Women-Only Training Program for Coach Developers."
13. Clarke, "Advancing Women's Careers through Leadership Development Programs"; Chuang, "Exploring Women-Only Training Program for Gender Equality and Women's Continuous Professional Development in the Workplace."
14. Carson et al., "Coach Like a Woman: Learnings From a Pilot Coach Education Program."
15. Clarke, "Advancing Women's Careers through Leadership Development Programs."
16. e.g., Katz, Walker, and Hindman, "Gendered Leadership Networks in the NCAA: Analyzing Affiliation Networks of Senior Woman Administrators and Athletic Directors'; Wells and Hancock, 'Networking, Mentoring, Sponsoring: Strategies to Support Women in Sport Leadership."
17. Dworkin, Maurer, and Schipani, "Career Mentoring for Women"; Wells and Hancock, "Networking, Mentoring, Sponsoring: Strategies to Support Women in Sport Leadership."
18. Ely, Ibarra, and Kolb, "Taking Gender Into Account: Theory and Design for Women's Leadership Development Programs"; Ibarra, Ely, and Kolb, "Women Rising: The Unseen Barriers."
19. Meyerson and Fletcher, "A Modest Manifesto for Shattering the Glass Ceiling"; De Vries, Webb, and Eveline, "Mentoring for Gender Equality and Organisational Change"; Pike et al., "Women and Sport Leadership: A Case Study of a Development Programme."
20. Kolb et al., "Making Change: A Framework for Promoting Gender Equity in Organization."
21. Dixon and Cunningham, "Data Aggregation in Multilevel Analysis: A Review of Conceptual and Statistical Issues"; Cunningham, *Diversity and Inclusion in Sport Organizations: A Multilevel Perspective*.
22. Kozlowski and Klein, "Multilevel Theory."

23. Black, Metzler, and Waldrum, "That Program Really Helped Me"; Black and Earnest, "Measuring the Outcomes of Leadership Development Programs."
24. Black and Earnest, "Measuring the Outcomes of Leadership Development Programs"; Black, Metzler, and Waldrum, "That Program Really Helped Me."
25. Black and Earnest, "Measuring the Outcomes of Leadership Development Programs'.
26. Ibid.; Grove et al., "EvaluLEAD: A Guide for Shaping and Evaluating Leadership Development Programs."
27. Cunningham, "Gender."
28. Stake, "Case Studies."
29. Creswell, *Research Design: Qualitative, Quantitative, and Mixed Methods Approaches.*
30. King and Nesbit, "Collusion with Denial: Leadership Development and Its Evaluation."
31. Braun, Clarke, and Weate, "Using Thematic Analysis in Sport and Exercise Research."
32. Ibid.
33. To protect the anonymity of the respondents, the exact years are not described.
34. Mikkonen, Stenvall, and Lehtonen, "The Paradox of Gender Diversity, Organizational Outcomes, and Recruitment in the Boards of National Governing Bodies of Sport."
35. Pike et al., "Women and Sport Leadership: A Case Study of a Development Programme."
36. Sartore and Cunningham, "Explaining the Under-Representation of Women in Leadership Positions of Sport Organizations: A Symbolic Interactionist Perspective"; Pike et al., "Women and Sport Leadership: A Case Study of a Development Programme."
37. Clarke, "Advancing Women's Careers through Leadership Development Programs."
38. Pike et al., "Women and Sport Leadership: A Case Study of a Development Programme."
39. See, e.g., Katz, Walker, and Hindman, "Gendered Leadership Networks in the NCAA: Analyzing Affiliation Networks of Senior Woman Administrators and Athletic Directors."
40. McPherson, Smith-Lovin, and Cook, "Birds of a Feather: Homophily in Social Networks."
41. Ibid.
42. See, e.g., Wenger, McDermott, and Snyder, *Cultivating Communities of Practice.*
43. See also Pike et al., "Women and Sport Leadership: A Case Study of a Development Programme."
44. Hovden, Elling, and Knoppers, "Meta-Analysis: Policies and Strategies"; Leberman and Burton, *Why This Book? Framing the Conversation about Women in Sport Leadership.* Routledge.
45. Kozlowski and Klein, "Multilevel Theory."
46. Mikkonen, "Understanding Gender (In)Equality in Leadership Positions in Sport: A Multilevel Perspective."

REFERENCES

Allen, Justine B., and Colleen Reid. "Scaffolding Women Coaches' Development: A Program to Build Coaches' Competence and Confidence." *Women in Sport and Physical Activity Journal* 27, no. 2 (1 October 2019): 101–109. https://doi.org/10.1123/WSPAJ.2018-0047.

Alsarve, Daniel. "Achieving Gender Equity: Barriers and Possibilities at Board Level in Swedish Sport." *European Sport Management Quarterly*, 16 August 2022. https://doi.org/10.1080/16184742.2022.2112256.

Belding, Madeline, and Ann Dodge. "Examining the Benefits of Female-to-Female Mentorship as a Result of Participation in a Female Coach Mentorship Program." *Canadian Journal for Women in Coaching* 16, no. 2 (2016): 1–5.

Black, Alice M., and Garee W. Earnest. "Measuring the Outcomes of Leadership Development Programs." *Journal of Leadership & Organizational Studies* 16, no. 2 (2009): 184–96. https://doi.org/10.4324/9781410604514-18.

Black, Alice M., Dianne P. Metzler, and Joseph Waldrum. "That Program Really Helped Me: Using Focus Group Research to Measure the Outcomes of Two Statewide Leadership Programs." *Journal of Leadership Education* 5, no. 3 (1 December 2006): 53–65. https://doi.org/10.12806/V5/I3/RF2.

Braun, Virginia, Victoria Clarke, and Paul Weate. "Using Thematic Analysis in Sport and Exercise Research." In *Routledge Handbook of Qualitative Research in Sport and Exercise*, edited by Brett Smith and Andrew C. Sparkes, 291–05. London: Routledge, 2016. https://doi.org/10.4324/9781315762012-26

Burton, Laura J. "Underrepresentation of Women in Sport Leadership: A Review of Research." *Sport Management Review* 18, no. 2 (2015): 155–65. https://doi.org/10.1016/j.smr.2014.02.004.

Carson, Fraser, Clara McCormack, Paula McGovern, Samara Ralston, and Julia Walsh. "Coach Like a Woman: Learnings From a Pilot Coach Education Program." *Women in Sport and Physical Activity Journal* 29, no. 1 (28 December 2021): 68–73. https://doi.org/10.1123/WSPAJ.2020-0047.

Chuang, Szufang. "Exploring Women-Only Training Program for Gender Equality and Women's Continuous Professional Development in the Workplace." In *Higher Education, Skills and Work-Based Learning*, 2019.

Clarke, Marilyn. "Advancing Women's Careers through Leadership Development Programs." *Employee Relations* 33, no. 5 (August 2011): 498–515. https://doi.org/10.1108/01425451111153871.

Creswell, John W. *Research Design: Qualitative, Quantitative, and Mixed Methods Approaches*. Los Angeles: SAGE, 2009.

Culver, Diane M., Erin Kraft, Cari Din, and Isabelle Cayer. "The Alberta Women in Sport Leadership Project: A Social Learning Intervention for Gender Equity and Leadership Development." *Women in Sport and Physical Activity Journal* 27, no. 2 (2019): 110–17. doi:10.1123/wspaj.2018-0059.

Cunningham, George B. *Diversity and Inclusion in Sport Organizations: A Multilevel Perspective*. New York, NY: Routledge, 2019.

Cunningham, George B. "Gender." In *Diversity and Inclusion in Sport Organization: A Multilevel Perspective*, edited by George B. Cunningham, 143–84. New York, NY: Routledge, 2019.

De Vries, Jennifer, Claire Webb, and Joan Eveline. "Mentoring for Gender Equality and Organisational Change." *Employee Relations* 28, no. 6 (2006): 573–587. https://doi.org/10.1108/01425450610704506

Dixon, Marlene A., and George B. Cunningham. "Data Aggregation in Multilevel Analysis: A Review of Conceptual and Statistical Issues." *Measurement in Physical Education and Exercise Science* 10, no. 2 (2006): 85–107. https://doi.org/10.1207/s15327841mpee1002_2

Dworkin, Terry Morehead, Virginia Maurer, and Cindy A. Schipani. "Career Mentoring for Women: New Horizons/Expanded Methods." *Business Horizons* 55, no. 4 (1 July 2012): 363–72. https://doi.org/10.1016/j.bushor.2012.03.001

Ely, Robin J., Herminia Ibarra, and Deborah M. Kolb. "Taking Gender into Account: Theory and Design for Women's Leadership Development Programs." *Academy of Management Learning & Education* 10, no. 3 (2011): 474–493.

Grove, John T., Barry M. Kibel, Taylor Haas, Bruce Avolio, Jennifer Martineau, Hallie Preskill, Margaret Neuse, Craig Russon, Richard Pearlstein, and Richard Kreuger. "EvaluLEAD: A Guide for Shaping and Evaluating Leadership Development Programs." Oakland: The Public Health Institute, 2005.

Hakamäki, Matti, Salla Turpeinen, and Kati Lehtonen. "A Strategy to Promote Gender Equality: The Number and Status of Women in Leadership and Decision-Making Positions in Finnish Sport." In *The Routledge Handbook of Gender Politics in Sport and Physical Activity*, edited by Győző Molnár and Rachael Bullingham, 2022. https://doi.org/10.4324/9781003093862-36.

Hovden, Jorid, Agnes Elling, and Annelies Knoppers. 'Meta-Analysis: Policies and Strategies'. In *Gender Diversity in European Sport Governance*, edited by A Elling, Jorid Hovden, and A Knoppers, 185–98. London: Routledge, 2019.

Ibarra, Herminia, Robin J. Ely, and Deborah M. Kolb. "Women Rising: The Unseen Barriers." *Harvard Business Review* 91, no. 9 (2013): 60–66.

Katz, Matthew, Nefertiti A. Walker, and Lauren C. Hindman. "Gendered Leadership Networks in the NCAA: Analyzing Affiliation Networks of Senior Woman Administrators and Athletic Directors." *Journal of Sport Management* 32, no. 2 (2018): 135–49.

King, Elizabeth, and Paul Nesbit. "Collusion with Denial: Leadership Development and its Evaluation." *Journal of Management Development* 34, no. 2 (2015): 134–52. https://doi.org/10.1108/JMD-02-2013-0023.

Kolb, Deborah, Joyce K. Fletcher, Debra E. Meyerson, Deborah Merrill-Sands, and Robin J. Ely. "Making Change: A Framework for Promoting Gender Equity in Organization." In *Reader in Work, Gender and Organization*, edited by Robin J Ely, Erica G. Foldy, and Maureen A. Scully, 10–15. Malden: Blackwell, 2003.

Kozlowski, Steve W. J., and Katherine J. Klein. "Multilevel Theory." San Francisco, CA: Wiley, 2000.

Kraft, Erin, Diane M. Culver, and Cari Din. "Exploring a Women-Only Training Program for Coach Developers." *Women in Sport and Physical Activity Journal* 28, no. 2 (22 July 2020): 173–79. https://doi.org/10.1123/WSPAJ.2019-0047.

Leberman, Sarah, and Laura J. Burton. "Why this Book? Framing the Conversation about Women in Sport Leadership." In *Women in Sport Leadership*, edited by Laura J. Burton and Sarah Leberman, 1–15. London: Routledge, 2017.

McPherson, Miller, Lynn Smith-Lovin, and James M. Cook. "Birds of a Feather: Homophily in Social Networks." *Annual Review of Sociology* 27 (2001): 415–44.

Megheirkouni, Majd, and Muhammad Azam Roomi. "Women's Leadership Development in Sport Settings: Factors Influencing the Transformational Learning Experience of Female Managers." *European Journal of Training and Development* 41, no. 5 (2017): 467–84. https://doi.org/10.1108/EJTD-12-2016-0085.

Meyerson, Debra E., and Joyce K. Fletcher. "A Modest Manifesto for Shattering the Glass Ceiling." *Harvard Business Review* 78, no. 1 (2000): 126–36.

Mikkonen, Marjukka. *"Understanding Gender (In)Equality in Leadership Positions in Sport: A Multilevel Perspective."* Doctoral thesis, University of Tampere, 2023.

Mikkonen, Marjukka. "'We Are Going to the Right Direction . . . but We Are Not in Ideal World yet': Understanding Gender (in)Equality within Leadership Positions in Nordic Football Governance'. *Sport in Society*, 2022. https://doi.org/10.1080/17430437.2022.2088358.

Mikkonen, Marjukka, Jari Stenvall, and Kati Lehtonen. "The Paradox of Gender Diversity, Organizational Outcomes, and Recruitment in the Boards of National Governing Bodies of Sport." *Administrative Sciences* 11, no. 4 (2021). https://doi.org/10.3390/admsci11040141.

Oakley, Judith. "Gender-Based Barriers to Senior Management Positions: Understanding the Scarcity of Female CEOs." *Journal of Business Ethics* 27, no. 4 (2000): 321–34. https://doi.org/10.1023/A:1006226129868.

Pike, Elizabeth, Anita White, Jordan Matthews, Samuel Southon, and Lucy Piggott. "Women and Sport Leadership: A Case Study of a Development Programme." In *The Palgrave Handbook of Feminism and Sport, Leisure and Physical Education*, edited by Louise Mansfield, Jayne Caudwell, Belinda Wheaton, and Beccy Watson, 809–23. London: Palgrave Macmillan, 2018. https://doi.org/10.1057/978-1-137-53318-0_51.

Sartore, Melanie L., and George B. Cunningham. "Explaining the Under-Representation of Women in Leadership Positions of Sport Organizations: A Symbolic Interactionist Perspective." *Quest* 59, no. 2 (2007): 244–65. https://doi.org/10.1080/00336297.2007.10483551.

Stake, Robert E. "Case Studies." In *Strategies of Qualitative Inquiry*, edited by Norman K. Denzin and Yvonna. S. Lincoln, 134–64. Thousand Oaks: Sage, 2003.

Wells, Janelle E., and Meg G. Hancock. "Networking, Mentoring, Sponsoring: Strategies to Support Women in Sport Leadership." In *Women in Sport Leadership: Research and Practice for Change*, edited by Laura J. Burton and Sarah Leberman. London: Routledge, 2017.

Wenger, Etienne, Richard A. McDermott, and William M. Snyder. *Cultivating Communities of Practice: A Guide to Managing Knowledge*. Boston, MA: Harvard Business School Press, 2002.

World Economic Forum. "Global Gender Gap Report 2022." 2022. http://reports.weforum.org/global-gender-gap-report-2022.

CHAPTER 3

REFLECTIONS ON EQUAL DEMOCRACY, EQUAL OPPORTUNITIES, AND PLURALISM

Against the Trivialization of Gender Quotas

Giovanna Iacovone
University of Basilicata

ABSTRACT

The scope of investigation and in-depth study of this contribution intends to highlight the lack of problematization inherent in the so-called 'pink quotas' and the consequent inability to address and resolve the complexity of the discriminatory reality. Reality that requires a systematization of those legal categories posed by the Constitution itself as functional guarantees, and a non-prejudicially ideological comparison with the related concepts that range from the valorization of differences to internal party democracy.

A PREMISE FOR THE FRAMING OF THE TOPIC

The issue of gender rebalancing in the decision-making processes of political bodies and public administrations involves the essence of the need for inclusion. That is, 'to be part', the expression of the relationship, the bond with the community to which one belongs. Article 2 of the Constitution acknowledges as inviolable this right. For its realization it imperatively 'requires the fulfilment of mandatory obligations for political, economic and social solidarity' as they are strictly functional to the development of each person's personality and progress of society (Article 4 of the Constitution).

The binding purpose of the Constitutional provision is completed and specified by Article 3, according to which, equality, in the substantive sense, is fulfilled through the guarantee of individual development in a two-way relationship, with effective involvement in the political, economic and social organization of the Country.

A correct and non-ideological reading of the scope of the Constitutional provisions referred to, would have been sufficient to grant centrality to the gender perspective, in the process of constructing the public interest. The relevance of the point of view linked to belonging to one of the two sexes, certainly contributes, in terms of outcome, in providing answers to the needs, interests and aspirations of all.

The issue of political representation and gender balance is relevant both in itself, as a fundamental right to access elected assemblies, and as a real chance for women to obtain an influential role in the government and decision-making processes that affect women's lives and the protection of their rights.

More specifically—and as a priority—we need to ask ourselves to which extent room is allowed to women in the shaping of policy content.

This is the point of observation to be favoured, if we want to grasp the limitations of the so-called 'pink quotas'[1] and the misunderstanding of the underlying substantial concept.

The intention is not to question the usefulness of the provision of instruments, that can more effectively promote gender equality, in all aspects of institutional action. But to question the interpretation that is given to the provision, not only by detractors, that does not favour substantive effectiveness as it continues to pursue the policy of formalism, thus causing an emptying of democracy and equality.

The scope of investigation and in-depth study of this contribution, therefore, intends to highlight the lack of problematization related to the so-called 'pink quotas'. The consequent inability to address the complexity of the discriminatory reality, requires a systematization of those legal categories posed by the Constitution itself as functional guarantees. Furthermore, a non-prejudicially ideological comparison with the related concepts that range from the valorization of differences, to internal party democracy.

EQUALITY IN THE FORMAL AND SUBSTANTIVE SENSE IN THE JURISPRUDENCE OF THE CONSTITUTIONAL COURT: EFFECTS OF INTERPRETATIVE UNCERTAINTIES

With this in mind, it is useful to first analyze—necessarily in brief—the evolution of Italian legislation and the interventions of the Constitutional Court. They have followed one after the other in the context of a difficult gestation. The dialectical confrontation between the legislature and the judicial body reviewing the constitutionality of laws, has taken place in the framework set out by the key concepts on which the current regulatory system is based.

The first set of regulations that attempted to rebalance gender in Italy, dates back to the years 1993-1995. The legislative rule, albeit expressed in a variegated sense, stated that in the lists for the elections to the representative assemblies of municipalities, regions and parliament, neither of the sexes could be present in excess of a certain proportion.[2]

The introduction of gender quotas, however, encountered an initial obstacle in Constitutional Court ruling no. 422/1995.[3] The detected unconstitutionality of the quotas in the law on the election of municipal councils (Article 5(2). Law no. 81/1993), consequently extended its effects to all the quota provisions in other electoral laws.

The orientation of the Constitutional Court was based on a partial reconstruction of the Constitutional principles of equality and pluralist democracy applied to the right to vote. That is, an 'oriented' interpretation of Articles 3 and 51 of the Constitution. The interpretation was based on the principle of formal equality[4] and on the consequent unconstitutionality of a direct attribution of the electoral result, in reality more presumed than actual, given the ignored distinction between candidacy and actual election.[5]

Judgment No. 422/1995, however, did not lack direct and indirect merits.

From the first point of view, it is interesting, in view of the analysis that follows, to make explicit reference to internal party democracy. The Constitutional Court, in fact, took the opportunity to emphasize that gender equality is preliminarily linked to cultural growth within parties and the choice of statutory instruments, aimed at gender balance, that could not be imposed by the State.[6]

Indirectly, however, the pronouncement had the merit of opening a season of Constitutional reforms that at first made the protection of equal democracy legitimate at regional level (Constitutional Laws No. 2/2001 and No. 3/2001) with the amendment of Article 117 of the Constitution. Subsequently, equal opportunities between women and men as a general principle were recognized for all elected offices with the amendment of Article 51 (Constitutional Law No. 1/2003).[7]

The aforementioned Constitutional assumptions have been read in a gradually more conscious manner by the Constitutional Court. It led to affirm that the purpose of achieving "effective equality" between men and women, also in access to elective representation, is "positively appreciable from a Constitutional point of view." This requirement is also expressly recognized in the regulatory context of the European Union and international law.[8] This important approach, however, appears to be tempered. Certain underlying principles still seem to constrain the legislature, in its choice of constitutionally compliant instruments, to protect equal opportunities in the electoral sphere.

Among these, the most important principle, which seems to constitute the parameter to which all electoral *technicalities are* related, is based on the assumption that fostering a greater presence of women in representative assemblies, contributes to strengthening the democratic principle (and the very 'quality' of democracy), provided, however, that the outcome is not predetermined.[9]

In the light of Constitutional jurisprudence, several instruments, deemed constitutionally compliant, can therefore be used to promote the rebalancing of gender representation in elected office: establishing quotas of candidacies reserved for the under-represented sex within non-blocked lists (with varying proportions of men and women, including, most frequently, 1/2 or 2/3 of the available candidacies); establishing, be the case more (exclusion or irrepresentability of the list) or less severe sanctions (fines) in the event of non-compliance with the candidacy quotas prefixed by law. Introducing methods of expressing preferences on the model of 'double gender preference'.

In any case, what is important is that measures are not introduced into the legal system that "do not aim to remove the obstacles that prevent women from achieving certain results, but rather to attribute those results directly to them" (Judgment No. 422 of 1995). "The constraints imposed by law to achieve a gender balance in political representation must not affect the "equality of *chances of* lists and candidates in electoral competition" (Judgment No. 49 of 2003).[10] These principles were in fact both reaffirmed in Judgment No. 4/2010 (point 3.2 of the considerations in law),[11] where it was stated that no rule may "prefigure an electoral result" or "artificially alter the composition of representation."

In other words, the Constitutional Court has considered Constitutional all those mechanisms, including in particular the double gender preference, which, while acting as rebalancing rules, are only 'indirectly and possibly, the result of a positive action' that, instead, directly pursues, and therefore inadmissible according to the aforementioned guideline, equality at the points of arrival, i.e., a rebalancing in results.[12]

This is an orientation in line with the general prudence shown by the Constitutional Court with regard to the application of Article 3(2), which has only in very rare cases upheld questions of Constitutional legitimacy for violation of the principle contained therein and in any case often in conjunction with other Constitutional provisions.[13]

The issue of affirmative action in the field of political representation is a very delicate one in the context of the interpretative framework of guarantees. Specially if we consider the combination of the new version of Article 51 of the Constitution, which commits the Republic to promote equal opportunities between women and men with appropriate measures and Article 3, paragraph 2, which instead sanctions precisely the relevance of mere de facto disparities, when they can be identified as "obstacles." But the Court intended to argue in relation to this specific area using a consideration of a general nature. In essence, a view of substantive equality as an objective that can be pursued exclusively through measures that act on opportunities, disquoting its role as a Constitutional parameter.

Uncertainties and perplexities of direction coming from the Constitutional Court itself, appear relevant, on another occasion, precisely by interpreting Article 51, it has in part contradicted what was affirmed in 1995. This is a further confirmation of the delicacy of the role recognized to affirmative action in the realization of *gender-sensitive* objectives. The reference is to Ordinance No. 39 of 2005, in which the Constitutional Court addressed a question, raised by the Council of State, concerning the legislative obligation to include at least one third of women in competition commissions, thus a real quota of results, albeit envisaged for an administrative body.[14]

On that occasion, in the light of the arguments made by the Council of State, based on the 1995 judgment in support of the unconstitutionality of the provision requiring the mandatory presence of women, the Constitutional Court held that the reference to the 1995 judgment was not sufficient in light of the amendment of Article 51 in 2003 and therefore declared the question manifestly inadmissible for lack of motivation.

An uncertainty emerged, probably due to the ideological friction in our Constitution between the liberal perspective, informed by an equidistant attitude, and the solidaristic one, which takes into account the differences and peculiarities of individuals. This friction had important negative repercussions causing the slow implementation of the Constitutional provisions on gender equality and on the genuine awareness of the advanced perspective taken on by our constituents. That is, the 'collective' dimension of gender equality, whereby the involvement (also) of women in every sphere is likely to produce an evolutionary improvement in society as a whole.[15]

The highlighted fluctuations of the Constitutional Court have blurred its guiding role. This has led to results that are not fully satisfactory to date, despite the fact that the recent legislative framework is beginning to envisage a holistic vision of gender equality with a clear provision for the application of positive actions.[16] In fact, encouraging an evident obstinacy—especially with regard to women's access to power (especially political power)—in interpreting the principles in a reductive manner, both on the side of the jurisprudence and on the side of the parties. As we shall try to show, parties do not make a suitable contribution to genuinely guarantee equal access to management positions and candidacies for men and women, sometimes using the wide meshes of the legislation to obliterate its effectiveness.[17]

THE EQUAL OPPORTUNITIES PARADOX: FROM REDISTRIBUTIVE TOOL TO PICK OF THE JURISPRUDENCE AGAINST EQUAL DEMOCRACY

This view seems to be confirmed in some interesting recent cases.

We are referring to the judgement with which the Council of State[18] rejected the appeal brought by a number of Apulian women's associations, fighting for equal representation in government bodies, against the first instance judgement[19] pronounced on a complaint against the electoral operations for the election of the regional council, in the part relating to the admission of lists and groups of lists composed *contra legem*, as well as against the election results.

The regional electoral law, amended on the basis of the substitutive intervention exercised by the State for failing to provide for double gender preference,[20] while setting out in the abstract the rule on the balanced composition of lists following the substitutive intervention of the State (Article 8(13)), allowed it to be violated in practice, in the absence of any mechanism to ensure its effectiveness.

In fact, it only provided for a fine to be paid after the election, i.e., once the council groups were formed, against lists that did not observe the 60/40 gender ratio and thus did not respect proportionality in the composition of the electoral lists.

The pecuniary sanction provided for by the regional law, moreover applicable *ex post facto*, did not constitute a deterrent capable of guaranteeing the full implementation of the Constitutional postulates, aimed at allowing the promotion of equal opportunities in access to elective public offices. Thus, frustrating the guarantee prescribed by Articles 51 and 3, paragraph 2, of the Constitution and pursued by Law No. 20 2016, proving to be unsuitable to safeguard 'gender equality' in the face of lists composed in a non-proportional manner and in fact conditioning the electoral result by inducing the association to challenge its outcome.

The administrative judge's failure to uphold the appeal, was based on two arguments from which emerges an instrumental tendency towards simplification and a difficulty in fully and satisfactorily thematizing the wealth of indications contained in the Constitutional text. This failure is also due to the aforementioned uncertain directions of the Constitutional Court.

The Council of State, in fact, firstly noted how the regional legislature had sufficiently implemented the state law, and in particular the fundamental principle of the promotion of equal opportunities, since the latter did not provide for direct sanctions against the presenters of lists with regard to their composition, but only against the voter who had his second preference cancelled if it did not concern a candidate of a different sex from the first.

This is clearly a fragile argument, to say the least, in the face of the mandatory rule according to which fundamental principles must not only be enunciated but also implemented. The regional legislator could not only have but should have provided for restorative and truly reparative consequences of the violation itself, in order to effectively protect the principle of equality.

It is evident, in fact, that in the face of what could be defined as 'essential levels' of protection identified by the State, the regional legislator is certainly legitimized to pursue more ambitious results, as demonstrated by the proliferation of experiments and models, mainly applied at local level.

Specific confirmation is drawn precisely from the strategic and wide-ranging vision that emerges from Article 51 of the Constitution, which, thanks to the reference to the 'Republic' and the use of the term 'measures', intended to involve all public powers in the promotion of equal democracy.

But even less acceptable is the further argument according to which "the non-implementation, by a list, of the relative provision, far from being in itself an element of (unique, as much as direct) vulnerating of equal access to elected public offices, rather integrates a non-compliance. The possible sanction of which cannot but be referred to the will that the electoral body is called upon, freely, to express [...] which, through the expression of the vote, may well "sanction," in an effectively "real" manner, those lists whose composition has not proved respectful of the gender balance."

The decision goes on to say that "even in the presence of lists not observing the proportional ratio in question, the final result could well prove to be "in line" with the aforesaid ratio (so as to ensure a "correct" composition of the assembly body); while, even in the face of compliance with the ratio in question, candidates all belonging to the same gender could nevertheless be elected, with the consequent compromise of the inspirational purpose of the provisions in question."

This reasoning is based on an obvious dichotomous and reductive view of the principles of formal and substantive equality considered, and completely decontextualized from environmental, cultural and social factors, the result of a lack of rigour in terms of technique, both legislative and applicative by case law.

In this regard, the failure to use the systematic method in the interpretation, has been emphasized. The method could have led to the valorization of the "link with the reference, in the combined provisions of articles 2 and 4, paragraph 2, of the Constitution, to the duties of solidarity, in particular if they are aimed at the progress of society," on which to base the perception of the binding scope of these provisions.[21] With the assumption of both legislative initiatives aimed at promptly removing the obstacles to the free expression of women's political and representative capacities, and jurisprudential interpretations in favour of satisfying the demand for 'equal freedom', as a principle of effective enjoyment for all of the inviolable freedoms and rights provided for by Article 2 of the Constitution, and which flows from our Constitutional Charter in disruptive terms.[22]

Adherence to this reading would have marked a more timely shift from a static dimension of equal treatment of men and women, to the dynamic perspective of equal opportunities. That is with the aim of achieving substantive equality in the spirit of the 1979 UN Convention on the Elimination of All Forms of Discrimination against Women (CEDAW) as well as the 1995 Beijing Declaration, acts that aim to achieve *de facto* equality.

It is clear that in a political, economic and cultural context that historically is not equidistant in the light of the concept of 'equal opportunities', mere enunciation is not suitable for meeting the requirements of the effectiveness of the principles and rules stemming directly from the Constitution, if not accompanied by measures. That is, positive actions, aimed at guaranteeing the result and which, in function of the role they perform, can only be of a transitional nature and are, therefore, destined to find their legal space until the objectives to which they are preordained, are achieved.

On the other hand, the theme of affirmative action and gender quotas, if properly declined by combining the liberal idea with the Constitutional concept of solidarity, far from postulating a levelling equality that aims to make results equal, tends to strengthen freedoms and related responsibilities.

In the perspective outlined above, a fundamental role, since they have been called upon several times by the Constitutional Court, can only be played by the parties, and the issue of equal democracy within them.

Indeed, the structuring of political competition and election campaigns, as well as the selection of political personnel, depends on them. The democratic organization of parties is therefore the 'indispensable prerequisite for true democracy also outside them.'[23]

As mentioned during the analysis of Constitutional jurisprudence, the Constitutional Court in its rulings No 422 of 1995 and No 49 of 2003 entrusted parties with important tasks of equal democracy.

In Judgment No. 422, the Court assesses positively, implicitly hoping for, the voluntary application of gender balance measures, based on the content of Article 49 of the Constitution, which in the light of the principles of substantive equality in Article 3 and of solidarity in Article 2, strongly values participation through parties as instruments that contribute to determining national policy.

It is in the parties that one builds that relationship of continuity with the citizens capable of providing content for national politics able to affect institutions.

Judgment No 49 of 2003 also considers the role of the parties in influencing the functioning of the institutions and thus, in line with Mortati's considerations, the need for democratic organization within the parties as a place of organic expression of the will of the citizens and selection of representatives.

The theme shifts to the transformation of parties into electoral machines that, for a long time now, have only functioned through a centralized (we could say "leaderistic") co-optation mechanism, especially with regard to the candidacies of women, thus losing the effective connection with citizenship and thus also much of democracy, and the equalitarian democracy that is an inseparable part of it.[24]

Without lingering over political analyses and remaining within the coordinates of the present analysis, it is not secondary to point out how the evolution of intermediate bodies, in the sense outlined, has triggered mechanisms that are not very virtuous in terms of participation in political life and the qualitative selection of the subjects called upon to represent them, with as many 'reactions' that are not functional, as we will try to argue, in posing and resolving the issue of gender equality.

We refer first of all to the predominantly quantitative approach by which the discipline of political representation is understood, which seems as likely to trigger conflicts with as many *actiones finium regundorum* as it is unsuitable for deconstructing the geography of domination that has been the basis of the distortion of democratic principles.

Secondly, and no less important and closely related to the first, there is a kind of homologation, or normalization, that is not conducive to the recognition and enhancement of the differences present in the society represented. Genuine recognition must lead to inclusive policies exercised in the 'public space' understood both in the institutional and in the concrete territorial sense and which, in the latter case, in addition to being a physical space, is also a relational space, in which public opinion is formed and manifested, suitable for expressing politically representative persons.

Both the profiles highlighted above are essential for an authentic reflection on gender quotas. To ignore them would mean to remain anchored to the sole representation of a destiny of exclusion to be redeemed, of a gap to be bridged, of inferiority to be overcome, leaving the concrete experience of women on the margins, and putting in place institutional policies that are abstract with respect to the multiform concrete reality of women.

EQUAL DEMOCRACY AND PURSUIT IN PURELY NUMERICAL TERMS: THE RELATIONSHIP BETWEEN AFFIRMATIVE ACTION AND PINK QUOTAS

The chosen survey perspective leads us to reflect on the results and potential of the albeit gradual reform process underway, since, despite the aforementioned dysfunctions, Italy is one of the States that have endowed themselves with a binding discipline, that is actually tending to produce some effects, also with regard to access to political-elective offices.

A sign of a turnaround began to be seen with the results of the 2013 general elections in which the overall average female presence in the Italian Parliament, historically far below the 30% threshold, considered the minimum value for gender representation to be effective, rose from 19.5 in the 16th legislature to 30.1 in the 17th legislature. This trend was reinforced with the 2018 elections, in which for the first time the measures provided for in Electoral Law No. 165 of 2017 to promote gender equality in political representation were tested. In 2018, in fact, 334 women were elected to Parliament, representing approximately 35% (of whom 225 in the Chamber and 109 in the Senate). A result that puts us above the EU average of 32.8%.

In the light of the most recent regulatory developments, it is therefore possible to say that we are in the midst of regulatory and cultural change, and the identification of mechanisms to measure the level of equality between women and men, seems to be moving in this direction. Think about the development of indicators and measures for the achievement of targets identified in the first National Strategy for Gender Equality developed in the implementation of the NRP.[25]

In this regard, however, a methodological *caveat* is in order, starting with the aforementioned strategy document.

The National Strategy for Gender Equality 2021/2026, adopted in August 2021, defines guidelines and measures to outline government action on equality issues over the next 5 years. Considering the 5 strategic priorities (work, income, skills, time and power), it defines a set of indicators to measure the main aspects of gender inequality, as well as *target* values (specific and measurable objectives to be achieved) and related actions or measures to achieve them.

The priority specifically relevant to the survey is 'power', within which the representation of women in political bodies is taken into account.

Faced with the observation of the backward position compared to more advanced countries (e.g., Sweden, Finland, France) that have by now achieved parity, which in Italy is accentuated at the level of regional and local authorities (below 20%),[26] the measures proposed essentially concern the reform of the so-called '*par condicio*' legislation, to ensure that candidates of both sexes for each party receive equal media exposure (e.g., equal air time) during the electoral campaign. As well as the implementation of the current legal provisions on regional electoral laws, with the introduction of gender preference mechanisms and gender parity requirements in the composition of electoral lists. Finally, with regard to municipalities and provinces, to provide for the introduction, by amending the single text of local authorities, in their statutes and regulations procedures to be followed in appointments to achieve gender balance and sanction instruments in the event of inactivity of the bodies.

The targets are therefore purely quantitative, just like the indicators, but are read in terms of 'progress for gender equality'.

While not intending to disavow the absolute priority of a rebalancing in terms of numbers and therefore the functionality of gender quotas, as evidently inferred from the above considerations, one cannot fail to emphasize how progress is a qualitative concept. As such it requires new and additional epistemological and methodological criteria to arrive at a correct interpretation of gender differences and the related needs to be met in order to create qualitatively acceptable living conditions for all.

In other words, an accomplished process of equal democracy implies the real expression, hence the recognition, of genders as ways of being of a single universality, to be considered together but in their specific identity at every level, including those of rule-making and public administration.

Focusing, as has been done so far, only on numerical balance has led to a misunderstanding of the real meaning of gender quotas and their function, triggering instrumentalizations and downward reactions even in terms of political quality. It is precisely this profile that needs to be monitored and correctly oriented, seeking to elaborate and metabolize the concept that equal opportunities is not the same thing as achieving a deplorable level of mediocrity, but on the contrary, it is functional to strengthening freedom and related responsibilities.

A sign of the instrumentalization is precisely in the trivialization through adjectivalization, often even in a derogatory sense, of them as 'pink' quotas.

There is thus a considerable risk of arriving at another expression of formalism, guaranteeing a false effectiveness insofar as it is not based on the real representative contributions that different identities can make politically and, therefore, on the side of social transformation.

This exposes us to conceptual deviations and the risk of a distorting and stereotypical use of the principle of differentiation and gender quotas.

Inequalities and discrimination, in fact, are of many different kinds and these play out on many different terrains and are generated by very different factors with respect to which measures must be put in place to overcome policies of a merely redistributive nature. These policies affect the structures by cancelling gender differences instead of enhancing them. It is necessary, in other words, to flank redistribution, which is necessary, with the valorization and therefore the empowerment of the individual.

And it is precisely on this terrain that we need to confront each other honestly and free from ideologies, party logics and stereotypes.

AN INTERSECTIONAL PERSPECTIVE TO BREAK OUT OF THE 'SIMILARITY/DIFFERENCE' STEREOTYPE

Studies on intersectionality, an important methodological landing place for reflections on gender issues and which, when applied to law, could help to unravel the ambiguities of politics and abandon those unsatisfactory interpretations based on the stereotype of formal equality, go in the direction represented.

Having questioned the paradigm of the neutrality of law (also and above all with respect to gender) and having become aware that the neutral subject it seemed to refer to, was in fact parametrial to the male subject, intersectionality shatters another belief, namely that of a falsely universal and neutral subject-woman' (Faralli 2003: 699).

It is not possible to give an account here of the now thirty-year debate on intersectionality,[27] which is, moreover, extremely composite, heterogeneous and articulated. The reflection that is proposed here, concerns the possibility that the intersectional perspective may rise to a legal-methodological category to overcome the unidirectional nature within which the issue of gender rebalancing in political representation, has been placed. That is, according to rigidly 'binary' paradigms that no longer appear functional for reading and interpreting the social and relational complexity in which we live, thus continuing to generate further asymmetries and discrimination justified by that indifference of results to which the liberal concept of formal equality tends.

It is, moreover, a methodology with a solid legal basis, identifiable both at European level, in Article 10 of the Treaty on the Functioning of the Union,[28] and national level in Article 3(1) of our Constitution. The Constitutional precept in considering the multiple causes of discrimination could well have been interpreted in an integrated and systematic perspective. It has instead been configured as merely programmatic, almost in contrast with the subsequent paragraph 2. The paragraph highlights the need to remove all obstacles to the development of the personality, and fully grasps the gender perspective, in which the architecture of the regulatory system must be constructed in all its social and political implications .

For several years now, European Union indications seem to have been moving in this direction[29] including, most recently, those contained in the European Commission's Communication of 5.3.2020 COM (2020) 152[30] in which explicit reference is made to intersectionality as a functional method for the adoption of the 2020–2025 gender equality strategy and which calls for the implementation of both European and Member State legislation in all areas, and, in particular, in those affected by clear and proven discrimination.

There is no doubt, in the light of the present analysis, that the field of electoral legislation can be strongly affected by such a heuristic tool, in the identification of criteria both for the composition of lists and in the results concerning gender quotas, with a view to a substantial rebalancing in a truly plural and all-encompassing perspective.

Perhaps the time is due for a modern contribution by legal science to interpret not a compartmentalized, but an integrated (and intersectional) reading of the multiple causes of discrimination and, consequently, of the multidimensionality of inequalities. An interpretation due to promote a political and legal vision, capable of activating a critical gaze able to identify gender implicitness and the stereotypes that are intertwined with it, questioning that kind of legal architecture that focuses on formal anti-discrimination and on the symmetrical equality between men and women, in terms of mere assimilation.

NOTES

1. M. D'Amico, *La lunga strada della parità, fra fatti, norme e principi giurisprudenziali*, in Riv. AIC, 2013, 3; id. *Gender Representation in Institutions. Strumenti di riequilibrio*, in *Centro di studi sulla giustizia/Facoltà di Giurisprudenza dell'università degli Studi di Milano*, 2017, vol. 27, 41 ff. ; A. Simonati, *Le "quote di genere" alla prova dei fatti: l'accesso delle donne al potere e i giudici amministrativi*, in *Giorn. dir. amm.*, 2014, 1001 ff.

2. Law No. 81 of 1993, concerning municipal councils, had initially provided that neither sex could be represented by more than 2/3 in the electoral lists (Art. 5(2)).

    Law no. 277 of 1993, concerning the election to the Chamber of Deputies, provided that in lists where candidates were voted for by the proportional system: lists bearing more than one name (up to 4) had to be made up of candidates and candidates in alternating order (amendment of Art. 4, para. 2 no. 2 of Presidential Decree no. 361 of 1957).

    Law No. 43 of 1995 regulating the regional elections provided that in the lists no sex could exceed two thirds of the candidates (Article 1(6)).

3. Const. court. 6-12.9.1995.

4. The Constitutional Court, in this well-known and criticised judgement, affirmed in fact that "on the subject of the right to vote, the mandatory rule

established by the Constituent Assembly itself, with the first paragraph of Article 51, and the first paragraph of Article 3, is that of absolute equality, so that any differentiation by reason of sex cannot but be objectively discriminatory, diminishing for some citizens [male citizens, ed.] the concrete content of a fundamental right in favour of others [female citizens, ed.], belonging to a group that is considered to be disadvantaged" thus ending up in establishing a "current discrimination as a remedy for past discrimination."

5. In particular, the Judge of Laws considered that those regulations, rather than removing the obstacles that in fact prevented women's political participation, tended to secure a result by directly awarding them the election. In this respect, they conflicted with the principles of political representation of pluralist democracy. The ruling was highly criticised for not distinguishing in any way between eligibility to stand as a candidate and actual election, and for ignoring the rationale of the norms ascribable to Article 3, paragraph 2 of the Italian Constitution (substantive equality), which was to try to remove the social obstacles that prevented women from participating on equal terms in the political organisation of the Italian Republic, thus giving precedence to the principle of formal equality as set out in Article 3, paragraph 1 of the Constitution.

6. Sentence No. 422 of 1995 states: "It is appropriate, finally, to observe that such measures, constitutionally illegitimate insofar as they are imposed by law, can instead be positively evaluated where they are freely adopted by political parties, associations or groups taking part in elections, even with specific provisions in their statutes or regulations concerning the presentation of candidacies. Valid results can therefore be achieved with an intense cultural growth action that leads parties and political forces to recognise the urgent need to pursue the effective equal presence of women in public life, and in representative offices in particular'. On the issue of the importance of the 'democratic method' in parties, A. Poggi, *La democrazia nei partiti,* in AIC, 2015.

7. Article 117, c. 7 of the Constitution, in fact, stipulated, for ordinary Regions, that 'Regional laws shall remove every obstacle that prevents the full equality of men and women in social, cultural and economic life and promote equal access of women and men to elected offices'; Article 51, c. 1 of the Constitution, on the other hand, was amended by specifying that 'All citizens of either sex may have access to public offices and elected positions on equal terms, according to the requirements established by law. For this purpose, the Republic shall promote equal opportunities for women and men by appropriate measures'.

From this point onwards, the regions, in particular the Campania region, began to experiment with various techniques to safeguard equality between men and women in the selection of candidates, which, in the face of constitutional amendments, succeeded in passing the constitutionality test of the Constitutional Court (see judgments No. 49/2003 and No. 4/2010).

On the constitutional amendments, T.E. Frosini, *La modifica dell'art. 51 Cost.: problemi e prospettive,* in www.archivio.rivistaaic.it, 17 March 2003; M. Cartabia, *Il principio della parità tra uomini e donne nell'art. 117, 7° comma,* in *La*

Repubblica delle autonomie. Regioni ed Enti locali nel nuovo Titolo V, edited by T. Groppi and M. Olivetti, Turin, Giappichelli, 2003, 129 ss.
8. C. Noto, *La rappresentanza di genere supera indenne il vaglio della Corte costituzionale*, in *Giurisd. amm.*, 2010, 83 ss.
9. This is because, according to the Consulta's assumption, pretending to predetermine the result—that is, to make it knowable and guarantee in advance how many women and how many men will concretely make up the representative bodies—ends up violating the democratic principle itself, which finds its maximum expression in the moment of voting, by definition free and personal (Article 48 of the Constitution).
10. Constitutional Court, 10–13 February 2003, No 49.
11. Constitutional Court, 14 January 2010, No 4.
12. L. Califano, *L'assenso 'coerente' della Consulta alla preferenza di genere*, in www.forumcostituzionale.it, 2010, 4; L. Carlassare, *La legittimità della 'preferenza di genere': una nuova sconfitta della linea del Governo contro la parità*, in *Giur. cost*, 2010, 81 ff.; S. Leone, *La preferenza di genere come strumento per ottenere, indirettamente ed eventualmente, il risultato di un'azione positiva*, in *Giur. cost.*, 2010, 84 ff.; G. Chiola, *Pari opportunità e riforme costituzionali: analisi e prospettive*, in *Soc. dir.*, 2008, 107 ff.
13. Some of these can be found in M. MANETTI, *La libertà eguale nella Costituzione italiana*, in. *Riv. trim. dir. pubbl.*, 2009, 635 ff, for an in-depth analysis of the logic behind the constitutional orientation: Constitutional Court no. 290 of 1974 with which the regulation of the penal code punishing political strikes was declared unconstitutional, which instead the Constitutional Court affirmed as an instrument of workers' participation in the political, economic and social organisation of the country; Constitutional Court no. 193 of 1976 with which the provision that allowed the institution responsible for assigning council housing an unjustified right of withdrawal was annulled, also because this aggravated the extreme difficulty of obtaining housing for the less well-off; Constitutional Court no. 364 of 1988 with which the principle *ignorantia legis poenalis non excusat* was declared illegitimate, also due to the fact that ignorance of the penal law may be due to the failure to remove the obstacles referred to in paragraph 2 of Article 3.
14. N. Pignatelli, *Parità di genere e commissioni di concorso pubblico: la dequotazione giurisprudenziale della quota*, in *Quad. cost.*, 2020, 404 ff.
15. A. Simonati, *La Costituzione "dimenticato" la parità di genere*, in *Riv. trim. dir. pubbl.*, 2021, 9 ff.
16. There is no doubt, however, that adherence to the parameter of gender equality is progressively taking root in the legislative fabric. At the supranational level, the Charter of Fundamental Rights of the European Union—which with the Treaty of Lisbon has become binding for our legal system—provides that equality between men and women must be ensured in all fields and that the principle of equality does not prevent the maintenance or adoption of measures that provide specific advantages in favour of the under-represented sex (Art. 23 inserted in Chapter III on equality).

Consistent with these indications is the Code for equal opportunities between men and women (Legislative Decree no. 198 of 11 April 2006), which brings together the current state legislation on gender equality in the areas of political, social and economic life. The Code deals with measures aimed at 'eliminating all discrimination based on sex, which has the consequence or purpose of compromising or preventing the recognition, enjoyment or exercise of human rights and fundamental freedoms in the political, economic, social, cultural and civil fields or in any other field' (Art. 1, para. 1). In particular, Art. 1 of the Equal Opportunities Code provides that: equal treatment and equal opportunities between women and men must be ensured in all fields, including employment, work and pay (para. 2); the principle of equality does not preclude the maintenance or adoption of measures that provide specific advantages in favour of the under-represented sex (para. 3); the objective of equal treatment and equal opportunities between women and men must be taken into account in the formulation and implementation, at all levels and by all actors, of laws, regulations, administrative acts, policies and activities (para. 4).

17. On this topic, the reflections of I. Carlotto, *L'ondivaga giurisprudenza amministrativa sulla promozione delle pari opportunità in ambito elettorale al cospetto della Corte costituzionale (a proposito di alcune recenti decisioni del giudice amministrativo)*, in *Osservatorio sulle fonti,* no. 3/2021, in http://www.osservatoriosullefonti.it

18. Cons. Stato, Sec. II, 25 June 2021, no. 4860.

19. Tribunale Amministrativo Regionale per la Puglia (Sede di Bari–Sezione Terza), no. 95 of 16 January 2021.

20. The Apulia Region, in fact, had not provided, in implementation of the State law, for the so-called double gender preference, thus rendering itself in default. This non-compliance led the national government to intervene in its stead, pursuant to Article 120, paragraph 2, of the Constitution, by introducing into the current regional law, by means of Decree-Law No. 86 of 31 July 2020 (converted into Law No. 98 of 7 August 2020), a provision for a second preference 'reserved for a candidate of the sex of the person elected'. 98), the provision of the second preference 'reserved for a candidate of a different sex from the other', considering that the holding of electoral competitions on the basis of a clearly illegitimate regulation would have led to the proliferation of appeals and jeopardised, with the regular course of operations, national unity. On the events in Puglia and the relative substitutive power exercised by the Government and the consequent appointment of a commissioner for the subsequent operational fulfilments: T. Groppi, "*La Costituzione si è mossa": la precettività dei principi costituzionali sulla parità di genere e l'utilizzo del potere sostitutivo del governo nei confronti della Regione Puglia*, in *federalismi.it*, 2020.

21. Anna Simonati, *La Costituzione "dimenticata" la parità di genere*, in *Riv. trim. dir. pubbl.*, 2021, notes that "From such a systematic reading it seems to follow, in fact, that the very constitutional provisions on gender equality require the application of positive actions, obviously in their naturally circumscribed transitional scope, as such destined to be expunged from the system when the objectives to the realisation of which they are preordained have settled."

22. M. MANETTI, *cit*.

23. P. CALAMANDREI, Discussion on the Draft Constitution, sitting of 4 March 1947, 1753 (http://www.camera.it/_dati/Costituente/Lavori/Assemblea/

sed049/sed049.pdf), cited by S. MERLINI, *I partiti politici, il metodo democratico e la politica nazionale*, in AA.VV., *Partiti politici e società civile a sessant anni dall'entrata in vigore della Costituzione*. AIC–Annuario 2008, Naples, 2009, 69.

24. M. Montalti, *La rappresentanza dei sessi in politica divenire rappresentanza protetta, tra riforme e interpretazione costituzionale*, in *Le reg.*, 2003, 491 ff.; *Donne e politica: la presenza femminile nei partiti politici dell'Italia repubblicana. Turin, 1945-1990*, edited by M.T. Silvestrini, C. Simiand and S. Urso, Milan, Giuffrè, 2005.

25. National Strategy for Gender Equality 2021-2026, in https://www.pariopportunita.gov.it/it/politiche-e-attivita/parita-di-genere-ed-empowerment-femminile/strategia-nazionale-per-la-parita-di-genere-2021-2026.

26. With the aim of ensuring equal gender representation in the different institutional and governmental levels, promoting an equal opportunity for political participation, they are measured:
    - the proportion of women appointed to public bodies, independent authorities and judicial guarantee bodies.
    - the share of women in regional councils, out of the total number of elected members in regional councils51—is now on average about 21%: the target is to reach at least about 40% on a national average level and ideally also for individual regional councils, following the example of regions such as Emilia Romagna where the share is already 38%;
    - the number of regional electoral laws that include principles of gender parity both in the electoral lists (i.e., gender requirements in the composition of the lists) and in the expression of the vote (e.g., gender preference or double preference), as defined by Law 165 of 2004 and according to the Senate of the Republic's feedback presented in its memo 220 of August 2020—to date, only 15 regional councils apply these principles, the goal is to see them applied in all 21 regional councils.
    - the proportion of women in the councils and collegiate bodies of municipalities and provinces, as well as in the bodies, companies and institutions dependent on them.

27. For an analysis of the concept of intersectionality, as well as its origin and the composite international and national debate, see the monographic work by B.G. Bello, *Intersectionality. Theories and practices between law and society*, Milan, 2020.

28. According to Article 10 TFEU, 'in defining and implementing its policies and activities, the Union shall aim to combat discrimination based on sex, racial or ethnic origin, religion or belief, disability, age or sexual orientation'.

29. Within the European Union, the debate on intersectionality began to emerge in the late 1990s. In particular, brief hints can be found in the anti-discrimination directives adopted in 2000: Directive 2000/43/EC regulating the principle of equal treatment between persons irrespective of racial or ethnic origin in the conditions of access to employment and occupation, vocational training, further training and retraining; Directive 2000/78/EC focusing on employment discrimination on the basis of religious beliefs, disability and sexual orientation, in which reference is made to multiple discrimination.

    There is also no lack of references in recent European Parliament Resolutions which, moreover, alongside the concept of multiple discrimination also use explicitly intersectional terminology: the first, *European Parliament Resolution on the Situation of women with disabilities* (2018/2685 (RSP99, 29.11.2018), concerns the situation with disabilities and in which it is recalled that "women and girls with disabilities experience double discrimination due to the intersection of gender and disability and may even often be exposed to multiple discrimination arising from the intersection of gender, disability and sexual orientation, gender identity, gender expression, sexual characteristics, country of origin, class, migration, status, age, religion or ethnicity" (para. 4); the second Resolution, on fundamental rights in the European *Union (European Parliament Resolution on the situation of fundamental rights in the European Union in 2017, (2018/2103 (INI), 16.1.2019)*, which expressly refers to behavioural obligations for States that "are required to address the main structural barriers to women's empowerment and their under-representation in work, decision-making and politics, which are the result of multiple and intersectional forms of inequalities, stereotypes and discrimination, both in the private and public sphere" (para. 22).

30. Communication from the Commission to the European Parliament, the Council, the European Economic and Social Committee and the Committee of the Regions, *A Union of Equality: The Strategy for Gender Equality 2020–2025*, makes explicit reference to both European and internal legislative implementation, in all areas and in particular in those affected by clear and proven discrimination: "The intersectionality aspect between gender and other causes of discrimination will be addressed in all EU policies. EU legislation and policies and their implementation should therefore respond to the specific needs and situations of women and girls belonging to different groups by taking the intersectional perspective into account," thus taking a policy perspective that embraces multiple struggles against all possible oppressions, without imposing a hierarchy between them but claiming the specificities of each.

CHAPTER 4

MUSLIM (MIGRANT) WOMEN WEARING THE HEADSCARF IN THE WORKPLACES

Does the 2021 *WABE* and *MH* Judgment of the EU Court of Justice Promote Equal Treatment in (Private) Employment and Occupation?

Arianna Pitino
Università degli Studi di Genova

ABSTRACT

The chapter analyses the judgment issued by the EU Court of Justice (Grand Chamber) on July 15th 2021, related to the cases *WABE*, C804/18 and *MH Müller Handels*, C341/19, following the requests by two German Courts for a preliminary ruling concerning Muslim women who wear headscarves in their workplaces.

The EUCJ determined the conditions under which an internal rule of a company/organization prohibiting workers from wearing any visible sign of political, philosophical or religious beliefs in the workplace, does not constitute direct discrimination on the grounds of religion or belief under EU law. The Author discusses about the application of the "neutrality rule" in private workplaces and the deep impact that this decision may have on Muslim women wearing a headscarf. In this judgment the requests for a preliminary ruling lodged by the two German Courts considered only the violation of the EU legislation dealing with discrimination on the grounds of religion. In the future, it is possible that the EUCJ will come to a different end by considering the legislation preventing discrimination on the grounds of gender which falls also under EU labor law.

AN OVERVIEW OF THE *WABE* AND *MH* JUDGMENT

Being employed is a means to fully develop one's personality and to achieve economic independence, as well as individual and social empowerment (Simonati, 2020; Parolari, 2019).[1] Working is also an important tool for people with a migrating background to integrate within the host States and their societies. This is why open and unconditional access to work seem to be particularly important for migrant women.

On July 15th 2021, the EU Court of Justice (Grand Chamber) issued a judgment related to the cases *WABE*, C804/18 and *MH Müller Handels*, C341/19[2] following the requests by two German Courts for a preliminary ruling concerning Muslim women who wear headscarves in their workplaces.

After two judgments having been pronounced in 2017,[3] these two recent joint cases have given the EUCJ the possibility to take stock of and to consolidate its previous jurisprudence regarding wearing visible symbols of political, philosophical or religious beliefs in the workplace, and they have also allowed it to better identify the limits and conditions to apply the "neutrality rule" in private workplaces.

The EUCJ determined that an internal rule of a company/organization, prohibiting workers from wearing any visible sign of political, philosophical or religious beliefs in the workplace, does not constitute—with regard to workers who observe certain dress codes based on religion—direct discrimination on the grounds of religion or belief provided that: the rule is applied in a general and undifferentiated way among employees; the employer pursues a policy of political, philosophical and religious neutrality in a consistent and systematic manner in relation to its customers or users; the employer demonstrates that in the absence of that policy, given the nature of his/her activities and the context in which they are carried out, he/she would suffer adverse consequences; the prohibition in question is limited to what is strictly necessary in view of the actual scale and severity of the adverse consequences that the employer is seeking to avoid by adopting that prohibition; the prohibition is not limited to conspicuous and/

or large-sized signs, but covers all visible forms of expression of political, philosophical or religious beliefs.

The EUCJ's judgment of 2021 is an opportunity to reflect on wearing religious symbols and clothing—and especially Muslim headscarves—in workplaces within the *private* sector. This chapter will attempt to answer a few questions that arise from this case-law, and it will do so from a public law perspective.

The first focus is on Muslim women, and the question that follows is: Are policies of neutrality pursued by employers targeting Muslim women in some way? Does the EUCJ's judgment put— either by law and/or *de facto*—Muslim migrant women who wear a headscarf in a more disadvantaged situation with regard to accessing work in the private sector compared to other women?

Secondly, it is necessary to investigate whether, under which conditions and to what extent, freedom of religion can be limited in the private sector according to EU law and jurisprudence. After examining this first point, another question follows: does the EUCJ consider the balance between the right to religious freedom and the other rights conflicting with it as a main responsibility of EU law, private employers and Courts, or as a matter which is primarily dependent on the margin of appreciation of National Legislators?

The answers to the questions listed above will constitute the necessary premise to try to understand how Muslim (migrant) women's rights and the integration of these women within the host States and the well-being of Western societies themselves, will be protected and enforced in the long run by policies of strict neutrality in employment and occupation or by other forms of neutrality that could prove to be more in compliance with the freedom of religion.

The final topic to be assessed is whether the EUCJ would have come to a different conclusion if the questions it was asked had been made on the grounds of gender discrimination and equal opportunities between men and women in employment and occupation as opposed to on the grounds of religion.

DRESSING IN COMPLIANCE WITH THE REQUIREMENTS SET BY RELIGION AND FAITH: FROM "NEUTRALITY OF PUBLIC SPACES" TO "NEUTRALITY OF PRIVATE SPACES"

The practice of covering one's head for religious purposes is an integral part of all three Monotheistic religions (Christianity, Judaism, and Islam) and of other religions and cultures. So that Muslim women are not the only ones who express their faith[4] and their membership in a religious community through their way of dressing, and by using headscarves to cover their heads and at times their necks (hijab) and faces (niqab and burqa).

Islam also requires men to follow a dress code which includes wearing tunic shirts, trousers, loose-fitting robes and different types of headscarves and hats. Jewish men cover their heads with a kippah and some ultra-Orthodox Jewish communities also require women to cover their heads (Moller Okin, 1998).[5] In Christian churches nuns are required to use a veil to cover their heads and habits to cover their bodies. In the Eastern Orthodox faith monks cover their heads with cylindrical hat covered with a veil (kamilavka). Christians may also wear religious symbols such as crucifixes and religious emblems representing saints. Sikh men are required to wear turbans covering their heads while Sikh women cover their heads with a headscarf, and both men and women usually wear other religious symbols such as the Kirpan (the Sikh "knife"). Even non-religious people can express their philosophical and ideological beliefs by wearing clothes with specific statements (e.g., against atomic energy, war, foreigners, etc.).

In all of the examples provided above one's dressing code becomes both the external expression of a personal belief and a religious symbol in the public sphere. Sometimes it is also a form of proselytism. Therefore, expressing one's religious belief through clothing is not an exclusive prerogative of Muslim women, but it also applies to many other religions. Some individuals prefer to keep their religious beliefs as a private matter without feeling the need to display them in public by wearing religious symbols or clothes. There are Muslim women who do not wear a headscarf just as there are Christians who do not wear a necklace with a crucifix or other Christian symbols.

However, there are two aspects that must be carefully considered with regard to Muslim people. In many European States, such as in Germany where the two cases analyzed in this chapter are drawn from, the Muslim community is the most numerous religious group after Christians.[6]

Another relevant aspect to consider is that in Western-European countries wearing a Muslim headscarf is perceived as being something more than just a religious symbol because it has also become a political symbol and an external sign of illiberal values. This is mostly due to the link between Islamic fundamentalism and terrorism as Islam is often seen as an illiberal religion, whose religious precepts go against the values and principles enshrined in the Constitutions of European States and which, above all, discriminate against women (Human Rights Watch, 2009; Helbling, 2014).[7]

Some evidence of this can be found by analyzing the number of European States that have passed laws prohibiting individuals from wearing religious symbols and dress in the public sphere in the last twenty years. Within the sphere of public employment these laws apply to many civil servants and workers in the public education sector. While the laws respond to the ideological and religious neutrality of public spaces as a means to protect the right to freedom of religion and to equality for all people, it cannot be denied that they indirectly target Muslim headscarves. In Germany there is evidence of this having occurred in the political debates held during the approval of such laws by the Legislatures of Landers. Furthermore, almost all the appellants in Court cases involving laws prohibiting individuals from wearing religious symbols in the public sector have been, to this date, Muslim women who wore headscarves and refused to take them off at work (Human Rights Watch, 2009).[8]

Although Muslim women are not the only ones to dress in accordance with religious precepts, they have become—*de facto*—the target of laws that prohibit the display of religious symbols in public spaces and workplaces.

The judgment issued by the EUCJ in 2021 on the joint cases *WABE* and *MH* is first and foremost interesting because it deals with the ban on religious symbols and dress codes in the *private* sphere, such as workplaces within the private sector. The EUCJ ruled that for the purpose of dir. 2000/78/EC an internal "neutrality rule" applied by a private employer does not constitute a direct discrimination on the grounds of religion or belief, "provided that that rule is applied in a general and undifferentiated way" to all employees (para. 55). Taking the EUCJ's reasoning to its extreme consequences, it empowers each employer in the private sector in any EU Member State to apply neutrality rules in the workplace.

This judgment is likely to have a more significant impact in those States which have already enacted bans on displaying religious symbols and clothing in the *public* sphere. Following this judgment Muslim women wearing headscarves will face greater barriers—not only in practice but also by law—in accessing employment not only in the public, but also in the private work sector.

The judgment may have disruptive effects even in States where bans on religious symbols and clothing in the public sphere are not yet in place. Without specific national laws regulating the use of religious symbols and dress in private workplaces, there does not seem to be any legal obstacle for private employers wishing to apply the "neutrality rule" in compliance with the legal framework established by the EUCJ.

In every case, even if applied by employers in a general and undifferentiated way as requested by the EUCJ, the neutrality rule seems likely to have a profound impact especially on Muslim women who wear the headscarf. Starting from now they will find themselves in a more disadvantageous situation compared to other women when accessing jobs in the private sector, and they will be forced to choose between employment (i.e., financial and individual empowerment) and displaying their religious beliefs (i.e., the respect of an individual's choice and social acceptance within the Muslim community).

Thus, the profile of indirect discrimination seems to emerge as it generally occurs when a seemingly neutral provision, criterion or practice applied by an employer puts people who have a specific religion or belief, such as

Muslim women wearing the headscarf, at a particular disadvantage. Regarding this, the EUCJ argued that differences of treatment indirectly based on religion may be justified "by the employer's *desire* to pursue a policy of political, philosophical and religious neutrality in the workplace, in order to take account of the *wishes* of its customers or users" (para. 59). Firstly, it is interesting to observe how the EUCJ seems to position its reasoning within the boundaries of private choices and interests protected under art. 16 of the EU Charter of fundamental rights that guarantee the right to conduct a business. The EUCJ uses words which are unrelated to legal language, such as *desire* and *wishes*, which are deemed sufficient to justify the differences in treatment on the grounds of religion and belief.

The EUCJ provides some further limits to the neutrality rule, which are identified as follows: the difference in treatment must be "objectively justified by a legitimate purpose" and the means to achieve it must be "appropriate" as well as limited to what is strictly necessary; the difference of treatment can be objectively justified when it corresponds to "a *genuine need* on the part of that employer, which the employer must demonstrate" (it can be the prevention of social conflicts in the workplaces and the presentation of a neutral image of the employer towards his/her users or customers, see para. 64 and 76); in the absence of the "neutrality rule" the employer would suffer adverse consequences (such as the loss of clients and/or of income). The limits imposed on employers by the EUCJ seem very general and extensive. The part relating to the burden of proof appears to be the only one with a more rigorous legal-procedural value since the employer is required to prove that the difference in treatment is objectively justified.

The reasoning of the EUCJ in the *MH* case adds little to the findings of the *WABE* case clarifying only that the neutrality rule must cover all visible forms of expression of political, philosophical, or religious beliefs and must not be limited to conspicuous or large-sized symbols only in order to be compliant with dir. 2000/78/EC.

THE "NEUTRALITY RULE" AND THE "RULE OF LAW"

In a well-known judgment pronounced in 2003[9] the German Constitutional Tribunal ruled that prohibiting the exhibition of religious symbols in public spaces (including public workplaces such as public schools) must be consistent with the rule of law and the principle of democracy, meaning that the prohibition can be provided for only under a specific law approved by the Legislature of the State (in Germany, it is a Länder's responsibility to regulate school policy, education and cultural affairs) and not by the decision of an authority within the public administration. In two judgments passed in 2015 (1 BvR 471/10 and 1 BvR1181/10), the same Constitutional

Tribunal ruled that the use of religious symbols in public workspaces can be limited only in cases where a "concrete risk" has been ascertained, and not in cases where there is a mere "abstract risk" of compromising the peace of the community within the school and the neutrality of the State (Di Martino, 2015; D'Amico, 2015).[10] In its last judgment passed in 2020 (2 BvR 1333/17), the German Constitutional Tribunal recognized the constitutionality of the ban on wearing a headscarf for judges but not for legal trainees: it considered the limitation of the right to religion justified under the principle of neutrality of the State in a matter that directly affects the proper functioning of the justice system (Gatti, 2020).[11]

On the one hand, in all three judgments the Constitutional Tribunal recognized that the freedom of religion is not an absolute fundamental right which is protected by German Basic Law; on the other hand, it pointed out that freedom of religion can be limited only if doing so is necessary in order to protect other substantive constitutional rights and interests of the State. Moreover, any limitation of the right to religious freedom must occur in strict compliance with the principle of proportionality. The responsibility to find a fair balance is dependent on the Legislatures and the laws approved by them in accordance with the rule of law.

Following the reasoning of the EUCJ in the *WABE* and *MH* judgment of 2021, it seems that as far as the right to religious freedom is concerned, there is no room for the rule of law at least in its more substantial meaning as provided for by specific National laws regulating the use of religious symbols in private workplaces. Starting from para. 79 of the judgment the EUCJ addresses the meaning and scope of the right to religious freedom as being protected under EU law (art. 10, 1 of the EU Charter of fundamental rights) and international law (art. 9 of the European Convention of Human Rights). The EUCJ highlights the need to find a fair balance among several fundamental rights and principles protected under the EU Charter of fundamental rights, such as the principle of non-discrimination (art. 21), the right to thought, conscience and religion (art. 10,1), the right of parents to educate and teach their children in accordance with their religion and values (art. 14,3) and the freedom to conduct a business (art. 16).

The EUCJ recognizes that Directive 2000/78/EC leaves a margin of discretion to Member States in granting the right to religious freedom a wider protection than that provided for under EU and international law. However, the EUCJ does not call on Member States to provide more detailed and specific National laws regulating the use of religious symbols in private spaces and especially in private workplaces.[12] Instead, it seems to consider the rights enshrined in the EU Charter of fundamental rights and the general provisions provided for by dir. 2000/78/EC—as the EUCJ itself interprets in this judgment—as a sufficient legal framework to regulate the ban on religious symbols in private workplaces.

While it asks National Courts to find a fair balance between the conflicting principles and rights in force at EU and national levels, it also declares its right to reserve the role of supervisor for itself "in determining whether the measures taken at the national level were justified in principle and whether they were proportionate."

According to the EUCJ, the legal framework concerning the prohibition of the use of religious symbols in private workplaces is already well established under EU and international law and jurisprudence and, most of all, it seems to recognize it direct horizontal effects among private individuals (Pitino, 2012).[13] National Courts are asked to apply those rules in their domestic legal systems. Private employers are given a high degree of responsibility in enforcing the neutrality rule and the display of religious symbols in the workplace according to their view on religion and ideological/philosophical beliefs. Although National Legislatures retain the main responsibility for regulating the freedom of religion, they seem to have been attributed only a marginal role under the supervision of the EUCJ.

In the *WABE* and *MH* case-law, the EUCJ seems to give more importance to employers' freedom in conducting a business, and to customers' rights rather than to workers' rights and to the right to religious freedom itself (Jackson, 2021).[14] The intervention of National laws is highly desirable in a matter which is not only the responsibility of States, but which also has a significant impact on social cohesion and the integration of people belonging to different religions and who live together within the same State.

The main objective of National legislations should be to prevent such an important issue from being mostly left to the individual choices—or *wishes*—of employers and clients, which are only limited by very general conditions established by the EUCJ.

The original objective, among others, of Directive 2000/78/EC was to lay down a general framework to combat discrimination on the grounds of religion and beliefs. After the EUCJ's judgment in the joint cases *WABE* and *MH*, that same Directive seems to have mostly become a legal basis to justify differences of treatment among workers in the private sector on grounds of religion through the neutrality rule, which is enforced by employers under the broad umbrella of EU law. This is an unexpected and controversial outcome for a directive whose objective was completely different.

"OPEN INCLUSIVE NEUTRALITY" VERSUS "STRICT DISTANCED NON-RELIGIOUS NEUTRALITY": WHICH OPTION IS MORE LIKELY TO BE AFFIRMED IN THE EUROPEAN UNION?

In the above mentioned judgment of 2003 the German Constitutional Tribunal referred to two different interpretations of neutrality that can be adopted by the State: "open inclusive neutrality," which accepts all religions and is tolerant to everybody in seeking to integrate all people notwithstanding their religion or ideological beliefs, and "strict distanced non-religious neutrality," which can lead to the banning on religious symbols after balancing many relevant rights and interests of the States, such as freedom of religion (positive freedom) and freedom from religion (negative freedom), the principle of equality, the freedom of education for pupils and the freedom of parents to educate their children in conformity with their religious, philosophical and pedagogical convictions, the protection of public order and security, societal peace and the neutrality of public employment.

Directive 2000/78/EC (Art. 2,5) provides that National laws, which lay down measures which are necessary in a democratic society for public security and for maintaining public order, the prevention of crime, the protection of health and the protection of the rights and freedoms of others, are not contrary to the principle of non-discrimination and to the purpose of the directive itself.

In its 2021 judgment the EUCJ seems to grant private employers broad power in interpreting and applying the neutrality rule in the workplace according to their clients' and their own wishes, under the freedom to conduct a business, which is protected by art. 16 of the EU Charter of Human Rights.

Therefore, there is a risk of there being different interpretations of religious neutrality both by public authorities on the one hand, and by private employers on the other hand, despite them being in the same State. This fact seems to be problematic since the interpretation of the principle of religious neutrality has an impact on migrants' integration and their empowerment, especially in the case of migrant women and Muslim women who wear headscarves, who appear to be the main target of the neutrality rules enforced in public as well as in private workplaces.

It seems that the two models of "open inclusive neutrality" and of "strict distanced non-religious neutrality" will coexist in the European Union depending on the more or less strict interpretation provided by each Member State to the principle of neutrality (e.g., a stricter interpretation is usually associated with France and less with Germany, whereas a more liberal interpretation is mostly associated with Italy, Spain and the United Kingdom).

This is not to say that one model should be always considered better than another as both models have positive and negative aspects that are worth considering. In principle the "open inclusive neutrality" seems to be more respectful of the right to religious freedom and it also seems to favor the peaceful societal coexistence and integration of people who belong to different religious groups within the spheres of occupation and employment. Nevertheless—when it leads to a State's indifference towards religious and cultural practices of minority groups—it can also result in a threat for individuals who belong to minority groups who risk being marginalized and suffering discrimination by people who are part of their own minority groups as well as by the majority (Moller Okin, 1997; Schmitt, 1972),[15] ultimately being forced to live within separate communities.

"Strict distanced non-religious neutrality" seems to be less respectful of the right to religious freedom, but it can help people who belong to minority religious groups to integrate into the host societies. One example is provided by Muslim women living in Western Countries who have abandoned the religious practice of wearing a headscarf even though it is still an obligation in their home countries—e.g., Saudi-Arabia and Afghanistan—and/or within their religious communities abroad (Jackson, 2021).[16] This can also encourage women who wear a headscarf to engage in self-employment in the private sector, leading to more job opportunities for other women who wear a headscarf (Human Rights Watch, 2009).[17] On the other hand, it can lead to fewer opportunities for Muslim women who wear a headscarf to find a job compared to women who do not follow religious precepts. It can also force Muslim (migrant) women to live or to move to EU states where National legislations and private employers' behavior guarantee working conditions which are more compatible with their religion.

CONCLUDING REMARKS ON RELIGIOUS NEUTRALITY AND GENDER EQUALITY BETWEEN WOMEN AND MEN IN OCCUPATION AND EMPLOYMENT

Given that it is very difficult to determine in abstract terms which of the two models of religious neutrality described above is the best in every circumstance, there is an urgent need for each EU Member State to intervene and regulate by law the application of the neutrality rule in the private sector in order to ensure the least sacrifice of the right to religious freedom and the best ways to promote the coexistence and peaceful integration of people who belong to different religious groups, and who live and work in the same State.

Regarding both of the neutrality models, women seem to be more frequently exposed to the risk of being discriminated against than men due to the disadvantages already arising from their gender. Therefore, it is of the utmost importance that National laws regulating the religious neutrality of the State—both in the public and in the private spheres—take the gender perspective into account.

As already stated above, the reasoning of the EUCJ in the *WABE* and *MH* is limited to a formal definition of non-discrimination, which states that the neutrality rule does not constitute discrimination on the grounds of religion provided that employers apply it to their employees in a general and undifferentiated fashion. However, the enforcement of the neutrality rule disproportionally affects women by reducing job opportunities in the private working sector for those who wear a headscarf. This ultimately results in indirect discrimination on the grounds of equality between men and women in occupation and employment.

The gender issue has remained in the background of the *WABE* case in consequence of the fact that—as noted by the EUCJ itself in para. 58—discrimination on the grounds of gender equality does not fall within the scope of dir. 2000/78/EU and the question referred to the EUCJ by the German Court relates only to this directive.[18]

It is well known that equality and non-discrimination between women and men are common and founding values of the European Union, which are firmly embedded in the Treaties of the European Union (art. 8, art. 153, para. 1, lett. i and art. 157 of the Treaty on the functioning of the EU), the EU Charter of Fundamental Rights and secondary legislation (see dir. 2006/54/EC on equal opportunities and equal treatment of women and men in employment and occupation).

If, in future, a request for a preliminary ruling, which is similar to those examined in *WABE* and *MH* cases, is referred again to the EUCJ by a National Court, the preliminary ruling will need to take into account not only the EU legislation dealing with discrimination on the grounds of religion but also that preventing discrimination on the grounds of gender which falls also under EU law.

In such a case, it is possible that the EUCJ will recognize the existence of an indirect discrimination against Muslim women wearing the headscarf on grounds of gender and equal opportunities between men and women in accessing employment and occupation.[19]

NOTES

1. On women empowerment and gender stereotipes see Simonati A. (2020), La 'cittadinanza di genere': una possibile chiave di lettura dell'evoluzione normativa. In Scarponi S. (Ed.), *Diritto e genere. Temi e questioni* (38). Napoli, ES e Parolari S. (2019), Stereotipi di genere, discriminazioni contro le donne e vulnerabilità come disempowerment. Riflessioni sul ruolo del diritto. *AG AboutGender*, 8(15), 102.
2. The WABE case concerned a Muslim teacher in a private child day care center who wore a headscarf. The MH case concerned a Muslim woman who wore a headscarf while working in a company operating a chain of drugstores in Germany.
3. In 2017 two National Courts in Belgium and France referred to the European Union Court of Justice (EUCJ) for a preliminary ruling asking whether prohibiting Muslim women from wearing headscarves in the workplace constituted a discrimination under the 2000/78/EC directive, establishing a

general framework for equal treatment in employment and occupation (*G4S*, C-157/15, and *Micropole*, C-188/15). In particular, the two questions focused on the interpretation of the 2000/78/EC directive prohibiting discrimination on the grounds of religion and belief, of art. 10 protecting the freedom of thought, conscience and religion and art. 16 protecting the freedom to conduct a business according to the Charter of Fundamental Rights of the European Union. The event constituted the very first time the EUCJ issued a judgment concerning the freedom of religion according to EU law.

4. In this chapter we will refer in general to the Muslim religion although the Muslim community is made of many religious orientations such as Sunnis, Shiites, Ahmadis, Alevi and secular Muslims.
5. Moller Okin, S. (1998). Feminism and multiculturalism: some tensions. *Ethics*, *108*(4), p. 673.
6. Muslims are the second religious group after Christians; this is also the case in France and Belgium, which referred to the EUCJ in the two first preliminary rulings regarding wearing headscarves in workplaces in 2017.
7. Human Rights Watch (2009). Discrimination in the name of neutrality. Headscarf bans for teachers and civil servants in Germany, p. 29 and 50. Accessed May 2023, from https://www.hrw.org/sites/default/files/reports/germany0209_webwcover.pdf, also reports that in Germany headscarf bans and the respective debate have aggravated discrimination against women who wear a headscarf even outside public employment. See also Helbling, M. (2014). Opposing Muslims and the Muslim Headscarf in Western Europe. *European Sociological Review*, *30*(2), pp. 243-44, who underlines that even people with liberal values tend to criticize "the role of women and the general lack of self-determination in Muslim societies."
8. Human Rights Watch (2009). Discrimination in the name of neutrality. Headscarf bans for teachers and civil servants in Germany, p. 8. Cit., which reports one judgment concerning a Sikh taxi driver wearing a turban who was confronted with the French law asking for bareheaded photographs on all identity documents, including driving licenses (ECHR, *Mann Sing v. France*, case 24479/07).
9. See the well-known *Fereshta Ludin*, 2 BvR 1436/02, concerning the first case of a German-Afghan teacher wearing a headscarf who was employed in public education.
10. Di Martino, A. (2015). L'ultima decisione sul velo del Bundesverfassungsgericht tra continuità e discontinuità giurisprudenziale. *diritticomparati.it*, p. 1. https://www.diritticomparati.it/lultima-decisione-sul-velo-del-bundesverfassungsgericht-tra-continuita-e-discontinuita-giurisprudenz/?print-posts=pdf e D'Amico, M. (2015). Laicità costituzionale e fondamentalismi tra Italia ed Europa: considerazioni a partire da alcune decisioni giurisprudenziali, *Rivista AIC*, 2, p. 30. https://www.rivistaaic.it/images/rivista/pdf/2_2015_DAmico.pdf
11. Gatti, A. (2020), Il divieto del velo per le giudici e le tirocinanti è costituzionale: per il Tribunale costituzionale tedesco "plurale" è prima di tutto "pubblico." *DPCE on line*, 1, p. 1037. https://www.dpceonline.it/index.php/dpceonline/article/view/950

12. Dir. 2000/78/EU, art. 2, para. 5 provides that "the directive shall be without prejudice to measures laid down by national law which, in a democratic society, are necessary for public security, for the maintenance of order and the prevention of criminal offences, for the protection of health and for the protection of the rights and freedoms of others."
13. On the horizontal direct effects of general principles of non-discrimination in EUCJ case-law see already Pitino, A. (2012). Riflessioni sull'efficacia diretta dei principi generali di non discriminazione nei rapporti di tipo verticale e orizzontale. in Pitino, A. (Ed.), *Profili attuali del principio di non discriminazione tra Unione europea e Regioni italiane* (p. 14), Roma, Aracne.
14. Jackson, E. (2021). Cases C-804/18 and C-341/19—The false neutrality of anti-intersectional interpretation. *Trinity College Law Review online*, https://trinitycollegelawreview.org/cases-c%E2%80%91804-18-and-c%E2%80%91341-19-the-false-neutrality-of-anti-intersectional-interpretation/, with regard to the EUCJ "rather than examining the effects of the ban on the applicant, they consider whether the employer had a 'legitimate' reason for excluding them from their workplace."
15. Moller Okin, S. (1997). Is multiculturalism bad for women? *Boston Review*. Accessed May 2023, from: https://bostonreview.net/forum/susan-moller-okin-multiculuralism-bad-women/, from a feminist perspective criticizes the approach of multiculturalism that provides for the protection of the rights of minority group or the right of minority group to be "let alone" in a liberal society since it usually limits the capacity of women and girls "to live with human dignity equal to that of men and boys." The A. highlights that monotheistic religions such as Judaism, Christianity and Islam justify the control of women by men at least in their most orthodox and fundamentalist beliefs, and that most cultures and traditions all around the world are patriarchal. Sometimes women's basic human rights are formally assured, but discrimination against women occurs in practice. On the concept of neutrality as "plurality relationship" which allows all groups to equally enjoy the State's rights and benefits see Schmitt, C. (1972). Rassegna dei diversi significati e funzioni del concetto di neutralità politica interna dello Stato (1931), in Miglio, G. and Schiera, P. (Eds.). *Le categorie del politico. Saggi di teoria politica* (p. 187), Il Mulino, Bologna.
16. Jackson, E. (2021), Cases C-804/18 and C-341/19—The false neutrality of anti-intersectional interpretation, Cit., considers that as an expression of Western feminism according to which the headscarf is a threat to womens' expression and empowerment.
17. Human Rights Watch (2009), p. 10, Cit.
18. Gender equality remained also in the background of some well-known judgments of the ECHR such as *Leyla Sahin v. Turkey* (2005) and *Dogru v. France* (2008).
19. After the 2021 judgment analyzed in this chapter, it seems less likely that the EUCJ will recognize the existence of a multiple discrimination against women both on grounds of religion and gender equality in employment and occupation.

REFERENCES

D'Amico, M. (2015). Laicità costituzionale e fondamentalismi tra Italia ed Europa: considerazioni a partire da alcune decisioni giurisprudenziali, *Rivista AIC, 2*, 1–35. Accessed May 2023, from https://www.rivistaaic.it/images/rivista/pdf/2_2015_DAmico.pdf

Di Martino, A. (2015). L'ultima decisione sul velo del Bundesverfassungsgericht tra continuità e discontinuità giurisprudenziale. *diritticomparati.it*, 1–6. Accessed May 2023, from https://www.diritticomparati.it/lultima-decisione-sul-velo-del-bundesverfassungsgericht-tra-continuita-e-discontinuita-giurisprudenz/?print-posts=pdf

Gatti, A. (2020), Il divieto del velo per le giudici e le tirocinanti è costituzionale: per il Tribunale costituzionale tedesco "plurale" è prima di tutto "pubblico." *DPCE on line, 1*, 1037–1044. Accessed May 2023, from https://www.dpceonline.it/index.php/dpceonline/article/view/950

Jackson, E. (2021). Cases C-804/18 and C-341/19—The false neutrality of anti-intersectional interpretation. *Trinity College Law Review online*. Accessed May 2023, from https://trinitycollegelawreview.org/cases-c%E2%80%91804-18-and-c%E2%80%91341-19-the-false-neutrality-of-anti-intersectional-interpretation/

Helbling, M. (2014). Opposing Muslims and the Muslim Headscarf in Western Europe. *European Sociological Review, 30*(2), 242–257.

Human Rights Watch (2009). Discrimination in the name of neutrality. Headscarf bans for teachers and civil servants in Germany, 1–68. Accessed May 2023, from https://www.hrw.org/sites/default/files/reports/germany0209_webwcover.pdf

Moller Okin, S. (1997). Is multiculturalism bad for women? *Boston Review*. Accessed May 2023, from: https://bostonreview.net/forum/susan-moller-okin-multiculuralism-bad-women/

Moller Okin, S. (1998). Feminism and multiculturalism: some tensions. *Ethics, 108*(4), 661–684.

Parolari S. (2019), Stereotipi di genere, discriminazioni contro le donne e vulnerabilità come disempowerment. Riflessioni sul ruolo del diritto. *AG AboutGender, 8*(15), 90–117.

Pitino, A. (2012). Riflessioni sull'efficacia diretta dei principi generali di non discriminazione nei rapporti di tipo verticale e orizzontale. in Pitino, A. (Ed.), *Profili attuali del principio di non discriminazione tra Unione europea e Regioni italiane* (pp. 9–32). Roma, Aracne.

Schmitt, C. (1972). Rassegna dei diversi significati e funzioni del concetto di neutralità politica interna dello Stato (1931), in Miglio, G. and Schiera, P. (Eds.). *Le categorie del politico. Saggi di teoria politica*, Bologna, Il Mulino.

Simonati A. (2020), La 'cittadinanza di genere': una possibile chiave di lettura dell'evoluzione normativa. In Scarponi S. (Ed.), *Diritto e genere. Temi e questioni* (pp. 27–48). Napoli, ES.

SECTION II

DIVERSITY, POLICIES, AND ADMINISTRATIVE ACTION

CHAPTER 5

ADVANCING SOCIAL EQUITY IN PUBLIC SERVICES

The Role of Artificial Intelligence

Anna Maria Chiariello
LUISS Guido Carli

Rocco Frondizi
University of Rome Tor Vergata

ABSTRACT

Artificial Intelligence (AI) has the potential to improve public administration and decision-making processes, as well as to solve problems in critical sectors. However, the use of AI also carries risks that must be addressed to uphold democratic values and human rights, with the protection of human dignity and privacy being particularly important. The adoption of AI solutions in public services can enhance the quality of services, generate savings, and offer greater guarantees to citizens. AI can also promote principles such as equality, equal treatment, and non-discrimination, as it allows for the provision of personalized services and can help break down societal divides. Nevertheless, the customization of public services through AI raises concerns about social equity, requiring ensuring that this principle is not undermined. This study aims to identify the risks and factors related to AI that can negatively affect public service provision and compliance with non-discrimination and social equity principles. The study also aims to identify tools that not only avoid discrimination but also promote diversity as a source of richness for society.

In the public sector, Artificial Intelligence (AI) is often used to improve the efficiency of public administration and its decision-making process, to foster positive relationships with citizens and businesses and to solve specific problems in critical sectors such as healthcare, mobility, and safety. Despite the many potential benefits of AI, there are also numerous risks, which must be addressed first of all in order to ensure respect for democratic values and human rights. In this regard, in consideration of the impact that emerging technologies have on society, a use of AI that safeguards human dignity and privacy appears to be of considerable importance.

Specifically in relation to public services, the adoption of AI solutions improves the quality of the services offered, generates savings, allows to reach larger production scales, is able to give greater guarantees to citizens, and, not least, leads to interesting benefits and positive effects in relation to the founding principles that govern them. In particular, among these principles, there are equality and equal treatment, according to which users all have an equal right of access to the service and to receive qualitatively equal services for the same need, and non-discrimination, according to which the service must be guaranteed to all without distinction of income, location, social class, and individual conditions. For example, the satisfaction of the need for non-discrimination based on location, social class, and individual conditions appears to be favored by the ability of algorithms to address the territorial and social divide and to break the isolation of certain populations, managing to provide them with public services more effectively, faster, and in a more personalized way. Furthermore, while the management of services by humans can generate more or less conscious and voluntary discrimination, AI, by allowing services to be customized and consequently to treat different situations differently, is able to allow greater implementation of the principle of substantive social equity.

At the same time, the use of new technologies for the purpose of providing public services may instead raise significant problems in relation to their compliance with the aforementioned principles. For example, given that algorithmic processing allows the customization of the public service and the better adaptation of administrative decisions to the specificities of each case, care must be taken to ensure that the principle of social equity is not endangered. It is no small matter. In fact, although today AI is a powerful tool capable of helping to improve the efficiency of public administration and public services, its use in this area cannot, however, result in a violation of the principles that govern them.

In this framework, this chapter intends to analyze the main risks and factors related to emerging technologies that can negatively affect the provision of public services and compliance with the principles relating to them, and in particular with non-discrimination and social equity. Furthermore, it intends to identify tools aimed not only at avoiding discrimination but also at enhancing diversity and promoting it as a source of richness for society.

ARTIFICIAL INTELLIGENCE (AI): DEFINITION, APPROACHES, AND DEVELOPMENT OVER TIME

Artificial Intelligence (AI) is a technology that has become ubiquitous in the daily lives of individuals, businesses, and organizations. Although AI encompasses a broad range of studies, theories, and methodologies, its ultimate objective is to enable machines to imitate human cognitive abilities such as decision-making, error-learning, reasoning, communication, problem-solving, and physical movement. Although there is no agreed definition of what AI is, it can be generally identified as the discipline that covers theorems and practical techniques for developing algorithms that let machines carry out clever tasks, involving specific domains and application areas. Based on this definition, distinctions need to be made according to the function associated with AI. Structural AI and functional AI are two approaches that can be taken. Structural AI simulates human brain activities and characteristics to obtain machine intelligence, while functional AI focuses on emulation and views intelligence as independent from the physical structure of the brain. Another classification can be made between the "top-down" and "bottom-up" approaches. The former uses a symbolic approach to manipulate symbols to produce results, while the latter starts from artificial neuron networks to create more complex reasoning structures. The final classification is between weak and strong AI. Weak AI refers to systems that can simulate some human cognitive functions but not achieve their full intellectual capabilities, while strong AI includes systems that can develop their own intelligence without emulating human thought processes. Finally, AI can be classified into four areas based on its intellectual abilities. These include comprehension, which involves identifying and extrapolating information from text, pictures, charts, screens, and voice; reasoning, which involves connecting different types of data using mathematical algorithms; learning, which involves processing incoming data and producing output, such as through machine learning; and interaction, which involves natural language computing.

But when and how was AI developed? The origins of Artificial Intelligence can be traced back to the 1950s, when there was a lot of interest in using computing technology for intelligent systems. A major event that contributed to the development of AI was a conference held in 1956 at Dartmouth College, which was attended by leading figures in computer science. During this conference, Alan Turing's work was highlighted. Turing, who is considered one of the pioneers of modern computing, published an article in 1950 called "Computing Machinery and Intelligence," which introduced what would later become known as the Turing test. This test determines whether a machine can be considered to have Artificial Intelligence, if it can imitate human responses and if it is able to produce feedback that is similar to that produced by a human. Turing's work on Artificial Intelligence attracted significant attention from the scientific community. In 1958, Franck Rosenblatt, a psychologist, introduced the Perceptron neural network scheme, which was designed for recognizing and classifying shapes. The Perceptron has an input, output, and learning rule based on error minimization. That same year, John McCarthy created Lisp, the first language to utilize virtual machines and virtual memory management for processing symbolic expressions. This progress led to a growing optimism about the future potential of Artificial Intelligence, with many debating whether AI could eventually match human intelligence. Some experts believed that AI had the ability to imitate and replicate the human brain's functioning perfectly. Joseph Weisenbaum created the first attempt at human-machine dialogue, called ELIZA, in 1966. It is considered to be the first example of a chatbot, even though it had some limitations in providing predetermined answers. In the 1970s, the first Expert Systems were developed. These AI systems were designed to solve specific tasks by emulating experts in specialized domains. The machine used a reasoning mechanism based on knowledge derived from domain experts and was developed through an inference engine that implemented appropriate reasoning algorithms. However, it was not until the 1980s that these systems were applied to fields such as diagnosis, design, monitoring, data interpretation, and planning. These systems proved to be excellent tools for industrial applications, leading to a period of intense technological development. In the latter part of the last century, there was a renewed interest in neural networks, with a focus on the Perceptron, which led to the development of the "connectionist" approach, whose aim was to use artificial neural networks as perfect substitutes for the human mind. The current phase of AI development is marked by the advancement of deep learning, which involves training artificial neural networks with massive amounts of data. This has enabled breakthroughs in various fields, including computer vision, natural language processing, and speech recognition. One of the key factors driving the progress in AI is the availability of large amounts of data, which enables better training of neural networks. Additionally, advancements in hardware, such as GPUs, are also contributing to the growth of AI.

AI AND THE PUBLIC SECTOR: STATE OF THE ART, OPPORTUNITIES, AND CHALLENGES

AI has emerged as a powerful tool for innovation and development in various sectors, including the public sector. Public administration is increasingly utilizing AI to carry out its numerous and complex tasks, reaping the numerous benefits that have previously been exclusive to the private sector (Misuraca & van Noordt, 2020): AI has the potential to revolutionize the way governments and public institutions operate by improving their efficiency, responsiveness, and decision-making capabilities.

One of the main areas where AI can be applied in the public sector is in the provision of public services. The public sector has been slow to adopt AI compared to the private sector, but there is increasing interest and investment in the potential of AI to improve public service delivery. Governments can leverage AI technologies to provide citizens with better and more personalized services, such as online self-service portals and chatbots that can answer citizens' questions and provide them with information. This can lead to significant cost savings for governments, as they can reduce the need for manual labor and streamline processes. Additionally, AI-powered tools can help governments better understand citizens' needs and preferences, leading to more effective and responsive policy-making. Therefore, AI improves the services provided, particularly those that are repetitive or have a high level of complexity, in terms of subjects involved, territorial areas concerned and technical characteristics (Masucci, 2019; Avanzini, 2019). Because of the use of AI, these services can now be provided in a more rapid, continuous, and efficient manner. In fact, AI allows for maximization of the use of human and material resources and, as a result, lowers costs associated with transactions as well as, most importantly, with the gathering and analysis of information and data. This enhances the relationship between public administration and citizens. The improvement of public service delivery is pursued through a variety of factors. These encompass the automation of routine government and administrative processes and the ability of AI to collect and analyze massive amounts of data (Galetta, 2020; Carullo, 2017), to weigh more variables in making complex decisions while erasing human errors, to allow for greater user participation, to personalize services, and to make them more accurate (Capdeferro Villagrasa, 2020).

Another potential application of AI in the public sector is in improving public safety and security. AI technologies such as facial recognition and predictive analytics can help law enforcement agencies prevent and respond to crimes more effectively. For example, AI-powered surveillance systems can automatically detect and alert authorities to suspicious activities, while predictive analytics can help police departments allocate resources more efficiently to areas where crimes are likely to occur. Additionally,

AI-powered tools can help governments respond more effectively to natural disasters and emergencies by providing real-time data and insights.

AI can also be used to improve healthcare services and outcomes. AI-powered tools can help healthcare providers diagnose and treat patients more effectively by analyzing large amounts of medical data, identifying patterns and trends, and providing personalized treatment recommendations. Additionally, AI can help healthcare providers predict and prevent diseases by analyzing patient data and identifying individuals who are at higher risk of developing certain conditions.

In the realm of environmental protection, AI can help governments better understand and address environmental challenges. For example, AI-powered sensors and monitoring systems can provide real-time data on air and water quality, enabling governments to identify and respond to environmental hazards more quickly. Additionally, AI can help governments develop more effective policies and strategies for addressing climate change by analyzing large amounts of data on energy consumption, greenhouse gas emissions, and other environmental factors.

Despite the potential benefits of AI in the public sector, there are also challenges and risks that must be addressed. One of the main challenges is ensuring that AI systems are transparent, accountable, and unbiased. This is particularly important in areas such as law enforcement and healthcare, where AI-powered tools can have significant impacts on people's lives. Additionally, there is a risk that AI could exacerbate existing inequalities and biases if it is not designed and implemented carefully. In fact, AI systems can reflect and even amplify the biases and prejudices of their developers and the data they are trained on. This can lead to discriminatory outcomes that perpetuate existing social inequalities, such as discrimination against certain races, genders, or socioeconomic groups. Moreover, the automation of jobs by AI can lead to displacement of human workers, creating new ethical considerations around the impact of AI on employment and labor practices. Finally, AI systems can make critical decisions that affect human lives, such as in autonomous vehicles or medical diagnosis systems. There are concerns about the safety and reliability of these systems, and how they can be held accountable if something goes wrong. Addressing these ethical risks requires a comprehensive approach that involves collaboration between developers, policymakers, and other stakeholders to ensure that AI is developed and deployed in ways that are ethical, transparent, and accountable.

Summarizing, AI has the potential to bring significant benefits to the public sector by improving the provision of public services, enhancing public safety and security, improving healthcare outcomes, and addressing environmental challenges. However, to realize these benefits, governments must be proactive in addressing the challenges and risks associated with AI and ensure that AI systems are transparent, accountable, and designed with the public interest in mind. These dangers cannot be understated; in fact, emerging technologies have such a profound effect on society that they threaten even the democratic principles and fundamental human rights upon which society is based, and not least also social equity.

GOVERNMENT INITIATIVES FOR AI IN THE PUBLIC SECTOR

In terms of using AI, the public sector falls behind the private sector. Governments are making an effort to remedy this imbalance by enacting a number of specific initiatives, declarations, policies, and rules. Almost forty nations have approved specific strategies in relation to the use of AI in the public sector, promoting its growth while protecting the interests and rights that such usage may infringe.

In the EU context, in 2018 the European Commission adopted the AI Strategy,[1] which addresses the socioeconomic implications of AI, both public and private. Based on the knowledge that AI has the potential to transform public services, it also develops a coordinated plan for the alignment of strategies intended to promote the development of AI in Europe (Coordinated Plan on Artificial Intelligence).[2]

In 2019 the same Commission adopted the Ethics Guidelines for Trustworthy AI, drafted by a group of AI experts which considered various issues, including equity, transparency, democracy, dignity and non-discrimination. The Guidelines are intended to offer direction on how to build and operate AI systems in an ethical and trustworthy manner and are based on the following four guiding principles: (i) respect for human autonomy; (ii) prevention of harm; (iii) fairness; and (iv) explicability processes.

The White Paper On Artificial Intelligence,[3] released by the Commission in 2020, lays the groundwork for the defense of consumer rights and the encouragement of innovation in the field of AI. With this White Paper, the Commission highlights the opportunity to choose, with regard to AI, a common European approach of such dimensions as to impede the fragmentation of the single market. This is based on the consideration that various and unrelated national initiatives run the risk of undermining legal certainty, eroding citizens' confidence, and impeding the emergence of a dynamic European industry. To achieve this goal, it is deemed necessary to adopt a strategic framework establishing measures intended to coordinate efforts at European, national, and regional level. Through a partnership between public and private sectors, the strategic framework should also mobilize resources to attain an "ecosystem of excellence" along the entire value chain and develop the right incentives to speed up the implementation of AI-based solutions (Marchianò, 2021).

In 2021 the European Commission adopted a Proposal for a regulation laying down harmonized rules on AI (AI Act).[4] This proposal outlines a route for the creation and application of AI systems intended to advance both innovation and fundamental human rights, as well as to create a suitable and uniform legal framework and impose on Member States a number of goals important to the public interest, besides the general goal of ensuring new technologies' reliability.

As far as the Member States are concerned, significant efforts have been made, for example, in Italy.

The White Paper on Artificial Intelligence at the Service of the Citizen (Libro Bianco sull'Intelligenza artificiale al servizio del Cittadino) was adopted by the Agency for Digital Italy in 2018. This soft law act analyzes how modern information technologies affect social interactions and the traditional model of administrative activity. It also addresses the issue of automating administrative tasks through the use of AI to enhance public services and the relationship between public administration and citizens (Tresca, 2018).

Furthermore, the Strategy for Technological Innovation and Digitalization of the Country, which targets three primary "challenges"—*i.e.* digitization of society, innovation of the country and the sustainable and ethical development of society as a whole—was adopted in 2019. The Strategy describes a broad process of structural transformation of Italy to address these challenges, which includes public administration services.

Moreover, the three-year Plan for Information Technology in Public Administration was adopted in 2020 to implement the Italian Digital Administration Code, which applies also to public service providers (Legislative Decree 7 March 2005, No. 82, art. 2, para. 2, lett. b, and art. 14-bis, para. 2, lett. b). The Plan lays out the goals as well as the primary management and development initiatives for the public administrations' information systems and pursues a number of goals in order to carry out the measures envisioned by the prior plans. First, it intends to accelerate the growth of a digital society where services prioritize customers and enterprises through the digitization of public administration. Second, it encourages innovation and digitization in the service of people, communities, and territories while preserving environmental sustainability. It also intends to promote standardization, innovation, and experimentation in the provision of public services, so helping to disseminate new digital technologies across the Italian productive system.

Despite their efforts, governments are still not sufficiently equipped to deal with issues that are highly specialized on both a practical and regulatory level. The lack of uniform laws governing the application of AI in the public sector is expected to result in dysfunctions. In fact, AI has the ability to alter how public services are delivered, generating complexity and uncertainty. In this context it seems vital to create a legal framework that is universal and comprehensive in order to enable the administration to completely and positively exploit the potential of AI on public services while also winning citizens' confidence.

PUBLIC SERVICE PRINCIPLES AND AI

Regarding public services, legislation, case law, and sector authorities have established a number of principles, among which there are: equality and equal treatment, which requires that users all have an equal right to access the service and to receive services that are qualitatively equal for the same need; non-discrimination, which requires that the service is provided to everyone without distinction of income, location, social class and individual conditions; universality, which requires that the service must be made accessible to all end users, regardless of location, at a specific quality level and at an affordable price (affordability).

In relation to the aforementioned principles, the application of AI in public administration, and especially in public services can have several advantages and good impacts. For instance, the ability of algorithms to contrast the territorial and social divide within States and to break the isolation of certain populations, managing to provide them with public services more effectively, faster, and in a more personalized way, favors the satisfaction of the need for universality (Barraud, 2018). Additionally, AI permits a wider implementation of the principle of substantive equality because it enables services to be customized and, as a result, treat different situations in different ways. This contrasts with humans' management of services, which can result in a more or less conscious and voluntary discrimination (Simoncini & Suweis, 2019).

In contrast, using new technology to deliver public services may present serious issues with respect to their adherence to the mentioned principles. For instance, caution is needed to guarantee that equity, equality and universality are not in danger given that algorithmic processing enables customization of the public service and adapts administrative decisions to the specifics of each situation. It other words, in spite of the fact that AI is a potent tool that can boost the effectiveness of public administration and public services, its application in this field cannot compromise the rules that govern the latters.

The provision of public services and adherence to the related principles can be negatively impacted by a variety of new technology-related factors.

For instance, an unevenly distributed connection on the territory runs the potential of creating inequalities and a subsequent "digital fracture" between citizens provided with good connection and those provided with low or no connection. On the contrary, a good connection that is distributed evenly must go hand in hand with the application of new technology to public services. In order to do this, it is essential to guarantee that there are appropriate infrastructures and also legal framework (Pesce, 2018).

Moreover, "low quality" databases, that exhibit discriminatory bias, such as those related to sex or gender stereotypes, might have a negative impact on the delivery of public services, and in the end on equity. For instance, when it comes to databases where some groups are either underrepresented or overrepresented, causing their existence to be ignored or overemphasized, the uncritical utilization of previous or current data might lead to or might perpetuate discrimination. The services offered might in fact inadvertently reflect data bias, which would go against equality and nondiscrimination. In order to avoid this, it seems vital to guarantee that humans can intervene and amend any disputed decisions, as well as that public administration can review the results produced by algorithmic systems in order to correct any unjust discrimination. This is undoubtedly a sensitive operation that needs significant means and resources which public administration often lacks, but it is nonetheless required (Molinari, van Noordt, Vaccari, Pignatelli & Tangi, 2021).

The importance of the aforementioned crucial topics is being emphasized more and more. For instance, in the United Kingdom the Committee on Standards in Public Life, in its Report on Artificial Intelligence and Its Impact on Public Standards (2020), is concerned that data bias poses a risk to objectivity, another principle that must guide public life. In Brazil a resolution of the Conselho Nacional de Justiça of 2020 emphasizes the significance of the compatibility of fundamental rights with AI development and believes it essential to respect principles like equality and non-discrimination (Resolução nº 332/2020).

In light of the above, it is appropriate to positively evaluate the numerous declarations, guidelines, and codes of ethics drafted by experts from the world's top institutions, which suggest measures to regulate the utilization of AI in the public sector in order to guarantee compliance with the aforementioned principles.

THE PRINCIPLE OF TRANSPARENCY

When applying AI (also) to public services, a large portion of the work is done without the public knowing and, as so, without it being involved. The foregoing contributes to a lack of trust in technology, confirmed by the fact that services to which technology has been applied have displayed disparity and inequity, especially during pandemic.

In order to remedy the aforesaid, it is essential to ensure the respect of the principle of transparency and of the related principle of accountability, according to which individuals should be allowed to contest inaccuracies in machine inputs, to present mitigating information, to enjoy a right of appeal that would provide the same degree of protection as an appeal process that is based on decisions made solely in a human decision of a similar type. To ensure that citizens can be aware about when algorithms are used, inquire about how they work, and identify the AI system and the institution in charge of it, transparency of the algorithms and publicity of the related decision-making processes are essential. Decisions based on AI must in fact be clearly understood and explicable to recipients for purposes of accountability, just like other public administration decisions.

Algorithms must be traceable and understandable in order for there to be transparency in the use of AI. This implies that it must be possible to comprehend the machine's decision-making process. To achieve this, the justification for the outcome generated by computers must be made public in a straightforward manner and in a clear language. Nevertheless, algorithms do not necessarily need to be made public. In fact, if an algorithm is exceptionally complicated, a non-expert audience would still be unable to understand it, which has the effect that its simple publishing may not be helpful for transparency purposes. In these situations of opacity it is crucial to be able to explain the algorithms, including the goal for which they are utilized, the key factors that affected the outcome, the kind of data used and their quality, as well as the decision-making rules adopted (Bublitz Camara, 2021).

Adequate steps are required to guarantee a fair level of transparency. For instance, in France the *loi pour une République numérique* (2016) treats the source codes of government software as administrative documents, so communicable under the same conditions as these. It also acknowledges individuals' right to information when an administration utilizes an algorithm to make a decision for them. In particular, citizens must be given the proper information about the algorithm's intended use, the extent and ways in which algorithm contributes to the decision-making process, the data processed and their sources, the processing parameters and, potentially, their weighting, and the operations performed. The administration must also clearly explain the rules governing data processing as well as the key aspects of its actions. In Spain and in the UK, administrations are recommended to adopt a catalog of all IT applications that can have an impact on citizens, including those that have an impact on the provision of public service (Berryhill & al., 2019). The European Commission stipulates a number of ethical imperatives and principles in its Ethics Guidelines for Trustworthy AI (2019), including explainability. The Commission specifically demands that decision-making procedures be openly disclosed, the capabilities and intent of AI systems be made clear, and that final decisions be as fully explicable to stakeholders as feasible.

Lately also the Italian Council of State has voiced its opinion on the necessity of ensuring that the administration uses algorithms in a transparent manner (decision 8 April 2019, No. 2270). It stated that a strengthened declination of the principle at stake requires that the algorithm, through which the robotic decision is made, must be "recognizable," in order to allow verifying that the results of the robotic procedure are in compliance with the prescriptions and purposes of law or administration and in such a way that the rules underlying the algorithm are clear (and therefore can be questioned).

When using AI results in the so-called "black box effect," compliance with the principle of transparency and the related obligation of motivation is severely compromised (Bathaee, 2018). In these situations, the decision-making and reasoning both occur in a "black box," with the effect that the machine learning algorithm—aimed at making computers capable of learning on their own, without being programmed—produces a result without being able to explain how it arrived at it (D. Desordi & C. Della Bona, 2020). In these cases, the provision of the source code or of the text written in non-programming computer language is unsatisfactory since it is not only illegible even by experts, but discloses just partially the dynamics of the decision. In contrast to the procedural principles and guarantees provided by law, which require that public administration justifies its acts and explains its decisions, particularly when a certain discretion is allowed, these technologies are scarcely predictable and are vulnerable to cyber security threats. Given the inability or extreme difficulty of explaining the algorithms and how they work, it is essential to guarantee that roles are clearly defined. In fact, the principle of accountability is inextricably related to the one of transparency, particularly in public action.

Furthermore, to address the black box effect, the EU General Data Protection Regulation No. 2016/679 (GDPR) states in Article 22 that "the data subject shall have the right not to be subject to a decision based solely on automated processing (...) which produces legal effects concerning him or her or similarly significantly affects him or her." The same Article does, however, establish a derogation system that states that the aforementioned does not apply to processings that are necessary for the execution of a task carried out in the public interest or in the exercise of official authority vested in the controller. The right not to be subject to a decision entirely based on automated processing may only be restricted under two circumstances, according to the following Article 23. First, the legality principle must be upheld, which means that either national or EU law must permit automated processing. Second, the proportionality principle needs to be adhered to: to protect a long list of listed public interests, such as defense and public security, the limitation must, in a democratic society, be a necessary and reasonable measure. In any case, automated processing must be "subject to suitable safeguards, which should include specific information to the data subject and the right to obtain human intervention, to express his or her point of view, to obtain an explanation of the decision reached after such assessment and to challenge the decision" (Recital 71 of GDPR). This is because it is crucial that public administration be able to provide adequate justification for its decisions. In other words, the principle of transparency and the associated accountability principle cannot be entirely surrendered by completely replacing human activity with that of AI when it comes to public activity.

In the light of the above, it is necessary to find solutions that can ensure the legitimacy and reliability of the use of new technologies in the public sector while fostering citizen confidence in them. In order to do this, it has been proposed that appropriate monitoring and auditing techniques of AI systems be used. The creation of a global, multi-sector, and independent certification authority or agency has also been urged. This agency would be tasked with validating ex ante and regularly checking the applications of new technologies to public services on the basis of security standards and global quality indicators, both still lacking today. It would allow for the correction of any erroneous computational reasoning and of the weight given to specific variables, fostering trust between users and public service providers as well as equity. Moreover, the creation of an independent international arbitration body that evaluates and settles conflicts between the parties involved in public service AI systems (i.e., developers, regulators, and users) also has been suggested (Oxford Commission on AI & Good Governance, 2021).

CONCLUSIONS

In conclusion, the potential benefits of using AI in the public sector are significant, as it can improve the efficiency of public administration and decision-making, foster positive relationships with citizens and businesses, and solve specific problems in critical sectors such as healthcare, mobility, and safety. However, there are also numerous risks that must be addressed to ensure respect for democratic values and human rights. A use of AI that safeguards human dignity and privacy is crucial, given the impact that emerging technologies have on society.

In relation to public services, the adoption of AI solutions can improve the quality of services offered, generate savings, reach larger production scales, and provide greater guarantees to citizens. AI can also help to address territorial and social divides within States, providing public services more effectively, faster, and in a more personalized way. However, care must be taken to ensure that the principles of equality, equal treatment, and non-discrimination are not endangered. Algorithmic processing should not result in a violation of these principles, and tools should be implemented to enhance diversity and promote it as a source of richness for society.

The use of AI in the public sector must be guided by a commitment to transparency, accountability, and fairness, with a focus on the promotion of human dignity and respect for human rights. As AI continues to evolve, it will be essential to monitor its impact on society and take proactive measures to address any negative consequences that may arise. It is important to involve citizens, civil society organizations, and other stakeholders in the development and deployment of AI solutions, to ensure that they meet the needs and expectations of all members of society.

Finally, the use of AI in the public sector holds great potential for improving public services, but it also poses significant risks that must be addressed. A human rights-based approach to the use of AI in public services is necessary to ensure that the principles of equality, non-discrimination, and social equity are upheld. By promoting diversity and respecting human dignity, AI can be a valuable tool for advancing the public good and building a more just and equitable society.

NOTES

1. COM(2018) 237, 25 April 2018.
2. COM(2018) 795, 7 December 2018.
3. COM(2020) 65, 19 February 2020.
4. COM(2021) 206, 21 April 2021.

REFERENCES

Andrews, R., & Van de Walle, S. (2012). "New Public Management and citizens' Perceptions of Local Service Efficiency, Responsiveness, Equity and Effectiveness," *Public Management Review, 15*(5), 762–783.

Gaynor, T. S., & Wilson, M. E. (2020). Social Vulnerability and Equity: The Disproportionate Impact of COVID-19. *Public Administration Review, 80*(5), 832–838.

Gooden, S., & Portillo, S., (2011). Advancing Social Equity in the Minnowbrook Tradition. *Journal of Public Administration Research and Theory, 21*(suppl_1), i61–76.

Guy, M. E., & McCandless, S. A. (2012). Social Equity: Its Legacy, Its Promise. *Public Administration Review, 72*(s1), S5–S13.

Jakobsen, M., & Andersen, S. C. (2013). Coproduction and Equity in Public Service Delivery. *Public Administration Review, 73*(5), 704–713.

Kroll, A. (2017). Can Performance Management Foster Social Equity? Stakeholder Power, Protective Institutions, and Minority Representation. *Public Administration, 95*(1), 22–38.

Resta, G. (2019). Governare l'innovazione tecnologica: decisioni algoritmiche, diritti digitali e principio di uguaglianza. *Politica del diritto, 2*, 199–236.

Riccucci, N. M., & Van Ryzin, G. G. (2017). Representative Bureaucracy: A Lever to Enhance Social Equity, Coproduction, and Democracy. *Public Administration Review, 77*(1), 21–30.

Simoncini, A., & Suweis, S. (2019). Il cambio di paradigma nell'intelligenza artificiale e il suo impatto sul diritto costituzionale. *Rivista di filosofia del diritto, 1*(8), 87–106.

Svara, J. H., & Brunet, J. R. (2004). Filling in the Skeletal Pillar: Addressing Social Equity in Introductory Courses in Public Administration. *Journal of Public Affairs Education, 10*(2), 99–109.

Zuddas, P. (2020). Intelligenza artificiale e discriminazioni, Liber amicorum per Pasquale Costanzo, www.giurcost.org., 457–476.

CHAPTER 6

EQUAL TREATMENT AND LAW RELATING TO RIGHT TO BE FORGOTTEN (RTBF)

An Examination of Some Judicial Decisions with Special Reference to the European Union and India

Jyoti Rattan
Panjab University

Vijay Rattan
Consultant to the United Nations

ABSTRACT

In the modern era of speedier Information and Communication Technology, the power of social media as an information dissemination tool and influencer is felt in the hands of each and every individual both inside as well as outside the organization. Earlier, organizations and the administration did not have easy and free access to positive or negative information about an employee or a would-be employee, but nowadays with the advent of all-pervasive social media, hardly any aspect can remain hidden about any individual, whether one likes it or not. This is where a new problem has arisen quite often to the detriment of an employee or a would-be employee of an organization. Many a time, information that has become infructuous, irrelevant, or not supposed to impact the future of an individual anymore, still keeps doing the rounds of social media creating a false narrative about the individual leading to unjustified harm to the individual within or outside an organization. In such situations, one may find oneself helpless. The speed and unlimited reach of social media have further stoked the fire of this new malady, with the potential to cause harm to anybody, where of late, the law had to intervene and come to the rescue of the affected party in the name of justice.

This article makes a humble attempt to analyze the law relating to the "Right To Be Forgotten" (RTBF), briefly covering the traditional forms of unequal treatment, emergence of a new and different form of unequal treatment that popped up its head not long ago in the 21st century largely due to the wide-spread and increasing use of modern information and communication technologies (ICTs), powerful influencer social media and the internet by citizens and organizations in every nation and across the continents, ultimately leading to the birth of the "Right To Erasure" (RTE), more often now called as the "Right To Be Forgotten," and further examine in this regard select European Union and Indian judicial decisions.

Since the area under examination is comparatively of recent origin in terms of national and international case law and is fast evolving its contours, it is by no means intended to be a comparative study between the European Union and India. The main focus here, however, is to study the emergence of a new and different form of unequal treatment of individuals in the 21st century, due the all-pervasive social media and the internet, consequent advent of "Right To Be Forgotten" (RTBF) or "Right To Erasure" (RTE), main relevant statutes, examine the broad spectrum of coverage of the "Right To Be Forgotten" (RTBF) in the European case law and the Indian case law, and touching upon select judicial decisions in the European Union and the Indian judicial systems, through the study of primary and secondary online and offline sources.

The widespread use, the world over, of the information and communication technologies, the internet, particularly the social media has no doubt vastly improved communication and digital human interactions in every country. However, at the same time, its instantaneous unlimited global reach has come as a blessing in disguise, with a subtle, and sometimes not so subtle, seamier side also.

For instance, sometimes by instant publishing of information, social media may violate the right to privacy of a person. In such a situation the moot question is whether the affected person can claim the right to privacy or the Right To Be Forgotten (RTBF), especially where information published is related to some specific incident and the affected person wants to forget it. Can he ask the social media to remove that information so as to avoid becoming an unwilling victim of some unfounded bias due to incomplete information circulating beyond his control on the social media?

Significantly, the right to be forgotten is a comparatively new concept or a new dimension of the right to privacy and a debate had been raging in this regard for quite some time, in many parts of the world. Various countries have enacted legislation in this regard and some landmark judgements are also there.

For instance, in Europe, the European Statute directly relating to the "Right To Be Forgotten" (RTBF) is the *General Data Protection Regulation (GDPR), 2018*. *Article 17* and *Recitals 65 and 66 of GDPR, 2018* deal with RTBF. Significantly, much earlier in 2011, the European Court on Human Rights in the case of *RTBF v Belgium* held that RTBF is covered under Article 10 (Freedom of Expression) of the *European Convention for the Protection of Human Rights and Fundamental Freedoms, 1950*.

Whereas, in India, the right to privacy is covered under *Article 21* of the Constitution as was held by the judiciary in a number of cases and one such recent example is *Puttaswamy v. Union of India, 2017*. However, unfortunately, in India there is no statute specifically and directly dealing with online data protection and RTBF, which gives a fundamental right to a citizen to get an objectionable information deleted, i.e, useless and defamatory private data to be deleted from a social media site. Even the provisions of India's *Information Technology Act, 2000* and *Rules* are silent and do not directly deal with the "Right to Be Forgotten" but jurists believe that some provisions indirectly cover this right.

Nevertheless, the RTBF has of late, attracted significant attention in India. However, the *Data Protection Bill, 2021* (withdrawn by the Indian Government on 3 August 2022) had provisions relating to the "Right To Be Forgotten" (RTBF).

Moreover, it has been aptly observed that Data powers the new information economy and the risks associated with it also continue to skyrocket. Data breaches, identity theft and loss of customer trust are posing a serious threat to organizations of all sizes, in all sectors, in the marketplace in today's digital world.[1] In this scenario, loss or intentional or unintentional misuse, or negligence in the handling or posting of personal data by legal entities are also raising new concerns and creating unforeseen problems for affected citizens across the globe, or rather in today's global village.

In this article, the researchers have made a humble attempt to analyze the law relating to the "Right To Be Forgotten" (RTBF), touching particularly upon the select case law in the European Union and India.

UNEQUAL TREATMENT

Different Shades of Unequal Treatment at Workplace

Unfair, or unequal treatment of employees in an organization, if practiced, could result in decreased motivation and drop in performance and productivity. Treating employees unfairly because of who they are, or rather perceived in a wrong manner, is discrimination and could result in their feeling upset, shamed, or even scared. This could lead to "their morale and their productivity levels to plummet," and "Academic studies have found that treating staff in an unfair way can drain them of energy and motivation," which is "Not good for results. Not good for your business," either. Further, not surprisingly, "You might even see absence levels rise. For some employees, feigning illness to stay off work will seem like a better option than facing a stressful situation that leaves them feeling mistreated."[2]

So, focusing on workplace situation, undoubtedly, "unequal" treatment often leads to perceived or actual problems in the lives of employees. In such a situation, an employee might feel discriminated against vis-à-vis his colleagues or other employees working in the organization. Such a treatment could be due to any reason and could acquire any form.

In Swedish, the expression "unequal" treatment includes 'insulting', and is defined as "to degrade others through words or actions," and "Unequal treatment means to be inexplicably and unfairly treated differently to others, carrying the risk of being pushed outside of the workplace community," further, examples of insulting, or unequal treatment include: "Deliberately insulting or ostracising a colleague, excluding a colleague or making things difficult for them by withholding important information or not inviting them to meetings that they should have joined, criticising and ridiculing a member of staff/colleague, and sexual harassment." In case a matter is based on any of the grounds of discrimination, it may additionally be considered a matter of discrimination. However, "short-term disagreements, conflicts or problems with cooperation are not considered unequal treatment."[3]

At the same time, some of the professional legal experts in the United States of America righty observe that everybody expects to be treated fairly and equitably at work and have legal rights and options, "This not only means that we have a basic expectation of being treated with dignity and respect, but we also operate with the belief that all employees will be afforded opportunities for pay raises, promotions and other opportunities based on their job performance and fulfillment of job duties.... we often see cases where people are treated poorly and unfairly because of who they are. Others are bullied or harassed in the workplace. While these instances might commonly occur in many workplaces, they are illegal."[4]

Further, "It is illegal to harass or discriminate against someone because of so-called "protected characteristics" such as age, disability, pregnancy, gender identity, sexual orientation, race, religion, color, nationality and sex," also "to engage in behavior that is harassing or discriminatory, which could create a hostile work environment, making it difficult for an employee to perform his or her job duties."[5] For example, unfair treatment at work, includes but is not limited to "Spreading rumors about an employee; Passing up someone for a training opportunity or promotion because of someone's race, color, gender or other protected characteristic; Creating offensive comments, emails or social media posts about an employee; Demoting, transferring or dismissing an employee without a fair, disciplinary process; Paying women lower wages for doing the same job, because of their sex; Firing or laying off older workers so the company can hire younger, cheaper workers to do their jobs,"[6] and so on.[7]

Unequal Treatment of a Different Kind: Newly Emerging Forms of Unequal Treatment Due to Social Media and the Internet

Unequal treatment at the workplace is turning out to be a polyhedral phenomenon, with the ever-new emerging forms of unequal treatment at the workplace. In other words, the influencing power of social media particularly over the last nearly two decades or so, has created a new kind of unheard of before unequal treatment at the workplace.

In other words, in the modern 21st century era of speedier Information and Communication Technology, the power of social media as a speedier and all-pervasive information dissemination tool and influencer in the hands of virtually every individual is strongly felt now-a-days. Earlier, organizations and the administration did not have easy and free access to positive or negative information about an employee or a would-be employee. But, whether one likes it or not, with the advent of all-pervasive social media, leading to the spread any kind of information at lightning speed not only across countries but continents with hardly any aspect remaining hidden about any individual, a new problem has arisen quite often to the detriment of an employee or a would-be employee of an organization.

Quite often, information that has become infructuous, irrelevant, or not supposed to impact the future of an individual anymore, still keeps doing the rounds of social media creating a false narrative about the individual leading to unjustified harm to the individual within or outside an organization. In such situations, one may find oneself helpless. The speed and unlimited reach of social media have further stoked the fire of this new malady, with the potential to cause harm to anybody, where of late, the law had to intervene and come to the rescue of the affected party in the name of justice.

The traditional and well-established areas of unequal treatment at workplace, as outlined earlier, have attracted adequate attention for quite some time and have legal provisions in place for dealing with the phenomena in almost every country, including Indian case law and the European case law.

THE EMERGENCE OF CONSEQUENT "RIGHT TO BE FORGOTTEN" (RTBF)

The "traditional" "unequal treatment" scenario explained earlier has been prevalent all over the world, perhaps, since times immemorial and individuals must have faced such situations at one time or another in almost every country or organization. Prior to the 21st century modern digital revolution, that all pervasive influencer, speedier and powerful modern information and communication technologies (ICTs), internet, emails, or social media, would also become an unintentional or intentional potent tool leading to a new solid cause of discrimination or "unequal treatment," was not foreseen earlier, and whose impact is now increasingly being felt across nations and continents.

Social media, in particular, due to very nature of its functioning, is such that it spreads any post like wildfire in the virtual world. Done either unintentionally or by design, within no time, thanks to the internet, a social media message is all over the world in a jiffy. This creates an immediate first impression in the mind of a person exposed to that post about the affected individual. And most likely, the impression tends to continue till countered with the subsequent truth about it. This is what is proving to be an Achilles heel for an affected party. The consequent concern being that in case such information is no longer true then how to ensure "instant" deletion of the same from all platforms, including all the links that may be there regarding that information. Till that is done, the "half-truth" or "wrong information" might keep coming back to bite an individual, an employee or even a potential employee to his detriment. Consequently, in order to salvage one's lost positive image, a remedy had to be found in the modern digital world. Somehow, the "untrue" negative image had to be erased, and consequently the "Right To Erasure" also known as the "Right To Be Forgotten" was born and came as a savior for an affected party.

Incidentally, the "Right To Be Forgotten" (RTBF) is a common name for a human right that first came into use in May 2014 in the European Union due to a ruling by the European Court of Justice (ECJ). Finding merit in the demand of an individual that internet search engines hide incorrect, out-of-date or potentially embarrassing information about them, in "a landmark decision in 2014 when a Spanish individual, who had his property repossessed and auctioned off in 1998 to recover social security debts, fought to have newspaper articles about the case removed from Google's search results," the European Court of Justice (ECJ) ruled in favour of the Spanish individual and held that "the material should be delisted if it was "inaccurate, inadequate, irrelevant or excessive"—a ruling that created what is commonly known as the right to be forgotten."[8] It is significant to note that after the European Court of Justice (ECJ) 2014 "Right To Be Forgotten" (RTBF) ruling, "Google created a compliance team to handle delisting requests. It has received nearly 722,000 applications to remove a total of 2.75m URLs since May 2014, according to the company's figures—almost 90 per cent of which were filed by private individuals. Google said it had complied with 44 per cent of the requests."[9]

Under the "Right To Be Forgotten" (RTBF), an individual could seek deletion of online private information from the Internet. Apart from the European Union (EU), the concept is recognized in some jurisdictions abroad. More specifically, sometimes while indulging in the instant publishing of information, social media may violate the right to privacy of a person. In such a situation the moot question is whether the affected person can claim the right to privacy or the "Right To Be Forgotten" (RTBF), especially where information published is related to some incident and the affected person wants to forget it and ask the social media to remove that information to avoid becoming an unwilling victim of some unfounded bias due to incomplete information circulating beyond his control on the social media and be subjected to unwarranted and unequal treatment within or outside the organization much to his discomfort leading to unjustified harm. For instance, the personal information of A is uploaded by B on social media (say Google, Instagram, Twitter etc.) which is related to any incident which A wants to forget or any personal information of A relating to a case, where he was convicted and subsequently acquitted in the appeal and wants to live peacefully in the society, is linked by the search engine without scrutiny. Here the moot question is whether A has the Right To Be Forgotten and can he request the social media to erase that personal information as he is trying to forget that incident and wants to live peacefully.

The "Right to Be Forgotten" (RTBF) and its Ambit

Especially after the beginning of the 21st century, it is increasingly being felt that everybody has a "Right To Be Forgotten" (RTBF). Every individual has a right to get "wrong," "incorrect," "half-correct," "outdated," "old," and "not currently relevant" information, "unwanted posts," about him or her removed from the internet that could be considered as detrimental to their image and which might subject them to prejudice or discrimination. Or there could be a previous conviction and how to get a criminal conviction removed from, say, Google searches, other platforms and related links. It is also seen that often articles are refused to be removed from the social media and the internet because the service providers maintain that such information needs to be shown to internet users in "public interest." And what could be more damaging is that there may be no time limit as for how long such information could be kept in the public domain by search engines or online service providers and the exposure to the information continues to be worldwide.

Such important developments in case law and legal solutions to emerging modern dilemmas due to the social media and the internet and invoking the now recognized "Right To Be Forgotten" (RTBF) in order not be a victim of unequal treatment is acquiring significance these days, besides other countries, in the European Union and India.

The Right to Be Forgotten and Professional People

The right to be forgotten for professional people is said to have come to the rescue of professional people. Before that, professionals continued to face serious problems due to adverse publicity in mainstream online and offline publications, links to which were not taken off the internet, even after having been acquitted of all charges eventually. Removal of all the links from Google was not so easy.

For instance, Google is said to "treat professional people much harsher than ordinary people when it comes to right to be forgotten applications. Google tends to cite public interest when it rejects right to be forgotten applications made by solicitors who ask Google to remove links to SDT (Solicitors Disciplinary Tribunal) decisions. It is however, possible to succeed with an application for a right to be forgotten for professional people."[10]

EUROPEAN CASE LAW: THE POSITION VIS-À-VIS "RIGHT TO BE FORGOTTEN" (RTBF)

General Data Protection Regulation (GDPR), 2018

In the European Union, the European Statute directly relating to the "Right To Be Forgotten" (RTBF) is the General Data Protection Regulation (GDPR), 2018. Article 17 and Recital 65[11] and Recital 66[12] of GDPR, 2018 deal with "Right To Be Forgotten" (RTBF). Significantly, much earlier in 2011, the European Court on Human Rights in the case of *RTBF v. Belgium* held that RTBF is covered under Article 10 (Freedom of Expression) of the European Convention for the Protection of Human Rights and Fundamental Freedoms, 1950.

Incidentally, the data protection package adopted in May 2016 aims at making Europe fit for the digital age and the European Union Charter of Fundamental Rights stipulates that EU citizens have the right to protection of their personal data.[13] In the European Union, the "Right To Be Forgotten" (RTBF) is covered under The *General Data Protection Regulation (GDPR), 2018* which deals with how personal data is required to be collected, processed, and erased.

A potent tool to counter unequal treatment due to wrong projection of one's image by the social media and the internet, the "Right To Be Forgotten" (RTBF) received a lot of media attention after the 2014 judgment from the European Union Court of Justice. This landmark judgment set the precedent for the right of erasure provision contained in the GDPR.[14] In other words, the "Right To Be Forgotten" (RTBF) empowers citizens to demand organizations to delete their personal data or that data which causes them unnecessary personal harm and is no longer required to be online for some valid reason. The RTBF is provided by the European Union's *General Data Protection Regulation (GDPR)*, a statute passed by the 28-member body in 2018.[15]

Circumstances When "Right To Be Forgotten" (RTBF) Can be Enforced

To rectify hosting of incorrect online information on social media and the internet leading to unequal treatment or hurting one's image unnecessarily, the "Right To Erasure," (RTE) also known as the "Right To Be Forgotten" RTBF, is a potent remedy under *Article 17* of the *GDPR, 2018*. Under *Article 17*, "the GDPR outlines the specific circumstances under which the right to be forgotten applies. An individual has the right to have their personal data erased," in case "The personal data is no longer necessary for the purpose an organization originally collected or processed it."[16]

It is significant to note that the "Right To Be Forgotten" (RTBF) dovetails with people's right to access their personal information in *Article 15*, and "The right to control one's data is meaningless if people cannot take action when they no longer consent to processing, when there are significant errors within the data, or if they believe information is being stored unnecessarily. In these cases, an individual can request that the data be erased. But this is not an absolute right. If it were, the critics who argue that the right to be forgotten amounts to nothing more than a rewriting of history would be correct. Thus, the GDPR walks a fine line on data erasure."[17]

In brief, *Article 17* lays down that an affected party has a right to have their data removed from a controller and/or processor for the following grounds: the original purpose for which the data was processed has been fulfilled, and the personal data in question is no longer needed, the data subject withdraws their consent, the data subject objects to the processing of their data, and there are no overriding legitimate interests, the personal data is collected and processed through unlawful means; The data must be removed to comply with a legal obligation, and the data is processed in relation to the offer of information society services to a child.[18]

More specifically, under *Article 17*, the GDPR outlines the specific circumstances under which the right to be forgotten can be enforced. "An individual has the right to have their personal data erased if: The personal data is no longer necessary for the purpose an organization originally collected or processed it; An organization is relying on an individual's consent as the lawful basis for processing the data and that individual withdraws their consent; An organization is relying on legitimate interests as its justification for processing an individual's data, the individual objects to this processing, and there is no overriding legitimate interest for the organization to continue with the processing; An organization is processing data for direct marketing purposes and the individual objects to this processing; An organization processed an individual's personal data unlawfully; An organization must erase personal data in order to comply with a legal ruling or obligation; An organization has processed a child's personal data to offer their information society services."[19]

However, at the same time, some experts rightly maintain that "given competing interests and the hyper-connected nature of the Internet, the right to be forgotten is much more complicated than an individual simply requesting that an organization erase their personal data."[20]

Circumstance Under Which the "Right To Be Forgotten" (RTBF) Does Not Apply

However, under certain circumstances, an organization's right to process someone's data might override their "Right To Be Forgotten." Here are the reasons cited in the *GDPR, 2018* that trump the Right To Erasure: "The data is being used to exercise the right of freedom of expression and information; The data is being used to comply with a legal ruling or obligation; The data is being used to perform a task that is being carried out in the public interest or when exercising an organization's official authority; The data being processed is necessary for public health purposes and serves in the public interest; The data being processed is necessary to perform preventative or occupational medicine. This only applies when the data is being processed by a health professional who is subject to a legal obligation of professional secrecy; The data represents important information that serves the public interest, scientific research, historical research, or statistical purposes and where erasure of the data would likely to impair or halt progress towards the achievement that was the goal of the processing; The data is being used for the establishment of a legal defense or in the exercise of other legal claims," furthermore, "an organization can request a "reasonable fee" or deny a request to erase personal data if the organization can justify that the request was unfounded or excessive."[21]

All said and done, it has also to be realized that "there are many variables at play and each request will have to be evaluated individually. Add to that the technical burden of keeping track of all the places an individual's personal data is stored or processed and it is easy to see why the GDPR's new privacy rights can be a significant compliance burden for some organizations."[22] However, these issues are not under the purview of this article.

The Response to the General Data Protection Regulation (GDPR), 2018

That pent up problems had been there amongst people regarding online data handling, or rather mishandling, is evident from the fact that ever since the GDPR came into effect, complaints spiralled throughout the European Union. For instance, the law firm DLA Piper survey about European data protection agencies to tally up data breaches and GDPR fines issued since the GDPR requirements went into effect in May 2018, revealed that the "Dutch, German, and British authorities all received over 10,000 reports of data breaches. Germany had the most, with over 15,000, while Liechtenstein had the fewest with 15. Per capita, the Netherlands had the most reported breaches, with nearly 90 incidents per 100,000 people, followed by Ireland and Denmark. Italy, meanwhile, has a suspiciously low level of data breaches for the size of its population and economy.[23] Helen Dixon, the Irish Commissioner for Data Protection, also reported that more complaints in the seven months after the GDPR took effect were there than in all of 2013, 2014, and 2015 combined and "The simple fact is that data privacy grows more important to people with every privacy scandal and data breach. Users are no longer willing to tolerate violations; they know their rights, and they know how to seek redress."[24]

General Data Protection Regulation (GDPR), 2018: A Strong Deterrent with Hefty Fines

The *General Data Protection Regulation (GDPR), 2018*, which had come into force on 25 May 2018, was drafted and passed by the European Union

(EU), and it "imposes obligations onto organizations anywhere, so long as they target or collect data related to people in the EU.... The GDPR will levy harsh fines against those who violate its privacy and security standards, with penalties reaching into the tens of millions of euros."[25]

The *GDPR, 2018* requires "data protection by design and by default,"[26] and "fines are administered by the data protection regulator in each EU country."[27] The more severe the violation greater the fine. Under the *GDPR, 2018* "fines are administered by the data protection regulator in each EU country. That authority will determine whether an infringement has occurred and the severity of the penalty."[28]

The law firm DLA Piper survey showed that "The German data protection authority, LfDI Baden-Württemberg, handed out 64 GDPR fines, which account for more than two-thirds of all the fines reported in the survey. The fines—91 of them in all—range in size from a €4,800 penalty for an unlawful CCTV system in Austria up to the recent €50 million fine the French data protection agency, CNIL, imposed on Google," and to expect "more fines in the coming months as the data protection agencies work through their backlog. Whether we can expect to see fines in excess of €50 million (the GDPR caps the penalty for serious infringements at €20 million or 4 percent of the offending company's worldwide annual revenue, whichever amount is higher) as a regular occurrence remains to be seen.[29]

Stringent fines are there for other lapses as well. The *GDPR, 2018* makes critical differences between personal data, pseudonymized data, and anonymized data. In a case relating to Data anonymization and GDPR compliance, the Danish taxi service Taxa 4×35 "faces a 1.2 million kroner fine (roughly €160,000) for not deleting or anonymizing its users' data."[30]

An expert has rightly observed that "taking the potentially gigantic financial and reputational damages that can come from non-compliance into account, the latest updates to the act will likely have the effect of promoting compliance amongst more companies."[31] Provisions for hefty fines for violations by the data handlers in the virtual world would certainly go not only go a long way in punishing the offenders but also prove to be strong deterrents in future.

European Judicial Pronouncements

The Court of Justice of the European Union ("the Court") in a Landmark Judgement,[32] on September 24, 2019, the Court held that the "right to be forgotten" does not require a search engine to de-list search results on all of its domains. However, a search engine operator is still required to de-list search results on domains for all of the European Union ("EU")

Member States. The ruling left the referring court, the Conseil d'État ("the Conseil"), to apply the Court's holding to Google's practices in France.

The events leading to this ruling began on May 21, 2015, when the President of the Commission nationale de l'informatique et des libertés ("CNIL"), the French data protection authority, served formal notice on Google that, when honoring a request to de-list search results, the company must apply the removal globally, rather than just to the domain of the requester's residence. Google refused, and limited removal only to the EU Member States. The company argued that global removal could be abused by authoritarian states. Google proposed a "geo-blocking technique" that would prevent a user in an EU Member State from accessing links de-listed in the EU.

CNIL found these steps inadequate and imposed a fine of €100,000. Google appealed to the Conseil for an annulment of CNIL's adjudication. The Conseil, in turn, referred several questions to the Court, resulting in the landmark holding above.

In deciding the case, the Court considered both the EU Data Protection Directive of 1995 ("DPD") and the EU General Data Protection Regulation of 2016 ("GDPR"). The Court first established that Google fell within the territorial scope of the DPD and the GDPR, given its activities in French territories. It then considered the goal of the relevant EU statute: guaranteeing a "high level of protection of personal data throughout the European Union." Even so, the right to protection of personal data is not absolute and must be balanced against other fundamental rights and the public interest in having access to information.

In September 2019, the Court of Justice of the European Union issued two judgments further delineating the scope of the right to be forgotten in the context of search engines. In *GC and Others*,[33] the Court decided that a search engine operator must only verify the lawfulness of its processing of sensitive data *ex post*, i.e., upon receiving a request for de-referencing. While lowering the level of protection of the right to data protection, this decision has to be understood as an act that brings the processing of sensitive data by search engines out of the grey area caused by the Court's decision in *Google Spain and Google*[34] and into the sphere of legality.

Some Latest Developments Relating to GDPR, 2018 With International Ramifications

It is well proven now that the *GDPR, 2018* is a robust statute that is making its presence felt beyond the European continent. In 2021, the European Commission introduced changes to the GDPR that are intended to further enhance the effectiveness of the statute. For instance, citing the removal of the privacy shield, an expert observed that "The GDPR's so-called privacy shield was intended to make it easier for data to be transferred from European companies and institutions to their U.S. counterparts. This facilitated a smoother business relationship and enabled tech companies such as Google, Yahoo, and Apple to easily share data on their customers with their U.S.-based parent corporations. However, the relative freedom the privacy shield gave to U.S. companies to process data under U.S. legal provisions has been revoked. Instead, U.S. companies that have previously used the privacy shield mechanism have now had to adopt standard EU GDPR contractual clauses to use the customer data of European citizens. Because the U.S. and EU have traditionally had polar opposite views regarding the requirement of consent to work with personal data, this development is important because it effectively forces U.S. companies to abide by much more stringent EU privacy laws," and further, "In the U.S., California was the first state to respond to the changes in the GDPR by implementing modifications to its own legal system. The state introduced the California Privacy Rights Act (CPRA), which gives citizens of the state more data privacy rights."[35]

INDIAN CASE LAW: THE POSITION VIS-À-VIS "RIGHT TO BE FORGOTTEN" (RTBF)

Like the other countries of the European Union, in fact the world over, more so in the 21st century, India too has been feeling the impact of the newly emerged menace of unequal treatment to individuals due to unnecessary and unchecked online information floating around on the social media and the internet whose only remedy seems to be the "Right To Erasure" (RTE) or the "Right To Be Forgotten" RTBF.

Whereas the "Right To Be Forgotten" RTBF is not yet recognized by stand-alone statute in India, the courts time and again have held it to be an intrinsic part of the "Right To Privacy." The "Right To Privacy" is covered under *Article 21* of the Indian Constitution as was held by the judiciary in a number of cases and one such recent example is *Puttaswamy v. Union of India*,[36] *2017*.

Meanwhile, to cover different forms of privacy in electronic form, India's *Information Technology Act, 2000* is there. Also, experts believe that the "The Information Technology Act, 2000 has recently been amended to meet challenges in cyber-crime, the amended Act is yet to come into force, it has introduced two important provisions that have a strong bearing on the legal regime for data protection. These are sections 43A and 72A, inserted into the IT Act by the Amendment Act. But the provisions pertaining to data security and confidentiality are grossly inadequate.... India has more to do with issues related to cyber-crimes and e-commerce transactions than data protection."[37]

A brief analysis of the provisions of the Indian Statute directly or indirectly relating to privacy and "Right To Be Forgotten" (RTBF) is as follows:

Provisions of the Information Technology Act, 2000 and Rules Indirectly Dealing With "Right To Be Forgotten" (RTBF)

Section 79 of the *Information Technology Act, 2000* deals with the liability of the Social media or intermediary for third-party information uploaded on its site, indirectly deals with privacy or RTBF. The general principle under Section 79 is that social media or intermediary is not liable for third-party information if due diligence is observed by the intermediary. Significantly, Due Diligence was initially defined in the *Intermediary Rules 2011* which are now repealed by the *Information Technology (Intermediary Guidelines and Digital Media Ethics Code) Rules, 2021*[38] *(the Intermediary Rules, 2021)*. Under These *Rules of 2021*, establishment and maintenance of Grievance Redressal Mechanisms by an intermediary operating (or looking to operate in India) is mandatory. *Rule 3(2)* of the *2021 Rules* provides that an intermediary shall appoint a Grievance Officer for handling grievances and complaints raised at least by Indian users (if such a mechanism is not already in place). This would include by prominently displaying the name and contact details of the Grievance Officer on its Website or Mobile Application, and by mentioning the method by which a complainant may be made to them by the aggrieved person. The said sub-rule further provides that the role of the Grievance Officer is to:

i. Acknowledge complaints received within 24 hours, and dispose of the same within 15 days;

ii. Acknowledge any order, notice or direction issued by a court or a government agency.

Furthermore, if the content is alleged to be exposing the complainant without consent then the same has to be taken down within 24 hours of receiving such a complaint. It also mandates implementing a mechanism for receiving such complaints, which may enable the individual or person to provide details, in relation to such content or share the link for the said content. This mechanism ensures that complaints are redressed expeditiously, especially those that are made by a specific individual alleging proliferation of his/her non-consensual images by a user of the said intermediary.

For example, where personal data or information of A is published on Google in India and A has requested to erase that information as it is objectionable then the grievance officer of Google India must acknowledge that request within 24 hours and dispose of the same within 15 days.

Recent Important Developments

Considering the urgency of the matter, the Indian Government is making sincere efforts for making a separate statute for data protection, also containing provisions for the "Right To Be Forgotten," as is evident from the following:

It is significant to note that although the "Right To Be Forgotten" (RTBF) is not expressly recognized as a constitutional fundamental right in India by the Supreme Court, but under the *Personal Data Protection Bill, 2021*, now withdrawn by the Indian Government on 3 August 2022, the "Right To Be Forgotten" (RTBF) was to become a statute of the land. An individual under the said Bill would have had greater freedom regarding control over the display of one's online personal information on the social media and the internet.

However, the Union Government withdrew the long-awaited *Personal Data Protection (PDP) Bill, 2021* submitting that it will be replaced with a new Bill with a 'comprehensive framework' and 'contemporary digital privacy laws,' and assuring that "The Bill will soon be replaced by a comprehensive framework of global standard laws for contemporary and future challenges."[39]

To get an idea of the recent efforts of the Indian Government, a quick glance at the two recent Bills in this regard is as follows:

The Personal Data Protection Bill, 2019

In India, the move to make "Right To Be Forgotten" RTBF a law of the land is of fairly recent origin. In August 2017, the nine-judge Bench of the Supreme Court of India affirmed the Right to Privacy in the *K.S. Puttaswamy vs. Union of India* (2017) "Right To Privacy Case." The Supreme Court pronounced that it was covered under the *Right to Life and Personal Liberty* under *Article 21* of the Indian Constitution. During the case, the Indian Union government set up a high-level Committee of Experts, chaired by Justice B.N. Srikrishna, to examine various issues related to data protection in India. In July 2018, the Committee submitted a draft *Personal Data Protection Bill* and an accompanying report titled: "*A Free and Fair Digital Economy: Protecting Privacy, Empowering Indians*" to the Indian Ministry of Electronics and Information Technology.[40]

Finally, after more than two years of debate, the *Personal Data Protection Bill, 2019* was introduced in the Lok Sabha on December 11, 2019. However, the Bill was sent for scrutiny by a Joint Parliamentary Committee (JPC) in consultation with industry experts and stakeholders. The Bill laid down the mechanisms for the protection of sensitive personal data and had proposed to establish a new and separate independent regulatory authority called the *Data Protection Authority* (DPA) in India. Significantly, certain new key provisions were introduced that were not in the 2018 Draft Bill, such as that the central government could exempt any government agency from the Bill and an individual's right to erasure also commonly known as the "Right to Be Forgotten" (RTBF). Like other data protection laws, the Bill had also proposed to have jurisdiction outside India besides covering any organization that did business in India. Thus, India due to its large population size with an ever-growing number of Internet users is said to have had a unique opportunity to shape a global privacy statute, along the lines of the General Data Protection Regulation (GDPR), 2018 of the European Union.[41]

However, unfortunately, in India there is no statute specifically and directly dealing with online data protection and "Right To Be Forgotten" RTBF, which gives a fundamental right to an affected individual to get the objectionable information deleted, such as useless and defamatory private data to be deleted from a social media Website and the internet. Even the provisions of the *Information Technology Act, 2000* and *Rules* are silent and do not directly deal with the "Right to Be Forgotten" RTBF, even though some jurists and legal experts claim that some provisions indirectly covered RTBF. Nevertheless, the "Right to Be Forgotten" RTBF has attracted significant attention in India and the Personal *Data Protection Bill, 2019* is said to have had provisions relating to the RTBF. However, the efforts thus far had resulted in a fresh draft of India's *Data Protection Bill, 2021*.

India's Data Protection Bill, 2021

Some judicial experts rightly maintain that the Joint Parliamentary Committee (JPC) Report in a true sense paved the way for data privacy and protection legal regime in India. The *Data Protection Bill, 2021*, now withdrawn by the Indian Parliament, is said to have proposed significant deviations from its earlier 2018 and 2019 versions. For instance, an exemption is said to have been extended to government agencies with respect to data processing. This is widely attributed to the Supreme Court judgment in the *Pegasus Spyware Case* that involved allegations against the Union government for indulging in surveillance on Indian citizens. The Supreme Court even constituted a committee to assess the violation of the right to privacy and come out with recommendations on the current surveillance laws in order to boost data protection practices. Others maintain that bringing government agencies under the umbrella of the *Data Protection Bill, 2021* is likely to ensure individual privacy and enhance cybersecurity.[42]

Briefly,[43] the latest draft, the now withdrawn *Data Protection Bill, 2021*, sought to regulate the collection, storage, transfer, and use of personal data. It also extended its ambit to foreign-based entities in case Indians are subjected to their data processing activities. The main provisions of the *Data Protection Bill, 2021*, included: Individual consent, data breach notification, transparency (prior notice and privacy policy describing data processing practices), purpose-based processing, technical security, and rights of individuals who part away with personal data such as name and email ID, or sensitive personal data such as a social security number. Individuals would have had more control over the processing of their data with these rights, as they would be able to remove, correct and access their data easily.

Interestingly, earlier in August 2021, the judiciary attempted privacy rights management under Indian case law. The Madras High Court dismissed a petitioner's "Right To Be Forgotten" (RTBF) who had prayed to have his criminal and court records expunged following his acquittal from a case. The court refused to accept the plea and dismissed it maintaining that the fulfillment of a task in public interest trumped the individual's right to privacy. The Court further stated that such Rights would be implemented more effectively after India passed a Data Privacy law.[44]

Some Indian Judicial Prouncements

Although there have not been many cases decided by courts in India yet, regarding this newly emerged issue of unequal treatment created due to the omnipresent online information even when not needed on the social media and the internet hurting one's image, leading to a growing demand for the "Right To Be Forgotten" RTBF or "Right To Erasure" RTE, however, a few important judgements are as follows:

In the *Jorawer Singh Mundy v Union of India & Ors.*[45] the moot question was whether the "Right To Be Forgotten" RTBF is covered under *Section 69A and 79* of the *Information Technology Act, 2000*. The Delhi High Court held that "the IT Act, 2000 provides for blocking the information for public access through any computer resource only under section 69A of the IT Act 2000. The IT Act also provides for the removal of certain unlawful information from an intermediary platform as per section 79.... The present case which pertains to the erasure of content under the doctrine of 'right to be forgotten' does not fall under any of the stipulated conditions."

In this case the Petitioner was an American citizen of Indian origin, who managed investments, dealt with real estate portfolios, etc. He travelled to India in 2009, a case under the *Narcotics Drugs and Psychotropic Substances Act (NDPS), 1985*, was lodged against him. In 2011, the trial court had acquitted him of all charges. In the appeal *Custom v Jorawar Singh Mundy*[46] was filed challenging, and the Delhi High Court upheld the order of the trial court and his acquittal. When the Petitioner thereafter went back to his home country, he faced significant hurdles in his professional life as the appellate judgment rendered by the High Court was available on Google and any potential employer who wanted to employ him can verify from Google. Accordingly, the Petitioner initially had requested Google India, Google LLC, Indian Kanoon, and other sites to take down the said judgment. However, except for Respondent No. 5, none of the other Respondents acted upon the Petitioner's request. Therefore, the present Writ Petition was filed, seeking directions to be issued to the Respondents to remove the said judgment from the entire Respondent's respective online platforms, recognizing the Right to Privacy of the Petitioner, under *Article 21* of the Constitution. The moot questions before the Court were: whether the "Right To Be Forgotten" RTBF was covered in right to privacy and whether transparency in judicial records be maintained if a Court order is removed from online platforms.

In Subhranshu *Rout v State of Odisha*,[47] the petitioner as well as the accused were village mates and classmates and on a fateful day, he committed rape on the informant and recorded the gruesome episode on his mobile phone. When the informant warned the petitioner, the petitioner threatened to kill her as well as to make viral the said photos/videos. Further, she has alleged for one year, the petitioner had maintained physical intimacy with the informant. Upon the informant narrating the incident to her parents, the petitioner opened a fake Facebook ID in the name of the informant and uploaded all the objectionable photos using the said ID in order to further traumatize her.

The Orissa High Court held that such objectionable photos and videos to remain on a social media platform, without the consent of a woman, is a direct affront on a woman's modesty and, more importantly, her right to privacy. In such cases, either the victim herself or the prosecution may, if so advised, seek appropriate orders to protect the victim's fundamental right to privacy, by seeking appropriate orders to have such offensive posts erased from the public platform, irrespective of the ongoing criminal process.

Regarding the statute on "Right To Be Forgotten" RTBF in India, the Court opined that *The Information Technology (Reasonable Security Practices and Procedures and Sensitive Personal Data or Information) Rules, 2011,* India's first legal framework recognized the need to protect the privacy of personal data, but it failed to capture the issue of the "Right To Be Forgotten" RTBF. The Hon'ble Supreme Court of India in the case of *K.S. Puttaswamy v Union of India,* held that purpose limitation is integral for executive projects involving data collection—unless prior permission is provided, third parties cannot be provided access to personal data. However, Section 5 of the now non-existent but earlier drafted *Personal Data Protection Bill, 2019* (later modified as *Data Protection Bill, 2021,* but now withdrawn on 3 August, 2022) had covered the "Right To Be Forgotten" RTBF.

Significantly, the Hon'ble Single Judge of the Orissa High Court also referred to the case of *Google Spain SL & Anr. v Agencia Espanola de Protection de Datos (AEPD) & Anr*[48] wherein the European Court of Justice had ruled that "the European citizens have a right to request that commercial search engines, such as Google, that gather personal information for profit should remove links to private information when asked, provided the information is no longer relevant. The Court, in that case, ruled that the fundamental right to privacy is greater than the economic interest of the commercial firm and, in some circumstances; the same would even override the public interest in access to information."

Further, the Court also observed that the aspect of the "Right To Be Forgotten" RTBF appears in the *General Data Protection Regulation (GDPR), 2018* which governs the manner in which personal data can be collected, processed, and erased. *Recitals 65 and 66* and in *Article 17 of the GDPR*, vests in the victim a right to the erasure of such material after due diligence by the controller expeditiously. In addition to this, *Article 5* of the GDPR requires data controllers to take every reasonable step to ensure that inaccurate data is "erased or rectified without delay." However, the Court observed that it cannot be expected that the victim in India shall approach the Court to get the inaccurate data or information erased every single time, regarding data that is within the control of data controllers such as Facebook or Twitter or any other social media platforms.

Earlier in *Zulfiqar Ahman Khan vs M/S Quintillion Business Media Pvt. Ltd., & Ors.*,[49] Plaintiff sought a permanent injunction against Quintillion Business Media Pvt. Ltd., its editor and its author, who had written two articles against the Plaintiff on the basis of harassment complaints claimed to have been received by them, against the Plaintiff, as part of the #MeToo campaign. The three individuals, who made allegations against Plaintiff, have remained anonymous and have not revealed their identity in the public domain. The stories, which had appeared on 12 October, 2018 as also on 31 October, 2018 were impugned in the present suit and an injunction was sought against the publication and re-publication of the said two articles. The Delhi High Court recognized the Plaintiff's "Right to Privacy," of which the "Right To Be Forgotten" RTBF and the "Right To Be Left Alone" are inherent aspects, and directed that any republication of the content of the originally impugned articles dated 12, October 2018 and 31, October 2018, or any extracts/ or excerpts thereof, as also modified versions thereof, on any print or digital/electronic platform shall stand restrained during the pendency of the present suit.[50]

Accordingly, Plaintiff was permitted to communicate this order to any print or electronic platform including various search engines in order to ensure that the articles or any excerpts/search results thereof are not republished in any manner whatsoever. Plaintiff was permitted to approach the grievance officers of the electronic platforms and portals to ensure immediate compliance with this order.[51] Further, the Court also gave a clear cut direction that where the said search engines do not take down/remove the objectionable content from their platforms within a period of 36 hours after receiving communication from the Plaintiff with a copy of this order, the Plaintiff is given liberty to approach this court forthwith — apart from approaching the appropriate authorities under the *Information Technology Act, 2000*.[52]

In 2016, in *Civil Writ Petition No. 9478 of 2016*, the Kerala High Court passed an interim order requiring Indian Kanoon to remove the name of a rape victim which was published on its website along with the two judgments rendered by the Kerala High Court in Writ petitions filed by her. The court recognized the Petitioner's right to privacy and reputation, without explicitly using the term "Right To Be Forgotten" RTBF.

However, in another interesting case, in 2017 *Dharamraj Bhanushankar Dave vs the State Of Gujarat*,[53] the Gujarat High Court dismissed a petition seeking "permanent restraint on a public exhibition of judgment and order" on an online repository of judgments and indexing by Google. It was the case of the Petitioner that he had been acquitted of several offences by the Sessions Court and High Court and the judgment in question was classified as "unreportable." The Court dismissed the petition on the grounds that the petitioner was not able to point out any provisions in the statute that posed a threat to his right to life and liberty, and that publication on a website did not amount to "reporting" of a judgment since it is not a law report.

So, in brief, undoubtedly, a "Right To Be Forgotten" RTBF is a need of the hour in India as well. In the absence of a legally enforceable RTBF, the only remedy available to an Indian citizen is the *Information Technology Act, 2000* read with *Supplementary Rules*, which act as the legal cornerstone to ensure the protection of personal information. However, a silver lining is that Lawmakers and Regulators progressively recognize the importance of data for economic and technological growth.[54] So fool-proof protection of all forms of data and preventing its intentional or unintentional abuse or misuse is being realized more and more in modern times. Going by the seriousness of the concerned authorities in the present times, an enforceable "Right To Be Forgotten" also seems to be a reality, hopefully, in not so distant future in India.

This is all the more important because, in the absence of an enforceable and foolproof "Right To Be Forgotten," or "Right to Erasure" in India too, citizens and those working in the public or private sector organizations, continue to suffer more and more from this new 21st century dimension of unequal treatment, rather a newly emerged malady, whereby an incorrect image projected by the social media and the internet, in the case of non-removal or timely deletion from the virtual world, places them in a disadvantageous or unequal position vis-à-vis others, thus making them suffer for no fault of theirs.

CONCLUSIONS AND SUGGESTIONS

In daily life, the traditional forms of discrimination and unequal treatment of individuals have been in vogue since times immemorial in almost every country be it on the basis of race, religion, colour, age, sex or various prejudices, among others, often flowing into organizational situations as well. In a workplace situation, whether public or private, the employees felt demotivated affecting their performance and productivity, even leading to actual sickness or depression.

As if all that was not enough, particularly in the 21st century, globally greater use of modern information and communication technologies (ICTs), internet and the mass communication tool of social media in various platforms by citizens and those working in organizations or potential employees, has led to new problems due to positive or negative information about anybody flashed at lightning speed across nations and continents, thus creating some sort of favourable or unfavourable image staying put in the minds of people, till something is done about it. When that happens, then in the absence of erasure of negative or incorrect information, or its timely subsequent modification in light of some important future positive developments making the negative information infructuous, the affected party may suffer or continue to suffer or may be made to suffer unjustifiably in workplace or daily life situations.

Or in other words, that may lead to a situation of "Unequal Treatment" where an unjustifiable negative image may be formed about an individual about whom certain obsolete or incorrect online information keeps doing uncontrolled rounds of social media and the internet, even if no longer true. It is this unfavourable situation for a citizen and the felt need of rectification of portrayal of a perceived negative image no longer valid, in case of an employee or a potential employee in the private or public sector, that gave birth to the "Right To Erasure" RTE also commonly known as "The Right To Be Forgotten" (RTBF).

In some digitally advanced countries including the United States of America, United Kingdom and the European Union, legal systems seem to be already in place for adequately tackling this comparatively new form of unequal treatment created by greater use of the social media and the internet in the 21st century, many a time blowing things out of proportion and to the detriment of an individual. To counter this new form of inequality, the "Right To Be Forgotten" RTBF or the "Right To Erasure" RTE have garnered global support.

Under the European Union Statute, the "Right To Be Forgotten" (RTBF) is covered under *Article 17* and *Recitals 65 and 66* of the *General Data Protection Regulation (GDPR), 2018*, which deals with how personal data is required to be collected, processed, and erased. The European Union "Right To Be Forgotten" (RTBF) empowers citizens to demand organizations to delete their personal data or that data which causes them unnecessary personal harm and is no longer required to be online for some valid reason.

In India, however, the problem seems to be deeper and a little tougher. To tackle this, newly emerged in the 21st century, modern form of unequal treatment due to the social media and the internet, experts have rightly warned that "the best solution can come from good legislative provisions along with suitable public and employee awareness. It is high time that we must pay attention to Data Security in India. Cyber Security in India is missing and the same requires rejuvenation.... we must at least now wake up. Data breaches and cybercrimes in India cannot be reduced until we make strong cyber laws.... Cyber law of India must also be supported by sound cyber security and effective cyber forensics," further, "The provisions purportedly for data protection jut out as an ugly patch work on the IT Act and do not offer any comprehensive protection to personal data in India. In these circumstances the question to be asked is, being a major IT power in the global map today, can India afford to deal with an important issue such as this in the manner in which it has dealt with in the amendments to the IT Act?"[55]

In the 21st century, given the rapid speed of advancements in the field of Information and communication technologies (ICTs), internet and the social media, a patch here and a patch there in the now almost obsolete India's *Information Technology Act, 2000*, won't do. What India needs is to completely revamp its *Information Technology Act, 2000*, in light of the latest developments and bring it in tune with the present-day situation and needs. At the same time, in a dynamic situation, besides the required infrastructure, India also needs to put in place fast, a stand-alone legally enforceable "Right To Be Forgotten" RTBF statute, on the lines of the European Union's *General Data Protection Regulation (GDPR), 2018*, with strong teeth and without any loopholes.

Most importantly, as this newly emerged form of unequal treatment is becoming omnipresent, with the world today technologically shrunk into a global village, in order to be effective, the above suggestions would be needed to be implemented fast and on priority not only in India but by every other country in the world as well to effectively tackle this new menace. And at the same time, there is an urgent need of spreading more awareness about this social media and internet generated modern form of unequal treatment and tackling it through the only, instantly implementable potent weapon called the "Right To Be Forgotten" RTBF, both among the legal fraternity as well as employees and potential job seekers in public or private sector, and even among common citizens so that wrong impressions don't prevail in the virtual world negatively impacting an individual in real life situations in any country.

NOTES

1. IAPP: The world's largest global information privacy community, https://iapp.org/about/, accessed 27 July 2022.
2. Bright HR. *Unfair treatment of an employee at work*, https://www.brighthr.com/articles/equality-and-discrimination/unfair-treatment-at-work/, accessed 1 August 2022.

3. Mittuniversitetet, MID Sweden University. *Unequal Treatment*, https://www.miun.se/en/staff/employee/health-and-safety-management-and-rehabilitation/systematic-health-and-safety-management/unequal-treatment/, accessed 3 August, 2022.
4. Kingslay, Eric. Kingslay & Kingslay. *How to Deal With An Unfair Workplace*, 26 July 2022, https://www.kingsleykingsley.com/blog/2020/january/how-to-deal-with-an-unfair-workplace, accessed 31 July 2022.
5. Ibid.
6. Ibid.
7. It is significant to note here that emails or social media posts about an employee, often resulting into discrimination of a new kind, rather a new kind of inequality, raising its head more and more in the 21st century—also seem to be covered and dealt with by the legal system in the United States. However, barring the European Union, the United Kingdom, and some other countries, in the absence of specific laws in place with sufficient teeth and no loopholes, most other countries are found wanting in effectively tackling this comparatively new menace.
8. Thompson, Barney. Financial Times: *Europe's top judges to hear 'right to be forgotten' cases: ECJ to consider whether search engines must delete links globally or only within the EU*, 10 September 2018, https://www.ft.com/content/86cd805c-b4d8-11e8-b3ef-799c8613f4a1, accessed 30 June 2022.
9. Ibid.
10. https://arighttobeforgotten.co.uk/right-to-be-forgotten-example/removing-links-to-sdt-decisions, reference to a 2012 trial in the Crown Court, in which The Solicitors Disciplinary Tribunal published its decision on the Solicitors Regulation Authority (the body which regulates solicitors in England and Wales) and on the Law Society Gazette websites.
11. Recital 65: Right of rectification and erasure: A data subject should have the right to have personal data concerning him or her rectified and a 'right to be forgotten' where the retention of such data infringes this Regulation or Union or Member State law to which the controller is subject. In particular, a data subject should have the right to have his or her personal data erased and no longer processed where the personal data are no longer necessary in relation to the purposes for which they are collected or otherwise processed, where a data subject has withdrawn his or her consent or objects to the processing of personal data concerning him or her, or where the processing of his or her personal data does not otherwise comply with this Regulation. That right is relevant in particular where the data subject has given his or her consent as a child and is not fully aware of the risks involved by the processing, and later wants to remove such personal data, especially on the internet. The data subject should be able to exercise that right notwithstanding the fact that he or she is no longer a child. However, the further retention of the personal data should be lawful where it is necessary, for exercising the right of freedom of expression and information, for compliance with a legal obligation, for the performance of a task carried out in the public interest or in the exercise of official authority vested in the controller, on the grounds of public interest in the area of public health, for archiving purposes in the public interest,

scientific or historical research purposes or statistical purposes, or for the establishment, exercise or defence of legal claims. GDPR.EU. https://gdpr.eu/Recital-65-Right-of-rectification-and-erasure.

12. Recital 66: Right To Be Forgotten: To strengthen the right to be forgotten in the online environment, the right to erasure should also be extended in such a way that a controller who has made the personal data public should be obliged to inform the controllers which are processing such personal data to erase any links to, or copies or replications of those personal data. In doing so, that controller should take reasonable steps, taking into account available technology and the means available to the controller, including technical measures, to inform the controllers which are processing the personal data of the data subject's request. GDPR.EU. https://gdpr.eu/Recital-66-Right-to-be-forgotten, accessed 7 July 2022.
13. European Commission. Data protection in the EU: The General Data Protection Regulation (GDPR), *The Data Protection Law Enforcement Directive and other rules concerning the protection of personal data,* https://ec.europa.eu/info/law/law-topic/data-protection/data-protection-eu_en, accessed 23 July 2022.
14. https://www.bing.com/search?q=right+to+be+forgotten+-+wikipedia&cvid=fa555722892345c1bf82789666ecdf32&aqs=edge.0.0.1575j0j1&pglt=43&FORM=ANSPA1&PC=EDGEDB, accessed 19 July 2022.
15. Ibid.
16. Ibid.
17. GDPR.EU. *Everything you need to know about the "Right to be forgotten"* This project is co-funded by the Horizon 2020 Framework of the European Union, https://gdpr.eu/right-to-be-forgotten/, accessed 21 July 2022.
18. Threat Stack: Part of F5, Boston, MA. GDPR: *What is the Right to Erasure?*, https://www.threatstack.com/blog/gdpr-what-is-the-right-to-erasure, accessed 5 August 2022.
19. GDPR.EU. *Everything you need to know about the "Right to be forgotten"* This project is co-funded by the Horizon 2020 Framework of the European Union, Op. cit.
20. https://gdpr.eu/right-to-be-forgotten/, accessed 22 July 2022.
21. GDPR.EU. *Everything you need to know about the "Right to be forgotten"* This project is co-funded by the Horizon 2020 Framework of the European Union, Op. cit.
22. GDPR.EU. *Everything you need to know about the "Right to be forgotten"* This project is co-funded by the Horizon 2020 Framework of the European Union, Op. cit.
23. GDPR.EU. *59,000 breaches reported in first eight months of new GPDR requirements,* https://gdpr.eu/gdpr-requirements-data-breach-reporting/, accessed 14 July 2022.
24. GDPR.EU. *Five takeaways for small businesses in Ireland's GDPR report,* https://gdpr.eu/ireland-gdpr-report-2019/, accessed 16 July 2022.
25. https://gdpr.eu/tag/gdpr/, accessed 7 July 2022.
26. https://gdpr.eu/email-encryption/, accessed 22 July 2022.
27. https://gdpr.eu/fines/, accessed 8 July 2022.
28. https://gdpr.eu/fines/, accessed 8 July 2022.

29. GDPR.EU. *59,000 breaches reported in first eight months of new GPDR requirements,* https://gdpr.eu/gdpr-requirements-data-breach-reporting/, accessed 18 July 2022.
30. https://gdpr.eu/data-anonymization-taxa-4x35/, accessed 22 July 2022, accessed 5 July 2022.
31. tdwi. Vojnic, Milica, *GDPR in 2021: Key Updates and Implications for Data Strategies,* https://tdwi.org/articles/2021/08/13/biz-all-gdpr-in-2021-key-updates.aspx#:~:text=In%20the%20new%20iteration%20of,for%20it%20to%20be%20valid, accessed 24 July 2022.
32. Jolt Digest. https://jolt.law.harvard.edu/digest/google-v-cnil-eu-rules-that-right-to-be-forgotten-does-not-apply-globally, Google v. CNIL: *EU Rules that Right to be Forgotten Does Not Apply Globally,* By Serena Wong—Edited by Chris Murray, October 17, 2019, C-507/17, Google LLC v. CNIL, 2019 EUR-Lex CELEX No. 62017CJ0507, 24 September, 2019, accessed 17 July 2022.
33. C-136/17 available at https://academic.oup.com/grurint/article/69/4/380/5732807 accessed on 23 February 2022.
34. C-131/12.
35. tdwi. Vojnic, Milica, *GDPR in 2021: Key Updates and Implications for Data Strategies,* https://tdwi.org/articles/2021/08/13/biz-all-gdpr-in-2021-key-updates.aspx#:~:text=In%20the%20new%20iteration%20of,for%20it%20to%20be%20valid, accessed 20 July 2022.
36. Writ Petition (Civil) No. 494 of 2012.
37. *Does India have a Data Protection law?* https://www.legalserviceindia.com/article/l406-Does-India-have-a-Data-Protection-law.html, accessed 27 July 2022.
38. Notified by the government of India on February 25, 2021.
39. Business Standard. *Govt withdraws Data Protection Bill, 2021, will present new legislation,* 3 August 2022, https://www.business-standard.com/article/economy-policy/centre-withdraws-personal-data-protection-bill-2019-to-present-new-bill-122080301226_1.html, accessed 8 August 2022.
40. Tunggal, Abi Tyas. *What Is the Personal Data Protection Bill 2019?,* https://www.upguard.com/blog/personal-data-protection-bill, accessed 27 July 2022.
41. Ibid.
42. IAPP: The world's largest global information privacy community. Wadhwa, Rishi, Bains, Grace. *The evolution of India's data privacy regime in 2021,* 17 March 2022, https://iapp.org/news/a/the-evolution-of-indias-data-privacy-regime-in-2021/, Portsmouth, U.S.A., accessed on 27 July 2022.
43. Ibid.
44. Ibid.
45. Writ P(C) 3918/2021.
46. Crl. A. No. 14/2013 t.
47. BLAPL No.4592/2020.
48. C-131/12[2014] QB 1022.
49. CS(OS) 642/2018.
50. CS(OS) 642/2018 para. 9.
51. CS(OS) 642/2018 para.10
52. CS(OS) 642/2018 para 11.
53. Special Civil Application No. 1854/2015.

54. IAPP: The world's largest global information privacy community. Wadhwa, Rishi, Bains, Grace. *The Evolution of India's Data Privacy Regime In 2021*, 17 March 2022, Op. cit.
55. *Does India have a Data Protection law?* https://www.legalserviceindia.com/article/l406-Does-India-have-a-Data-Protection-law.html, accessed 27 July 2022.

CHAPTER 7

MISSION UNITED—ORGANIZATIONALLY DIVIDED

Inter-Sectorial Collaboration in the Hungarian Approach to Servicing Ukrainian Refugees

Agnes Jenei
University of Public Service, Hungary

Réka Zsuzsánna Máthé
University of Public Service, Hungary

Maliga Reddy
Durban University of Technology

Strinivasan Pillay
Durban University of Technology

ABSTRACT

The Ukrainian–Russian war exposed the governments of neighboring countries to situations they never experienced in peacetime; situations for which they had little or no preparation. The reception and servicing (meeting various and diverse needs) of masses of refugees required a completely new approach. In Hungary unexpected and unprecedented close cooperation took place among actors that previously were not in contact with each other. The focus of this research is this exceptional inter-sectoral collaboration among territorial government offices, municipalities, and charity organizations aimed at providing basic needs for refugees in five transitory care centers (*Help Points*), set up near the Ukrainian border as a response to the emergency situation caused by the outbreak of the war.

The purpose of this paper is to examine the barriers to collaboration that might arise in teams with high cognitive diversity. Based on a series of semi-structured interviews, the study offers insights into different challenges to collaboration. Using Bayesian process tracing, our results show that inter-organizational collaboration is highly facilitated by managing similarly diverse teams, clearly delimiting tasks, creating adequate organizational structures, and building trusting relationships.

PRELIMINARY REMARKS

Inter-sectorial/interorganizational collaboration, either successful or ineffective, has extremely high stakes in emergency management. Collaboration among various organizations is often a very challenging imperative. Several case studies describe the enablers and stoppers of collaboration in different circumstances. Since the number of disasters (natural and human-induced hazards) is increasing, the importance of a deeper understanding of the phenomena of inter-organizational collaboration is growing. Present study aims to contribute to the understanding of the possible barriers to inter-organizational collaboration in disaster management and managing cognitive diversity.

The objective of this paper is to analyze a temporarily established inter-organizational collaboration in an emergency/disaster situation. It focuses on leadership challenges and good practices related to managing cognitive diversity of the partners. In the case presented in this chapter we analyze the inter-organizational collaboration within a specific program designed by the Humanitarian Committee and set up by the Hungarian Government immediately after the outbreak of the war in Ukraine.

The chapter is structured as follows: the description of the background of the emergency situation is followed by a short overview of the literature highlighting findings related to emergency/disaster management, diversity management, and cognitive diversity management. The methodological section presents the research design, the method of data collection and data analysis. This is followed by the presentation of the findings. Finally, the concluding arguments of the research are summarized, highlighting key limitations, and raising possible directions for further consideration.

BACKGROUND OF THE COLLABORATION: REFUGEE CRISIS

First Stage: February 24–25–26, 2022

Starting 2022 February 24th, thousands of refugees (typically mothers with children or elderly people) were arriving to the Hungarian border, many of them on foot. Once they crossed the border, a majority waited to unite with their relatives (husbands). Often, thousands of people were just staying there, near the border crossings in a small open-air area, in cold weather without any concrete goals. Five small local municipalities (200-4000 inhabitants) near the five cross-bordering points tried to help the refugees, but the crowd of people was overwhelming.

Since the war surprised even security policy experts, there was no plan how to respond to this human disaster. The Hungarian government was searching for appropriate solutions to deal with the influx of refugees. Meantime, the thousands of vulnerable young women and children attracted a mass of unidentified people coming with good or bad intentions, as it regularly happens is similar situations. NGOs, volunteers, people by car, companies with buses moved from the whole country willing to offer help, but the spontaneous efforts turned into chaos.

Second Stage: From February 27 to the End of April

The Government set up the Humanitarian Committee to coordinate the crisis and established five transit care centers, called officially *Help Points*, based on the consultation in the field with the stakeholders (municipalities, NGOs). Involving stakeholders to such a degree in the decision-making processes is quite unusual. As a result, five refugee transit centers were established near to the five border crossings. Managers of the centers had to transport the refugees arriving on foot from the border to the newly established centers and had to provide for their basic needs and accommodation for 24–72 hours.

Actors Running the Help Points

Three types of organizations were appointed at each center to co-manage the Help Points:

1. Local Municipality (ensuring the building and infrastructure for the Help Points): at Lónya, Záhony, Barabás, Beregsurány, Tiszabecs
2. Humanitarian organizations: Relief Service of the Reformed Church, Caritas Hungary, Baptist Relief Service, Hungarian Charity Service of the Order of Malta, Hungarian Red Cross
3. Territorial Government Offices

Different types of organizations are different in terms of organizational structure, number of staff, responsibilities, available equipment, qualifications, competencies, experiences, communication styles, resources. The workforce coming from different types of organizations is used to different organizational culture, internalized different organizational values and norms and internal procedures. Municipalities and Government Offices have never faced situations like this. Some NGOs had similar international experience, but not all of them.

These organizations usually don't work together, at least, not in Hungary. They don't know each other, they don't have contacts with each other, yet, they were mandated to work together. Hence, in this research we call these organizations atypical partners. The context of their collaboration was unusual also because of the unusual working hours, as they are completely different from the office hours: the care centers were open 24 hours a day for several months.

Operation of the Help Points

For several weeks approximately 3,000–5,000 refugees per day attended the Help Points situated in settlements with 200–4,000 inhabitants. During this period, most refugees stayed 1–3 nights or in case of illnesses, they stayed a week or more. The workforce of the three organizations had to provide hot meal, drinks, accommodation, needs-specific enabling information, health care and free transportation to their Hungarian destinations. They assured the continuous cleaning of the reception areas, welcoming, registration, orientation of the refugees, selection and provision of the domestic and international donations. Additionally, they provided information related to EU regulations for refugees coming from outside EU countries.

The tasks were new and something unexpected turned up every day: continuous re-adjustment was needed in an ongoing process. However, from the improvised, ad-hoc solutions they managed to get to standardization of the tasks in about three weeks. Managers had to be available 24 hours, answer the phone in the middle of the night, manage the acute stress as no one knew how long the influx of refugees would continue, keep the staff mentally and physically healthy while in service 24 hours for unforeseeable period of time.

Performance of the Help Points

The services provided by the centers can be considered adequate and their collaboration a successful one, according to both objective and subjective considerations. There were no complaints against service providers neither from the clients, nor from the international observers. The only case initiated by the Hungarian Ombudsman for Minority Rights was subsequently withdrawn. The subjective perception of the service providers was that the refugees were satisfied with the services rendered to them: they received high number and high level of expression of gratitude (many drawings made by children) and moved adults. In some cases, a few international refugees became volunteer providers for several months.

THE ROLE OF DIVERSITY MANAGEMENT IN COLLABORATION DURING EMERGENCY

When referring to emergency management, Federal Emergency Management Agency (FEMA) defines it as: "the managerial function charged with creating the framework within which communities reduce vulnerability to hazards and cope with disasters" (FEMA, 2007). The emergency management cycle on which modern emergency management is based, defines four phases of emergency management: (a) prevention/mitigation; (b) preparedness; (c) response; and recovery (FEMA, 2007). The examined Hungarian case can be regarded as the response phase of the emergency cycle.

Emergency management necessitates the communities and organizations from the nonprofit, public and private sectors to work together to strengthen the society's capacity to prevent or mitigate, prepare for, respond to, and recover from disasters. Emergency situations requires collaboration between actors of different background and cultural organizations. Baker (2020) as cited by Wolf-Fordham (2020) inspects how representatives of emergency management, public health preparedness, and public administration might improve their collaboration. She examines similarities and differences in practitioner demographics, professional competencies, organizational goals, and culture. In her findings, the barriers to collaboration are the dissimilar role interpretations of the various actors belonging to different types of organizations. For example, public health professionals look to understand the scientific evidence in the field, and their interpretation becomes political (cites Baker, 2020). As opposed to this, emergency managers act more as government representatives. The two contrasting role perceptions might lead to weakened collaboration and, thus, less effective emergency response.

The response to similar challenges is the establishment of collaborative management which occurs when people from different organizations create and sustain relationships that encourage trust, build consensus, produce, and share ownership of a collective objective (FEMA, 2007; Kamensky & Burlin, 2004). The willingness to collaborate as an indispensable tool in emergency management to deal with uncertainty and complex extreme events was highlighted by several authors (Arklay, 2015; Waugh & Streib, 2006; Curnin and O'Hara, 2019). Given the increased number of disasters and humanitarian crises occurring in the face of diminishing global resources, contemporary disaster management and humanitarian organizations face greater challenges to optimize cooperation and coordination processes among actors.

The literature on diversity management is extensive—a thorough examination of it is not the current purpose of the authors. There is no single universally accepted definition of diversity. Usually, it refers to the inclusion of age, education, background, function, and personality. It also includes lifestyles, sexual orientation, geographic origin, tenure with an organization, management and non-management values, beliefs, and opinions (Robbins, 2019). Demographics mostly reflect surface level diversity that can lead employees to perceive one another through stereotypes and assumptions. Yet, evidence has shown that as people get to know one another, they become less concerned about demographic differences once they see themselves as sharing more important characteristics, such as personality and values, which represent deep-level diversity.

The literature on cognitive diversity management, in the context of diversity management is less elaborated. It is important to note that this paper does not aim to use the term as in brain sciences or psychology. For our purpose, the distinction of Milliken and Martins (1996) seem most relevant. The authors distinguish two types of diversity: observable individual differences (such as race, ethnicity, gender, age), respectively, and differences in underlying attributes. The latter characteristic is divided into three main categories. Firstly, personality characteristics such as values and socioeconomic background. Secondly is the subgroup based on skills and knowledge, that refers to differences in educational, functional, occupational background, industry experience. Lastly, the authors differentiate based on organizational and group tenure. In the case of the first type of diversity, evidence suggests that groups' level of integration is relatively low and the likelihood of turnover is higher. Nonetheless, in the case of non-observable differences, the result are not conclusive.

According to the authors, there are four types of effects of diversity on an organization: affective, cognitive, symbolic, and communicative. The cognitive effects of diversity refer to the consequences diversity "might have on the group's ability to process information, perceive and interpret stimuli, and make decisions" (Milliken and Martins, 1996:416). In other words, it's the ability of group members to put all information together, process it and then reach common conclusions, thus make higher quality decisions. The authors found that this type of diversity in effect works well in heterogeneous groups, as the cognitive variety of these groups involves a multitude of differing and new possibilities, with a strong cross-pollination of ideas, that can lead to creativity. Phillips and Loyd (2006) arrive to a similar conclusion: heterogeneous groups can be beneficial for group decision-making when individuals who look different on the surface bring different task perspectives to the table. This study aims to explore exclusively on the cognitive effects of the above-described Hungarian emergency situation collaboration.

In the 21st century employees with different backgrounds, mindsets, desires, needs, interests, and personal opinions are acknowledged as the main available source of innovative ideas that companies can implement towards profitable performance and expanded market (Seliverstova, Pierog 2021). Reynolds and Lewis (2017) stated that there is a strong positive correlation between cognitive diversity and performance. However, diversity at the group-level can cause conflicts, as well, not only cohesion, creativity, group performance and idea generation. Cognitive diversity can increase task conflict. In addition, task conflict mediates the effects of cognitive diversity on decision outcomes (Olson et al. 2007). Diversity can have negative effects like social exclusion, miscommunication, conflicts, and high turnover (Williams and O'Reilly 1998).

Managing diversity in an effective way means to foster personal development practices that bring out the skills and abilities of all workers, acknowledging how differences in perspective can be a valuable way to improve performance for everyone. (Robbins et al. 2016). Researchers suggest that diversity experiences are more likely to lead to positive adaptation for all parties in four cases. Firstly, the diversity experience undermines stereotypical attitudes, secondly, if the perceiver is motivated and able to consider a new perspective on others. Thirdly, if the perceiver engages in stereotype suppression and generative thought in response to the diversity experience, and lastly, if the positive experience of stereotype undermining is repeated frequently. (Robbins et al 2016).

Managing diversity while very different organizations need to work together is a tremendous managerial challenge. The collaboration and the provision of quality services depends on the level of successful collaboration. In this research, the authors consider the collaboration of the three unlikely Hungarian partners as a successful one. The concept of collaboration and cooperation are extensively deliberated in the literature. The key difference between these approaches is that cooperation is more focused on working together to create an end product, while successful collaboration requires participants to share in the process of knowledge creation (Dillenbourg et al. 1996; Roschelle and Teasley 1995).

Thomson and Perry (2006) state that collaboration "suggest a higher level of collective action than cooperation" "Collaboration is a term used to describe the relationships between organizations when partners need to work towards a common goal to solve complex societal problems. These relationships are characterized by high levels of interaction (Gray 1989; Cigler, 2001; Huxham an Vangen 2005; AbouAssi et al. 2016). The high levels of interaction needed for collaborative partnerships require several intrinsically linked dimensions.

As identified in the literature, inter-organizational structures can be either a barrier to, or an enabler of inter-organizational collaboration in the nonprofit and public sectors in disaster recovery. Curnin and O'Hara examined the collaboration among three partners. The authors pointed out that in the case examined by them, there were three different factors responsible for enabling successful collaboration between the various partners: interorganizational structures, trusting relationships between the various actors; and role clarity. Their study stressed that role clarity is fundamental for inter-organizational collaboration; it needs to be articulated in the administrative arrangements of the interorganizational structures and needs to be expressed when forming trusting relationships. In addition, individuals must clearly understand their own role and that of their own organization to ensure credibility and build trust between stakeholders.

At this stage, the present article uses the atypical Hungarian partnership to examine the barriers of collaboration. Since the case presented by Cumin and O'Hara (2019) is very similar to the Hungarian case, the authors will use the dimensions of collaboration as purported by Cumin and O'Hara (2019) as major anchoring points.

RESEARCH QUESTIONS AND HYPOTHESIS

The research presented by Curnin and O'Hara (2019) stresses that the most important variables influencing collaboration in disaster management would be inter-organizational structures, trusting relationships, and role clarity. This study is part of a more extended research aiming to explore the enablers and the barriers of the collaborations that took place in the Hungarian case, with a particular attention to the leaders' challenge of managing cognitive diversity.

Hence, the main research question investigates the factors that challenged or enabled the collaboration between government offices, local councils, and non-governmental organizations. At this preliminary stage, the authors were interested in determining the factors that hindered managing the diverse collaboration and can be identified as the decisive components. Hence, the first research question reads as follows:

RQ1: *Which factors were the biggest obstacles to collaboration in the atypical Hungarian case?*

Professional literature suggests that in some cases individuals in diverse groups with differences in socio-economic background, industry, and organizational membership, industry or organizational tenure might look at each other through stereotypes. This has a negative effect on the generation of ideas and reaching common solutions. Similarly, the dissimilar role interpretations of the leaders might lead to misaligned managerial goals, which, in turn, have negative effect on collaboration. Stemming from the differences of role perceptions, tasks conflicts might emerge which additionally might hamper collaboration. It is likely, that in the Hungarian case similar obstacles were encountered during collaboration, at least at the very beginning, and that these had to be overcome. Based on literature, we created the hypothesis stating that the most important barriers to collaboration in the Hungarian case were the initial stereotypes, the dissimilar role interpretations, and the task conflicts. Therefore, our first hypothesis reads as follows:

H1: *The most important barriers to collaboration were the initial stereotypes, the dissimilar role interpretations, and the task conflicts.*

The null hypothesis suggests that no relationship exists in the set of variables suggested by the literature and the observed outcome.

$H_{(1)}0$: *The collaboration was smooth, there were no barriers due to stereotypes, dissimilar role interpretations or task conflicts to overcome.*

As an effort to formalize Bayesian process tracing, we explicitly stated the alternative hypothesis, which could have been observed, if our $H_{(1)}$ would not hold. In order to do this, we specified a set of mutually exclusive and exhaustive rival hypotheses that will allow us to meaningfully reason about the likelihood of observing evidence in the light of our $H_{(1)}$. Therefore, we formulate three rival hypotheses.

Given that these three actors do not usually collaborate and there is a significant diversity in personality characteristics among them, we can assume that the major obstacle was posed by the stereotypes. However, since there are some examples of successful similar collaboration in Hungary, it is possible that stereotypes might not be a major obstacle in this case. Rather, the diversity regarding organizational tenure and membership can have a great influence on how various individuals perceive their own role during the emergency. Stemming from this, we can suppose that each of the three different types of actors had very different approaches to managing the emergency situation. This might have posed the greatest challenge to collaboration, which leads us to our next hypothesis.

$H_{(R)}$: *The biggest challenge in the collaboration was presented by the dissimilar role interpretations, however, once these were sorted out, the collaboration was smooth.*

Another alternative might be that there were no task conflicts among the participants—their differences in role perceptions and their organizational culture would direct the collaborating organizations to assume only specific tasks, which do not overlap. Additionally, the Hungarian government gave the framework to the collaboration and roles and responsibilities were established at the very beginning of the collaboration. The next hypothesis reads:

$H_{(T)}$: *Due to obvious differences in roles and experiences, there were no task conflicts among the various actors. The collaboration among the highly atypical partners was smooth.*

Lastly, in order to be able to argue in favor of our $H_{(1)}$ we include another alternative hypothesis referring to additional causal mechanisms.

$H_{(N)}$: *There were no other significant sources of possible barriers to the collaboration.*

Once we have formulated our mutually exclusive and exhausting alternative hypothesis, we can state that only one of the mechanisms might operate, thus we can maintain $H_{(1)}0 = H_{(R)} + H_{(T)} + H_{(N)}$.

Since we know that, overall, the Hungarian collaboration was a successful one, it is worth examining the factors which contributed most to the success of collaboration. Our second research question would aim to explore that specific causal mechanism. However, at this preliminary stage we only examine the possible obstacles to collaboration.

RESEARCH DESIGN AND METHODOLOGY

In answering our research question, we used process tracing with Bayesian inference (Fairfield and Charman 2017 and 2022). We chose the method of process tracing as it allowed us to establish whether, and how, a potential cause or causes influenced the specific outcome, namely, the successful collaboration. Additionally, by applying the Bayesian inference, we aimed to interpret the probability of individual competing hypothesis, considering the knowledge stemming from the relevant literature, and the evidence gathered (Fairfield and Charman, 2019). Therefore, we compared the numerical estimate of the degree of belief in a hypothesis before evidence (the prior distribution) to the numerical estimate of the degree of belief after considering the evidence (posterior distribution).

The first step in our analysis was to consider three different scenarios for the prior distribution for the four hypotheses:

1. the indifferent principle, form a position of maximum ignorance I(0).
2. the case described as "Interested in collaboration"
3. the case considering the role of the government mandate

The logic of assigning the particular frequencies to the hypothesis stems from the Bayesian logic of assigning degrees of belief in certain explanations, in the light of our prior knowledge considering the relevant literature. Accordingly, based on relevant literature, the collaboration could have been successful even without the government's mandate (Nemec et all, 2019) and the gathered evidence from the field. Thus, we try to formally evaluate competing explanations of complex sociopolitical phenomena, relative to each other.

Being an atypical emergency situation, the case selection on theoretical consideration is less relevant. Rather, the study examined all five Help Points and conducted case studies at each site. The primary sources of information were semi-structured interviews with leaders of all three types of organizations. Fifteen semi-structured interviews, each for a duration of approximately one hour, were carried out between 20 June and 18 August 2022.

The interviews were transcribed and then coded in the first round using inductive methods. Second, specific codes (the inductively created codes for *Differences due to diversity* were recoded deductively, according to the theoretical framework as presented in the literature review. The codes not directly related to the collaboration among the three main actors were not included in the analysis. Additionally, sections deductively coded as Development during process were similarly revised and adjusted.

The authors consider as evidence the results code coverage and cross-tabulation, supported by recollection of events based on the narratives and on hard evidence, such as reports of international organizations. The evidence was weighted, taking into account even the possible biases of the respondents.

RESULTS: BARRIERS TO COLLABORATION

Diversity in the Groups

As presented earlier, the emergency management group was formed by five different Humanitarian organizations, the representatives of the municipality where the Help Points were located, respectively, the representatives of the territorial Government Offices.

There was no significant surface level diversity in terms of race and ethnicity, however, there were some differences regarding age and gender. Regarding differences in personality characteristics, the diversity was more significant (presented in the Appendix).

There were considerable differences regarding the level of education, educational background, tenure in the organization, professional experience and experience with emergency case management.

Assigning Priors

The first step in our analysis was to consider three different scenarios for the prior distribution for the four hypotheses. Firstly, we apply the indifferent principle, form a position of maximum ignorance $I_{(0)}$. This scenario aims to approach the objective Bayesianism and it ignores all background information, hence we assign equal probabilities to the distribution of our five hypotheses. In the second scenario, we draw form the cases discussed in the literature presenting successful collaboration of similar Hungarian actors. In these circumstances, we can see that there is an existing will to work closely with other actors in order to achieve a greater good. Additionally, we approach this case with the background knowledge that non-governmental organizations were the first ones to offer humanitarian services to the Ukrainian refugees. Moreover, as it has been documented in the literature, there are cases when governmental actors initiate collaboration to be able to provide better quality services. We labeled this case as "Interested in collaboration" and treated this background information as our second scenario.

Based on this previous knowledge, we can assume that there were some barriers to collaboration; however, it was not due to stereotypes or task conflicts, rather due to dissimilar role interpretations. In this case, we assign a higher probability to this hypothesis and almost equal probabilities to the other hypotheses. Still, the probability that in a collaboration there would be no task conflicts and stereotypes to overcome is very low; therefore, we assigned a greater probability to our H1 than to our alternative hypothesis—although the assignment is inevitably subjective in nature.

Lastly, we considered a third scenario. This case draws on the mandate of the Hungarian government that required the three atypical partners to work together, even though they did not choose their partners for themselves. We believe that in this case task conflicts should have been minimal due to the government's intervention. Rather, stereotypes and dissimilar role perceptions were more prevalent during collaboration. Hence, we assign a slightly highest relativity to $H_{(T)}$ and a lower relativity to H1, with almost equally high probability $H_{(R)}$. In this case we estimated a lower probability for $H_{(N)}$, considering that several unforeseen issues might have arrived under a mandated collaboration. We convert the probabilities into log-odds to allow easier work with weights in the future.

Finding Evidence

The authors consider as evidence the results code coverage and cross-tabulation, supported by recollection of events based on the narratives and on hard evidence, such as reports of international organizations. The evidence was weighted, taking into account even the possible biases of the respondents. Firstly, crosstabs for the recoded elements of *Differences due to diversity* (as mentioned above) and the main actors (NGOs, Local councils, and Government offices) respectively, the five locations were executed. The results were analyzed and as a result, the following pieces of evidence were found:

- E_1 = Task conflicts were existent at least at the beginning of the collaboration
- E_2 = Differences in role perceptions were present not only at organizational level, but also at individual, micro level.
- E_3 = At least at the beginning, there were some stereotypes which were gradually broken down.
- E_4 = Other challenges reported did not pose a barrier to collaboration.

Assessing Weight to Evidence

Once we have our evidence, we proceed to assigning weights (WoE) to each piece of evidence (E_X) to be found under our hypothesis (H_J). In this order, we quantify how likely a piece of evidence is to be found under each of the hypothesis, conditional on the pieces of evidence previously incorporated in our analysis and on our background information (presented as scenarios and further denoted as *I*). Since we only have four pieces of evidence and four rival hypotheses, it makes a reasonable choice to use a less formal Bayesian process tracing.

As Fairfield and Charman (2017, 2022) proposed, we assigned weight to our individual pieces of evidence on a logarithmic scale, using decibels. The reason why they propose the logarithmic scale over a linear scale is that human perception is more accustomed to differentiate between barely noticeable changes in relative and not absolute changes (think of brightness of light or loudness of sound). Sound measured in decibels is in a logarithmic scale and it expresses ratios making able to calculate very small differences in likelihood rations easier. For instance, Fairfield and Charman (2017:11) note that a change in 5 decibels is clearly noticeable, while an increase of 10 decibels is perceived about twice as loud, and 20 decibels is roughly four times louder, while 30 decibels about eight times louder. The authors suggest regarding decisive evidence that clearly favors one hypothesis over the other as a rough equivalent to 30 decibels. The likelihood estimated with the help of decibel analogy as used by the authors in Fairfield and Charman (2022) .

Our goal in weighting evidence is to assess their relative values in favor of two rival hypotheses. While assessing their values expressed in decibels is inherently subjective in nature, it is important to note, that for our qualitative research the *likelihood ratio* matters and not *the absolute value of the probabilities.*

In the next stage we proceed at counting the weight of evidence for the hypothesis where we simply add the various weights that supported any given hypothesis. Our evidence did not support $H_{(T)}$ and $H_{(R)}$ and only one piece of evidence weighing 20 dB supported $H_{(N)}$. The majority of evidence favored H1 when compared to its rivals, the total weight of evidence amounting to 126 dB. We found that in the three cases evidence overwhelmingly supports our H1.

Once we have our weights in decibels, we need to add the total weight of evidence supporting each hypothesis to our prior log-odds to obtain the posterior log odds ratios. With changing from the state of total ignorance, the log-odds of $H_{(N)}$ are decreasing, making it less likely that no other conflicts might arise during a similar real-life collaboration. Since we did not find evidence supporting $H_{(R)}$ and $H_{(T)}$, the probability that biggest challenge in a similar collaboration would be presented by the dissimilar role interpretations, and that no task conflicts will arise is extremely low.

The evidence very strongly supports our H1 stating that the barriers to collaboration in this diverse team was a combination of initial stereotypes, the dissimilar role interpretations, and the task conflicts. This is in line with the result found by Cumin and O'Hara (2019), who stress the role of inter-organizational structures, trusting relationships and role clarity. Our posterior H1 has a higher value in the case when partners would choose to freely collaborate without a strict mandate coming from a government. This means that in similar cases the probability of having these three barriers is greater when compared to the scenario where stricter, imposed rules are in place.

Our results are drawn from evidence provided by the interviewees, and we tried to quantify these qualitative results in order to affect a fairly formal Bayesian process tracing. By using logarithmic scales, we tried to better assess the very small likelihoods of evidence when faced two competing hypotheses. Further fine graining the research could be done by reordering the evidence and test that the reordering of evidence incorporated into our analysis does not affect the final posterior probabilities on the hypothesis. At this stage, however, given the types of evidence found, rearranging the evidence will not show too much arbitrariness, which is inherent in assessing numerical values.

Lastly, we consider that by differentiating between the two scenarios and assigning accordingly different priors to our hypothesis does make the differences in likelihood ratios (especially expressed on logarithmic scale) more evident. We do not claim that these are absolute ratios but aim to point at the differences between them. The several orders of magnitude supporting our H1 stress that the posterior probability on H1 remains higher than its rivals.

CONCLUSIONS

Our research examined the inter-organizational collaboration that took place as a response to an emergency situation in Hungary: the three atypical partners offered services to the refugees affected by the Russian-Ukrainian war. The three different types of organizations—humanitarian organizations, local government offices and municipalities were mandated by the government to provide services in a collaborative way. Formal and informal evidence point out that the collaboration was a successful one. At this stage our examination concerned the barriers that, at least at the beginning of the collaboration, might have posed some challenges in managing the teams. In this order, we tested the most likely barriers as suggested by the literature. We collected evidence from semi-structured interviews that we weighted. With the help of tools used in formal Bayesian process tracing we assessed the probabilities of alternative hypotheses against the one suggested by the literature. In order to refine our research, we tested it in three different scenarios, the results of which strongly supported our hypothesis.

Based on these, it seems that in case of the Hungarian disaster management, the central government's intervention, and decision to mandate collaboration helped reduce the likelihood of frictions and facilitated the foundations of better inter-organizational structures. It seems that the clear definition of roles, with some flexibility to manage them, has also contributed greatly to the robustness of collaboration. The stereotyped image of each other that had previously existed over a very short period has evolved into a collaboration based on swift trust, partly in seeing each other's commitment and determination to help. The technique of defining a "higher order goal," for which all parties are willing to work, as recognized in conflict management, mediation and negotiation techniques, worked very well in this crisis situation, however, without the boundaries set by the government it would have been harder to manage it.

The interviews also show that to maintain trust in the long term, it is essential to ensure transparency so that the parties can agree on equal burden sharing and balanced access to financial resources.

ACKNOWLEDGEMENT

We are greatly indebted to Dr. István György prof. Gergely Deli, Dr. Péter Domokos, prof. Gyula Vastag, Dr. István Román, and Dr. Ágota Dobos for their invaluable support, and to everyone who contributed to the realization of the data collection.

APPENDIX
Diversity in Groups

Gender	Age	Organizational membership	Background and experience	Tenure
Female	41–45	Head of the District Office (belonging to the County Government Office) Kisvárda	jurist, public services competency development trainer	public administration, 20 years in leadership position
Male	41–45	Head of the District Office (belonging to the County Government Office) Fehérgyarmat	agronomist, TQM expert, administration manager	public administration for 21 years, some of it in leadership position, current tenure for one year.
Female	36–40	Head of the District Office (belonging to the County Government Office) Záhony	administration manager	20 years leadership position in public administration, current position for seven years
Male	51–55	Head of the District Office (belonging to the County Government Office) Vásárosnamény (responsible for two help points)	jurist	20 years leadership position in public administration
Female	41–45	Head of Unit in the District Office (belonging to the County Government Office) Vásárosnamény (responsible for two help points)	jurist	20 years in public administration, 12 years in mid-leader position
Male	51–55	Mayor Municipality Záhony	IT specialist	more than 20 years as IT specialist, manager in the railway sector and at the own company
Male	56–60	Mayor Municipality Beregsurány	entrepreneur, entrepreneur for the majority	24 years in this position

(continued)

Gender	Age	Organizational membership	Background and experience	Tenure
Male	61–65	Mayor Municipality Tiszabecs	trade qualification entrepreneur in agriculture and livestock farming	24 years tenure
Male	46–50	Mayor Municipality Lónya	teacher in primary school and religion teacher	3 years in the current position
Male	46–50	Mayor Municipality Barabás	mechanical engineer and entrepreneur	12 years in this position
Male	31–35	Relief Service of the Reformed Church	geographer, urban developer, working experience in the Labor Office	less than six months in this position
Male	46–50	Head of the Greek-Catholic Caritas Nyíregyháza Diocesi	jurist, criminologist, economic law, contractual law, 4 years	one-year in this position
Female	41–45	Relief Program Director, Baptist Relief Service	special education/needs teacher; 22 years at the Relief Service, experience in international emergency management; international development programs, special needs children, human traffic victims	three years in the current position
Male	35–40	Hungarian Charity Service of the Order of Malta Head of Emergency Management Department	studies in Humanities (English and Central European Studies) IMT emergency medical technician participation in EU disaster management and emergency management training programs	more than 3 years in this position 10 years in similar positions
Female	46–50	Hungarian Red Cross, Head of the Szabolcs-Szatmár-Bereg County	sociologist, geographer, rural developer, community developer, strategist, project manager	six years in this position previously project manager, mid-manager in many different projects

REFERENCES

AbouAssi, Khaldoun, Nadeen Makhlouf, and Page Whalen. "NGOs' resource capacity antecedents for partnerships." *Nonprofit Management and Leadership* 26.4 (2016): 435–451.
Arklay, Tracey. "What Happened to Queensland's Disaster Management Arrangements?: From 'Global Best Practice'to 'Unsustainable'in 3 Years." *Australian Journal of Public Administration* 74.2 (2015): 187–198.
Baker, Sarah "The Chance for Sustained Bipartisanship for Emergency Preparedness and Response," Morning Consult, April 17, 2020, Online: https://morningconsult.com/opinions/the-chance-for-sustained-bipartisanship-for-emergency-preparedness-and-response/, cited by Wolf-Fordham, Susan. "Integrating government silos: Local emergency management and public health department collaboration for emergency planning and response." *The American Review of Public Administration* 50.6–7 (2020): 560–567.
Cigler, Beverly A. "Multiorganizational, Multisector, and Multi-Community Organizations: Setting theResearch Agenda" In: *Getting Results Through Collaboration: Networks and Network Structures Public Policy Management*, ed. by M. Mandell, 50–71. Westport, CT: Quorum Books, 2001.
Curnin, Steven, and Danielle O'Hara. "Nonprofit and public sector interorganizational collaboration in disaster recovery: Lessons from the field." *Nonprofit Management and Leadership* 30.2 (2019): 277–297.
Dillenbourg, Pierre. "What do you mean by collaborative learning?." (1999): 1–19.
Fairfield, Tasha, and Andrew Charman. "A dialogue with the data: The Bayesian foundations of iterative research in qualitative social science." Perspectives on Politics 17.1 (2019): 154–167.
Fairfield, Tasha, and Andrew Charman. "Explicit Bayesian analysis for process tracing: Guidelines, opportunities, and caveats." Political Analysis 25.3 (2017): 363–380.
Fairfield, Tasha, and Andrew E. Charman. Social Inquiry and Bayesian Inference: Rethinking Qualitative Research. Cambridge University Press, 2022.
Federal Emergency Management Agency (Blanchard, & Wayne, B., & Canton, & C., Lucien & Cwiak, & L., Carol & Goss, & C., Kay & McEntire, David & A., David & Newsom, & Lee, & Selves, & D., Michael & Sorchik, & A., Eric & Stenson, & Kim, & III, Turner & Dewayne,) Principles of Emergency Management Supplement. 2007. Online: https://www.researchgate.net/publication/313441915_Principles_of_Emergency_Management_Supplement
Gray, Barbara. *Collaborating: Finding Common Ground for Multiparty Problems*.San Francisco, CA:Jossy-Bass, 1989.
Huxham, Chris, and Siv Vangen. *Managing to collaborate: The theory and practice of collaborative advantage*. Routledge, 2005
Kamensky, John M., and Thomas J. Burlin, eds. *Collaboration: Using networks and partnerships*. Rowman & Littlefield Publishers, 2004.
Mathe, Reka Zsuzsanna, and György Hajnal. "Civil-Society Organizations' Capacity Building in the Local Governmental Sector: Is It Working? A Case Study." NISPAcee Journal of Public Administration and Policy 10.1 (2017): 61–80.

Milliken, Frances J., and Luis L. Martins. "Searching for common threads: Understanding the multiple effects of diversity in organizational groups." *Academy of management review* 21.2 (1996): 402–433.

Nemec, Juraj, Mária Murray Svidroňová, and Éva Kovács. "Welfare co-production: Hungarian and Slovak reality." NISPAcee Journal of Public Administration and Policy 12.2 (2019): 195–215.

Olson, Bradley J., Satyanarayana Parayitam, and Yongjian Bao. "Strategic decision making: The effects of cognitive diversity, conflict, and trust on decision outcomes." *Journal of management* 33.2 (2007): 196–222.

Phillips, Katherine W., and Denise Lewin Loyd. "When surface and deep-level diversity collide: The effects on dissenting group members." Organizational behavior and human decision processes 99.2 (2006): 143–160.

Reynolds, Alison, and David Lewis. "Teams solve problems faster when they're more cognitively diverse." *Harvard Business Review* 30 (2017): 1–8.

Robbins, Ira P. "Lessons from Hurricane Katrina: Prison emergency preparedness as a constitutional imperative." *U. Mich. JL Reform* 42 (2008): 1.

Robbins, Stephen P, Timothy A Judge, Bruce Millett, Maree Boyle.: Organisational behaviour. Pearson Australia (2016).

Robbins, Steve, L. *What If? : Short Stories to Spark Inclusion.* John Murray Press (2019)

Roschelle, Jeremy, and Stephanie D. Teasley. "The construction of shared knowledge in collaborative problem solving." *Computer supported collaborative learning.* Springer Berlin Heidelberg, (1995).

Savage, Grant T., et al. "Stakeholder collaboration: Implications for stakeholder theory and practice." *Journal of business ethics* 96 (2010): 21–26.

Seliverstova, Yana, and Anita Pierog. "A theoretical study on global workforce diversity management, its benefits and challenges." (2021).

Thomson, Ann Marie, and James L. Perry. "Collaboration processes: Inside the black box." *Public administration review* 66 (2006): 20–32.

Vangen, Siv, and Chris Huxham. "Aiming for collaborative advantage: Challenging the concept of shared vision." *Advanced Institute of Management Research Paper* 015 (2005).

Waugh Jr, William L., and Gregory Streib. "Collaboration and leadership for effective emergency management." *Public administration review* 66 (2006): 131–140.

Williams Katherine, Y., and A. O'Reilly Charles. "Demography and diversity in organizations: A review of 40 years of research." *Research in Organizational Behavior* 20 (1998): 77–140.

Wolf-Fordham, Susan. "Integrating government silos: Local emergency management and public health department collaboration for emergency planning and response." *The American Review of Public Administration* 50.6–7 (2020): 560–567.

CHAPTER 8

EQUAL TREATMENT AND ENHANCEMENT OF DIVERSITY

The Role of Urban Regeneration Practices

Annalisa Giusti
University of Perugia

ABSTRACT

In Italy, the awareness of a renewed "territorial question" has converged in the debate on urban regeneration as a new approach to urban policies and a synthesis capable of unifying diverse needs.

In fact, it has progressively become the key concept under which the emerging problems of the territories have been brought under: reducing land consumption, reusing buildings, redeveloping parts of cities that have lost their original function, and improving the quality of life of the inhabitants.

Thus, many initiatives, sometimes very distant from each other, have been characterized as "urban regeneration," from regulations to revive the construction sector, which has always been central in the Italian economy, to some experiments in civic engagement, promoted by communities of citizens who take care of their neighbourhoods.

Such a wealth of content risks producing two effects: that urban regeneration becomes only a verbal synthesis and is incapable of directing urban regeneration processes toward goals of economic and social solidarity; that it is a cause of social segregation, generating further inequality.

For this reason, the chapter aims to describe what the Italian legal instruments for urban regeneration are and under what conditions these measures could improve equality and enhance diversities in the urban context.

TERRITORY AND INEQUALITY: THE ROLE OF URBAN REGENERATION

The territory—broadly understood to include cities, towns, and suburban areas—can be a cause of discrimination but also a privileged field that enhances diversity. An Italian academic, Bernardo Secchi (2013), an urban planner, wrote "*The City of the Rich and the City of the Poor*" to point out how urban policies can increase inequality, but also how the consolidation of this situation can hinder a new vision of urban policies.

In Italy, awareness of a renewed "territorial question" has converged in the debate on urban regeneration as a new approach to urban policies and a synthesis capable of unifying diverse needs (Giusti, 2018).

The metaphor most often used to describe the main goal of urban regeneration is the "mending of the suburbs," drawing inspiration from the program of Life-Senator and architect Renzo Piano (2016), who aspired to give a new identity to those parts of the city (not necessarily far from the centre), to reduce inequality and to ensure urban security (Secchi,1983). To achieve these goals, it would first have been necessary to redevelop areas where people in difficult conditions live (Fontanari-Piperata 2017, edited by; Di Lascio-Giglioni 2017, edited by); these measures would not have been sufficient if they were not linked to others that could improve the quality of life of the inhabitants and the socio-economic conditions of the areas concerned.

The health emergency and the ensuing general crisis caused by COVID-19 have given greater prominence to this situation because they have also increased inequality at the spatial level: a large part of the population has experienced the daily difficulties of living in places without adequate infrastructure or in uncomfortable homes (Giusti, 2021a). These are not only people living in the suburbs but also middle-class people living in neighbourhoods without efficient public services or green areas, the result of low-quality urban choices. Progressively, urban regeneration has become the key concept under which the emerging problems of the territories have been brought under: reducing land consumption, reusing buildings, redeveloping parts of cities that have lost their original function, and improving the quality of life of the inhabitants.

Thus, many initiatives, sometimes very distant from each other, have been characterized as "urban regeneration," from statutes introduced to revive the construction sector, which has always been central to the Italian economy, to some experiments in civic engagement, promoted by communities of citizens who take care of their neighbourhoods. The common denominator of these measures is to "give a second chance" to parts of cities that have lost their original function, due to the passage of time, economic and social changes, or abandonment by institutions. Finally, urban regeneration is one of the pillars of Mission No. 5 "Cohesion and Inclusion" of Italy's National Recovery and Resilience Plan (NRP) and has, at the same time, a central role in achieving the Plan's cross-cutting objectives: supporting women's empowerment, addressing gender discrimination, improving the job prospects of young people, territorial rebalancing and the development of Southern Italy and inland areas (Giusti, 2021b).

Because of this polysemous nature, urban regeneration risks becoming only an expression of effect, but it does not emerge how the practices that lead back to it can be a tool for reducing inequality. For this reason, the chapter aims to describe what the Italian legal instruments for urban regeneration are and under what conditions these measures could improve equality in the urban context. To this end, it will first describe an overview of Italian initiatives for urban regeneration, highlighting their strengths and weaknesses.

THE ITALIAN TOOLS FOR URBAN REGENERATION: THE BOTTOM-UP INITIATIVES

To describe Italian tools for urban regeneration, it is useful to distinguish between two different categories: bottom-up and top-down initiatives.

The first one has been defined as experiences of "informal public law" (Giglioni, 2017) because they were born as spontaneous initiatives of citizens who take care of their cities and, particularly, of urban common goods. Cities, in fact, became the privileged ground to experiment with the theories of commons (Bombardelli, 2016; Arena-Iaione edited by, 2017): taking care of the neighbourhood and recovering abandoned or underutilized buildings for cultural and creative initiatives were considered significant expressions of the relationship between good and fundamental rights that is on the base of that doctrine (Cortese, 2016).

All those practices have been progressively institutionalized and new administrative tools have been created (Foster-Iaione, 2022).

One of the most important was the "regulation for the collaboration between municipalities and their citizens for managing common urban goods," adopted for the first time in Bologna, in 2014. Enhancing the constitutional principle of horizontal subsidiarity (Arena, 2017), this regulation promotes a model of "shared administration," where citizens and Municipalities collaborate and take care of urban commons according to the contents of a specific pact, called "pacts of collaboration." These pacts can have different objects (Chirulli-Iaione edited by, 2018), but "urban regeneration" is their common denominator. Taking care of urban spaces, reusing abandoned buildings, or organizing social activities (for children or elderly people, for example) are all considered different ways to use urban commons and to improve the conditions of people who live in the interested parts of the cities.

Another important practice took place in the City of Naples (Masella, 2018), that is the first city in Italy to establish a Department of Common Goods to enhance forms of heritage use for the preeminent collective interest. In 2011, the Municipal Statute was amended and the legal category of common good was introduced among the goals, objectives and fundamental values of the City of Naples. Many disused buildings that have been firstly spontaneously occupied by groups of citizens for cultural and social activities, often for poor and underprivileged people, have been declared "common goods," where the collective use of the space is regulated by participative democracy instruments. Initial informal experiences became formal: as of 2015, the City of Naples took note of the "Community Civic Use Statements" of the former Filangieri Nursery School (in Italian, *ex Asilo*), of Villa Medusa, the Liberated Garden (in Italian, *Il Giardino Liberato*), former Lido Pola (in Italian, *ex Lido Polo*), former OPG (in Italian, *ex OPG*), Liberated Scugnizzo (in Italian, *Lo scugnizzo liberato*), and Saint Faith Liberated (in Italian, Santa Fede Liberata).

Initiatives for shared administration have also been gradually formalized: more than 200 Italian municipalities have adopted regulations (as you can read at www.labsus.org); the Lazio region has also introduced a law (Lazio regional law, n. 10/2019) governing such instruments. In addition, State (art. 21 *quarter* D.P.R. 380/2001) and regional laws (for example: Emilia Romagna regional law n.24/2017 or Veneto regional law n. 14/2017) currently regulate one of the typical practices of shared administration, namely the temporary use of unused buildings for economic, social, cultural or environmental recovery (Torelli, 2021).

URBAN REGENERATION IN STATE BUILDING REGULATIONS AND REGIONAL LEGISLATION

The "top-down" instruments for urban regeneration are a very broad category, because it includes different tools, that have different aims.

The real estate crisis of 2008 and the consequent urgency to relaunch the building activity sector, transformed urban regeneration into a strategy for the economic recovery of the Country. So, it has become one of the principles that have inspired some of the most important decrees adopted to increase Italian competitiveness, to "unlock" public and private constructions (Decree law n. 32/2019 converted to law no. 55/2019), and, finally, to recover the national economic situation after the pandemic crisis caused by Sars COVID-19 virus (Decree law n. 76/2020 converted to law no. 120/2020).

The significance of building activity has caused a general phenomenon of identification between urban regeneration and the various interventions aimed at reusing, renovating or upgrading existing buildings, which Italian building legislation regulates. In addition, some initiatives developed to encourage the start of private works have been considered urban regeneration tools: this is the case of the "110 percent super bonus" (Decree law n. 34/2020 converted to law no. 1 17 77/2020) which raises to 110 percent the rate of deduction of expenses incurred for energy efficiency works (also including demolition and reconstruction), earthquake interventions and similar renovation initiatives. Other similar measures, such as the "facade bonus" (Law no.190/2019), for the renovation of building facades in historic downtowns or the "eco-bonus" (for energy efficiency works), have also been qualified as urban regeneration.

The latitude of this category has created an overlay between the tools and the purposes of urban regeneration, which causes the risk of its loss of identity. Despite building activity being central in every process of urban regeneration, not all the renewal or re-use works can be qualified as such.

Another important part of urban regeneration tools is regulated by regional legislation (Stella Richter 2019, edited by ; Id 2021, edited by).

Under Article 117 of the Italian Constitution, legislative power belongs to both the State and the Regions; this article enumerates which matters belong to the exclusive legislative power of the State and which are those shared with the Regions, of which it establishes the fundamental principles. Urban regeneration falls under the broad subject of "land-use planning," which is shared by the State and the Regions: for this reason, many Regions have regulated "urban regeneration" within the general framework of State law. In fact, there is still no State law on urban regeneration, and the Regions have been forerunners of central land-related issues.

Although the regional context is varied, there are some frequent themes that can be traced back to urban regeneration. Many statutes see urban regeneration as a strategic alternative to land consumption: the priority is to avoid new construction and reuse existing ones. The concrete initiatives for urban regeneration are focused on degraded areas, under different points: urban, economic, cultural, or social; they are realized by implementing plans, often based on an agreement by privates and administration. To encourage private interventions, these laws often introduce some exceptions to the general urban discipline; many of them, finally, provide for new forms of participation, with the specific purpose of realizing projects shared with the inhabitants.

URBAN REGENERATION IN MEASURES FOR ECONOMIC AND SOCIAL COHESION

The boundaries of urban regeneration have been best delimited by the policy instruments for measures of economic and social cohesion.

Among these, some of the most important are the initiatives aimed at "mending suburbs," the so-called, in Italian, "Bando Periferie." The first one was published in 2017 and it was directly inspired by the just-mentioned "mending of the suburbs" of Mr. Renzo Piano (Boscolo, 2020). It was an extraordinary program for the "urban regeneration and safety of the suburbs of the cities" and it created a sort of competition between municipalities (in particular, those that Italian legislation identifies as "provincial capitals" or "metropolitan cities," thus with a large territorial extension and a substantial number of inhabitants) that were to submit projects that a State Committee would have to evaluate. These proposals could have had different objectives—redeveloping public spaces, improving urban decor, enhancing urban services—but, finally, they should have been able to give greater security to the areas involved and reduce inequalities. The short time available for municipalities to submit projects and the limited sums available (not enough for all applicants) led to a different outcome than expected. Most municipalities submitted projects that were ready to be implemented, residents were not involved in the designs, and private investors instead played a significant role: if they had contributed at least 25 percent of the amount, the project could have received the maximum score and had a better chance of success than others.

Although this program has had many problems, largely caused by the inability of public administrations to manage projects, this experience has been repeated, in a more structured way, in 2020. The financial law for 2020 (art. 1, par. 43, Law n. 160/2019) has provided for the period from 2021 to 2034 increasing amounts for urban regeneration (150 million of Euro for 2021, 250 millions of Euro for 2022, 550 millions of Euro for each year for 2023 and 2024, 700 millions of Euro for each year from 2025 to 2034). This is an important difference from the first call, which was an episodic experience and excluded the planning that is necessary to develop a serious strategy for the territories that must be regenerated. Another important difference concerns the contents. Projects must be included in the ordinary public works program to be approved by the municipalities every three years and updated every year; this provision is important to avoid these sums being used for projects that have "in the drawer" and have no real urban regeneration goals. In addition, this call is specifically focused on social goals: one of the elements that give a higher score is the "rate of social and material vulnerability" calculated by the Italian Statistical Institute. The new "suburban call" aims to reduce inequalities through a massive program that, of course, gives building interventions a central role, but considers them a driver for an additional goal, which is to reduce the social and economic distance from the inhabitants of the different parts of the Municipality. More schools, a better quality of public services, adequate public spaces, and modern infrastructures can be solid contributions to urban regeneration to ensure equal treatment and eliminate inequalities.

In order to give effect to the programme, the Decree includes some contents useful for measuring the results and verifying whether all the objectives have been achieved. There is a monitoring system for financed projects and severe administrative control to ensure their implementation.

The financial law for 2020 has also introduced an urban regeneration programme focused on the housing issue. It is the Innovative Programme for housing Quality, in Italian *Programma Innovativo per la Qualità dell'Abitare* (Italian acronym P.IN.QU.A.) that assigns funds to the Municipalities that apply for projects that aim to reduce housing discomfort, with specific attention to suburbs. These projects must be drawn up according to specific criteria: sustainability, soil consumption reduction, densification, intelligent—inclusive and sustainable cities (smart cities). Special attention is also given to the ability to involve residents in the participatory design of interventions.

Both programs P.IN.QU.A and "*Bando Periferie*" have been incorporated into the Italian NRP, whose Mission No. 5, dedicated to "inclusion and cohesion," in component No. 2.2. deals with "urban regeneration and social housing." The measures in Mission No. 5, component No. 2, involve municipalities and metropolitan cities, where conditions of social distress or vulnerability are most widespread. The component includes three investment lines (inv.), which have different but related objects:

- inv. 1: these sums are allocated to municipalities with more than 15000 inhabitants to develop projects that reduce situations of marginalization and social degradation and improve the urban décor and the quality of the social—economic environment
- inv. 2: this investment is named "Urban Integrated Plans," in Italian "*Piani Urbani Integrati*" and it promotes participatory planning processes in Metropolitan cities; these initiatives start from the redevelopment of parts of cities but aim to increase their value by improving services for their inhabitants and encouraging new activities:

that is why these processes must be participatory and must be based on a continuous dialogue between public and private actors
- inv. 3: realizes the development of an innovative housing program from public housing. Again, the starting point is the redevelopment of the existing housing stock; it also provides for the construction of new houses. The added value of the projects is the experimentation with a new form of housing, in which people share common spaces, co-manage houses and try to implement a supportive lifestyle.

Independently of individual measures, the Italian NRP develops a clear strategy for urban regeneration. The primary objective is to recover urban areas or existing buildings so that they become a vehicle for promoting economic, cultural and social activities, which could improve the quality of life of the inhabitants. To this end, urban regeneration initiatives mainly involve the so-called "public city," namely public areas, public buildings, public services and infrastructure. Public administrations have the direction of the program, because they must identify the needs of communities, the objectives to achieve and guide private initiatives. Private individuals can be involved in different ways, from co-design to project co-financing: in the latter case, the amount cannot exceed 30%.

The first two tranches of projects were approved in 2021 and 2022 and are to be completed by 31 March 2026: by that date, the municipalities that have been awarded the funds must transmit the acceptance certificate, which demonstrates the completion of the work and its perfect execution. The projects have yet to be implemented and it is too early to try to take stock of what has been planned and what has been done and to verify if urban regeneration practices can really be an instrument to overcome or reduce inequalities. Of course, it is considered a central achievement, as evidenced by the importance given to the rate of social and material vulnerability.

As mentioned, these measures are essential to enhance the transversal goal of the plan: supporting women's empowerment, facing gender discrimination, improving the job perspective of young people, territorial rebalancing and South Italy and inner areas development.

Some brief examples can explain the transversal relevance of these measures.

One of the planned urban regeneration interventions is the construction of new kindergartens: if their number increases, women do not have to leave their jobs to be with their children and women's employment grows.

Building new schools or sports facilities improves the environment in which young people live, promotes their social inclusion and helps prevent the crime phenomena often prevalent in the suburbs.

Urban regeneration of southern Italian areas, through the construction of new infrastructure and the redevelopment of degraded urban areas, can be useful in reducing the gap between northern and southern Italy, because it creates more favourable conditions for inhabitants, encourages young people to stay where they were born and avoids mass urbanization processes (and the abandonment of inland areas).

Under What Conditions Urban Regeneration Can Generate Inequality

The analysis of the different legal instruments for urban regeneration showed the richness of the current debate, and the centrality of the topic, but also the risk that it will lose its identity and remain just a formula without real meaning (Cartei, 2022).

This is not just a problem of definition: grasping its essential core is crucial to understanding how these urban policies can ensure equality of treatment and value diversity.

It could happen if every intervention that includes building renovation or urban rehabilitation and has as its goal the reduction of land consumption is qualified as urban regeneration. Their overlap not only doesn't evidence the characteristics of urban regeneration but also risks undermining its objectives.

In fact, if every process of urban redevelopment is treated in the same way there are no differences between the interventions in cities areas that could be more attractive and those in "suburbs," using this expression to identify the areas, not necessarily far from the centre, that have low-quality services, infrastructure deficit and economic distress. This means that these latter parts of the city could remain in such a situation and also become the places to which residents of neighbourhoods that have increased in value as a result of redevelopment and have become too expensive for the people who used to live there are forced to move.

This is what has been described as gentrification (Glass 1964), the phenomenon whereby the original inhabitants have been excluded because of the high cost of the renovated buildings and have to move to where life is less expensive.

That situation of "urban substitution" causes new segregation: people who can pay for houses in the renovated parts of cities, reasonably of the same social class, replace the original ones, eliminating any social, political, and ethnic differences. Urban regeneration doesn't appear as a tool for improving territorial cohesion and enhancing diversities, but risks becoming the way to a new "city of the rich and city of poor."

To avoid these consequences, it is necessary to focus on what elements give urban regeneration its own characterization.

Under What Conditions Urban Regeneration Can Ensure Equal Treatment and Enhance Diversities

Urban regeneration practices in the Italian experience are not new in the field of urban planning studies, both legal and technical: we can recall the recovery plans introduced in 1978 or the "*contratti di quartiere*," Italian for "neighbourhood contracts" developed in 1998. The former aimed to overcome urban decay by recovering the existing urban and built heritage; the latter considered physical interventions in urban areas, public or private construction as the vehicle to promote the economic and social reactivation of critical areas of cities.

Bottom-up initiatives, on the other hand, are heirs to the tradition of Italian volunteering, currently enhanced by the constitutionalization (art. 118 Cost.) of the principle of horizontal subsidiarity.

The polysemic nature of urban regeneration is its peculiarity; the wealth of legal and technical tools is its strength and allows for a combination of different actions, from bottom-up to top-down.

Among the practices reviewed, therefore, it is not necessary to select which can be traced back to it and which cannot. Instead, we need to identify what characteristic should guide the coordination of all these initiatives and enable urban regeneration to take on an autonomous heuristic value.

The bottom-up practices and the various economic and social cohesion measures examined have shown that, in these cases, the concrete public interest that should be realized is not only in governing the construction sector; urban and physical transformations aim at economic and social cohesion and must be able to reduce inequalities. Frequently, the interested urban areas are those where middle classes live, that often have law quality services, infrastructure deficit. These are spaces that need to be connected to the city, giving them an identity; they need to be mended indeed, to avoid segregation on a geographical basis.

Going more concrete, we can give an example of what the different factors that generate inequality might be. These are cross-cutting indicators: housing conditions, educational attainment, labour market participation, economic conditions, family structures, also with reference to welfare problems related to the aging population. Many of these indicators have a higher rate for immigrants or, more generally, for people of specific ethnicities; others are higher for women or young people. A large proportion of them concerns the elderly.

In all these cases, building interventions are key elements of urban regeneration processes, both public and private, but they cannot be considered the only vehicle for urban regeneration if they do not also have a social value, if they are not able to reduce spatial inequalities, to improve the social and environmental context in which they are implemented. Otherwise, it is simply renovating a building or reusing it for a different purpose, but it is not urban regeneration.

The reorientation of urban regeneration allows an initial distinction to be made.

First of all, not all of today's urban planning can be summarized in urban regeneration, but only that part that also considers territories as a tool to reduce inequalities, to guarantee equal dignity to citizens, beyond the places where they live.

Another part of it deals with the governance of the built environment, albeit in a "new relationship between territorial communities and their surrounding environment" (according to Italian Constitutional Court, decision Oct. 6, 2021 No. 202), inspired by the principles of sustainable development, no more land consumption and reuse of the existing.

Those profiles do not conflict with each other, but they should not be overlapped and equally managed.

From this distinction comes the need to use some of the urban regeneration tools we have discussed differently.

We can give a few examples, starting with the principle of reducing land consumption.

Regional laws often introduce it as a general statement, without specifying implementation criteria. Some of them list when it is allowed (for example, for urban redevelopment purposes) or set a percentage of new land to be consumed that each municipality has available.

If urban regeneration goals allow for new land consumption, the principle must be interpreted to enhance its intergenerational solidarity component and allow new construction or infrastructure only if it is necessary to overcome inequality. It means, for example, overcoming a frequent Italian practice of building affordable housing in marginal areas of cities, with low market value, and insufficient or low-quality infrastructure. Such environmental sacrifices must be able to guarantee the quality of life.

If we read this statement through the lens of administrative principles, it is an application to urban policies of the principle of proportionality (Galetta 2019). And it could also be the criterion for modulating the application of some regional law provisions that introduce special and derogatory discipline to incentivize private regeneration initiatives.

The reference is to those provisions of exemption from the payment of fees related to construction activities or other obligations that correspond to the increased urban load generated by regeneration interventions. Since these sums are necessary for the functioning of the city, such facilities should be applied not to all redevelopment practices, but only to those in the least attractive parts of cities. The presence of lower charges should direct private investment to the less attractive parts of cities, encouraging urban regeneration processes. On the contrary, a blanket application could become just a tool to give more value to private rents, without a positive social effect.

FINAL REMARKS

Rediscovering the essential core of urban regeneration has been central to understanding how urban policies, while seemingly different from the past, can increase spatial inequalities. It has shown, in fact, that if every urban process that includes redevelopment practices is considered urban regeneration, it can generate effects opposite to those for which it was created. To avoid this, it is not necessary (and would also be unrealistic) to think that all urban practices should aim at urban regeneration goals. On the contrary, it is necessary for administrations to differentiate individual actions and coordinate urban regeneration goals in governing the urban transformation.

Using urban regeneration tools well and balancing the different objectives of urban practices is the most difficult and, at the same time, the most demanding challenge for administrations (Stella Richter, 2016).

It means that, first of all, they must regain ownership of urban planning procedures and the direction of choices affecting the territories, which for many years have been tied only to the needs of the market and the necessity to find resources for the management of the city, especially from private individuals. Second, there is a need for a different approach to urban issues, capable of selecting different interests, balancing them, and devising solutions that can avoid the main mistakes of the past, which can be summarized as high endowment differentials between different parts of the city, spatial segregation, enhancement of private rents, and lack of attention to environmental issues.

Last but not least, administrations must regain technical expertise and return to making good projects.

Alongside expert knowledge, there is also a need for widespread knowledge, which only participatory techniques can guarantee. They should be new ways of involving inhabitants, enabling them to understand projects, collaborate in their definition, and present and discuss alternatives.

What has opened is a fruitful season for Italy, in which it will be possible to experiment with this different approach to urban policies, also thanks to the great availability of resources, coming from the NPR. In fact, the programme establishes specific objectives that may really be gained only if the projects are able to have social effects.

We can give an example. The Italian NPR invests in the construction of sports facilities: the spread of sports culture can develop the resilience of the most vulnerable people; the creation of urban parks can combine sports and entertainment activities, and the whole community will benefit.

To achieve the goals of the plan, therefore, it is not enough just to implement the facilities.

The same example can be made with interventions involving public buildings, public streets or squares: it is not enough to renovate existing buildings or areas. Instead, these interventions should be able to create a new identity for those areas, because they can become new common spaces where people meet and recognize themselves as an integral part of that area. With this new infrastructure, neighbourhoods would become safer (Simonati, 2019), and people would return to spend their time there, and this would cause a positive proactive effect.

Finally, these interventions will have to be reconciled and coordinated with the "ordinary" governance of urban transformation, with the aim of not operating by separate parts but reconnecting and, finally, mending the different souls of the city.

If the projects succeed in achieving their goals, they will be the best demonstration of how urban policies can also be an effective vehicle for valuing diversity and ensuring equal treatment.

They will also be an effective stimulus so that administrations, once these extraordinary resources are finished, will be able to differentiate strategies for governing urban transformations according to the aforementioned guideline of proportionality, truly balancing the different interests present on the territory and thus restoring urban regeneration its identity traits, beyond a mere statement of principle.

REFERENCES

Arena, G., & Iaione, C. (Eds.). L'età della condivisione, Roma, 2017.
Arena G., Democrazia partecipativa e amministrazione condivisa, in A. Valastro (edited by), Le regole locali della democrazia partecipativa. Tendenze e prospettive dei regolamenti comunali, Naples, 2016, 236.
Bombardelli M. (edited by), Prendersi cura dei beni comuni per uscire dalla crisi. Nuove risorse e nuovi modelli di amministrazione, Naple, 2016.
Boscolo E., Le periferie e i fallimenti dell'urbanistica italiana, in M. Immordino, G. De Giorgi Cezzi, N. Gullo e M. Brocca (edited by), Periferie e diritti fondamentali, Naples, 2020.
Cartei G. F., Note critiche a margine di un disegno di legge in materia di rigenerazione urbana, in Munus, 1, 2022, 133.
Chirulli P.- Iaione C. (edited by), La co-città. Diritto urbano e politiche pubbliche per i beni comuni e la rigenerazione urbana, Naples, 2018.
Cortese F., Che cosa sono i beni comuni?, in Bombardelli M. (edited by), Prendersi cura dei beni comuni per uscire dalla crisi. Nuove risorse e nuovi modelli di amministrazione, Naple, 2016, 37.
Di Lascio F., & Giglioni F. (edited by), La rigenerazione di beni e spazi urbani. Contributo al diritto delle città. Bologna, 2017.

Fontanari E., & Piperata G. (edited by), Agenda RE-CYCLE. Proposte per reinventare la città, Bologna, 2017.
Foster S., & Iaione C., Co-cities. Innovative Transitions toward Just and Self-Sustaining Communities., The MIT Press, 2022.
Galetta Diana-Urania, Il principio di proporzionalità fra diritto nazionale e diritto europeo (e con uno sguardo anche al di là dei confini dell'Unione Europea), in Riv.it.dir.pub.com., 2019, 6, 903.
Giglioni F., Order Without Law In The Experience Of Italian Cities, in IJPL, 2017, 2, 2017, 291.
Giusti A., La rigenerazione urbana come strategia di ripresa e resilienza, in Munus, 2, 2021, 329.
Giusti A., La rigenerazione urbana fra consolidamento dei paradigmi e nuove contingenze, in Dir.amm., 2, 2021, 439.
Giusti A., La rigenerazione urbana. Temi, questioni e approcci nell'urbanistica di nuova generazione, Napoli, 2018.
Glass R., London: Aspects of Change, edited by Centre for Urban Studies, London 1964
Labsus.org, accessed in February 2023.
Masella N., Politiche urbane e strumenti per la promozione degli usi civici: il caso studio di Napoli, in Chirulli P.- Iaione C. (edited by), La co-città. Diritto urbano e politiche pubbliche per i beni comuni e la rigenerazione urbana, Naples, 2018, 297.
Piano R., Il rammendo delle periferie, in Il sole 24 ore, 24.01.2016.
Secchi B., Cucire e Legare, in Casabella, n.490, 1983.
Secchi B., La città dei ricchi e la città dei poveri, Bari, 2013.
Simonati A., Rigenerazione urbana, politiche di sicurezza e governo del territorio: quale ruolo per la cittadinanza?, in Riv. giur. ed., 2019, 1, 31.
Stella Richter P. (edited by), La nuova urbanistica regionale, Milan, 2021.
Stella Richter P. (edited by), Verso le leggi regionali di IV generazione, Milan, 2019.
Stella Richter P., Profili funzionali dell'urbanistica, Naples, 2016 reprint.
Torelli G., Le ultime frontiere del recupero e della valorizzazione del patrimonio urbano: gli usi temporanei, in Dir. amm., 2, 2021, 475.

SECTION III

DIVERSITY AND EQUAL TREATMENT
IN THE EDUCATIONAL SYSTEM

CHAPTER 9

DIVERSITY AND DIVERSITY MANAGEMENT AT AUSTRIAN UNIVERSITIES

Esther Happacher
University of Innsbruck

Lamiss Khakzadeh
University of Innsbruck

Alexandra Weiss
University of Innsbruck

ABSTRACT

This chapter outlines the current state of diversity management at Austrian Universities. For this purpose, it will give an overview of the most important provisions of the Austrian legal system regarding equality and non-discrimination in general. Furthermore, it will refer to the University of Innsbruck and give concrete examples of measures promoting Diversity and Diversity management.

During the last decades, diversity and diversity management have become increasingly the subject of legal, managerial and other reflections.

To discuss what diversity management is about we first need to define the meaning of diversity. We understand it to refer to diversity by gender, age, ethnicity, religion, culture, social origins, disabilities, social background... Frequently, more than one dimension applies to the same case, therefore underlining the intersectional aspect of diversity. A central aspect in dealing with diversity is equal treatment and non-discrimination to ensure equality. Especially the topics of equality and non-discrimination concerning gender have been in the focus of the legislator and they reflect in legal standards set out for administrations as much as for private actors. Diversity management supports compliance with these standards: "Diversity Management is an intersectional approach to a targeted perception, use and promotion of plurality in social systems as e.g., profit and non-profit organisations, public organisations and groups and teams. The aim of Diversity Management is to optimize the use of staff's competences and resources by promoting equality of opportunity and a professional handling of diversity."[1]

As a first step, we would like to outline the most important provisions of the Austrian legal system regarding equality and non-discrimination in general, as they are the basis for the development of diversity management measures. As a second step, specific provisions regarding Austrian universities will be illustrated, putting the focus on diversity and diversity management. By referring to the University of Innsbruck, examples of initiatives of promoting Diversity and Diversity management will be given. Short remarks conclude the contribution.

EQUALITY AND NON-DISCRIMINATION—AN OVERVIEW ON THE AUSTRIAN LEGAL SYSTEM

International and European Level

In 1948 the General Assembly of the UN adopted the Universal Declaration of Human Rights. In regard to equal treatment several provisions are of particular interest: Article 2 states that all rights and freedoms set forth in this Declaration apply to any person "without distinction of any kind, such as race, colour, sex, language, religion, political or other opinion, national or social origin, property, birth or other status." Supplementary, Article 7 states that all humans "are equal before the law and are entitled without any discrimination to equal protection of the law." Furthermore, all "are entitled to equal protection against any discrimination in violation of this Declaration and against any incitement to such discrimination.."

In 1958 Austria joined the European Convention on Human Rights. In Austria this treaty has a very particular legal status: it is a law of constitutional rank.[2] Article 14 ECHR contains an accessory prohibition of discrimination, according to which the "enjoyment of the rights and freedoms set forth in this Convention shall be secured without discrimination on any ground such as sex, race, colour, language, religion, political or other opinion, national or social origin, association with a national minority, property, birth or other status." These different grounds for discrimination are non-exhaustive.[3] Due to its accessory character Article 14 does not guarantee a general principle of equality but can only be applied in connection with another right laid down in the ECHR.[4]

Protocol No 12 to the ECHR enshrines a general prohibition of discrimination: Article 1 prohibits discrimination irrespective of the rights and freedoms laid down in the European convention on Human Rights.[5] Austria signed this Protocol in 2000, it has, however, not been ratified yet.

Beside the ECHR there are several UN-Treaties in regard to equality and anti-discrimination. Compared to the ECHR they do however differ in their legal status: most of them are not self-executing and in addition, most of them do not have constitutional rank but only the status of a simple national law.

Several of these UN-Treaties have particular relevance for questions of equality. This is e.g., the case with the International Convention on the Elimination of All Forms of Racial Discrimination. Austria ratified this treaty in 1972.

Furthermore, the UN Convention on the Rights of Persons with Disabilities has to be named. In Austria it entered into force in 2008 and it involves a set of rules opposing discrimination against people with disabilities. Article 4 lays down a general obligation: The contracting States have "to ensure and promote the full realization of all human rights and fundamental freedoms for all persons with disabilities without discrimination of any kind on the basis of disability."

The UN Convention on the Rights of Women of 1979—Austria ratified this Convention in 1982—focuses on the elimination of discrimination against women and obliges the contracting states to take, inter alia, legislative measures (Article 2).

When we turn to European Union law there is of course one regulation that is of particular importance in regard to equality and diversity: this is the Charter of Fundamental Rights which entered into force in 2009. According to Article 20 everyone "is equal before the law." This general principle of equality[6] is complemented by specific prohibitions of discrimination laid down in Article 21: §1 prohibits any "discrimination based on any ground such as sex, race, colour, ethnic or social origin, genetic features, language, religion or belief, political or any other opinion, membership of a national minority, property, birth, disability, age or sexual orientation." This list of discrimination grounds is non-exhaustive ("such as"). Due to the objectives of the European Union Article 21 §2 enshrines a specific prohibition of discrimination on grounds of nationality.[7] Beside this general principle of non-discrimination the Charter of Fundamental Rights of the European

Union contains also specific provisions. Article 23 safeguards the equality of men and women, Article 26 ensures the rights of disabled persons.

In addition, EU-Directives have been issued that relate to specific subject areas such as the Council Directive 2000/78/EC of 27 November 2000 establishing a general framework for equal treatment in employment and occupation, the Directive 2000/43/EC of 29 June 2000 implementing the principle of equal treatment between persons irrespective of racial or ethnic origin and the Directive 2004/113/EC of 13 December 2004 implementing the principle of equal treatment between men and women in access to and supply of goods and services.

National Level

Regarding the national Austrian law first of all the "principle of equality"—as it is enshrined in the constitution—has to be named. Its legal basis can be found in two provisions: First it is laid down in Article 2 Staatsgrundgesetz, which dates back to 1867. Secondly, it is guaranteed in Article 7 Bundes-Verfassungsgesetz (B-VG, Federal Constitution). Both provisions guarantee a general principle of equality:[8] all citizens are equal before the law.

These provisions apply to Austrian citizens and—according to the principle of non-discrimination—also to EU- and EEA-citizens.[9]

In order to implement the International Convention on the Elimination of All Forms of Racial Discrimination Austria implemented a constitutional law, namely the BVG zur Durchführung des Internationalen Übereinkommens über die Beseitigung aller Formen rassischer Diskriminierung (Constitutional Law for the Implementation of the International Convention on the Elimination of All Forms of Racial Discrimination). Art I extends the general principle of equality to persons who are neither Austrian nor EU-/EEA-citizens.[10]

In addition to the general principle of equality Article 7 §1 B-VG also enshrines specific prohibitions of discrimination: privileges based upon birth, sex, estate, class or religion are prohibited. Furthermore it explicitly prohibits discrimination of persons with disabilities. Therefore the State (Bund, Länder and municipalities) commits itself to ensuring the equal treatment of disabled and non-disabled persons in all spheres of everyday life.

In addition there are provisions concerning gender: according to Article 7 §2 the State (Bund, Länder and municipalities) acknowledges gender-equality. Measures that promote factual equality of women and men, in particular by eliminating actually existing inequalities, are expressly permitted. Besides, gender-equality also has to be secured when it comes to budgeting (Article 13 §3 B-VG).

Subordinate to constitutional law there are of course numerous legal provisions to secure non-discrimination. Examples include the Bundes-Gleichbehandlungsgesetz[11] (Federal Equal Opportunities Act) and the Gleichbehandlungsgesetz (Equal Opportunities Act) which apply to employment relationships. In addition there is the Bundes-Behindertengleichstellungsgesetz[12] (Federal Disability Equality Act), which aims at eliminating and preventing discrimination against people with disabilities (§1).

THE UNIVERSITIES ACT 2002

In 2002, a comprehensive reform of the Austrian university system took place by the Universities Act 2002.[13] This Federal law specifies the goals, the guiding principles and the tasks for the Austrian universities. Among the provisions, several references to equality can be detected. Firstly, §1 para. 1 Universities Act 2002 sees the "... helping a society in transition to master the challenges it faces in a humane and gender-equal fashion" as one of the goals of the Austrian Universities.[14] Among the guiding principle defined by §2 Universities Act 2000 "equality of the sexes; equality of social opportunity; special attention to the needs of the handicapped" 8§2 n.9) are set out. With regard to tasks, §3 n.9 Universities Act 2002 enumerates "gender equality, and the advancement of women" amidst the functions of Austrian Universities. Therefore, the Universities Act 2002 underlines not only gender equality, but as well equality relating to other dimensions of diversity.

Nonetheless, the element of gender equality is the most prominent. §41 Universities Act 2002 obliges Universities to work towards a balanced representation of men and women, by reaching and maintaining a 50% quota of women in all categories, functions and organisation units.[15] This includes promoting the career advancement of women. These obligations regard all bodies or organs responsible for the recruitment process, e.g., heads of department, deans or members of the Rectorate responsible for Human Resources. In addition, the Federal Equal Opportunities Act applies to the universities, prohibiting any discrimination based on gender, ethnic origin, religion or political opinion, age or sexual orientation in relation with employment or training at university (§44 Universities Act 2002). Another measure to ensure gender equality is the 50% quota of women in collegial bodies and in electable positions in the election proposals, e.g., candidate lists for the Academic Senate (§20a Universities Act 2002). The control of the fulfilment of these objectives is vested in the Working Group on Equal Opportunities (§42 para. 8 a–d Universities Act 2002).

The Working Group on Equal Opportunities (first introduced in 1991) is regulated in §42 Universities Act 2002[16] and is "responsible for combating gender discrimination as well as discrimination on the basis of ethnicity, religion or conviction, age, or sexual orientation by university governing bodies and for advising and supporting the university's members and governing bodies in connection with these issues." In particular, the Working Group controls all texts of advertisement for posts, the invitations of candidates and the candidates interviewed (§42 para. 6 Universities Act 2002). The Working Group on Equal Opportunities has the right to invoke the decision of an arbitration board, if it "has reason to believe that a decision made by a university governing body reflects a discrimination against a person on the basis of gender, ethnicity, religion or conviction, age, or sexual orientation" (§42 para. 8). Is the decision found to be discriminating, it is void (§43 para. 6 Universities Act 2002). Therefore, this independent body, whose members come from all groups represented at the university (professors, researchers, administrative personnel, students) is a main element in the fight against discrimination and for diversity (with exception of people with handicap[17]).

Two compulsory elements of each University Statute play an important role in enhancing diversity in the academia: the Affirmative Action Plan for Women and the Equal Opportunities Plan. The Affirmative Action Plan (§§20b and 44 Universities Act 2002[18]) sets out more detailed measures to implement the aforementioned duty to promote women, inter alia by promoting measures to create awareness about work–life reconciliation issues or provisions on gender mainstreaming and incentive systems in budgeting. The Equal Opportunities Plan (§20b Universities Act 2002) aims to render all dimensions of equality more visible, therefore promoting diversity as a task and an objective of the whole university. The Equal Opportunities Plan is closely linked to the Affermative Action Plan for Women. Therefore, some Universities have merged both compulsory elements and apply all instruments intended for the advancement of women also in the interests of an anti-discriminatory, diversity-promoting and equality-promoting policy.[19]

On a more general level, the Austrian National Development Plan for Public Universities (GUEP) 2022–2027[20] declares gender equality, diversity und social inclusion as a systemic goal, including promotion of competencies in the field of gender and diversity.[21] The GUEP constitutes the framework for the Performance Agreements each university has to negotiate on a three-year basis with the Federal Ministry for Science and Research in accordance with §13 Universities Act 2002. The scope of the Performance Agreement is to define the public funding by the Federal Government to enact the aims set out by the Universities Act. Among them, we find enhancing social diversity and inclusion and increasing the percentage of women in leadership positions (§13 para. 1 g Universities Act 2002). Therefore, these Agreements offer an efficient tool to the Ministry for pursuing specific aims as e.g., the compatibility of child care and academic careers, promoting women in leadership positions and female junior researchers, social permeability, inclusion of underrepresented groups, gender mainstreaming and diversity management.[22] Another governance tool is the Ministerial Report on the Universities to the National Council (§11 Universities Act 2002).[23] It has to relate on the achievements in the sector of Gender equality as well as in Diversity management insofar as "Achieving equal opportunities and educational equity in science and research goes beyond the issue of gender: Proactive diversity management allows universities to harness the diversity of students and staff as an opportunity and resource as they compete in the higher education sector."[24] Therefore, it monitors the progress made in the field of diversity management.

In addition, within the framework set out by the Austrian National Development Plan for Public Universities, each University has to elaborate its own Development Plan 8§13 b Universities Act 20002). Therefore, all Development plans contain references to diversity and gender mainstreaming, some refer to these topics in more general terms or by detailing a number of projects, means and structures.

As far as the social dimension of higher education is concerned, since 2001 this topic was given more attention within the framework of the Bologna-Process, In addition, in 2013 the Council of the European Union invited its Member States in its Conclusions on the social dimension of higher education to "adopt national objectives which are aimed at increasing the access, participation and completion rates of under-represented and disadvantaged groups in higher education, with a view to progressing towards the Bologna Process goal that the student body entering, participating in and completing higher education at all levels should reflect the diversity of Member States' populations."[25] The Austrian Strategy set out in 2017 aims to create a variety of learning opportunities for different students, to increase the freedom to choose between the different educational sectors, to achieve a balance between the sexes and to promote access and degree for disadvantaged groups.[26]

Another tool concerning Diversity management has to be mentioned. Since 2016, the Federal Ministry for Research and Science hands out the "Diversitas Award" for projects regarding diversity and equality, thereby promoting best practices at Austrian Universities raising the awareness on this topic.[27] Among the award-winning projects are "You've got talent!", a checklist developed by the Technical University of Graz on diversity in teaching with simple questions and suggestions how to consider the dimensions of diversity in teaching. Another award was attributed to the Center for Interdisciplinary Gender Studies at Innsbruck University which brings together members from different faculties and external organisations in research on topics related to women, gender, feminist and queer research.

DIVERSITY MANAGEMENT AT INNSBRUCK UNIVERSITY

In accordance with the indications on the national level, the governance documents of the University of Innsbruck implement a diversity management based on the concept of intersectionality. Recently, both the Development Plan 2022–2027[28] and the Performance Agreement 2022–2024[29] dedicate sections to Diversity management, picking up on the strategy already laid down in the Development Plan 2019–2021 and the Performance Agreement 2018–2021. In particular, the Development Plan focus on social inclusion, gender and enhancing knowledge and awareness in diversity.[30] The Performance Agreement puts the focus on equality in all diversity dimensions.[31]

In addition to the aforementioned instruments, the University of Innsbruck is dedicating more attention to Diversity and to Diversity Management. In Spring 2017 a "Steering Group Diversity Management" coordinated by the Unit of Equality and Gender Studies was set up, using its expertise in the field of equal treatment and gender. The group encompasses the members of the Rectorate responsible for Human Resources and for Teaching and Students as well as experts stemming from central administrative units as Human Resources Development unit or Public Relations and includes the Students' representation Österreichische Hochschülerschaft, the staff councils for administration and for researchers and last but not least the Working Group on Equal Opportunities. As a first step, already existing measures, projects and contact points were rendered more visible by establishing an own homepage dedicated to the Diversity management at the University of Innsbruck.[32]

In 2021, the University started a broad participation process to develop a comprehensive diversity strategy under the lead of the Vice Rectorate of Human Resources involving more than 50 external and internal experts from different administrative and scientific organizational units. Presented at a university-wide strategy-day, the diversity strategy was published in spring 2022.[33] Putting the focus on the dimension of social background and gender diversity the main targets of the strategy are (a) awareness raising, (b) strengthening equal opportunities and transparency in the recruitment processes, (c) improve access to university for disadvantaged student groups, and (d) establish a diversity-monitoring for staff and students.

It has to be pointed out that since 2016, a particular focus has been put on the social diversity in relation to students by taking up on the strategy set out within the European Higher Education Area on promoting access to higher education of disadvantaged groups and regardless of social background the access. Initiatives include monitoring about the situation of first generation students, consulting in schools for parents and first generation students, courses about "First Generation Students. Exclusion Mechanisms in the Austrian Educational System" for students of all faculties, a research project about the promotion of non-traditional students. Other measures include setting up a mailing-list on diversity issues and organizing lecture series, e.g., within the AURORA-Network[34] about "Doing Diversity in Higher Education in the Aurora European Universities Alliance. To increase awareness on diversity, a compulsory training unit on diversity has been introduced in the obligatory formation on teaching for incoming researcher and on general administrative issues for administrative personnel as well as volunteer trainings in diversity issues are offered to all categories of personnel, aiming in particular at people in managerial positions as Deans and Head of departments. Calls to present projects for diversity promotion at the University of Innsbruck aim at stimulating interest and knowledge on diversity issues. Other initiatives as a lecture series about excellency and its societal dimensions and a Working group on competences in gender and diversity in appointment procedures for Tenure tracks are on the way.

CONCLUDING REMARKS

Austrian Universities must meet a series of legal and budgetary requirements regarding equal treatment, antidiscrimination and equality, in particular in relation to gender. However, in addition to gender and anti-discrimination policies, Austrian Universities have taken more and more action in the field of diversity. In 2006, a study on the status quo on gender and diversity management at Austrian Universities concluded that "the task related to gender and diversity management still remain largely the burden of committed individuals" and stated that "gender and diversity management is still suppressed by traditional value of identity and role construction."[35]

Nowadays, the Austrian Universities have recognized diversity as an enriching potential for all dimensions of academia, from the field of teaching and learning to the field of research and with regard to personnel management. Therefore, encouraged by the strategic instruments laid down in the Universities Act 2002, they have developed strategies and programmes to enhance and manage diversity.

This development shows a raise in the awareness of diversity issues. Nevertheless, it has to be stressed that Diversity management at Austrian Universities is still at the beginning. The same applies to diversity as a guiding principle in all action and policies at University level. Therefore, challenges in the years to come will be manifold. They include enhancing the awareness for diversity and diversity management, tackling situations of multiple discrimination issues and promoting an equal level of protection against all discrimination by striving for a more comprehensive legal basis in relation to all diversity elements.

NOTES

1. Translation of the definition given by the Austrian Society for Diversity—ASD: "Diversity Management ist ein intersektionaler Ansatz zur gezielten Wahrnehmung, Nutzung und Förderung von Vielfalt in sozialen Systemen wie Profit- und Nonprofit-Unternehmen, öffentlichen Organisationen sowie Gruppen und Teams. Ziel von Diversity Management ist es, durch die Förderung von Chancengleichheit und den kompetenten Umgang mit Vielfalt personelle Kompetenz und Ressourcen in Organisationen optimal zu nutzen." see https://www.societyfordiversity.at/show_content.php?hid=1 (03.03.2023).
2. See BGBl 1964/59, by which the European Convention on Human Rights was retroactively elevated to constitutional law in 1964.
3. *Forster*, Art 14 EMRK, in Kahl/Khakzadeh/Schmid (ed), Bundesverfassungsrecht (2021) para. 7; *Meyer-Ladewig/Lehner*, Art 14 EMRK, in Meyer-Ladewig/Nettesheim/von Raumer (ed), EMRK4 (2017) para. 16; *Schilling*, Internationaler Menschenrechtsschutz[4] (2022) para. 802; *Grabenwarter/Frank*, B-VG (2020) Art 14 EMRK para. 2.
4. *Meyer-Ladewig/Lehner*, Art 14 EMRK para. 5; *Forster*, Art 14 EMRK para. 1 f; *Schilling*, Menschenrechtsschutz Rn 783; *Grabenwarter/Frank*, B-VG Art 14 EMRK para. 1; see also *Köchle*, Art 21 GRC, in Holoubek/Lienbacher (ed), GRC Kommentar[2] (2019) para. 17.
5. *Forster*, Art 14 EMRK para. 5; *Schilling*, Menschenrechtsschutz para. 783; *Grabenwarter/Frank*, B-VG Art 14 EMRK para. 4.
6. *Schmahl*, §20 Gleichheitsgarantien, in Grabenwarter (ed), Europäischer Grundrechteschutz[2] (2022) para. 18; *Köchle/Pavlidis*, Art 20 GRC, in Holoubek/Lienbacher, GRC Kommentar[2] (2019) para. 1; *Lemke*, Art 20 GRC, in von der Groeben/Schwarze/Hatje (Hrsg), Europäisches Unionsrecht[7] (2015) para. 2; *Folz*, Art 20 GRC, in Vedder/Heintschel von Heinegg (ed), Europäisches Unionsrecht[2] (2018) para. 1.
7. *Schmahl*, §20 para. 60; *Köchle*, Art 21GRC para. 24.
8. *Khakzadeh*, Art 7 B-VG, in Kahl/Khakzadeh/Schmid (ed), Bundesverfassungsrecht (2021) para. 4; *Muzak*, B-VG[6] (2020) Art 2 StGG para. 1; *Grabenwarter/Frank*, B-VG Art 7 para. 1.
9. *Khakzadeh*, Art 7 B-VG para. 9 f; *Grabenwarter/Frank*, B-VG Art 7 para. 4 f; *Muzak*, B-VG Art 2 StGG para. 2.
10. *Khakzadeh*, Art 7 B-VG para. 6; *Kutsche*, Art. 3 BVG-RD, in Kahl/Khakzadeh/Schmid (ed), Bundesverfassungsrecht (2021) para. 9.
11. BGBl 1993/100 as amended by BGBl I 2020/24.
12. BGBl I 2005/82 as amended by BGBl I 2018/32.
13. Bundesgesetz über die Organisation der Universitäten und ihre Studien (Universitätsgesetz 2002—UG 2002), BGBl I 2002/120 as amended by BGBl I 2021/177. See in general
14. Faulhammer, §1 UG, in Kommentar
15. See in general *Kucsko-Stadlmayer/Haslinger*, §41, in Perthold-Stoitzner, UG (2018) n.1–7.
16. See in general *Kucsko-Stadlmayer/Haslinger*, §42 in *Perthold-Stoitzner*, UG (2018).
17. They are protected by the Federal Disability Equality Act.

18. See as well §41 Federal Equal Opportunities Act. See in general *Benke/Holzleithner,* §20b in Perthold-Stoitzner, UG (2018).
19. See §6 Affirmative Action Plan for the Advancement of Women and Gender Equality of the University of Vienna: "As far as possible, all instruments intended for the advancement of women are also used in the interests of an anti-discriminatory, diversity-promoting and equality-promoting university policy (e.g., awarding scholarships, developing and implementing mentoring programs, coaching and similar measures)." https://satzung.univie.ac.at/en/more-parts-of-the-statutes/affirmative-action-plan-for-the-advancement-of-women-and-gender-equality/ (3.3.2023).
20. See Bundesministerium für Bildung, Wissenschaft und Forschung , Der Gesamtösterreichische Universitätsentwicklungsplan 2022-2017 (GUEP 2022-2027) (2019), https://www.bmbwf.gv.at/Themen/HS-Uni/Hochschulgovernance/Steuerungsinstrumente/GUEP.html (3.3.2023).
21. See GUEP 2022–2027, pp. 27–28. A first assessment of this strategy can be found in Bundesministerium für Bildung, Wissenschaft und Forschung (2023), *Von der Geschlechterpolitik zur diversitätsorientierten Gleichstellungspolitik im österreichischen Hochschul- und Forschungsraum,* published after the editorial deadline for this article.
22. See for example Performance Agreement Innsbruck University 2018-2021, point A.2.2.1.
23. See Federal Ministry Education, Science and Research, University Report 2020 Executive Summary pp. 41–44 (https://www.bmbwf.gv.at/Themen/HS-Uni/Hochschulgovernance/Steuerungsinstrumente/Universit%C3%A4tsbericht.html, 3.3.2023).
24. See Federal Ministry Education, Science and Research, University Report 2020 Executive Summary, p. 44.
25. 2013/C 168/02, OJEU 14.06.2013, C 168/02.
26. BMWFW (2017). Nationale Strategie zur sozialen Dimension in der Hochschulbildung, Für einen integrativen Zugang und eine breite Teilhabe, Wien, pp. 9–10.
27. See https://www.bmbwf.gv.at/Themen/HS-Uni/Gleichstellung-und-Diversit%C3%A4t/Policy-und-Ma%C3%9Fnahmen/Diversit%C3%A4tsmanagement/DMP-Diversitas.html
28. See Universität Innsbruck, Entwicklungsplan 2022–2027, pp. 48–49 (see https://www.uibk.ac.at/universitaet/leitung/dokumente/entwicklungsplan-2022-2027.pdf, 3.3.2023).
29. Universität Innsbruck, Entwicklungsplan 2022–2027, p. 49.
30. Universität Innsbruck, Bundesministerium für Bildung, Wissenschaft und Forschung, Leistungsvereinbarung 2022–2023 (https://www.uibk.ac.at/universitaet/mitteilungsblatt/pdf-dateien/universitaet_innsbruck_lv_2022-2024.pdf)
31. Leistungsvereinbarung 2022–2023, p. 14.
32. See https://www.uibk.ac.at/universitaet/diversitaet/.
33. See https://www.uibk.ac.at/universitaet/diversitaet/diversitaetsstrategie/index.html.de
34. See https://aurora-universities.eu/.

35. Hanappi-Eggger/Hoffmann, Gender and Diversity Management at Austrian Universities in Vedder (eds.) Managing Equity and Diversity at Universitites, 2006, pp. 111–126 (p. 121).

REFERENCES

Benke N., Holzleithner E. (2018). §20b. In Perthold-Stoitzner B. (Ed.), *Universitätsgesetz 2002*. Vienna: MANZ'sche Verlags- und Universitätsbuchhandlung.
Folz H.-P. (2018). Art 20 GRC. In Vedder C., Heintschel von Heinegg, W. (Eds.), *Europäisches Unionsrecht: EUV/AEUV/GRCh/EAGV* (2nd edition). Baden-Baden, Vienna, Zürich: Nomos, facultas, Dike.
Forster A. (2021). Art 14 EMRK. In Kahl A., Khakzadeh L., Schmid S. (Eds.), *Bundesverfassungsrecht: B-VG und Grundrechte*. Vienna: Jan Sramek Verlag.
Grabenwarter C., Frank S. L. (2020). B-VG: Bundes-Verfassungsgesetz und Grundrechte. Vienna: MANZ'sche Verlags- und Universitätsbuchhandlung.
Hanappi-Egger W., Hoffmann R. (2006). Gender and Diversity Management at Austrian Universities.In Vedder G. (Ed.), *Managing Equity and Diversity at Universities*. Munich: Hampp Verlag, pp. 111-126.
Khakzadeh, L. (2021). Art 7 B-VG. In Kahl A., Khakzadeh L., Schmid S. (Eds.), *Bundesverfassungsrecht: B-VG und Grundrechte*. Vienna: Jan Sramek Verlag.
Köchle C. (2019), Art 21 GRC. In Holoubek M., Lienbacher G. (ed), *Charta der Grundrechte der Europäischen Union: GRC-Kommentar* (2nd edition). Vienna: MANZ'sche Verlags- und Universitätsbuchhandlung.
Köchle C., Pavlidis L. (2019), Art 20 GR. In Holoubek M., Lienbacher G. (Eds.), *Charta der Grundrechte der Europäischen Union: GRC-Kommentar* (2nd edition). Vienna: MANZ'sche Verlags- und Universitätsbuchhandlung.
Kucsko-Stadlmayer G., Haslinger K. (2018), §41. In Perthold-Stoitzner B. (Ed.), *Universitätsgesetz 2002*. Vienna: MANZ'sche Verlags- und Universitätsbuchhandlung.
Kucsko-Stadlmayer G., Haslinger K. (2018), §42.In Perthold-Stoitzner B. (Ed.), *Universitätsgesetz 2002*. Vienna: MANZ'sche Verlags- und Universitätsbuchhandlung.
Kutsche S. (2021), Art 3 BVG-RD. In Kahl A., Khakzadeh L., Schmid S. (Eds.), *Bundesverfassungsrecht: B-VG und Grundrechte*. Vienna: Jan Sramek Verlag.
Lemke S. (2015), Art 20 GRC.In von der Groeben H., Schwarze J., Hatje A (Eds.), *Europäisches Unionsrecht: Vertrag über die Europäische Union, Vertrag über die Arbeitsweise der Europäischen Union, Charta der Grundrechte der Europäischen Union* (7th edition), Baden-Baden: Nomos.
Meyer-Ladewig J., Lehner R. (2017), Art 14 EMRK. In Meyer-Ladewig J., Nettesheim M., von Raumer S. (Eds.), *EMRK: Europäische Menschenrechtskonvention* (4th edition), Baden-Baden, Vienna, Basel: Nomos, Manz, Helbing Lichtenhahn Verlag.
Muzak G. (2020), Das österreichische Bundes-Verfassungsrecht: B-VG, F-VG, Grundrechte, Verfassungsgerichtsbarkeit (6th edition). Vienna: MANZ'sche Verlags- und Universitätsbuchhandlung.
Schilling T. (2022), Internationaler Menschenrechtsschutz: das Recht der EMRK und des IPbpR (4th edition). Tübingen: Mohr Siebeck.
Schmahl S. (2022), §20 Gleichheitsgarantien. In: Grabenwarter C. (Ed.), *Europäischer Grundrechteschutz* (2nd edition). Baden-Baden: Nomos.

CHAPTER 10

GENDER MATTERS IN GENDER DIFFERENCE PERCEPTIONS

The Case of University of Rome Tor Vergata

Marianna Brunetti
Tor Vergata University of Rome

Nathalie Colasanti
University of Rome Unitelma Sapienza

Annalisa Fabretti
Tor Vergata University of Rome

Mariangela Zoli
Tor Vergata University of Rome

Diversity as Strategic Opportunity, pages 171–193
Copyright © 2024 by Information Age Publishing
www.infoagepub.com
All rights of reproduction in any form reserved.

ABSTRACT

This chapter investigates students' perceptions and awareness of gender disparity in academia and the labor market, based on a survey administered to a sample of students in the Faculty of Economics at a big University in the Center of Italy. The questionnaire aimed at detecting potentially different perceptions of men and women regarding gender differences by considering both their actual experiences as students and their expectations about labor market conditions. The questions of the survey were the result of the joint work of a group of students and instructors that discussed gender issues together and shared individual perceptions of disparity experienced at different steps of their academic life. A brief description of the genesis of the focus group serves as a foundation for describing the structure and the questions of the survey and for explaining the rationale behind them. Then, the main results of the survey are discussed, highlighting the most significant differences in perceptions of gender issues for male and female students.

Gender discrimination, sexual harassment, and gender violence are still too recurrent phenomena in any institution or organization. Universities, like any other social system, suffer from discrimination and stereotyped dynamics related to gender issues at any level. Sometimes the analysis of specific cases allows us to shed light on broader issues: e.g., looking at universities as one social environment in which educational, occupational, and cultural processes mix up can offer new insights into how gender schemes are perceived, produced, and reproduced in social organizations.

The latest available data show that in Italy, female students represent 56.3% of students, 56.9% of graduates, and 48% of the doctorates, in line with the European average. The distribution of the student population concerning the study area differentiated by gender shows the typical horizontal segregation, which sees women prevailing in the humanities and men in the Science, Technology, Engineering, Mathematics, or STEM (report MUR 2022). Despite no relevant differences are observed in graduation rate, time, and performance, one year after graduation, ceteris paribus, men are 17.8% more likely to be employed than women, and they receive an average of 89€ net more per month (report Almalaurea, 2021). Overall, these data reveal a demeaning picture that, on the one hand, shows the persistence of solid cultural stereotypes that influence the choice of study path and job opportunities, and on the other hand, it asks to be still profoundly understood: where are the barriers still? As Miller et al. (2015) observed, despite their educational role, universities reproduce gender schemes and reinforce stereotypes while exposing students to gender segregation. Moreover, the low level of structural pressures and the higher job opportunities given by tertiary education allow gender schemes, transmitted by social interactions, to be reproduced undisturbed. Considering that inequalities have deep cultural roots, we wonder how and to what extent these inequalities are perceived by students. Gender disparities are often invisible, or made invisible, so many people struggle to recognize or accept them.

In the following section, we summarize some of the most relevant contributions on these issues and argue that it is necessary to further investigate people's perceptions and consciousness of the gender gap inside academia, especially within the student population. This work aims at providing a contribution in this direction. In order to do so, we examine responses to a questionnaire administered to a sample of students enrolled in the Faculty of Economics at a big University in the Center of Italy and developed in a focus group including both students and instructors. The experience of the focus group and the questionnaire design are explained in the third section, while the main findings are presented in the fourth one. Finally, last section concludes.

LITERATURE REVIEW

Despite the relevance of the issue, perceptions of gender disparities among university students have yet to be examined in depth. There is, however, growing interest in the subject since differences in students' perceptions shape the scientific culture in universities and affect educational choices, which in turn affects the attitudes to gender roles of future workers and determines the different treatment of women and men in the labor market (Pla-Julián and Díez, 2019).

Concerning educational choices, recent studies show that despite improvements in women's representation in higher education, horizontal gender segregation in subject choices and fields of study persists. Women continue to be overrepresented in social sciences and the humanities and underrepresented in STEM fields like engineering and ICT. This segregation in educational choices is considered critical in explaining gender inequalities in earnings, career opportunities and access to leadership positions. Indeed, labor market prospects are less favorable regarding employment rates, risks of overeducation and wages for graduates in humanities and social sciences compared to graduates from STEM fields (Barone and Ortiz, 2011; Núñez and Livanos 2010). Bertrand (2018), for instance, finds that the potential gender gap in education-based earnings for women born in 1985 is still relevant (about 6% for expected average earnings and 10% for expected ninetieth percentile earnings), even though it has decreased compared to the one experienced by women born in 1950 (14% and 22%, respectively). The underrepresentation of women in STEM disciplines is a matter of concern because STEM occupations provide higher wages and are characterized by particularly small gender differences in earnings. Goldin (2014), using data from the 2009-2011 American Community

Survey and considering full-time salaries for the top occupations (ranked by male incomes), finds that technology and science occupations have the lowest gender pay gap and that, in some of these occupations, women have even higher average earnings than men.

Some studies have tried to understand the mechanisms behind gender segregation in higher education, a phenomenon which reflects cultural forces and the tendency to conform to gender stereotypes (Barone, 2011). Previous contributions generally agree in explaining the segregation in education choices with the persistence of gender essentialism, i.e., the belief that men's and women's capacities and interests are profoundly different (Levanon and Grusky, 2016). Even though the actual average performance of men and women in math and science do not significantly explain gender segregation (Morgan et al., 2013), perceived differences in skills and outcomes continue to have a significant impact (Correll, 2004). Perceptions about gendered preferences, especially those related to the different orientations of men and women for career opportunities versus family duties, are often considered possible explanations for different educational choices (Ceci and Williams, 2010), even though the empirical evidence provides mixed results on the impact of these perceptions. For instance, Barone and Assirelli (2020), using data from a sample of Italian high school students interviewed during their last year of high school and at the beginning of their first year at the university, find that preferences for career prospects reduce the probability of choosing humanities and social sciences as fields of study, but in the same way for both genders. On the contrary, the authors find that expressive preferences for school subjects and specific occupations, i.e., preferences which reflect the emotional value assigned to specific fields of study and professions independently from their potential economic value, contribute significantly to explaining why women enroll more in the humanities and social sciences than men. Other studies show that these gendered preferences reflect not only psychological but also cultural factors that perpetuate gender inequality: boys and girls are often encouraged to follow different educational pathways by "significant" adults, like teachers, parents, and school counsellors, whose influence reflects stereotypes about gendered talents and the desire to conform to the reference group (Gabay-Egozi et al., 2015; Zafar, 2013).

Another strand of literature which is relevant to our work is the one investigating students' perceptions of discrimination and stereotypes at the university and in the workplace. Steele et al. (2002) examine, for instance, the perceptions of undergraduate female students at a U.S. university in male-dominated academic fields, such as math and science, finding that, in these fields, women report higher levels of discrimination than women in female-dominated fields (like social science and humanities) and men in both male and female-dominated areas. Similarly, female students in traditionally male domains are more likely to feel threatened by the gender stereotype that "women are not as capable as men" and to consider changing their study area as a result. According to Schmitt et al. (2002), perceptions of discrimination against one's gender tend to adversely affect the psychological well-being of female undergraduate students but not men. Along the same line, Sipe et al. (2009) investigate students' perceptions of the gender discrimination they could experience after their studies in the workplace. In a survey administered in 2006 in a public U.S. university, they find that overall students do not perceive gender discrimination as a problem both for their and for women's careers. In particular, around 90% of all students do not think they would experience gender-specific barriers in terms of advancement opportunities, networking, mentoring and wage. Similar perceptions are also reported concerning opportunities for women in the workplace. On the other hand, female students are more likely to anticipate gender discrimination, both for them and for women in general, than male students. For instance, half of the female students anticipate that women may experience a gender bias at work, against only one-third of the male students. In a follow-up paper which extends the data collection period to 2013, the authors find increased students' awareness and concerns about gender discrimination both against women and men. However, results still confirm high percentages of students that do not correctly anticipate the risk of being personally discriminated against (Sipe et al., 2016).

THE WORKING GROUP EXPERIENCE AND THE GENESIS OF THE QUESTIONNAIRE

The idea of investigating perceptions of gender inequality among the student population arose after a seminar held on March 6th, 2019, at the Library of the Faculty of Economics, University of Rome Tor Vergata. As suggested by the title, "Gender (UN)balances" ("(S)bilanci di genere" in the Italian version), the seminar aimed at identifying the main issues and limits of gender-sensitive reporting in universities, with a specific focus on the university which hosted the event. Thanks to the interventions of some female professors, who presented their personal experiences of gender discrimination in academia, the seminar highlighted the existence of significant gender disparities at the university, especially with regards to academic and employment segregation, as well as to the glass ceiling. Educational segregation indicates the perception that certain subjects are more "feminine" (e.g., humanities, psychology), while others are more "masculine" (e.g., engineering): students might thus tend to choose their academic path based on such perceptions, following the internalized prejudice that only specific subjects are suitable for, or aligned with, their gender. Another point raised referred to the glass ceiling: despite girls graduate more (and faster) than boys, and despite more women apply for PhDs and hold junior researcher positions than men, the role of full professor is largely reserved to men.

At the end of the event, the two moderators, who are also authors of this chapter, launched an open call to the audience to involve interested students to further investigate gender issues within the university. A working group was thus formed, composed of three associate professors and one post-doc fellow (the authors of this chapter) and four students (Ilaria Romani, Sara Scollo, Noemi Viggiano, and Chiara Zangrilli), enrolled in courses of economics, finance, and banking. Despite the call was open to all students and professors, without gender limitations, all working group members ended up being women, most of whom engaged in improving gender equality at different levels, and some even active within feminist organizations.

The group worked together, cooperatively and horizontally, without distinctions due to the different roles. Professors supported students' ideas and suggestions, providing materials and methods to carry out the research. The general objective was to create a network, an alliance of women, all at the same level, to investigate perceptions of gender equality, or inequality, among the student population.

Several meetings were held between March and November 2019. At first, the group discussed issues that emerged during the seminar and the personal experiences both inside and outside the university, concluding that gender inequalities were routine rather than episodic accidents. Group members also used emails to stay in touch, follow up on specific issues and circulate papers and information.

Then, the group decided to look up similar projects that were carried out in other universities and to develop a survey to investigate students' perceptions. Again, the survey was designed jointly by instructors and students, whereby the contribution of the latter was essential to obtain questions that were easy to understand and likely to be answered by the respondents. Specifically, the continuous and meticulous confrontation between all the working group members was aimed at choosing, on the one hand, the questions dealing with the issues that could be among the most sensible for the student community and, on the other, at avoiding excessively long or pedantic questions that could divert the attention of the students.

Once the survey was finalized, the professors contacted several administrative offices at the university (such as the office of the Central Committee for equal opportunities, CUG, in charge of ensuring gender equality) to inform about the initiative and obtain their support in spreading the survey to the broadest possible population.

The group also decided to have two versions of the survey, one physical and one online (through Google Forms, both in Italian and English), in order to reach a broader audience and facilitate distribution.

The physical questionnaire was distributed, at the beginning of the lectures, in four classes on November 25th (International Day for the Elimination of Violence Against Women) and 26th, 2019. The selected population included first and second-year bachelor students, thus representing a sufficiently broad group of students. After briefly explaining the overall project, a professor and a student of the working group together administered the survey in each class.

On November 28th, 2019, the Library of the Faculty of Economics sent out a newsletter with the links to the Italian and English versions of the survey, accompanied by a brief presentation of the working group and the project, encouraging students to participate. Most responses were received within the first four days, although the links remained active for one month, until December 27th, 2019.

Participation in the survey was incentivized by the possibility of receiving a gadget, consisting of a highlighter or pen holder: for surveys completed in presence, gadgets were given at the end of the survey; for those who participated online, specific meetings were set where participants could receive their gadget upon showing a screenshot indicating survey completion. In both instances, gadgets were given out by students in the working group.

Once the survey was conducted, the group met again in January 2020 to decide how to create a database that could be used to investigate the results and carry out further research. Then, the Covid-19 pandemic and subsequent lockdown slowed the activities down and made it more complicated to keep up with the project. Finally, one student member of the working group (Ilaria Romani) decided to dedicate her graduate thesis to the project, completing data analysis and interpreting the survey results.

Overall, the experience has been very enriching for all group members, both students and professors, had something to learn from others. Working with other women to study a current issue that affected everyone's life directly was quite empowering. Moreover, the results that were firstly presented in the master's degree thesis of Ilaria Romani, were also presented in an international conference in 2022 (Gender R-Evolutions, held in Trento, Italy), spreading the word to a broader academic community.

SURVEY DESCRIPTION

The survey was organized into four different sections, namely:

1. Perception of gender gaps at the university (9 multiple-choice questions)
2. Perception of gender gaps in the job market (7 multiple-choice questions)

3. Knowledge of gender gaps and roles of institutions (4 multiple-choice questions)
4. Demographics (5 multiple-choice + 3 open questions)

The survey was designed to commit to two specific principles: to have wording as inclusive as possible and to avoid any possible conditioning in the answers. For instance, all multiple-choice questions included the alternative "I don't know" and "Refusal" among the possible answers, in order to guarantee that the respondents felt free while answering and that the survey captured answers and opinions really meant by the respondents. Besides, the section on demographic characteristics was on purpose positioned at the end of the questionnaire to avoid any type of conditioning of the answers during the survey completion.

A more detailed description of each section and the rationale behind each question are described in what follows.

Perception of Gender Gaps at the University of Rome Tor Vergata

The first three questions of this first section aimed at capturing the students' perception of potential differences between males and females along several dimensions: (a) students' final marks for the exams, (b) students' time to accomplish the final graduation, and (c) professors' teaching abilities. The set of possible answers included parity and disparity between genders, specifying in the latter case the direction of the difference, i.e., whether women on average get higher marks/graduate sooner/teach better than men, or the other way around. With reference to students' final marks, the answer "It depends on the exam" was also included to capture the perception that students might have different innate abilities and propensities depending on their gender.

The fourth and fifth questions aimed at capturing the diffusion of another deeply-rooted stereotype, which leads to horizontal segregation, i.e., women are less able to successfully engage in STEM than men. This view has been reproduced within the field of Economics by exploiting the traditional dichotomy between the subfields of Management, whose more qualitative approach is typically considered "easier" and hence more adapt to women, and the one of Economics, which instead relies more on quantitative methods and is thus considered more appropriate for men.

A related stereotype, i.e., that male students typically succeed because of their (innate) talent while female students succeed because of their dedication (to the study), is the object of another set of questions. In the first question, the students faced a hypothetical situation: they are informed that a male student, Pierre, got the maximum score on an exam. They were then asked to indicate which, according to them, was the main factor that led Pierre to that result, by choosing between three options: (a) Pierre studied hard and was strongly committed, (b) Pierre is smart and brilliant, with an innate aptitude for that exam, (c) I don't know. Then, the same question, with the same alternative answers, was repeated referring to a female student, Marie (the students were named after Pierre and Marie Curie, Nobel prizes in Physics in 1903 for their pioneering research on radioactivity). The idea is that differences in the answers referring to Pierre or Marie provided by male and female students can be reconducted to traditional stereotypes about the different innate abilities and attitudes in how they approach their studies and exams.

The last two questions aimed at capturing students' perceptions of potential gender differences in terms of motivations behind the choice of the academic curriculum and career opportunities. As for the former, the students were asked to select which aspects, among the following, were considered by males and females when choosing the program to enroll in: (a) career opportunities, (b) wage, (c) work–life balance opportunities, and (d) personal attitudes (regardless of job opportunities). The answers to this question allow to test whether the presumption that men are slanted towards career opportunities and good earning potential while women are more concerned about work–life balance and personal attitudes is actually there and, if so, whether it is equally widespread among male and female students. Besides, a significantly higher share of (both males and females) students indicating work–life balance for women would confirm the assumption that unpaid domestic work and care services are perceived to be primarily in charge of women.

Finally, the students were asked whether in the private sector men and women have the same career opportunities or not, and—if not—which among the two has the better opportunities in order to evaluate the actual awareness of students about the remarkably different opportunities and career paths that men and women often face once on the job market.

Perceptions of Gender Gaps in the Job Market

This second section was designed to evaluate the students' perception of gender differences in the job market in Italy and if and how these perceptions change once suitable data on the phenomena are provided.

Specifically, the first three questions asked the respondent to provide his/her opinion about potential differences among men and women in terms of: (a) working conditions one year after graduation; (b) salary conditions (conditional on having the same job), and; (c) achieving managerial positions (conditional on having the same degree of education). In all cases, the possible answers included a gender gap in favor of men (men having more chances of working/higher salaries/higher chances of being managers than women), the other way around (women having more options of working/higher salaries/higher chances of being managers than men), or parity.

The same issues were investigated in the following four questions. In this case, however, respondents were preliminarily provided with official data strictly related to the questions. Specifically, before asking students about the presence of gender inequality, they were informed that in 2018 men had an 8.2 percentage-point higher probability of working one year after graduation than women. Then, the same question was asked after specifying that the 8.2 percentage-points gap was observed despite males and females achieved graduation at the same time and with the same average final mark. In the first two questions, official data were taken from Almalaurea, a consortium of Italian universities gathering data on Italian graduates. In the other two cases, data were from Eurostat, which currently reports an average gender pay gap of around 20%, and a remarkable glass ceiling, as only 29% of managers working in Italy are women.

Exploring if and how the awareness of gender differences changes in the light of these data, also across the gender of the respondents, might be of interest as it sheds some light on the actual receptiveness of—thus giving useful targeting suggestions on—the potential recipients of awareness campaigns.

Awareness of Gender Gaps and Roles of Institutions

Whilst the first two sections focused on the perception of gender gaps during the university period and on the job market respectively, the third one focused more on actual awareness of gender gaps and on the actual and potential role of the institutions that might deal with them, both in the context of the university and nationwide.

Specifically, in the first two questions, the respondents were asked if they are informed of the existence of two important committees that are present in (any Italian) university, namely the Central Committee for equal opportunities and the Joint Committee of students and professors (in Italian, Comitato Unico di Garanzia or CUG, and Commissione Paritetica, respectively), and whether they know their aims and functions. As briefly already explained, the CUG ensures the protection and promotion of individual dignity and of the rights to equal opportunities, non-discrimination, well-being, health, and safety of all people at the university, staff, and students. Individuating and removing any form of direct and indirect discrimination, including gender discrimination, is one of its declared objectives. The Joint Committee of students and professors is composed of four professors and four students who jointly monitor the quality of the curricula offered by the different degree courses to guarantee the implementation of good practices in the teaching activities and solve potential disputes. The two survey questions allowed to estimate the share of students aware of the existence in the academic environment of institutions they can speak to in order to signal and remove any kind of discrimination related to their sexual identity or orientation, religion, or ethnicity.

The third question of this section focused on the concept of "equal opportunities." This is a comprehensive notion, set off in the Italian Constitution, indicating the condition in which individuals face no discrimination, for any reason whatsoever, in all possible aspects of life, political, social, economic etc. Despite its wideness, this concept is often identified with (and hence reduced to) the abolition of any form of gender discrimination.

Respondents were thus asked to indicate which, among the following, describes the concept of "equal opportunity" at best: i) a condition in which each person, regardless of gender, nationality, religion, political viewpoint, and sexual preferences, has the same life perspective and opportunities; ii) a condition in which men and women work under the same rules, earn the same salary for the same job, and have the same career opportunities; iii) a condition in which no type of discrimination exists (besides, as usual, the choice "I don't know" as well). Hence, the most comprehensive definition was coupled with two other possibilities: one restricting this condition to the abolition of any form of gender difference (i.e., of one single type of discrimination) on the job market (i.e., in one single aspect of life), and one referring to an utterly undetailed condition. The former definition has been chosen to investigate whether, also among students, this concept is indeed typically interpreted in a quite lessened way. The latter definition has been intentionally left extremely vague to assess students' propensity to think deeper about equal opportunities.

The last question of this section aims at assessing the actual knowledge of students about the gender gap in Italy, whether they are aware of the situation or whether they underestimate it. The question refers to the Global Gender Gap Report, published yearly by the World Economic Forum, which evaluates about 150 countries based on several indicators of gender gaps in the economy, politics, education, and health. These indicators are then summarized into a final index, which ranges between 0, i.e., total gender disparity, and 1, i.e., total gender parity, and allows for a final rank. Respondents were asked to indicate their opinion about the position of Italy in this ranking, whether they think Italy is among the best 50 countries, the worst 50 countries, somewhere in the middle, or "I don't know." Answers allow us to have an idea of the distribution of students in terms of their overestimation, underestimation, or awareness of gender issues in Italy. In the 2018 Global Gender Gap Report, the most recent one at the time the survey was administered, Italy ranked as the 70th country (with a final index of 0.706) out of the 149 considered, i.e., in the middle of the distribution.

Demographics

The latter section aimed at collecting information about the demographics of the respondents. Specifically, respondents were asked to provide information on their gender, year and course of enrollment, and nationality as well as the year of birth and educational level of (both) parents.

The gender of the respondent is among the covariates of most interest, as the sensibility to the gender gaps, and hence the distribution of the answers to some of the questions in the survey, is expected to be remarkably different between male and female students. The year and course of enrolment are helpful to control how much the students are "experienced" with the academic environment, and if perceptions and awareness change according to how students self-select in one field or another, whilst nationality has been asked, taking advantage of the large international environment of the Faculty of Economics at the university of Rome Tor Vergata, to account for the potentially relevant role of different cultural backgrounds. The birth year and education level of both parents has also been solicited. In doing so, the wording has intentionally avoided the canonical use of terms like "Father" and "Mother," leaving the respondents free to indicate the gender of Parent 1 and Parent 2. This with the twofold aim of being as inclusive as possible, allowing for the possibility that students might have grown up with same-sex couples of parents and of studying the diffusion of the bias according to which the male parent typically comes first. Besides, the answers to this question were of high interest as the level of education of the parents, along with the potential inequality between the two, act as a proxy of the cultural context and family models within which students grow up, which are expected to sensibly affect their sensibility and awareness of gender-related issues.

RESULTS AND DISCUSSION

This section briefly summarizes the main evidence drawn from the survey, starting from the demographics of the respondents and then moving to their perception of gender differences at the university and in the labor market.

Demographics

The questionnaire was completed by 814 individuals, 216 of whom in presence and 598 via the web. Among the latter, 434 were completed in Italian and 164 in English. The online questionnaire was distributed through the library's Faculty mailing list which counted, at the time of the questionnaire administration, roughly 5800 addresses, leading to a response rate of around 14% (or 19,4% if one considers only the 4196 students actually enrolled at the time the questionnaire was administered).

Table 10.1 summarizes the distribution of the answers in terms of administration and language of the survey, as well as of gender, course, year,

TABLE 10.1 Demographic Characteristics, Overall and by Gender of the Respondent

Variable	Full Sample Absolute frequency	Share	Males Absolute frequency	Share	Female Absolute frequency	Share
Language						
Italian	650	79.85%	292	80.66%	328	78.66%
English	164	20.15%	70	19.34%	89	21.34%
Administered						
Online	**598**	**73.46%**	**237**	**65.47%**	**346**	**82.97%**
In person	**216**	**26.54%**	**125**	**34.53%**	**71**	**17.03%**
Gender						
Male	362	45.08%	362	100.00%	—	—
Female	417	51.93%	—	—	417	100.00%
No Answer	35	4.33%	—	—	—	—
Course						
Under-grad	484	59.46%	228	62.98%	240	57.55%
Post-grad	242	29.73%	100	27.62%	135	32.37%
PhD	8	0.98%	5	1.38%	3	0.72%
No answer	80	9.83%	29	8.01%	39	9.35%
Year						
1	323	40.07%	161	44.60%	156	37.50%
2	231	28.66%	97	26.87%	124	29.81%
3	88	10.92%	36	9.97%	50	12.02%
4	57	7.07%	28	7.76%	29	6.97%
5	107	13.28%	39	10.80%	57	13.70%
Graduate Parent						
No	401	53.89%	171	51.81%	222	57.00%
Yes	343	46.11%	159	48.19%	168	43.00%
Nationality						
Italian	598	86.04%	265	85.48%	310	86.11%
Non-Italian	97	13.96%	45	14.52%	50	13.89%

Note: The table reports the distribution of the demographic characteristics, over the full sample and by gender of the respondent. In bold, the variables for which the difference between the responses given by males and females is statistically significant.

nationality, and parents' demographics of the respondents, both overall and by gender of the respondent.

While the share of men is higher among the respondents in class, the digital answers are mainly provided by women (statistically significant difference). Most students are Italian, are currently enrolled in an undergraduate course, and only half of them has at least one parent with a university degree. Along none of these demographics though a statistical difference is observed between male and female respondents, meaning that our sample is in this respect gender-balanced.

Perception of Gender Gaps at the University

Table 10.2 reports the distributions of the answers to the questions on the perception of gender differences, again over the entire sample and by gender of the respondent. No statistically significant difference between gender is observed with respect to the graduation time of the students or the teaching abilities of the teacher, while the picture changes when it comes to the exams' final marks. In that respect, about half of the sample perceive no difference between girls and boys, while 21% of the students perceive an advantage for the girls, and another 17% believe that it depends on the topic of the course. Besides, these perceptions are not equally engrained among students: the first is more widespread among male (27.6% against 15.1%), while the latter among female (13.3% against 20.1%).

Two other typical stereotypes are confirmed: on the one hand, that the predisposition towards some disciplines depends on the gender of the student, and, on the other, that males typically succeed because they are brilliant while females succeed because they study hard. Moreover, the perception of the different career opportunities is significantly more widespread among female students than among their male counterparts.

Finally, Figure 10.1 shows the deeply rooted perception that the motivations behind the choice of a certain study path are remarkably different depending on the student's gender: men choose having their career opportunities and salary in mind, while women do so mostly focusing on work–life balance (differences are statistically significant except for "personal attitudes and passions").

Perceptions of Gender Gaps in the Job Market

Figure 10.2 shows that in all the questions about differences in job conditions and opportunities, female perceive significantly more than male students the disparities in terms of lower chances of getting a job (panel A),

Gender Matters in Gender Difference Perceptions • 185

TABLE 10.2 Perception of Gender Differences, Overall and by Gender of the Respondents

Variable	Full Sample Absolute frequency	Full Sample Share	Males Absolute frequency	Males Share	Female Absolute frequency	Female Share
Mark						
Women higher	170	20.88%	100	27.62%	63	15.11%
Men higher	29	3.56%	14	3.87%	15	3.60%
No difference	362	44.47%	149	41.16%	196	47.00%
It depends on the exam	135	16.58%	48	13.26%	84	20.14%
I don't know	118	14.50%	51	14.09%	59	14.15%
Graduation time						
Women sooner	186	22.85%	78	21.55%	101	24.22%
Men sooner	40	4.91%	17	4.70%	23	5.52%
No difference	438	53.81%	213	58.84%	211	50.60%
I don't know	150	18.43%	54	14.92%	82	19.66%
Teachers						
Male better	120	14.76%	61	16.90%	52	12.47%
Female better	68	8.36%	28	7.76%	38	9.11%
No difference	568	69.86%	246	68.14%	300	71.94%
I don't know	57	7.01%	26	7.20%	27	6.47%
Aptitude towards Management						
Women better	89	11.03%	22	6.11%	65	15.70%
Men better	96	11.90%	58	16.11%	29	7.00%
No difference	468	57.99%	206	57.22%	248	59.90%
I don't know	154	19.08%	74	20.56%	72	17.39%

(continued)

TABLE 10.2 Perception of Gender Differences, Overall and by Gender of the Respondents (cont.)

Variable	Full Sample Absolute frequency	Full Sample Share	Males Absolute frequency	Males Share	Female Absolute frequency	Female Share
Aptitude towards Economics						
Women better	44	5.41%	15	4.14%	28	6.71%
Men better	143	17.57%	62	17.13%	73	17.51%
No difference	431	52.95%	188	51.93%	227	54.44%
I don't know	196	24.08%	97	26.80%	89	21.34%
Pierre						
Study hard and very committed	664	81.67%	289	80.06%	347	83.21%
Had good aptitude	93	11.44%	37	10.25%	53	12.71%
I don't know	56	6.89%	35	9.70%	17	4.08%
Marie						
Study hard and very committed	683	84.01%	297	82.27%	359	86.09%
Had good aptitude	67	8.24%	23	6.37%	40	9.59%
I don't know	63	7.75%	41	11.36%	18	4.32%
Opportunities on the private sector						
Men better opportunities	459	56.60%	164	45.56%	281	67.55%
Women better opportunities	36	4.44%	20	5.56%	14	3.37%
No difference	245	30.21%	140	38.89%	95	22.84%
I don't know	71	8.75%	36	10.00%	26	6.25%

Note: The table reports the number of observations and the relative share of the respondents by the answers given to the questions on perception, over the entire sample and by gender of the respondent. In bold, the variables where the difference between the responses given by males and females are statistically significant.

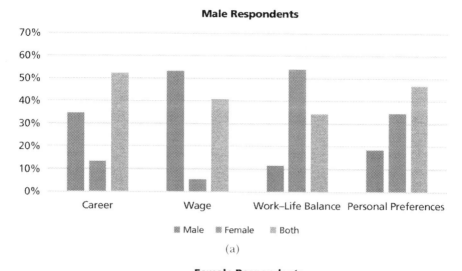

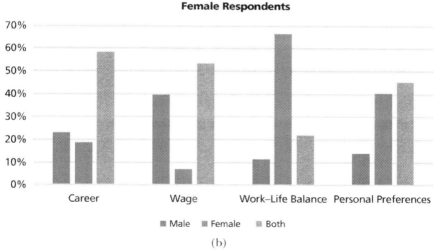

Figure 10.1 Motivations considered when choosing the University program to enroll.

of lower salary (panel B) and of lower chances of accessing management roles (panel C).

This significant difference persists even when the respondents are provided with specific data on gender gaps from Almalaurea and Eurostat, whereby again female students show greater awareness and sensitivity to the data, while male students typically underestimate the issue of different gender opportunities in the workplace, see Figure 10.3.

188 • M. BRUNETTI et al.

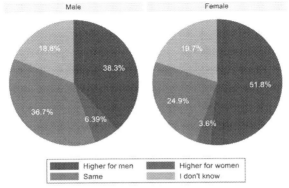

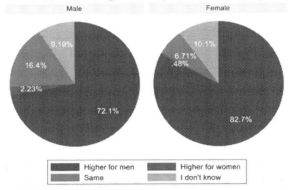

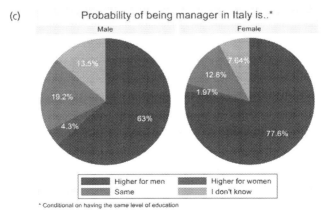

Figure 10.2 Perceptions of gender differences in the labor market.

Gender Matters in Gender Difference Perceptions ▪ 189

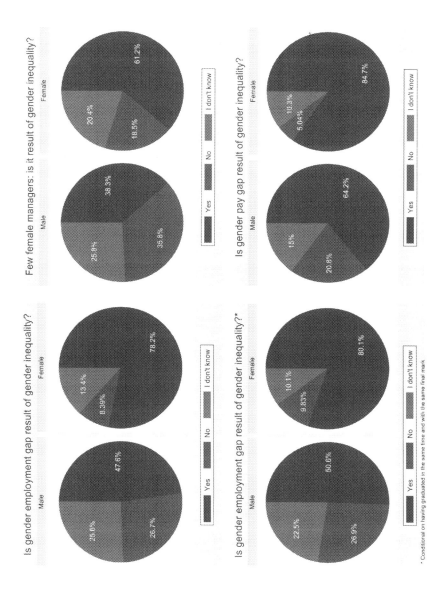

Figure 10.3 Perceptions of labor market gender gaps, after information provision.

Awareness of Gender Gaps and the Role of Institutions

Most of the respondents, in this case without significant distinctions between genders, know neither the existence of CUG and Commissione Paritetica, the two institutional bodies devoted to guaranteeing equal opportunity and participation in academia, nor their goals and functioning (92,5% and 83.8% for the two committees, respectively, as shown in panel A of Figure 10.4). The awareness slightly increases with students' seniority, probably thanks to the longer stay within the University, but remains quite low even among PhD students, suggesting the need to spread information about the central roles of these boards, their role and activities throughout the student community.

Similarly, panel B of Figure 10.4 shows that less than half of students, again with no significant difference between males and females, is able to

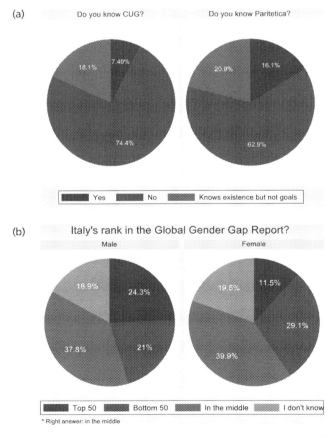

Figure 10.4 Knowledge of CUG and Paritetica and of Global Gender Gap Report Italy's rank.

collocate Italy in its right ranking according to the Global Gender Gap Report (GGR).

CONCLUSION

The activities of the focus group and the survey presented in this chapter allowed to unveil the perceptions of gender issues in a university environment, with a specific focus on the student's population. This is still quite an unexplored issue, especially in Italian academia, despite gender gaps are observed at different levels. While gender disparities have now been explored with reference to the access to the academic career and promotions of professors (Filandri and Pasqua, 2021), perceptions and experiences of gender discrimination among students have not been studied yet. Our study is a first step in filling this gap in the literature.

The results of the survey administered to the students of the Faculty of Economics of a large Italian University are in line with what reported in the literature (e.g., by Sipe et al., 2009, or Sipe et al., 2016) and show that both male and female students tend to underestimate the existence of gender disparities, even though female students tend to perceive and recognize gender imbalances more than their male counterparts, even when they receive specific information about the data related to gender disparities. On the other hand, and again in line with what reported in previous studies (see e.g., Schmitt et al., 2002), female students are aware of their gender membership and of their limitations in their employment opportunities. There remains a strong polarization in what many perceive as innate differences, i.e., in the determining factors of the choice of study path; such a finding confirms that among young adults and adolescents, a conventional family arrangement (a husband working full time and a wife staying home with children) remains the most desired and expected (Dernberger and Pepin 2020). Finally, a high percentage of students, no matter the gender, ignore the existence of the CUG, the only institutional body within universities in charge of ensuring equal opportunities.

Our findings suggest that while working to contrast gender discrimination in any form and to un-build gender stereotypes, we should also take care of enhancing students' awareness about these issues through specific actions since the very beginning of their stay in the university environment.

REFERENCES

Almalaurea (2021). XXIII Indagine Condizione occupazionale dei Laureati. Available at: https://www.almalaurea.it/sites/almalaurea.it/files/docs/universita/occupazione/occupazione19/almalaurea_occupazione_rapporto2021.pdf

Barone, C. (2011). Some things never change: Gender segregation in higher education across eight nations and three decades. *Sociology of Education*, *84*(2), 157–176.

Barone, C., & Assirelli, G. (2020). Gender segregation in higher education: an empirical test of seven explanations. *Higher Education*, *79*, 55–78.

Barone, C., & Ortiz, L. (2011). Overeducation among European University Graduates: a comparative analysis of its incidence and the importance of higher education differentiation. *Higher Education*, *61*, 325–337.

Bertrand, M. (2018). Coase lecture—The glass ceiling. *Economica*, *85*(338), 205–231.

Ceci, S. J., & Williams, W. M. (2010). Sex differences in math-intensive fields. *Current Directions in Psychological Science*, *19*(5), 275–279.

Correll, S. J. (2004). Constraints into preferences: Gender, status, and emerging career aspirations. *American Sociological Review*, *69*(1), 93–113.

Dernberger, B. N., & Pepin, J. R. (2020). Gender Flexibility, but not Equality: Young Adults' Division of Labor Preferences. *Sociological Science*, *7*, 36–56.

Filandri, M., & Pasqua, S. (2021). 'Being good isn't good enough': gender discrimination in Italian academia. *Studies in Higher Education*, *46*(8), 1533–1551.

Gabay-Egozi, L., Shavit, Y., & Yaish, M. (2015). Gender differences in fields of study: The role of significant others and rational choice motivations. *European Sociological Review*, *31*(3), 284–297.

Goldin, C. (2014). A grand gender convergence: Its last chapter. *American Economic Review*, *104*(4), 1091–1119.

Levanon, A., & Grusky, D. B. (2016). The persistence of extreme gender segregation in the twenty-first century. *American Journal of Sociology*, *122*(2), 573–619.

Miller, D. I., Eagly, A. H., & Linn, M. C. (2015). Women's representation in science predicts national gender-science stereotypes: Evidence from 66 nations. *Journal of Educational Psychology*, *107*(3), 631.

Morgan, S. L., Gelbgiser, D., & Weeden, K. A. (2013). Feeding the pipeline: Gender, occupational plans, and college major selection. *Social Science Research*, *42*(4), 989–1005.

MUR (2022). Focus le carriere femminili in ambito accademico (2022). Available at http://ustat.miur.it/media/1218/focus_carrierefemminili_universit%C3%A0_2022.pdf

Núñez, I., & Livanos, I. (2010). Higher education and unemployment in Europe: an analysis of the academic subject and national effects. *Higher Education*, *59*, 475–487.

Pla-Julián, I., & Díez, J. L. (2019). Equality plans and gender perception in university students. *Mediterranean Journal of Social Sciences*, *10*(4), 39.

Schmitt, M. T., Branscombe, N. R., Kobrynowicz, D., & Owen, S. (2002). Perceiving discrimination against one's gender group has different implications for well-being in women and men. *Personality and Social Psychology Bulletin*, *28*(2), 197–210.

Sipe, S. R., Larson, L., Mckay, B. A., & Moss, J. (2016). Taking off the blinders: A comparative study of university students' changing perceptions of gender discrimination in the workplace from 2006 to 2013. *Academy of Management Learning & Education, 15*(2), 232–249.

Sipe, S. R., Johnson, C. D., & Fisher, D. K. (2009). University students' perceptions of gender discrimination in the workplace: Reality versus fiction. *Journal of Education for Business, 84*(6), 339–349.

Steele, J., James, J. B., & Barnett, R. C. (2002). Learning in a Man'S world: Examining the perceptions of undergraduate women in Male-dominated academic areas. *Psychology of Women Quarterly, 26*(1), 46–50.

Zafar, B. (2013). College major choice and the gender gap. *Journal of Human Resources, 48*(3), 545–595.

CHAPTER 11

INCLUSION AND DIVERSITIES IN ITALIAN SCHOOLS BETWEEN THEORY AND PRACTICE

A Legal Analysis

Stefania Baroncelli
Free University of Bozen-Bolzano

ABSTRACT

This chapter aims to analyse the diversities that exist among students in Italian schools and the degree of legal protection afforded to them within the Italian and European legal frameworks. After conducting an analysis of the concept of inclusion and how it is applied, the article examines the factors that create the most discrimination in schools, focusing on a specific aspect of diversity and inequality. Thus, the focus is on diversity stemming from disability, specific learning needs, migration background, and socio-economic status of students. The analysis seeks to identify the degree of legal protection that the legal system accords to these diversities, in the light of international, Constitutional, and legislative provisions, and the evolution of jurisprudence.

This article sets out to analyse the different types of diversities that characterise students in Italian schools and the degree of legal protection afforded to them in the Italian and European legal frameworks. To do so, it refers to an interdisciplinary research project on "Diversity and Inclusion in Schools: Legal Solutions and Good Practices" which, in addition to legal experts, involves pedagogists, in order to better understand whether the legal regulations are suitable for responding to the demands made by pedagogists under the concept of inclusion.[1] Differences among students are thus analysed within the broader framework of inclusive education, considering that schools must consider all human differences and overcome a category-based approach that could generate labelling and discrimination.

After conducting an analysis of the concept of inclusion and how it is applied in the European and Italian legal frameworks, the article addresses the factors that create the most discrimination in schools, focusing on a specific aspect of diversity and inequality. Thus, the focus will be on diversity stemming from disability, migration background, and socio-economic status of students. The analysis will seek to identify the degree of protection that the legal system accords to these diversities, in the light of international, Constitutional, and legislative provisions and the evolution of jurisprudence.

EDUCATION: FROM INTEGRATION TO INCLUSION

In the past, schools used to accommodate disadvantaged students by segregating them from mainstream schools. Today, they are included within the classroom, which has to adapt to the needs of the students. We have therefore moved from the 'school of segregation' to the 'school of integration' to then reach the 'school of inclusion'.[2] The concept of integration within a classroom refers to the addition of disadvantaged students in existing mainstream educational institutions, with the understanding that they can adapt to the standardised requirements of these establishments. The term 'inclusion', on the other hand, places more emphasis on the status of the classroom and the school, which must take into account the needs of all students when planning the structure and curriculum. At the same time, inclusive education recognises certain specific rights for disadvantaged children, such as those with special educational needs.

But what are the implications of inclusive education?[3] Inclusion requires extensive improvements to the structure, teaching methods and curricula of mainstream schools and consists of a process of continuous efforts to remove obstacles to the enjoyment of the right to education, in theory and in practice, to effectively include all students.

THE INTERNATIONAL INSTRUMENTS OF PROTECTION

Several international instruments and treaties underpin this turn towards inclusive schools. The *Salamanca Declaration* and the related *Framework for Action on Special Needs Education* adopted in 1994 are the first comprehensive texts that specify the characteristics of inclusive education and offer some paths to transformation.[4] These texts promote the idea that all children have the right to an education, even if the conference's main focus was more specific and centred on youngsters with special needs. The framework has had significant effects because it outlines standards, guidelines, and procedures for governments, international organizations, and local entities to achieve the goal of an inclusive education. It has been approved by 92 Governments and 25 organizations that were present at the conference.

The first principle of the framework is based on the concept of 'education for all'. Schools have a responsibility to meet the needs of all students, regardless of their physical, intellectual, social, emotional, linguistic, or other needs. This concept dates to the well-known *UN Universal Declaration of Human Rights* adopted in 1948, according to which (art. 26) "everyone has the right to education." Furthermore, schooling should be free and compulsory, at least in the elementary and fundamental stages. Despite the adoption of the declaration, universal access to education has encountered difficulties in its implementation. In 1990, according to UNESCO, more than 100 million children did not have access to primary school.[5] This is why the United Nations, with the support of States and some international organisations, decided in 1990 to adopt a *World Declaration on Education for All*.[6] The declaration advocates greater equity in educational services, which means achieving an acceptable level of learning, but also recognises the need to provide special protection for children and young people with disabilities as an integral part of the education system. Children with disabilities and giftedness, children who work or live on the streets, kids from rural or nomadic populations, kids from linguistic, ethnic, or cultural minorities, and kids from other underprivileged or marginalized locations or groups should all be considered. The broad principle of non-discrimination is thus projected through the idea of everyone having the right to education. The *Salamanca Declaration* thus recognizes that all children are guaranteed social dignity, regardless of their abilities or backgrounds.

A second idea of the *Salamanca Declaration* and *Framework for Action* assumes that the best way to eliminate discrimination is to include children with special educational needs in the provision made for the majority of children, on the basis of child-centred pedagogy, i.e., on the basis of inclusive education. This is a crucial point: experience has shown that inclusive education can significantly reduce school repeat and drop-out rates typical of many education systems and is particularly beneficial for students with disabilities or special educational needs. Furthermore, experience has shown that only a small proportion of students—who usually live in cities - benefit from special schools due to their high cost, especially in developing countries. As a result, the vast majority of special education students, especially those attending schools in remote areas, do not receive any services. This is why enrolment in special schools or in special classes within the school should be considered as an exception: only in extraordinary cases, when attendance of normal classes is not advantageous to these students' needs because of the seriousness of the disability or if it necessary for the welfare of the child or of that of other children. However, this alternative must be understood extremely strictly: not only is it only feasible in very rare circumstances, but it must also be "clearly demonstrated" that the educational needs of children cannot be met through attendance at regular schools.[7] Even in his case, children should not be completely segregated.

Such schools have also the advantage of spreading a culture of respect and non-discrimination for all the differences in the society, and help in creating a welcoming and respectful community, against stereotypes; that is, an inclusive society. This factor stresses the link between the school and the society, which should act hand in hand, and makes education the main factor which enables children and young people to participate in the community. Education is thus considered not only a technical mission to be accomplished by teachers and professors: a successful social reform implies a united effort by students, parents, families, associations, and volunteer, as it depends "above all, upon the conviction, commitment and good will of the individuals who constitute society."[8]

The concept of 'inclusive school' implies a systematic reform or, rather, a process involving educational content, teaching methodologies, organisational structures and strategies to eliminate barriers to provide all students, according to their age, with an equitable learning mode and environment that reflects their needs and, also, their preferences. This approach, as we have seen, is based on the idea of the 'right to education for all', with reference to the need to accept students who are at a disadvantage in normal classes and has been constructed considering in particular the condition of children with disabilities or special educational needs.

The *United Nations Convention on the Rights of Persons with Disabilities* enacted in 2007 in New York provided a significant impetus for change in Italy and the European States.[9] The Convention represents the culmination of decades of UN efforts to alter perceptions and methods of dealing with people with disabilities.[10] Behind this convention is the idea of moving away from the old model of seeing people with disabilities as 'objects' of charity, medical care, and social protection toward considering them as 'subjects' with rights. It adopts a broad definition of people with disabilities and restates the requirement that people with all different kinds of disabilities be granted access to all fundamental freedoms and human rights.

Article 24 of the Convention is focused on education. It states that "States Parties recognise the right to education of persons with disabilities. In order to realise this right without discrimination and on the basis of equal opportunities, States Parties shall ensure an inclusive education system at all levels and lifelong learning." This means not excluding pupils with disabilities from the mainstream education system on the grounds of disability and guaranteeing them access, on an equal basis, within their community.

Article 24 stipulates that integration within the class shall make use of a "reasonable accommodation" determined according to the specific needs of each student. Thus, the adaptations that are necessary for each student on the basis of his or her disability condition must be ensured, without imposing a disproportionate or excessive burden on the school. In this way, it is also possible for these students to enjoy human rights and fundamental freedoms on an equal basis with others.[11]

THE EUROPEAN CONVENTION FOR HUMAN RIGHTS (ECHR) AND THE CHARTER OF FUNDAMENTAL RIGHTS OF THE EUROPEAN UNION (EU CHARTER)

At the European level, discriminatory conducts are clearly prohibited by Article 14 of the ECHR and Article 21 of the EU Charter. Art. 14 of the ECHR is particularity relevant, as it ensures that the rights secured by the Convention should be guaranteed without discrimination whatsoever, and especially for ground of sex, race, colour, language, religion, political or other opinion, national or social origin, association with a national minority, property, birth or other status. Art. 21 of the EU Charter, being more recent, makes reference to new grounds for discrimination, such as genetical features, disability, age and sexual orientation.[12] Both articles forbid a list of possible grounds for discrimination by way of example only, effectively prohibiting discriminatory rules and conduct for any other condition even if not included in the categories of the articles.

A maximum degree of protection for discriminatory treatments in school has been granted by the European Court of Human Rights (ECtHR) combining Article 14 of the ECHR with Article 2 of the Protocol 1 of the ECHR on the right to education. Under such articles a difference in treatment is not always discriminatory, as it can be justified by a *legitimate aim* pursued by the State.[13] The issue was tackled by the ECtHR already in 1968 in the *Belgian linguistic case*.[14] In this judgment children with French mother tongue living in a Dutch-speaking area of Belgium could not attend French speaking schools, while the reverse by Dutch children living in French speaking area in Belgium was possible. The Court decided that contrary to Belgium's arguments legal measures governing access to the education in French in the communes with special facilities were not established in the interest of the schools or for financial or administrative reasons but were originated only from considerations related to the language spoken by pupils. As such, they were not legitimate and amounted to discrimination forbidden by Article 2 of Protocol No. 1 taken together with Article 14 of the ECHR. The ECtHR clarified more recently that the existence of a legitimate goal alone is not sufficient, as the disparity in treatment must also be proportionate. Thus, in the case *Altinay v. Turkey* a change in the university's access rules was deemed justified in light of the enhancement of higher education, but the implementation of such changes was judged out of proportion because it wasn't anticipated and no corrective measures were taken.[15]

Recently, a violation of the ECHR has conducted the ECtHR to strike down as discriminatory national provisions relating to education. In the landmark case *G.L. v. Italy* an Italian pupil affected by autism was denied by the school of the right to enjoy the help of a support teacher for disabled during the first two years of primary school.[16] The Strasbourg Court decided that the Italian State decision was discriminatory as cuts in funds for financial reasons fell only on disabled children and not on non-disabled ones. We will analyze this judgment more in depth in the part dedicated to the Italian case.[17] However, we anticipate that this judgment can be considered a turning point in the jurisprudence of the ECtHR. The novelty lies in the fact that the ECtHR linked the violation to the obligations and rights under the UN Convention on Disabilities, giving fundamental value to its inclusive approach. Previously, the Court's decisions on the subject had been marked by a very cautious approach that had rewarded the margin of appreciation (discretion) of States in their choice of educational policies, showing to give credit more to the doctrine of integration than to that of inclusion.

In *Sanlsoy v. Turkey* the applicant claimed that his right to an education had been violated because of his autism. The ECtHR however determined that there had not been a systematic denial of the applicant's right to education because of his autism or a violation of the State's obligations under Article 2 of Protocol No. 1 taken together with Article 14 of the ECHR. As a result, the application was denied. Similar findings were made in *Dupin v. France*,[18] a case concerning an autistic child who had been denied admission to a mainstream school and directed to a specialised institution. The ECtHR emphasised the State's wide margin of appreciation in this matter and accepted an essentially medical-pathological perspective of disability, to the detriment of any profile of effective socialisation and inclusion in the community context.[19] The same conclusion was reached by the ECtHR in 2019 in the case *Stoian v. Romania*, where a disabled son and his mother applied against the Romanian authorities, claiming that they had failed to provide suitable access to education for the pupil.[20] In fact, the schools were not suited to the special needs of the students, as they lacked adequate facilities. In addition, the curriculum had not been adjusted to the pupil's needs. Notwithstanding this, the ECtHR decided that the Romanian authorities had complied with their obligation to make reasonable accommodation. Additionally, within the parameters of their margin of appreciation, they had also committed resources to address the educational requirements of children with impairments.

ITALIAN CONSTITUTIONAL AND LEGAL PROVISIONS

Article 34 of the Italian Constitution, recognising that "school is open to all," lays the foundation for an inclusive school. Being "open to all" means that there is a right but also a duty to attend school that develops especially in the first years of life. In fact, Article 34 of the Constitution continues, schooling is free and compulsory for at least eight years. This period has now been extended by law to twelve years or, alternatively, until a three-year diploma is obtained by the age of eighteen.

The education and upbringing of young people are the task of the Republic (Article 33 of the Constitution): the State establishes schools for all types and levels. Following the Constitutional reform of 2001 which has entrusted more legislative power to Regions, general rules on education and the setting of essential levels of performance are set by the State, while it is up to the Regions to intervene in detail with laws in the field of education. Full legislative competence lies with the Regions in vocational training. At the same time, the autonomy of schools is recognised.[21] The building of schools is however the task of the municipalities. Finally, also the right of private entities to create and establish schools and educational institutions is acknowledged, in accordance with the principle of pluralist society enshrined in the Constitution.

Articles 33 and 34 of the Constitution apply the principle of the centrality of the person referred to in Article 2 of the Constitution to schools; indeed, it can be said that schools, as social forms protected in general by Article 2 of the Constitution, are the very prerequisite for the enjoyment of other Constitutional rights, as they enable the development of pupils' personalities and the acquisition of the professional skills and educational abilities that will enable young people, once they become adults, to enter the job market and self-sustain themselves or continue their education in higher education institutions.[22]

The application of the principle of non-discrimination in Article 3 of the Constitution is also fundamental for a constitutionally oriented school notion. This is relevant, first of all, in its liberal component (first paragraph), which prohibits discrimination that may be contained in laws on the basis of skin colour, social origin or citizenship, gender or sexual orientation, language, religion or citizenship (or statelessness) of students. Such discrimination may affect students already in the admission process and teachers at the time of recruitment, but also later, once the student has been admitted or the teacher recruited.

More recently, the principle of equity or substantive equality recognised by Article 3, paragraph 2, of the Constitution has taken on increasing importance. The right to education provided by current legislation for all in some cases is not sufficient, since some categories of students cannot actually benefit from it due to their condition—the presence of an "economic and social obstacle"—that must be removed through appropriate public policy interventions. Thus, because of equality, positive actions and differentiated assessments are legitimized for students with mental and physical disabilities of varying degrees of severity. Some specific programmes can be organized for students who do not speak the national language either in the case of immigrants or in the case of children who are part of a linguistic minority, or who live far away and in isolated places or in economically or socially disadvantaged conditions, for instance, through scholarships and students' housing.

The Italian Constitution clearly states the legislator's obligation to provide specific guarantees to protect disabled people, both in the employment and educational spheres (art. 38 Constitution). Such principles are enshrined in the section devoted to social rights. On the basis of art. 38 the integration within school of disabled students was initiated.[23]

Previously, the Italian legal system provided for segregated classes inspired by the logic of separation between normal and handicapped pupils: the latter were seen as a cause of disturbance with respect to the progress of the class and for this reason entrusted to teacher-doctors.[24] The separation of classes dates back to the Gentile reform of 1923 which, while extending compulsory schooling up to the age of fourteen, established segregated education for the blind and visually impaired in separate facilities with specialised teachers.[25] This separation was later made more articulated during the Fascist period with the creation of differentiated classes, reserved for pupils with mild disorders, and special schools, dedicated to deaf, blind and mentally impaired children.[26]

Awareness of the negative and ghettoising consequences of this system began to emerge in the 1960s, leading in the 1970s to the legislative reform that, at least in theory, provided for the possibility of including the disabled in mainstream classes. A new Law of 1971 (Law No. 118 of 1971) affirmed, in fact, the principle of inclusion of the disabled, ensuring them free transport, classroom assistance in the most serious cases and access to school premises. The legislative path towards an inclusive school then continued with laws that specified how disabled children should be included and treated in mainstream classes. Law No. 517 of 1977 represents a real quantum leap, providing for the right of disabled pupils to be enrolled in primary and middle schools on a normal basis and the provision of specific forms of integration tools. The right to integration of disabled pupils was then clarified and extended by the intervention of the Constitutional Court, which extended the obligation to integration in normal classes to secondary schools and universities as well, declaring the Constitutional illegitimacy of Article 28(3) of Law No 118 of 30 March 1971—"new provisions in favour of the disabled and invalids"—in the part where, with reference to disabled persons, it provided that "attendance at secondary schools will be facilitated," instead of providing that "attendance at secondary schools is ensured."[27] Subsequently, the Constitutional Court extended the accompanying allowance to disabled children in kindergarten.[28]

The latest legislative reform adopted in Italy is Law No. 107 of 2015 (so-called *'Good School'* Law), which conforms to the paradigm shift introduced by international law.[29] An inclusive school is an organization that not only respects, but values diversity, marked by respect, where discriminations are forbidden. The principles of individualization and personalization—understood as prohibition of discrimination, freedom, and differentiation—are applied. This step is fundamental, because an inclusive school manages to question certain dogmas that are accepted and implemented and accepts the suggestions and needs expressed by the school community, making them a value.[30]

THE CASE-LAW OF THE ITALIAN CONSTITUTIONAL COURT

School inclusion has been strengthened thanks to the jurisprudence of the Italian Constitutional Court. Its contribution has been essential, since it has on several occasions anticipated principles subsequently acquired by legislation. Moreover, it defined an "*essential core of rights*" that cannot be compressed by the legislature for reasons of public spending restraint, especially in the case of the most serious cases of disabled pupils.[31] In addition, this "core" was interpreted extensively by the Court, considering it not limited to educational and didactic activities, but also including other activities that must be considered a precondition whose guarantee is necessary for disabled pupils to fully enjoy their right to education.

The Italian Constitutional jurisprudence has undergone a profound transformation over the last 50 years. In the 1970s the Court had declared manifestly unfounded the questions of Constitutional legitimacy based on the principle of equality because of the objective diversity of the two groups of pupils (on the one hand, sighted children, on the other, blind children) or because of budgetary limits in the case of non-implementation of the right to education under Article 34 of the Constitution.[32] In subsequent years, however, as the legal and social framework changed, Constitutional jurisprudence also became increasingly inclusive, especially with reference to the protection of the rights of disabled students.

The Court, rejecting the thesis, now obsolete in the scientific field, that a disabled status is irreversible, identifies the school as the true game-changer, responsible for the recovery and development of the personality of disabled children and their preparation for integration into society and the world of work. Following this reasoning, the Court goes so far as to provide for the right of disabled students to pursue higher studies, including university (which Article 38 of the Constitution, on the basis of a literal interpretation, would only guarantee to the "able and deserving"), arguing on the basis of Article 2 and Article 3, para. 2, of the Constitution.[33] School inclusion, in fact, is recognised both through the provisions on combating situations of socio-economic and cultural hardship and in those that protect persons with psychophysical and mental disabilities.

The Constitutional Court has interpreted the specific articles of the Constitution dedicated to schools also in conjunction with the other Constitutional provisions that deal more specifically with the organizational aspects of schools. These include the rules on administrative efficiency, subsidiarity and school autonomy.[34] In recent times, the limit of financial resources has also taken on a significance of its own, following the inclusion of the principle of balanced budget in the Constitution.[35] Its impact was, however, limited thanks to the jurisprudence of the Constitutional Court, which made the rights of disabled pupils prevail over financial needs, with a landmark ruling (judgment 275/2016) that places a clear limit on the incursion of the principle of balanced budget on the effectiveness of education.[36] As a consequence, the Constitutional Court annulled a regional law enacted by the Region Abruzzo on the ground that the regional contribution for transportation of disabled students was limited by the financial availability. The lack of financial resources amounted to denying access to school for the more vulnerable, i.e., disabled children.

An inclusive school is also a quality school, i.e., it succeeds in preparing its students to the best of their ability for higher education, putting into practice the Constitutional design according to which the '"capable and deserving, even if deprived of means, have the right to attain the highest levels of studies" (Article 34 of the Constitution). While compulsory education is free, higher education does not have to be free, but the effectiveness of the right is ensured through scholarships, family allowances and other provisions to be granted by the State and the Regions. The methods of disbursement are subject to formal administrative procedures, since the Constitution requires a public competition, i.e., an administrative procedure based on predetermined requirements. Provisions and scholarships are an essential character of the right to study, so much so that the Court extended the possibility of obtaining provisions to pupils in private schools, considering the limitation to public schools to be unjustifiably discriminatory.[37]

PRACTICAL DIFFICULTIES IN IMPLEMENTATION: THE CASE *G.L. V. ITALY*

The legal framework on school inclusion of disabled pupils in Italy is assessed as well-advanced even by external evaluators. This is the case of the *United Nations Committee on the Rights of Persons with Disabilities*, which appreciates the fact that Italy, over the last thirty years, has made an effort to implement an inclusive and segregation-free education system.[38] However, there are still difficulties in the implementation of laws, decrees and regulations on inclusive education and in the quality of teacher training, including pre-service and in-service training on inclusive education. Other problems relate to pedagogy and communication used in the classroom. For example, schools do not provide deaf children with sign language interpreters and other pupils with accessible teaching materials and technology, which makes real inclusion in schools difficult. Other difficulties lie in the obsolescence and lack of accessibility of school buildings, which prevents and makes it difficult for pupils and students with disabilities to attend school. Accessibility refers not only to buildings, but also to other premises and spaces that are considered an integral part of education, such as school facilities, canteens, recreational spaces and school transport, which must be accessible and safe, according to the principles of universal design. Fortunately, the adoption of the Next Generation EU (NGEU) and the National Plan for Recovery and Resilience (NPRR) aim to improve this situation by providing funds to municipalities to renovate school buildings to make them more accessible.[39]

Other difficulties lie in the scarcity of funds allocated to pay support teachers and other professionals. Mainly due to the economic crisis that started in 2008 and the subsequent austerity policies adopted in Italy in the 2010s, the State reduced funds to the Regions and consequently to the Municipalities, which are responsible for organising social services.[40] Public services dedicated to disabled and disadvantaged children and students have consequently been reduced or even eliminated. One example is the elimination of funds for school transport for disabled pupils.

As anticipated before, a recent ECtHR judgment is particularly relevant in this context. It is the case *G.L. v. Italy* of 2020.[41] The court noted that inclusive education is guaranteed by Italian law, which also safeguards a child's right to an education if they have a disability. Italian Law ensures that impaired students attend regular classes at public schools and provides for psycho-pedagogical services that guarantee the presence of a support teacher in the classroom. In addition, if needed, other professionals are foreseen by law, such as communication assistants whose mission is to "eliminate perceptual and sensory barriers" and educational assistants who accompany the students to promote their autonomy and socialization. Despite the letter of the law, the ECtHR found an enforcement problem: Italy's failure to implement the rights meant that it exceeded any margin of appreciation, especially because restrictions on the fundamental rights of particularly vulnerable groups, such as persons with disabilities, must be considered significantly limited.

The Strasbourg Court discussed also the issue of the balance between right to education for disabled pupils and the need to reduce public spending. The Court emphasised how, as a general rule, the ECHR does not exclude limitations related to budgetary needs, but on condition that such interventions are distributed in a non-discriminatory manner over all the beneficiaries of the school service, regardless of their disability status. In this respect, it considered that, in view of the model of inclusive education adopted in Italy and in accordance with the case-law of the Italian Court of Cassation, any budgetary restrictions should have an equivalent impact on the provision of education for pupils with and without disabilities.[42] In *G.L. v. Italy* therefore the ECtHR held that the ECHR provisions had been infringed, pointing out that the discrimination suffered by the person concerned was to be considered all the more serious because it took place at a particularly delicate stage for individual development, such as during primary education.

OTHER DIVERSITIES

The principle and practice of inclusion concerns all students, no one excluded, although particular attention is paid to needs arising from personal or social situations that affect learning abilities such as disabilities and learning disorders, health conditions, refugee or immigrant status and socio-linguistic or family disadvantages. Moreover, the practice of inclusion does not mean reducing the level of learning, since education must also be of quality, i.e., guarantee the educational success of all pupils.[43]

Special Educational Needs

The protection of students with disadvantages began with reference to the category of the disabled, with laws 118/1971 and 517/1977. It was only later that Italian legislation opened up protection to other weaknesses, based on the assumption that it was necessary to go beyond the differentiation between able-bodied and disabled pupils. Thus the large 'container' category of pupils with 'Special Educational Needs' (BES in Italian)[44] was formulated, which includes (a) certified disabled students;[45] (b) 'Specific Learning Disorders' (DSA in Italian) and other less serious disorders (such as deficits in the use of language, deficits in non-verbal skills, physical coordination, borderline cognitive functioning, attention disorders); and, more generally, 3) students with socio-economic, linguistic and cultural disadvantages, including pupils with a migrant background.

Types of fragility other than disabilities began to be recognised through Law No. 53 of 2003 (so-called 'Moratti reform'), which provides for the right to an individualized approach and training through ad hoc study plans. However, it was Law No. 170 of 2010 that recognized specific learning disorders (DSA: dyslexia, dysgraphia, dysorthographia and dyscalculia) for which specific learning and protection measures were envisaged.[46] The actions to be taken in the case of pupils with DSA are described in the *Guidelines on Specific Learning Disorders* issued in 2011 by the Italian Ministry of Education, which prescribes individualized education plans, with specific support and assistive compensatory aids, dispensatory measures and appropriate testing and assessment measures. The two cases of 'students with disabilities' and 'students with DSA' are only partially overlapping: it is true that in both cases a certification is required (from a doctor and/or a psychologist) but the procedure to be followed is different and the rights recognised are also different, in particular students with DSA are not entitled to a support teacher.[47]

Finally, in 2013, a directive was issued by the Italian Ministry of Education that provides measures for intervention in favour of students with BES (Special Educational Needs).[48] These needs are not or may not be certified under Law No. 104 of 1992 for disabled students, thus not entitling them to the benefits and measures provided for by the same law, and among these, to the support teacher. The directive also includes within BES the area of socio-economic, linguistic and cultural disadvantage, establishing certain principles to be followed by the teaching staff.

Students With a Migrant Background

Since the 1983/1984 school year, there has been an upward trend in the number of students with a migration background in the Italian schools.[49] The peak was in 2007/2008 with an increase of almost 73,000 students. In the 2020/21 school year, there was a decrease (−1.3%), but despite this reduction probably due to the lock-down of the pandemic, the presence of pupils with non-Italian citizenship remained unchanged in percentage terms compared to the 2019/20 school year (10.3%).[50] In absolute terms, the number of pupils with non-Italian citizenship in the 2020/21 school year amounted to 865,388. This survey does not consider students with language difficulties who have Italian citizenship, such as adopted children, children from linguistic minorities or second-generation immigrants.

Foreign pupils are asked to acquire certain language skills and civic values during their integration process, based on the duties established by the Italian *Code on Immigration*.[51] According to this code, immigrants should integrate in the Italian society, through a process aimed at promoting the coexistence of Italian and foreign citizens, with respect for the values enshrined in the Italian Constitution, with the mutual commitment to participate in the economic, social and cultural life of society. To obtain a residence permit, foreigners must sign an '*integration agreement*' with a commitment to achieve specific integration objectives.

The Immigration Code considers the educational status of foreigners and intercultural education. Foreign minors are subject to the same rights and duties as Italian pupils, and the right to schooling must also be guaranteed to them by the State, the Regions and other local authorities, including through the organisation of specific Italian courses. Linguistic and cultural differences must be considered as a value underpinning mutual respect and tolerance on the part of schools, which must promote initiatives aimed at including them, protecting the culture and language of origin of pupils and organising intercultural activities.[52]

For students with migration background, learning the Italian language is a major obstacle. This is why Law No. 107 of 2015 recognizes the teaching of Italian as L2 as part of the educational offer.[53] However, the implementation of this objective is still difficult to implement. Italian legislation favours the organization of Italian language teaching projects for the benefit of students with migrant backgrounds; however, this is merely an opportunity that each school may or may not take advantage of, depending on its financial resources and established priorities. In fact, Law No. 107 of 2015 refers to the autonomy of schools and does not allocate fees for organizing such courses.

Some didactic and organisational suggestions to foster the inclusion and educational success of pupils with immigration background are contained in the *Guidelines for the admission and integration of foreign pupils* issued by the Italian Ministry in 2014.[54] The document divides pupils into various categories, according to their different integration needs: pupils with non-Italian citizenship, pupils with non-Italian-speaking family background, unaccompanied minors, pupils who are children of mixed couples, pupils who have arrived by international adoption, and Roma, Sinti and Caminanti pupils. The guidelines give a series of advice to schools of great practical relevance: how to distribute foreign pupils in schools, how to involve families in the education process, rules on the teaching of Italian as L2, plurilingualism, and teacher training.

The Italian legal system, therefore, lays down specific rules for foreign pupils that prioritise the language aspect. However, language difficulties are part of a broader framework of inclusion, since pupils with a migrant background normally have other social, psychological or cultural difficulties that affect their school performance. Therefore, disadvantages in the socio-economic, linguistic and cultural spheres are part of BES and must be addressed with the tools of the inclusive school. Schools can therefore intervene by organising a customised and individualised pathway, as well as using compensatory and dispensatory tools (e.g., avoiding reading aloud or fast dictation). However, these are transitional interventions that serve students to 'get back on track' in order to continue as soon as possible following the mainstream programme together with the other students. Therefore, the effectiveness of the interventions must be monitored so that they are applied "for as long as strictly necessary."[55] Thus, dispensatory measures will be entirely transitional in nature; teachers will have to give priority to pedagogically and educationally customised paths and use fewer dispensatory or compensatory measures.

An important impetus for protection against discrimination based on racial or ethnic origin in education comes from the European Union (EU). Pursuant to Directive 2000/43/EC on the principle of equal treatment between persons irrespective of racial or ethnic origin, Italy approved Legislative Decree No. 215 of 2003 establishing an office for discrimination within the government, with the aim of promoting activities for the fostering of equality and the removal of any form of discrimination based on racial or ethnic origin, with reference also to cultural and religious forms of racism.[56] The EU has also adopted the *Action Plan on Integration and Inclusion 2021–2027*, which suggests targeted and personalised support that takes into consideration personal features, such as gender or religious background, that may offer particular problems to those with a migratory history. Early intervention and sustained commitment are both necessary for successful inclusion and integration.[57] The Action Plan does not suggest any integration and inclusion model to be followed, limiting itself to supporting Member States' initiatives with funding, dissemination and exchange of best practices, not least because the Union has only been granted a complementary competence in this area.

The Action Plan devotes special attention to schools. It identifies a number of situations in which pupils with a migrant background are disadvantaged: they run a higher risk of dropping out of school, in many cases they only achieve a lower level of education than their native peers and many of them are in families exposed to poverty and social exclusion.[58] Schools have the potential to provide the tools for the improvement of the social position of many pupils. Moreover, schools can also act as hubs, as they can connect pupils and their families, on the one hand, and associations or institutions facilitating integration and inclusion, on the other. In fact, if schools want to be successful and build cohesive communities, they cannot act in isolation, but must be able to count on the cooperation of other actors, also involving the local community.

Considering the importance of language acquisition up to an advanced level for students with a migratory background, it is hoped that Italian legislation guarantees every pupil with language gaps access to a learning path that lasts over time until the acquisition of an advanced level of knowledge of the language. In this process, a key role can be played by teachers and tutors who can guide and support students on their way to an advanced level of knowledge.

Students With Socio-Economic Difficulties

Students' socio-economic difficulties are a factor that can hinder the implementation of the right to education. This is why Article 34 of the Italian Constitution recognises the right of able and deserving students to attain the highest levels of education, even in the event of financial hardship. This provision is made effective by the same Article 34, which stipulates the State's obligation to intervene through scholarships, family allowances and other benefits, which must be awarded through competitive examinations.[59]

In the period following the approval of the Italian Constitution, the Constitutional Court interpreted the principle of the right to education free of charge in a reductive manner, essentially considering the provisions of Article 34 of the Constitution as a political programme. In addition, the right to education was considered very narrowly and limited to teaching activities to the exclusion of other related services, such as books availability, school canteens, and school transport. The legal doctrine of the time also interpreted Article 34 narrowly, arguing that it only included the administrative right to be admitted to the school, under the conditions laid down by law; however, there was no duty on the part of the State to set up and implement the school service. The position of private individuals was therefore one of mere interest and not of right. However, this approach was not shared by all. For instance, Pototschnig in the 1970s argued that Article 34 of the Constitution recognised a real subjective right to education.[60] This interpretation linked Article 34 with the Constitution's articles on fundamental rights, and the principle of equality and was later shared by the Constitutional Court.

The most recent rulings of the Italian Constitutional Court and the Italian legislation[61] emphasise a broad notion of the right to study, according to which everyone, on the basis of their abilities and merits, can have access to the highest levels of studies: an expression that indicates every level and type of education, including the university.[62] Requisites for the award of scholarships that discriminate directly or indirectly between national and foreign students are not legitimate, on the basis of EU Law, Constitutional and legal principles.[63] The Constitutional Court has consequently stricken down as unconstitutional those regional laws which required the residency in the Region as prerequisite for applying to the scholarship,[64] as in the case of the Province of Bolzano/Bozen[65] and the Province of Trento.[66] In the case of disabled students, ability and merit must be assessed on the basis of specific parameters tailored to the individual disability situation.

The Italian Ministry of Education guarantees the right to study throughout the country and defines the essential levels of services.[67] A State fund is established for the disbursement of scholarships for low-income secondary school students to combat school dropout.[68] Each year, the Ministry of Education, the Regions, and the local authorities establish the regional allocation of resources on the basis of the number of students and the regional school dropout index.

While the State has the task of identifying the levels of essential services, the Regions have full competence on the right to study. However, an examination of the levels of implementation of the various Regions poses a problem for the uneven level of implementation of the right to study throughout the country, as some Regions are much more efficient and generous than others.[69]

During the period of lock-down due to COVID-19, the right to study has acquired even more relevance, considering the need to ensure the availability of PCs, wi-fi, and communication and teaching software for students to attend classes. However, in some cases Regions have reduced or withdrawn scholarships for merit.[70]

CONCLUSIONS

In this article we have analysed the diversities that exist among students in Italian schools and the degree of legal protection afforded to them within the Italian and European legal frameworks based on the principle of non-discrimination and inclusion. We have highlighted how the intensity of protection varies according to the type of diversity.

Regulatory guarantees against discrimination based on students' disability conditions are the strong core of legislation and jurisprudential interventions. This stems from the fact that disability should be certified by a doctor. Until the 1970s, the management of disability had been entrusted to the exclusive medical monopoly; following the regulatory reforms adopted from 1971 onwards, an important social and psychological component was added, based on the evolution of scientific research and the indications of the World Health Organisation, which accept a bio-psycho-social model of disability. Another reason why this category of pupils is particularly protected stems from the presence of international treaty - the *United Nations Convention on the Rights of Persons with Disabilities* - which has been ratified by Italy and is binding. Notwithstanding the high level of legal protection, some Regions still encounter practical difficulties in enforcing the legislation, as demonstrated by the recent *G.L. v. Italy* case decided by the ECtHR. This case shows how social rights, such as the right to education, are increasingly restricted by legislative imperatives linked to the budget balancing requirements of the Italian State and Regions.

Less severe cases of disability and specific learning disorders (SLD) also require a certified clinical diagnosis in order to enjoy the rights guaranteed by law (dispensatory measures, compensatory aids, timing). However, there is no juxtaposition between these cases and those of disability, as the procedures are different, and the diagnosis for specific learning disorders does not entitle the child to support teachers.

Legislation protecting against other types of diversity not certified by a medical certificate is less strong; this is the case of discrimination on the grounds of skin colour and migratory background, which is left more to the choices of schools and general legislation than to actual regulatory obligations. Nevertheless, there are interesting initiatives aimed at promoting respect for differences in children at school, essentially through guidelines and plans adopted by the State and the EU. The greatest difficulty encountered by these students is that of the Italian language; this is why the regulations provide for the teaching of Italian as L2. However, these students do not only have problems in the language but are also bearers of multiple diversities, such as economic, social and cultural difficulties.

The intervention of the State and the Regions to guarantee the right to study for students with economic and social difficulties is very relevant. Although guaranteed by the Constitution, the right to study has struggled to take hold because it is conditioned by the State's financial restrictions and because it has been interpreted in a very narrow way by case law and doctrine. The situation has changed only recently, with the passing of more advanced legislation that has provided for personalized intervention to enable the cultural and personal development of each student. Jurisprudence has managed to limit discrimination between Italians and foreigners or between residents and non-residents. Here again, however, the right to study is continually threatened by the lack of public resources and by the fact that the type of protection depends on the type of Region, which is highly differentiated in contrast to the need to provide uniform services throughout Italy.

More recently, the Italian legal system has introduced promotional regulations to foster a set of both training and educational actions in schools of all levels to overcome new inequalities and prejudices, through the "*National Plan for Respect Education*" launched by the State in 2017.[71] The actions cover themes such as gender discrimination, race and religion, homophobia, bullying, STEM (promoting science education for female students). The implementation of the pact shows that the transmission of the principles of social coexistence and respect between people is fully among the tasks of the school, which exercises them together with the families.

NOTES

1. This research project resulted in the publication of the special issue: S. Baroncelli (Ed.) (2022) Diritto all'istruzione e inclusione nelle scuole dopo la pandemia. Quali diseguaglianze, quale autonomia? *federalismi.it*. 32/2022, 1–154, from: https://www.federalismi.it/focus/index_focus.cfm?FOCUS_ID=156. The special issue contains the following articles: S. Baroncelli. Diritto alla diversità e inclusione nelle scuole: disabilità, condizioni economico-sociali, background migratorio, genere e minoranze linguistiche, iv–xx; G. Matucci. Fra nuove resistenze e manifestazioni di resilienza. Scuola e inclusione in tempo di Covid,1-16; G. Chiara. L'inclusione scolastica negli sviluppi normativi e della giurisprudenza costituzionale: brevi notazioni,17–34; A. Simonati. Dal "piano nazionale per l'educazione al rispetto" all'autonomia scolastica: il metodo "reticolare" per l'inclusione e l'integrazione, 35–48; A. Poggi. L'autonomia scolastica come autonomia funzionale: promessa mancata o rivoluzione fallita?, 49–66; M. Rosini. Capacità, merito e carenza di mezzi. Riflessioni critiche sul diritto allo studio, 67-93; O. Farkas. Integrazione nella scuola inclusiva: alunni con background migratorio nella scuola italiana in una prospettiva europea, 94–114; M. Cosulich & E. Happacher. Scuola e minoranze linguistiche nelle autonomie speciali alpine, 115–137; M. Falanga. Il principio di inclusione sociale e suo riverbero nella materia della pubblica istruzione, 138–154.

    The results and publications of the research are also visible on the research project website from: https://diversityatschool.project.unibz.it
2. B. Bouquet (2015). L'inclusion: approche socio-sémantique. *Vie sociale, 11(3)*, 15–25.
3. United Nations, Committee on the Rights of Persons with Disabilities (2016). General comment No. 4 (2016) on the right to inclusive education, 10: "Inclusive education is to be understood as:

    (a) A fundamental human right of all learners. Notably, education is the right of the individual learner and not, in the case of children, the right of a parent or caregiver. Parental responsibilities in this regard are subordinate to the rights of the child; (b) A principle that values the well-being of all students, respects their inherent dignity and autonomy, and acknowledges individuals' requirements and their ability to effectively be included in and contribute to society; (c) A means of realizing other human rights. It is the primary means by which persons with disabilities can lift themselves out of poverty, obtain the means to participate fully in their communities and be safeguarded from exploitation. It is also the primary means of achieving inclusive societies; (d) The result of a process of continuing and proactive commitment to eliminating barriers impeding the right to education, together with changes to culture, policy and practice of regular schools to accommodate and effectively include all students."

4. UNESCO (1994). The Salamanca Statement and Framework for Action on Special Needs Education, Salamanca, Spagna, from: https://unesdoc.unesco.org/ark:/48223/pf0000098427

    The Salamanca Framework was adopted by the World Conference on Special Needs Education. Such conference was organized by the Government of Spain in cooperation with UNESCO and held in Salamanca in 1994 with the aim to give to States and institutions guidance in the implementation of the Salamanca Declaration.

5. Data by UNESCO (1990). World Declaration on Education for All and Framework for Action to Meet Basic Learning Needs, adopted by the World Conference on Education for All, Meeting Basic Learning Needs, Jomtien, Thailand 5–9 March 1990, 2, from: https://www.humanium.org/en/wp-content/uploads/2017/03/Education_for_all.pdf

6. UNESCO (1990). World Declaration on Education for All.

7. UNESCO (1990). World Declaration on Education for All, 12.

8. UNESCO (1990). World Declaration on Education for All, 11.

9. United Nations (2006). Convention on the Rights of Persons with Disabilities, New York, 2006, https://www.ohchr.org/en/instruments-mechanisms/instruments/convention-rights-persons-disabilities

10. The Convention became effective on May 3, 2008 and has been ratified by 164 States while 89 States have ratified both the Convention and the Optional Protocol. As for Italy, see Law No. 18 of 2009.

11. S. Favalli (2018). The United Nations Convention on the Rights of Persons with Disabilities in the Case Law of the European Court of Human Rights and in the Council of Europe Disability Strategy 2017–2023: 'from Zero to Hero'. *Human Rights Law Review, 18(3)*, 517–538, from: https://doi.org/10.1093/hrlr/ngy026

12. Art. 21 of the EU Charter: "Any discrimination based on any ground such as sex, race, colour, ethnic or social origin, genetic features, language, religion or belief, political or any other opinion, membership of a national minority, property, birth, disability, age or sexual orientation shall be prohibited."

13. Council of Europe (2022). Guide on Article 2 of Protocol No. 1 to the European Convention on Human Rights, Right to Education, 31 August 2022.

14. ECtHR, case *relating to certain aspects of the laws on the use of languages in education in Belgium v. Belgium (merits)* (application no 1474/62; 1677/62; 1691/62; 1769/63; 1994/63; 2126/64), 23 July 1968.

15. ECtHR, *Altinay v. Turkey*, application no. 37222/04, 9 July 2013.

16. ECtHR, *G.L. v. Italy*, application no. 59751/15, 10 September 2020.

17. See para. on "Practical difficulties in implementation."

Inclusion and Diversities in Italian Schools Between Theory and Practice ▪ **215**

18. ECtHR, *Dupin v. France*, application no. 2282/17, 24 January 2019.
19. A. Patti (2020). Il diritto all'istruzione delle persone con disabilità: le pronunce Dupin contro Francia e Stoian contro Romania. *Forum di Quaderni costituzionali*, 1, 188.
20. ECtHR, *Stoian v. Romania*, application no. 289/14, 25 June 2019.
21. See A.M. Poggi (2019). Per un «diverso» stato sociale. La parabola del diritto all'istruzione nel nostro Paese, Bologna; M. Falanga (2017). *Diritto scolastico. Analisi e profilo*. ELS La Scuola, 11–36.
22. See G. Chiara (2020). Scuola e nuove problematiche di inclusione sociale. In A. Ciancio (Ed.), *Ripensare o "rinnovare" le formazioni sociali? Legislatori e giudici di fronte alle sfide del pluralismo sociale nelle democrazie contemporanee*. Turin, 77–96.
23. S. Penasa (2014). La persona e la funzione promozionale della scuola: la realizzazione del disegno costituzionale e il necessario ruolo dei poteri pubblici. I casi dell'istruzione delle persone disabili e degli alunni stranieri. In F. Cortese (Ed.), *Tra amministrazione e scuola. Snodi e crocevia del diritto scolastico italiano*. Naples: Editoriale Scientifica, 1–40.
24. D. Bellocco (2021). La persona con disabilità alla luce dei risvolti costituzionali. *Ratio Iuris*, 3.
25. Royal Decree No. 3126 of 1923.
26. Royal Decree No. 786 of 1933.
27. Italian Constitutional Court, Judgment No. 215 of 1987.
28. Italian Constitutional Court, Judgment No. 467 of 2002.
29. Law n. 107 of 13.7.2015.
30. See the aims to be pursued by the school enshrined in Law No. 107 of 2015: preventing and combating early school leaving, all forms of discrimination and bullying, including cyberbullying; strengthening of school inclusion and the right to study of pupils with special educational needs through individualised and personalised paths, also with the support and collaboration of the local social, health and educational services and sector associations [...] promotion of individualised training paths and involvement of pupils and students; identification of pathways and systems functional to the enhancement of pupils' and students' merit; literacy and improvement of Italian as a second language through courses and workshops for students of non-Italian language, to be organised also in collaboration with local authorities and the third sector, with the contribution of communities of origin, families and cultural mediators.
31. This concept was enunciated and deepened especially by G. Zagrebelsky (1993). Problemi in ordine ai costi delle sentenze costituzionali. In AA. VV. (Eds.), *Le sentenze della Corte costituzionale e l'art. 81, u.c., della Costituzione* (p. 123). Milano: Giuffrè. According to Zagrebelsky, a former judge of the Italian Constitutional Court, when it comes to the overriding values of the welfare state, the principle of budgetary balance cannot in any way condition spending decisions of the Constitutional Court.
32. Italian Constitutional Court, Judgment No. 125 of 1975.
33. Italian Constitutional Court, Judgment No. 215/1987. On this case, see S. Troilo (2012). I "nuovi" diritti sociali: la parabola dell'integrazione scolastica dei disabili. *Associazione Gruppo di Pisa*, *3*, 2012, from: https://www.gruppo-

dipisa.it/8-rivista/263-silvio-troilo-i-nuovi-diritti-sociali-la-parabola-dell-integrazione-scolastica-dei-disabili
34. Article 97, Article 120, Article 117, paragraph 3, of the Italian Constitution. See F. Angelini, & M. Benvenuti (2014). *Le dimensioni costituzionali dell'istruzione*. Naples: Jovene.
35. Article 81 of the Constitution provides for the principle of balanced budget.
36. Italian Constitutional Court, Judgment No. 80 of 2010, Judgment No. 275 of 2016, Judgment No. 83 of 2019. Judgment No. 275 of 2016 has been widely analysed by scholars. See E. Vivaldi (2019). Il diritto all'istruzione delle persone con disabilità: continuità dei finanziamenti e tutela del nucleo essenziale del diritto. *Le Regioni*, 3, 814–823; E. Furno (2017). Pareggio di bilancio e diritti sociali: la ridefinizione dei confini nella recente giurisprudenza costituzionale in tema di diritto all'istruzione dei disabili. *Nomos*, 1, 1–22; L. Madau (2017). "È la garanzia dei diritti incomprimibili ad incidere sul bilancio, e non l'equilibrio di questo a condizionarne la doverosa erogazione." Nota a Corte cost. n. 275/2016. *Osservatorio AIC*, 1, 1–13; A. Longo (2016). Una concezione del bilancio costituzionalmente orientata: prime riflessioni sulla sentenza della Corte costituzionale n. 275 del 2016. *federalismi.it*, 10, 1–14; R. Cabazzi (2017). Diritti incomprimibili degli studenti con disabilità ed equilibrio di bilancio nella finanza locale secondo la sent. della Corte costituzionale n. 275/2016. *Le Regioni*, 3, 593–608; L. Ardizzone & R. Di Maria (2017). La tutela dei diritti fondamentali ed il "totem" della programmazione: il bilanciamento (possibile) fra equilibrio economico-finanziario e prestazioni sociali (brevi riflessioni a margine di Corte cost., sent. 275/2016). *Diritti Regionali*, 2, 173–190; F. Blando (2017). Soggetti disabili e istruzione: la lotta per il diritto. *federalismi.it*, 10, 1–17.
37. Italian Constitutional Court, Judgment No. 454 of 1994.
38. United Nations. Committee on the Rights of Persons with Disabilities (2016). Concluding observations on the initial report of Italy, 31.8.2016, 1.
39. Mission 4 (Education and Research) of the NPRR provides for 100.000 classrooms transformed into connected learning environments, school renovations for a total of 2.4 million square meters, and the wiring of 40.000 school buildings. See https://pnrr.istruzione.it
40. L. Trucco (2012). Livelli essenziali delle prestazioni e sostenibilità finanziaria dei diritti sociali. www.*gruppodipisa.it*, 3, 2.
41. ECtHR, *G.L. v. Italy*, Application no. 59751/15, 10 September 2020.
42. ECtHR, *G.L. v. Italy*, § 68.
43. Article 1, paragraph 2, Presidential Decree No. 275 of 1999: "2. The autonomy of educational institutions is a guarantee of freedom of teaching and cultural pluralism and is embodied in the planning and implementation of educational training and education aimed at the development of the human person, adapted to different contexts, to the demands of families and to the specific characteristics of the subjects involved, in order to guarantee their educational success, in line with the general aims and objectives of the education system and with the need to improve the effectiveness of the teaching and learning process" (ToA).
44. Law No. 53 of 2003.

45. Disabled students are protected by Law No. 104 of 1992 and DPR 24.02.1994.
46. Law No. 170 of 2010.
47. G. Arconzo (2021). Disabilità e diritto all'istruzione. *Forum di Quaderni Costituzionali Rassegna*, 510.
48. MIUR (Italian Ministry of Education), Ministerial Decree 27 December 2012 and Ministerial Internal Regulation (Circolare) No. 8, 6 March 2013.
49. MIUR. Ufficio statistico (2021). Gli alunni con cittadinanza non italiana. Anno scolastico 2020–21, 8.
50. Since, while the number of pupils with non-Italian citizenship decreased, the total number of pupils also decreased by almost 121,000 (or -1.4%).
51. Article 4 bis of Legislative Decree No. 286 of 1998.
52. Article 38 of the Italian Immigration Code.
53. Law No. 107 of 2015 has as a general object the literacy and improvement of Italian as a second language through courses and workshops for students with non-Italian citizenship or language. Such courses should be organised also in cooperation with local authorities and the third sector, with the contribution of communities of origin, families and cultural mediators.
54. MIUR, Linee guida per l'accoglienza e l'integrazione degli alunni stranieri, 2014, https://www.miur.gov.it/documents/20182/2223566/linee_guida_integrazione_alunni_stranieri.p%20df/5e41fc48-3c68-2a17-ae75-1b5da6a55667?t=1564667201890
55. MIUR (Italian Ministry of Education), Ministerial Internal Regulation (Circolare) No. 8, 6 March 2013, 3.
56. Legislative Decree No. 215 of 2003—Implementation of Directive 2000/43/EC implementing the principle of equal treatment between persons irrespective of racial or ethnic origin.
57. European Commission (2020). Communication to the European Parliament, the Council, the European Economic and Social Committee and the Committee of the Regions, Action plan on Integration and Inclusion 2021-2027, COM/2020/758 final.
58. Farkas, *Integrazione nella scuola inclusiva: alunni con background migratorio nella scuola italiana in una prospettiva europea*, 94.
59. For general comments on Article 34 of the Constitution see Q. Camerlengo (2008). Art. 34 Cost. In S. Bartole & R. Bin (Eds.) *Commentario breve alla Costituzione*, Padova, 341; A. Poggi (2006). Art. 34. In R. Bifulco, A. Celotto, M. Olivetti (Eds.). *Commentario alla Costituzione*, vol. I, Torino, 704; B. Caravita (1990). Art. 33 e 34. In V. Crisafulli & L. Paladin (Eds.) *Commentario breve alla Costituzione*, Padova, 232; S. Cassese & A. Mura (1976). Art. 33 e 34. In M. Bessone, L. Montuschi, D. Vincenzi Amato, S. Cassese, A. Mura (1976). *Rapporti etico-sociali. Commentario della Costituzione*, diretto da G. Branca, Roma, 252.
60. U. Pototschnig (1973). Istruzione (diritto alla). In *Enciclopedia del diritto*, vol. XXIII, Milano, 98: "The right provided for in Article 34 is not merely formal (right to be enrolled in a school), but is a right to enjoy the necessary education, 'in spite of' any possible economic and social obstacles that individuals may come up against in practice."
61. See Legislative Decree No. 63 of 2017.

62. Even the Court of Justice of the EU uses a large interpretation of 'education' in the implementation of Council Directive 2000/43/EC of 29 June 2000 on the principle of equal treatment between persons irrespective of racial or ethnic origin, including also the award by a private foundation of scholarships to support research projects or studies abroad. However, the Court requires a close link between the financial payments and participation to research projects, which also fall within the concept of 'education'. See Court of Justice of the EU, *Heiko Jonny Maniero v. Studienstiftung des deutschen Volkes*, Case C-457/17.
63. As for EU Law, see Council Directive 2000/43/EC of 29 June 2000 implementing the principle of equal treatment between persons irrespective of racial or ethnic origin, which forbids direct and indirect discrimination also in the field of education and vocational training.
64. The residence clause was provided for by some regional laws as a condition or even only as a favourable element for access to university courses.
65. See Italian Constitutional Court, Judgment No. 2 of 2013, delivered against the Law of the Autonomous Province of Bolzano No. 12 of 2011 ('Integration of foreign citizens'), which required a minimum period of five years of uninterrupted residence for citizens of non-EU countries in order to have access to the facilities provided for attendance at a school located outside the province and to financial benefits for the right to university study.
66. Italian Constitutional Court, Judgment No. 42 of 2021, concerning the Trento provincial Law No. 13 of 2019, insofar as it provided that the province could reserve a number of places not inferior to 10% to candidates residing in the province of Trento, in the case of equal merit with non-resident candidates in the university entrance tests.
67. Art. 1, para. 181 f), Law No. 107 of 2015 establishes some general principles implemented by Legislative Decree No. 63 of 2017.
68. Article 9 of Legislative Decree No. 63 of 2017.
69. Rosini, *Capacità, merito e carenza di mezzi. Riflessioni critiche sul diritto allo studio*, 67.
70. This is the case for South Tyrol for university students, see: https://civis.bz.it/it/servizi/servizio.html?id=1002940
71. Simonati, *Dal "piano nazionale per l'educazione al rispetto" all'autonomia scolastica: il metodo "reticolare" per l'inclusione e l'integrazione*, 35.

REFERENCES

Angelini, F., & Benvenuti, M. (2014). *Le dimensioni costituzionali dell'istruzione*. Naples: Jovene.

Arconzo, G. (2021). Disabilità e diritto all'istruzione. *Forum di Quaderni Costituzionali Rassegna*, from www.forumcostituzionale.it

Ardizzone, L., & Di Maria, R. (2017). La tutela dei diritti fondamentali ed il "totem" della programmazione: il bilanciamento (possibile) fra equilibrio economico-finanziario e prestazioni sociali (brevi riflessioni a margine di Corte cost., sent. 275/2016). *Diritti Regionali*, 2, 173–190, from: https://www.dirittiregionali.it/wp-content/uploads/2017/04/documento-integrale3.pdf

Baroncelli, S. (2022). Diritto alla diversità e inclusione nelle scuole: disabilità, condizioni economico-sociali, background migratorio, genere e minoranze linguistiche. In S. Baroncelli (Ed.) Diritto all'istruzione e inclusione nelle scuole dopo la pandemia. Quali diseguaglianze, quale autonomia? *federalismi.it*. 32/2022, iv–xx, from: https://www.federalismi.it/focus/index_focus.cfm?FOCUS_ID=156.

Bellocco, D. (2021). La persona con disabilità alla luce dei risvolti costituzionali. *Ratio Iuris*, from: https://www.ratioiuris.it/la-persona-con-disabilita-alla-luce-dei-risvolti-costituzionali

Blando, F. (2017). Soggetti disabili e istruzione: la lotta per il diritto. *federalismi.it*, *10*, 1–17, from: https://www.federalismi.it/nv14/articolo-documento.cfm?Artid=34010&content=&content_author=

Bouquet, B. (2015). L'inclusion: approche socio-sémantique. *Vie sociale*, *11*(3), 15–25, from: https://www.cairn.info/revue-vie-sociale-2015-3-page-15.htm.

Cabazzi, R. (2017). Diritti incomprimibili degli studenti con disabilità ed equilibrio di bilancio nella finanza locale secondo la sent. della Corte costituzionale n. 275/2016. *Le Regioni*, *3*, 593–608.

Camerlengo, Q. (2008). Art. 34 Cost. In S. Bartole, & R. Bin (Eds.) *Commentario breve alla Costituzione*, Padova, 322–341.

Caravita, B. (1990). Art. 33 e 34. In V. Crisafulli & L. Paladin (Eds.) *Commentario breve alla Costituzione*, Padova, 224–232.

Cassese, S., & Mura, A. (1976). Art. 33 e 34. In M. Bessone, L. Montuschi, D. Vincenzi Amato, S. Cassese, & A. Mura (1976). *Rapporti etico-sociali. Commentario della Costituzione*, diretto da G. Branca, Roma.

Chiara, G. (2022) L'inclusione scolastica negli sviluppi normativi e della giurisprudenza costituzionale: brevi notazioni. In S. Baroncelli (Ed.) Diritto all'istruzione e inclusione nelle scuole dopo la pandemia. Quali diseguaglianze, quale autonomia? *federalismi.it*. 32/2022, 17–34, from: https://www.federalismi.it/focus/index_focus.cfm?FOCUS_ID=156.

Chiara, G. (2020). Scuola e nuove problematiche di inclusione sociale. In A. Ciancio (Ed.), *Ripensare o "rinnovare" le formazioni sociali? Legislatori e giudici di fronte alle sfide del pluralismo sociale nelle democrazie contemporanee*. Turin, 77–96.

Cortese, F. (Ed.). (2014). *Tra amministrazione e scuola. Snodi e crocevia del diritto scolastico italiano*. Naples: Editoriale Scientifica.

Cosulich, M., & Happacher, E. (2022) Scuola e minoranze linguistiche nelle autonomie speciali alpine. In S. Baroncelli (Ed.) Diritto all'istruzione e inclusione nelle scuole dopo la pandemia. Quali diseguaglianze, quale autonomia? *federalismi.it*. 32/2022, 115–137, from: https://www.federalismi.it/focus/index_focus.cfm?FOCUS_ID=156.

European Commission. (2020). Communication to the European Parliament, the Council, the European Economic and Social Committee and the Committee of the Regions, Action plan on Integration and Inclusion 2021–2027, COM/2020/758 final.

Falanga, M. (2022). Il principio di inclusione sociale e suo riverbero nella materia della pubblica istruzione. In S. Baroncelli (Ed.) Diritto all'istruzione e inclusione nelle scuole dopo la pandemia. Quali diseguaglianze, quale autonomia?

federalismi.it. 32/2022, 138-154, from: https://www.federalismi.it/focus/index_focus.cfm?FOCUS_ID=156.
Falanga, M. (2017). *Diritto scolastico. Analisi e profilo.* ELS La Scuola.
Farkas, O. (2022) Integrazione nella scuola inclusiva: alunni con background migratorio nella scuola italiana in una prospettiva europea. In S. Baroncelli (Ed.) Diritto all'istruzione e inclusione nelle scuole dopo la pandemia. Quali diseguaglianze, quale autonomia? *federalismi.it.* 32/2022, 94–114, from: https://www.federalismi.it/focus/index_focus.cfm?FOCUS_ID=156.
Favalli, S. (2018). The United Nations Convention on the Rights of Persons with Disabilities in the Case Law of the European Court of Human Rights and in the Council of Europe Disability Strategy 2017–2023: 'from Zero to Hero'. *Human Rights Law Review,* 18(3), 517–538, from: https://doi.org/10.1093/hrlr/ngy026
Furno, E. (2017). Pareggio di bilancio e diritti sociali: la ridefinizione dei confini nella recente giurisprudenza costituzionale in tema di diritto all'istruzione dei disabili. *Nomos,* 1, 1–22.
Longo, A. (2016). Una concezione del bilancio costituzionalmente orientata: prime riflessioni sulla sentenza della Corte costituzionale n. 275 del 2016. *federalismi.it,* 10, 1–14.
Madau, L. (2017). "È la garanzia dei diritti incomprimibili ad incidere sul bilancio, e non l'equilibrio di questo a condizionarne la doverosa erogazione." Nota a Corte cost. n. 275/2016. *Osservatorio AIC,* 1, 1–13.
Matucci, G. (2022) Fra nuove resistenze e manifestazioni di resilienza. Scuola e inclusione in tempo di Covid. In S. Baroncelli (Ed.) Diritto all'istruzione e inclusione nelle scuole dopo la pandemia. Quali diseguaglianze, quale autonomia? *federalismi.it.* 32/2022, 1–16, from: https://www.federalismi.it/focus/index_focus.cfm?FOCUS_ID=156.
Patti, A. (2020). Il diritto all'istruzione delle persone con disabilità: le pronunce Dupin contro Francia e Stoian contro Romania. *Forum di Quaderni costituzionali,* 1, from: https://www.forumcostituzionale.it/wordpress/
Penasa, S. (2014). La persona e la funzione promozionale della scuola: la realizzazione del disegno costituzionale e il necessario ruolo dei poteri pubblici. I casi dell'istruzione delle persone disabili e degli alunni stranieri. In F. Cortese (Ed.), *Tra amministrazione e scuola. Snodi e crocevia del diritto scolastico italiano.* Naples: Editoriale Scientifica, 1–40.
Poggi, A. (2022) L'autonomia scolastica come autonomia funzionale: promessa mancata o rivoluzione fallita? In S. Baroncelli (Ed.) (2022) Diritto all'istruzione e inclusione nelle scuole dopo la pandemia. Quali diseguaglianze, quale autonomia? *federalismi.it.* 32/2022, 49–66, from: https://www.federalismi.it/focus/index_focus.cfm?FOCUS_ID=156.
Poggi, A. (2019). *Per un «diverso» stato sociale. La parabola del diritto all'istruzione nel nostro Paese.* Bologna: il Mulino.
Poggi, A. (2006). Art. 34. In R. Bifulco, A. Celotto, & M. Olivetti (Eds.). *Commentario alla Costituzione,* vol. I, Torino, 699–716.
Pototschnig, U. (1973). Istruzione (diritto alla). In *Enciclopedia del diritto,* vol. XXIII, Milano.

Simonati, A. (2022) Dal "piano nazionale per l'educazione al rispetto" all'autonomia scolastica: il metodo "reticolare" per l'inclusione e l'integrazione. In S. Baroncelli (Ed.) Diritto all'istruzione e inclusione nelle scuole dopo la pandemia. Quali diseguaglianze, quale autonomia? *federalismi.it.* 32/2022, 35–48, from: https://www.federalismi.it/focus/index_focus.cfm?FOCUS_ID=156

Rosini, M. (2022) Capacità, merito e carenza di mezzi. Riflessioni critiche sul diritto allo studio. In S. Baroncelli (Ed.) Diritto all'istruzione e inclusione nelle scuole dopo la pandemia. Quali diseguaglianze, quale autonomia? *federalismi.it.* 32/2022, 67–93, from: https://www.federalismi.it/focus/index_focus.cfm?FOCUS_ID=156.

Troilo, S. (2012). I "nuovi" diritti sociali: la parabola dell'integrazione scolastica dei disabili. *Associazione Gruppo di Pisa, 3,* 1–14, from: www.*gruppodipisa.it*.

Trucco, L. (2012). Livelli essenziali delle prestazioni e sostenibilità finanziaria dei diritti sociali. *Associazione Gruppo di Pisa, 3,* 1–92, from: www.*gruppodipisa.it*.

UNESCO. (1994). The Salamanca Statement and Framework for Action on Special Needs Education, Salamanca, Spagna, from: https://unesdoc.unesco.org/ark:/48223/pf0000098427

UNESCO. (1990).World Declaration on Education for All and Framework for Action to Meet Basic Learning Needs, adopted by the World Conference on Education for All, Meeting Basic Learning Needs, Jomtien, Thailand 5–9 March 1990, 2, from: https://www.humanium.org/en/wp-content/uploads/2017/03/Education_for_all.pdf

United Nations, Committee on the Rights of Persons with Disabilities. (2016). General comment No. 4 (2016) on the right to inclusive education.

United Nations. (2006). Convention on the Rights of Persons with Disabilities, New York, 2006, from: https://www.ohchr.org/en/instruments-mechanisms/instruments/convention-rights-persons-disabilities.

Vivaldi, E. (2019). Il diritto all'istruzione delle persone con disabilità: continuità dei finanziamenti e tutela del nucleo essenziale del diritto. *Le Regioni, 3,* 814–823.

Zagrebelsky, G. (1993). Problemi in ordine ai costi delle sentenze costituzionali. In AA. VV. (Eds.). *Le sentenze della Corte costituzionale e l'art. 81, u.c., della Costituzione,* Milano: Giuffrè, 327–382.

Zagrebelsky, G. (2022). *La lezione.* Torino: Einaudi.

CHAPTER 12

DIGITALIZATION AND THE EDUCATION SYSTEM

What Prospects for Building a Truly Inclusive System?

Loredana Giani
Università Europea di Roma

ABSTRACT

This chapter addresses the issue of digitalization in the education system by examining the potential and criticalities inherent in this transition, also in the light of the elements of reflection that emerged during the COVID-19 pandemic.

The analysis also aims to verify the various components that are at the origin of the so-called digital divide, which is not to be traced back to the skills profile alone, or to merely economic factors, but also to the very characteristics of the territories and, therefore, infrastructural data.

Given this key, we proceeded to read the contents of the National Plan for the Digital School, and the impact that the PNRR has had on the context of digitalization, above all using a key of interpretation that aims at to exploit the existing tools, including digitalization, being careful to avoid them becoming an instrument of inequality, rather than a tool aimed at bridging existing inequalities.

DIGITAL TRANSITION AND INCLUSION: A POSSIBLE MARRIAGE?

Any discourse that wishes to address the issue of the digital transition of an inclusive educational system requires that reference be made to a model that necessarily moves away—and it could not be otherwise—from a sphere of inquiry limited to the single reality considered, specifically that of the school, to make way for a necessarily broader vision, in which various co-ordinates are intercepted, ranging from the preliminary consideration of what should be meant by an inclusive educational system, from a perspective in which inclusion becomes a tool for the realisation of the more general objective of cohesion, to the consideration of transition in a broad dimension in which digitalisation is not, and could not, be considered only with reference to what takes place within the educational system, but in a broader sense, considering the educational system as part of a broader institutional *framework*.

Moving on from the first element mentioned, that of inclusion—understood as a projection of cohesion (economic and, above all, social), in turn an element that underpins sustainability itself, of which, from many sides, we hear multiple declinations—it is clear that we cannot ignore the need to take an overall view in which a relationship of logical presupposition emerges between inclusion, understood as a tool with (necessarily) organisational value, and the realisation of the other two objectives (cohesion and sustainability), in a substantive sense that has, however, struggled to assert itself in the context of ordinary legislation.[1]

School inclusion represents, in fact, only one of the possible declinations in which the macro-category can be understood, and it is based on the recognition of the relevance of full participation in life (at school, but not only, if we consider the school as part of a "network" on which society is based) of all individuals, configuring itself as a process that presupposes the enhancement of individual differences and the facilitation of social participation and learning; a process in which the school, part of a broader organisation, becomes a key player in eliminating the barriers that stand between the individual and the exercise of their fundamental rights.[2]

POVERTY AND INCLUSION

In this context, in order to understand whether, and to what extent, the digital transition can support and promote the achievement of 'inclusion', it is necessary to focus on "poverty,"[3] understood in a plural and interconnected declination, from a perspective that certainly cannot be reduced to the merely material or materialistic, and, I would say, reductively economic dimension. It has to be understood according to a relational point of view that, while not ignoring the merely material dimension mentioned, understands poverty in an overall dimension, referring to "weakness," understood as a datum that requires the intervention of the public subject in the guise of the implementer of the duty of social solidarity, highlighting, among other things, that multidimensionality that shows the non-bi-univocity of the single poverty-inequality relationship, but, on the contrary, reveals an internal incrementality between poverty and its consequences on inequality, an obstacle to any inclusive process.[4]

And so, especially in the context of defining the focal variable of the survey, i.e., the evaluative space on the basis of which inequalities are to be assessed, following Sen's teachings, two questions emerge that need to be answered: "equality of what?" and "equality for what?."

Two questions the autonomous relevance of which immediately emerges in the framework of the educational context and, above all, where the profiles related to digitalisation are integrated in it, which, if considered from the content profile (referring to the potential that the implementation of digital tools can present), can mark a qualitative leap in the education sector. A potential that is immediately resized and relativised if we consider the negative potential of the so-called digital divide[5] which, among other things, cannot be linked solely to the capacity-related aspects, but must, as we will see, take into consideration a multiplicity of factors, including the infrastructural data and, therefore, the characteristics of the territorial systems. A context, the one just referred to, in which equality of capacity, referring to the "individual's freedom to lead a certain type of life rather than another"[6] is referred not only to the space of "capacities," but also to that of "functioning," i.e., the states and ways of being and doing that people can acquire in the course of their lives such as, for example, being nourished, enjoying good health, enjoying self-respect, taking part in community life.[7]

From the perspective considered, in which the areas of education and digitalisation are examined from a binary perspective, the answer to the first question cannot be reductively summarised by referring to access to educational processes and, in parallel, to digital systems, understood as components of the pedagogical path.

Starting from the first element, in the context of the education system, rivers of ink have been used, and not only in the legal context, to investigate the instruments aimed at guaranteeing access, first, and then that series of interventions of a substantial nature that have significantly delineated the characteristics of the right to education, or the right to school (recalling in both cases the relevance of training courses),[8] in order to ensure the fulfilment of those duties of solidarity and those obligations imposed by the principle of substantive equality that constitute the essential prerequisite for the full development of the person and, therefore, as a guarantee of that unswerving, essential and undeniable core of fundamental rights, among which the right to education (which is not understood here from the perspective limited to education) and training is fully included. This same nucleus has as its counterpart the constitutional requirement for public intervention, a requirement the recognition of which has led the Constitutional Court to affirm the balancing of the budget, which cannot in any way be limited to temporary interventions of a welfarist nature, but should be developed in a systemic dimension. A profile that is precisely the main criticality of the public intervention carried out so far.

Following this line of exposition leads to the second question posed at the beginning.

Starting from the current and specific context of the education system, equality cannot be referred to the overall purposes that are enclosed in the multiform concept of the "right to education" correlated to the (guarantee of a) construction of (real) citizenship paths in a democratic system and, therefore the concept itself of inclusion cannot be limited only to those aspects that are of immediate impact related to the hypothesis in which the subject has disabilities or falls into the broad category of BES,[9] but must be understood in a broader sense and must be referred to the individual understood in their complexity from a perspective in which the need cannot be understood in a way that is parcelled out, but as a prismatic projection of different needs that, however, belong to the same subject.[10]

Therefore, considering the premises outlined above, it is clear that equality must be referred to the project of building those capabilities[11] that allow the realisation of that substantial equality that enables the individual to express their personality, even in the social formations of which they are part, regardless of their starting conditions. And so, in the relationship between inclusion and diversity, in the context of inclusive processes, it is necessary to shun uniforming dynamics, which in themselves contain the germ of inequality, inherent in the choice of a single reference model, guaranteeing an inclusion that is "sensitive to differences" that, in the words of Habermas, ensures "cultural autonomy, rights relating to certain groups, programmes of legal equalisation, as well as arrangements aimed at effective protection of minorities."[12]

From this perspective, as mentioned above, the relevance of the issue of poverty emerges in a multifaceted and multidimensional form that finds a positive projection in the construction of inclusive processes with respect to which education clearly plays a central role. Poverty, and specifically educational poverty, should not be understood only in terms of weakness,[13] but should also be examined with a view to enhancing the potential of a digital transition process, in a different dimension, as an evidently broader phenomenon, which refers to a state of vulnerability linked to a level of deprivation that does not guarantee appropriate and just opportunities.

And it is certainly no coincidence that over the years the fight against educational poverty has become a central objective of European, OECD and UN policy, with the intention of considering education and training as key elements for the achievement of economic and social objectives, precisely because of the recognition of the impact that educational poverty itself has on the development and growth of states.

An analysis conducted by Save the Children Italy,[14] on the basis of 14 indicators referring specifically to the digital transition of education systems, reveals less than comforting data on educational poverty, mainly understood as deprivation of the possibility to learn, experiment, freely develop skills, talents and aspirations in the early stages of life, a period in which people is more malleable and receptive.

The highest levels of educational poverty are recorded in the South, both in terms of the supply of services and in terms of participation in cultural and educational activities. And the same regional differentials in educational achievement, in the availability of public services for children, in the incidence of economic and educational poverty, offer the image of a deeply divided country. A country in which regional gaps in human capital, levels and quality of education are not only a symptom of inequality and unequal opportunities, but are insidious ways through which poverty and inequality are transmitted between generations.[15]

It is, indeed, well known that poverty does not only mean a reduced economic sphere, but fewer opportunities that accentuate starting inequalities, contributing to the intergenerational transmission of poverty and the various gaps that are connected to it. And the reduction of inequalities at the outset— moving from early childhood—would not only lead to the achievement of greater social equity,[16] but would also have positive effects on the welfare of the territories, thus having virtuous impacts not only on future education, but also on the reduction of crime rates, on the improvement of productivity at work and on various other social profiles.

THE PANDEMIC CRISIS AND DIGITAL DIVIDE

The pandemic crisis, which has certainly given a significant boost to digitalisation processes, has revealed the weakness of the reference model, its inability to find resilient formulae, without exacerbating differences, contributing, on the contrary, to increase the distances between the parts of the system.

This trait is particularly evident with regard to digitalisation processes, in respect of which, despite the potential, numerous criticalities have emerged that, in practice, have generated inequalities instead of the inclusion that was intended.

To this end, we need only look at the data on educational poverty, i.e., "the deprivation on the part of children and adolescents of the possibility of learning, experimenting, developing and allowing their capacities, talents and aspirations to flourish freely," i.e., the impossibility of enjoying effective protection and guarantee of the right to education, understood in an overall dimension, as mentioned, of guaranteeing a path that allows each individual to develop their personality, aptitudes, and therefore a way for building citizenship.

With the pandemic, not only did the risk of material poverty of a part of the citizenry increase, but access to educational tools was precluded, or not properly used, for certain segments of the population, generating a real and substantial loss in terms of cognitive, socio-emotional and physical development. In fact, the difference between those who have internet access and those who do not has been highlighted, a difference that adds to the sources of inequality and social exclusion, revealing one of the most dangerous tendencies of the current economic system: the ability to push those on the margins of society towards the abyss, increasing wealth and poverty, interconnectedness and marginalisation.

The thesis according to which the spread of the internet, together with the digital divide it implies and presupposes, would amplify already existing inequalities within an already highly polarised society such as ours, is usually identified as the stratification thesis. Taking its cue from the so-called St. Matthew effect (those who have will be given and will be in abundance; those who have not will also be deprived of what they have), a part of the doctrine has pointed out that some citizens, enjoying higher cultural and economic status than the rest of the population, would be able to further improve their condition by capitalising on and taking full advantage of the opportunities offered by the net, with the consequence that the digital divide would increase.

In other words, the digital divide stands as the typical, post-modern form of poverty, the source of its own incrementality.[17]

Just a few references to give an idea of the scale of the phenomenon. Consider, for example, the DESI (*Digital Economy and Society Index*), the tool through which the European Commission monitors the digital progress of Member States. There are five dimensions taken into consideration: *(i)* connectivity (in particular broadband development); *(ii)* human capital (i.e., the skills and digital inclusion of citizens); *(iii)* the use of internet services; *(iv)* digital technology integration (an objective linked to the digitalisation of the economy); and *(v)* the development of digital public services.

Looking at the data, Italy ranks fourth last in the ranking that assesses connectivity, human capital, internet use, digital technology integration and digital public services.[18]

If we look at the reasons for this huge gap, the causes are multiple, being conditioning elements for the correct access and use of digital tools, which according to the provisions of EU Regulation 2120/2015 is a real right, or rather a fundamental prerogative for the exercise of rights, not only the economic conditions of households, but also the territorial data, highlighting the impact that choices on infrastructure policy have on the issue.

From the analysis conducted by Openopolis[19]—with children on Eurostat data, the criticality of the Italian situation compared to other European countries clearly emerges.

Looking at the percentage of households with internet access at home, Italy ranks fourth last of the countries considered, with 96% of households with minors and around 90% of singles.

This is a critical issue that, examined with specific reference to the Italian territorial context, reveals a strong impact of territorial characteristics and, therefore, not only of economic conditions. Differences that multiply if we look at data relating to inland areas, or to the peripheries of cities, where in 2019 only 79% of households have internet access from home, compared to 80.4% in metropolitan areas.

The critical situation linked to the territorial context is even more evident if we look at the availability of broadband, with respect to which Umbria stands out in the negative, even recording 6.8% of households declaring that they do not have internet precisely because of the absence of broadband, Liguria and Molise. This is certainly a critical situation, also noted by the EU Court of Auditors which, not surprisingly, in its Broadband Report 2018 highlighted how "investment in broadband will also contribute to providing quality education, promote social inclusion and benefit rural and remote regions. Some stakeholders believe that broadband is so important that it should be considered an essential public service, in the same way as other services such as road, water, electricity and gas networks."

An objective shared by Italy, which laid down the targets set by the European Commission in 2010 (basic broadband (up to 30 Mbps) for all by 2013; fast broadband (at least 30 Mbps or more) for all by 2020; ultrafast broadband (over 100 Mbps) for at least 50% of European households by 2020 in the national digital growth strategy (2014-20) and in the ultra-wideband strategy. Targets raised by the Commission in 2016 (connectivity of at least one gigabit per second for schools, libraries and public offices to full 5g coverage in urban areas and along major terrestrial transport routes. By that date, the minimum connectivity reached will have to be 100 megabits per second for all European households) and which, as the figures show, are still far from full achievement. In fact, the Italian average number of households reached by the fixed network at 30 Mbps is lower than the European average; in the Val d'Aosta and Molise the quota does not reach the 40 per cent threshold. In the case of Molise, 18 per cent of households are not reached by the fixed network, compared with the national average of around 5 per cent. Wired network coverage is also low in other regions (Basilicata and Abruzzo 12%, Umbria 11% and Calabria 9%), which are two times lower than the national average, in which the situation as regards educational poverty is further aggravated also because of the economic conditions of the territories.[20]

The overall picture becomes even bleaker if we also consider the structural endowments of educational institutions and families and the digital skills of pupils and families with respect to which Italy ranks third last, with 64% compared to the European average of 83%.

And it is no coincidence, for example, that many of the interventions carried out during the pandemic also concerned the purchase of PCs, tablets and devices for internet connection in schools, and for the digital equipment of students. Think of Lombardy's family package, or the connectivity bonus for students living in Lazio, or even Campania's #conlefamiglie announcement.

TOWARDS THE CONSTRUCTION OF INCLUSIVE EDUCATION SYSTEMS

Already from these brief outlines emerge not only the real critical profiles that exist in the area, and with which the digital transition process has and will have to deal, but also the complexity of the process, in which various interdependent plans are intercepted that cannot but move in parallel, according to a unitary design aimed at the territorial system. A system in which the parts, even if autonomous, cannot but interrelate, generating virtuous paths. An intersection of plans, actors and competences, functional to the construction of a renewed 'educational environment'.

And, thus, the digitalisation process will necessarily have to develop taking into account the infrastructural plan, the organisational plan, referring to the system and to the individual educational institutions and, more generally, to the network institutions, the skills plan (of institutions, families and learners) and the methodologies plan. Plans that in different ways are taken into consideration in the various documents that over the years have addressed the issue of the digitalisation of education systems, which represents a central node of the European Pillar of Social Rights in which, in fact, one of the principles concerns precisely quality and inclusive education and lifelong learning in order to maintain and acquire skills that enable full participation in society and successful transitions in the labour market.[21] A dimension, the one embodied in the European Pillar of Social Rights, to which is related the European Agenda for Skills itself, related, in turn, to the European Digital Strategy.

We also think of the positions expressed by the Organisation for Economic Co-operation and Development (OECD), which already in 2017[22] defined the characteristics of an 'innovative learning environment', an environment defined as an organic whole that embraces the learning experience organised for specific groups of students around a single 'pedagogical core' that goes beyond a predefined classroom or programme, including activities and learning outcomes, thus recognising, a central role for teachers.[23]

Significant are the seven principles defined there, which evidently reflect a comprehensive approach, recognising a central role for educational systems in the construction of citizenship processes:

> (i) the learning environment recognises learners as the main participants, encourages their active engagement and develops in them an awareness of their activities as learners; (ii) the learning environment is grounded in the social nature of learning and actively encourages properly organised cooperative learning; (iii) the learning professionals within the learning environment are fully attuned to both the motivations of learners and the crucial ground that emotions have in achievement; (iv) the learning environment is highly sensitive to the individual differences between the students within it, including their prior knowledge; (v) the learning environment develops programmes that require constant commitment by putting everyone on the line without causing undue overload (vi) the learning environment operates with expectations in mind and implements assessment strategies consistent with those expectations; it also places a strong emphasis on formative feedback to support learning; (vii) the learning environment strongly promotes 'horizontal connection' between knowledge areas and subjects, as well as with the community and the wider world.

In this context, it is clear that the process does not, and could not, concern only the infrastructure, but must be managed in a systemic manner, involving the organisation that makes use of the infrastructure, as well, to the point of including the pedagogical core of the learning environment itself, projecting the school into a different dimension, as a 'training organisation' that places the learner at the centre, embedded in an adaptive system of a technological type so as to improve their learning experiences according to personal characteristics, preferences and progress.

Also in line with this are the positions expressed by the Council of Europe, which, in order to realise Goal 4 on the quality of education in the Sustainable Development Goals of the 2030 Agenda, emphasises the need to build and improve educational facilities that are sensitive to children, disabilities and gender, and that provide safe, non-violent, inclusive and effective learning environments for all.

A model also inspired by the *European Schoolnet* within the *Future Classroom Lab* initiative.

But the centrality of an appropriate digitalisation process also emerges in the Council Conclusions on Digital Education in the European Knowledge Societies (2020/C 425/10) in which the need to focus on the competences of teachers and trainers is emphasised, both in the creation of learning environments that promote the critical and creative thinking of each learner, and in the creation of safe, inclusive and high-quality content and learning environments. A conclusion that rests on the knowledge that "well-trained teachers, capable of using digital technologies in a pedagogically appropriate and age- and gender-sensitive manner, are a key factor in achieving digital, inclusive and high-quality education for all."

In this context, therefore, it is evident how the digital transition of the education system itself acts as an engine for social change, at least in its intentions.

PATHS TO THE DIGITALIZATION OF EDUCATION SYSTEMS

With the pandemic crisis, as mentioned above, the potential, but also the very critical aspects of the digital transition of the education system emerged in all their positivity and drama. Assessments on the first profile are easy, those on the second much more complex for the reasons mentioned. On the one hand, infrastructural inadequacy, on the other, the profile of individual endowments in terms of access to infrastructures and skills have in many cases increased that gap not only between territories but also between population groups, running the risk of transforming a process, that of digital transition, from an engine for the construction of an inclusive and quality system, into a source of inequalities.[24]

It is certainly no coincidence that, for instance, the Council Conclusions on Countering the COVID-19 Crisis in Education and Training (2020/C 212 I/03) are inspired by the need to make further efforts to accelerate the digital transformation of education and training systems, strengthen the digital capacity of education and training institutions and reduce the digital divide, including by further supporting the development of digital skills and competences of teachers and trainers,[25] in order to facilitate the teaching and assessment of the framework of digital learning contexts.

The Digital Education Action Plan 2021–2027—Rethinking Education and Training for the Digital Age (Communication from the Commission to the European Parliament, the Council, the European Economic and Social Committee and the Committee of the Regions[26]) also follows these lines. In it, various measures, coordinated at European level, are envisaged for the construction of a high-quality, inclusive and accessible European digital education system in which the critical issues that emerged during the emergency period are recalled and partially resolved.

The plan presents a vision of comprehensive education aimed at improving digital literacy, competences and skills at all levels of education and training and for all levels of digital competences and, quite significantly, emphasises the need to make education systems ready for the digital age by specifying some basic principles that are also fundamental for improving the quality and inclusiveness of education in Europe:

a. inclusive, high-quality digital education that respects data protection and ethics;
b. transforming education for the digital age also through enhanced dialogue and stronger partnerships between educators, the private sector, researchers, municipalities and public authorities;
c. adequate investment in connectivity, equipment and organisational skills and competences to ensure access to digital education for all. Specifically, the document emphasises that: "education is a fundamental human right and access to it must be guaranteed, regardless of the environment in which it takes place, whether physical, digital or a combination of both. The right to quality and inclusive education, training and lifelong learning is the first principle of the European pillar of social rights, while the fifth principle of the pillar gives workers the right to training";
d. Digital education should play a central role in enhancing equality and inclusiveness: "Digital skills are essential to be able to develop and implement digitally inclusive and accessible systems. Similarly, due to the lack of digital skills and accessibility, many disadvantaged groups, families and teachers have been unable to continue working and learning during lockdown. This not only increased the risk of poverty and disadvantage, but also widened inequalities in education and training";
e. e-skills should be core competences for all educators and training staff and be integrated into all areas of teachers' professional development, including initial training;
f. Digital educators play a key role in digital education;
g. Digital literacy is essential for living in a digitised world;
h. Basic digital competences should become an integral part of the core transferable competences everyone should have in order to realise their personal development, actively engage in society as a citizen, use public services and exercise fundamental rights;
i. the centrality of advanced digital skills in transition processes;
j. there is a need for high-quality educational content to increase the relevance, quality and inclusiveness of European education and training at all levels.

The document identifies priorities (2) and numerous actions (17) to be achieved:

   a. Promote the development of a highly efficient digital education ecosystem, including six actions covering strategic dialogue with Member States, the proposal for a Council Recommendation on blended learning, the European digital education content framework, digital connectivity and equipment for education, digital transformation plans for education and training institutions, the use of artificial intelligence systems in education and, thus, ultra-high-capacity internet connectivity and digital educational content, and digital skills training, including digital teaching methods.[27]
   b. Improve digital competences and skills for the digital transformation (7 actions including (i) common guidelines for teachers and educators to promote digital literacy; (ii) the updating of the European Digital Competence Framework; (iii) the establishment of the European Digital Competence Certificate—EDSC; (iv) the proposal for a Council Recommendation on improving the supply of digital competences in education and training; (v) the transnational collection of data on students' digital competences; (vi) 'Digital Opportunities' placements in higher education in Erasmus+, promoting women's participation in STEM disciplines; (vi) the European eLearning Cluster to support Member States by creating a network of national eLearning advisory services to exchange experiences and good practices on e-inclusion enablers.

Also in the Communication from the Commission to the European Parliament, the Council, the European Economic and Social Committee and the Committee of the Regions,[28] *realization of the European educational area by 2025*, cooperation between states is promoted in order to enrich the quality and inclusiveness of national systems.

OUTLINE OF THE NATIONAL DIGITAL SCHOOL PLAN AND THE THRUST OF THE NRP

Looking at the Italian situation, a recent survey on the degree of digitalisation of facilities placed Italy 20th in the ranking.

With reference to our system, the digital transition process dates back to 2015, the year of implementation of the National Plan for the Digital School, which made it possible to have a unified planning tool that, in synergy with the structural funds of the 2014-2020 Operational Programme, has been greatly accelerated thanks to the identification of 35 specific actions that have been implemented to different degrees within the country.

The PNSD focused on four areas: that of *connectivity*, which should be seen as the backbone of the entire transformation process, and on this we also have to say thanks to the resources allocated, first for ultra-broadband, and, then, also integrated by the PNRR that have affected a large part of school buildings, with the goal of almost total coverage by 2024, infrastructural problems, which have not been resolved to date, notwithstanding; *that of (digital and innovative) environments and tools* enriched also thanks to European funds; *that of skills and*, finally, *that of teacher training and support*, which has seen the introduction of the figure of the digital animator flanked as well by the teachers of the Digital Innovation team and supported, for some years now, by the territorial training teams as well.

It is in this context that the PNRR fits in, reflecting the approach of the PNSD, by including several areas in the transition process: that relating to the computerisation of structures, the declared aim of which is to achieve an improvement in the efficiency of the administrative system, also from an organisational point of view; that relating to information technology, understood as technology to support teaching; and the third relating to the teaching of information technology.

With the PNRR, thanks to the new scenarios initiated by the PNSD, we would like to complete the picture but also relaunch some actions.

Specifically, Mission 4 of the NRP is dedicated to education and research, aimed at strengthening the conditions for the development of a knowledge-intensive, competitive and resilient economy, and is divided into 2 components

- M4C1 Strengthening the supply of education services, from kindergartens to universities, divided into 4 action areas (qualitative improvement and quantitative expansion of education and training services; improvement of recruitment processes and teacher training; skills expansion and infrastructure enhancement; reform and enhancement of doctorates), with 9 reforms and 14 investments.
- M4C2 from research to enterprise, broken down into 11 investments, grouped into three lines of action (strengthening research and dissemination of innovative models for basic and applied research conducted in synergy between universities and enterprises; support for innovation processes and technology transfer; strengthening of support conditions for research and innovation).

In particular, the line on broadening skills and upgrading infrastructure includes four investments: (i) new skills and new languages; (ii) school

4.0—innovative schools, new classrooms and laboratories; (iii) school building safety and upgrading plan; (iv) advanced university teaching and skills.

It is in this context that the School 4.0 Plan sees the light, whose inspiring principles, enumerated at the beginning, recall two quotations from Montessori and Malaguzzi, by way of a request for methodological legitimisation for the valorisation of the role of space in the educational process, taking up, at least in its intentions, what had already been envisaged in the document *Teachers as Designers of Learning Environments. The Importance of Innovative Pedagogies* (Center for Educational Research and Innovation, OECD).[29]

The document refers to the 'learning ecosystem, formed by the intersection of places, times, people, learning activities, tools and resources', to emphasise that it is not enough 'only space and technology to create an innovative environment, but training, organisation of time and teaching methodologies are fundamental'.

The Plan is divided into three sections:

- *Background*, defines the context of the intervention, tracing the stages of the educational and digital transformation process in Italian schools and the European reference scenarios;
- *Framework*, divided into two parts aimed at presenting the framework and main guidelines for the design of innovative learning environments (*Next Generation Classrooms*) and laboratories for the digital professions of the future (*Net Generation Labs*);
- *Roadmap*, in which the stages of the implementation of the School 4.0 investment line are outlined.

With specific reference to the School 4.0 Plan, the intention is to overcome the boundary between the physical and the virtual learning environment, ensuring an integration between the two.[30]

This is a measure that intends to transform classrooms into innovative learning environments, turning digitalisation into a pillar of teaching, starting precisely by adapting classrooms understood as infrastructures, first of all by making them flexible and adapted to the new learning methodologies, and secondly by equipping them with advanced technological systems. Physical learning spaces to which virtual spaces will have to be added.

The approach is universalistic, so as to guarantee equal opportunities for all schools, according to the number of classes present, while preserving the autonomy of the schools that are called upon to design this type of intervention.

Alongside the infrastructural and organisational plan is that of skills, the subject of another and, in part autonomous, line of intervention that directly concerns the digital transition of school personnel, leaving the choice of activities to the autonomy of the schools, entrusted to a planning nucleus that works alongside the school principal to plan interventions in parallel with the adaptation of environments. This is a measure that aims to promote a system for the development of digital teaching and the training of school personnel on the digital transition by developing a national digital education hub for the training of teachers and school personnel and an integrated network of territorial training hubs.

A final measure is the one on new skills and new languages, which aims to ensure equal opportunities and gender equality in terms of teaching and guidance for all school cycles in order to grow scientific culture and the approach to computational thinking in schools and to strengthen internationalisation.[31]

The Decree of the Minister of Education No. 89/2020 introduced the Guidelines on Integrated Digital Education that provided for the adoption, in each institute, of a school plan for integrated digital education within the PTOF, providing specific indications on how it should be organised, and Budget Law 2021, No. 178/2020 increased the staffing of technical assistants in order to ensure the functionality of IT equipment in the various orders and grades. The same law strengthened the territorial information teams to promote actions to train teaching staff and enhance students' skills on innovative teaching methodologies. The teams, pursuant to Article 47 of Decree-Law No 36/2022, provide ongoing support to educational institutions for the implementation of the PNRR investments, with the functional coordination of the PNRR Mission Unit.

In addition to these funding lines, there are also those included in Mission 5, Component 3, Investment 3 of the PNRR to combat educational poverty in the southern regions for which, in the last call for proposals published, were aimed at expanding and enhancing educational and care services for the 0-6 age bracket, in order to strengthen the acquisition of fundamental skills for the wellbeing of children and their families; at promoting the wellbeing and harmonious growth of minors, guaranteeing effective educational opportunities and anticipating, at an early stage, forms of social hardship and educational poverty combating school drop-outs, especially in the 11–17 age group, by promoting not only the improvement of the educational offer, also thanks to the activation of individualised paths, complementary to the traditional ones, functional to the insertion into the world of work, but also by foreseeing joint actions 'inside and outside school' aimed specifically at managing and stemming the phenomenon of school drop-outs.

Law 233/2021, finally, in Art. 24 *bis*, provided for three distinct actions for the development of digital skills in the coming school years: (i) updating of the National Plan for the training of teachers in schools of all levels, which will have to include, among the national priorities, the approach to the learning of computer programming (coding) and digital didactics, in line with the PNRR investment dedicated to *New skills and new languages*; the updating and integration of computer programming and digital skills in the specific learning objectives and competence targets of the National Indications for the curricula of pre-school and first cycle of education and of the National Indications and Guidelines in force for the educational institutions of the second cycle of education; the development of digital skills, also by fostering the learning of computer programming (coding), within existing teaching. And the Budget Law 2022, in a very significant way, reconfirmed the fund for the fight against child educational poverty, created in 2016, based on a memorandum of understanding for its management between banking foundations and the government, for the two-year period 2023-2024, with the recognition of a contribution, in the form of a tax credit, for the payments made by the fund to the banking foundations which, from 2016 to 2021, have financed numerous innovative projects aimed essentially at meeting the needs of the territories. Leaving aside the huge amount of funding, which to date amounts to 607 million euros, what is relevant for the purposes of this discussion is the method that has proved to be successful, thanks to the bottom-up dynamic of project expression, and which has also been replicated in the Fund for the Digital Republic. The fund is intended 'to support experimental interventions aimed at removing the economic, social and cultural obstacles that prevent minors from fully benefiting from educational processes'. The intervention strategy is based on the role of the 'educating community', which includes the various actors in the network: schools, local authorities, the third sector, families and children. It is a tool that has been valorised by doctrine precisely because of its potential[32] underlined in the recently published guidelines that aim to promote an integrated, replicable and sustainable intervention model, based on the synergic involvement of all the territorial actors.

Without going into the details of the guidelines, which are the result of research carried out in a number of locations, what in my opinion deserves to be emphasised is precisely the role that is acknowledged for the members of the community, which ceases to be a mere container and background context, but becomes an active and capacitating subject capable of stimulating growth and functioning, by emphasising the capabilities of the subjects involved, understood as the internal power of individuals, and as external power, i.e., as the possibility of taking advantage of favourable circumstances and opportunities, enhancing the specificities of the individual and the putting into circulation of each one's skills, with a view to cooperative learning and connected to current events and what happens outside the school. And very significantly, the text emphasises how "*the individualist approach to social and educational issues, even in its most vital version made up of enthusiasm and self-denial, is proving increasingly inadequate to tackle highly complex problems such as school drop-outs and educational poverty,*" and this on both a personal and organisational level. The educating communities are placed at the centre of the processes of building educational and community agreements.[33]

CONCLUSIONS

In this context, if we agree with the main function of education systems, which is to guarantee the effectiveness of the right to education and upbringing in its value referring to the very existence of the individual, it is indispensable to adopt a system perspective in which the infrastructural and organisational dimension goes hand in hand with the construction of competences.

A necessary integrated vision is essential in order not to dissipate the unrepeatable opportunity offered by the NRP: "to increase productivity, innovation and employment, to ensure wider access to education and culture and to close territorial gaps."

A unitary dimension that, as mentioned at the outset, is a precondition for guaranteeing the development of a system that is truly inclusive, where inclusion, in the words of Habermas, indicates the way in which belonging to the community, to society, acquires full value: an "intersubjectively shared context of a possible understanding."[34] A dimension in which inclusion and equality are posited as pathways that allow the boundaries of community to open up.

This is, evidently, an approach that considers otherness, a constitutive condition of any reality, overcoming the opposition with which it would be understood in a non-inclusive dimension, crowning the Hegelian dialectical movement by guaranteeing a synthesis that cannot fail to have an impact on the way of understanding schooling and didactics itself.

In this context, digitalisation undoubtedly has a great deal of potential, but there is no denying the risks linked to the different profiles it covers, from structural deficiencies, which limit access, to inadequacies also in terms of skills. These are all elements that inevitably affect the weaker sections of the population (I am thinking of BES or the disabled) who, as already highlighted in the PNSD, should instead be among the first recipients of those learning environments that, taking advantage of the flexibility of configurations, should adapt to users.

But, if we consider precisely what emerged during the pandemic emergency, digitalisation at present appears more as a source of inequalities and thus as a brake with respect to the effectiveness of the (fundamental) right to education. In this period, in fact, the great distance could be seen between those who had digital tools at their disposal and those who, for various reasons, did not have such tools, and therefore, the projects, the lines of intervention will have to be oriented in a systemic dimension, in fact, that enhances the multidimensional perspective, a prerequisite for an inclusive process, enhancing, or rather leveraging the autonomies that have to be placed in the conditions to create that organisational and cultural substratum, functional to guarantee the operability of citizenship rights by ensuring, the various actors, a model that guarantees equal opportunities for all, while respecting differences.

NOTES

1. Cf. Nazareno Panichella, "Diseguaglianze territoriali e stratificazione sociale," *Il Mulino*, no. 1 (2022): 61-65; in the same issue, Stefania Sabatinelli, "Le disparità nell'accesso ai servizi per l'infanzia," *Il Mulino*, no. 1 (2022): 78–86.
2. In these terms, Loredana Sciolla, "La classe senza regole," *Il Mulino*, no. 2 (2008): 259–266.
3. On this point, see the analysis by Claudio Franchini, *L'intervento pubblico di contrasto alla povertà* (Naples: Editoriale scientifica, 2021), 11-41; Larysa Minzyuk and Felice Russo, "La misurazione multidimensionale della povertà in istruzione in Italia. Multidimensional Measurement of Educational Poverty in Italy," *Politica economica*, no. 1 (2016): 65–122.
4. See the focus by Stefania Baroncelli, "Diritto alle diversità e inclusione nelle scuole. Disabilità, condizioni economico-sociali, background migratorio, genere, e minoranza linguistiche," *Federalismi*, no. 32 (September 2022): 1–11.
5. Of possible interest, Anna Maria Pinna, "L'economia digital divide," *Equilibri*, no. 3 (2001): 219–226.
6. Amartya Sen, *La diseguaglianza. Un riesame critico* (Bologna: Il Mulino, 1994), 64.
7. Sen, *La diseguaglianza,* 63–69.
8. Cf. Lucia Valente, "Contrasto alla povertà e promozione del lavoro tra buoni propositi e vecchi vizi," *Diritto delle relazioni industriali,* no. 4 (2018): 1081–1095.
9. Gisella Decarli, Laura Franchin, Beatrice Bozzetto, Luca Surian, "Un'indagine sulle buone prassi per la didattica online e per l'insegnamento della matematica indicate dagli insegnanti in epoca di COVID-19," *Psicologia clinica dello sviluppo*, no. 2 (2021): 347–354.
10. On this subject let us refer to Loredana Giani, "Disabilità e diritto all'istruzione: alla ricerca di un difficile equilibrio tra persona e valore economico della prestazione (pubblica)," in *Funzione amministrativa e diritti delle persone con disabilità*, ed. Margherita Interlandi (Naples:Editoriale scientifica, 2022) 139-155; Loredana Giani, "Dalla multilevel governance alla governance reticolare. Esigenze dei territori, capability e appropriatezza degli interventi," in *Scritti in onore di Aldo Carosi* (Naples: Editoriale Scientifica, 2021): 463-490; Loredana Giani, La normativa in materia di Disturbi Specifici dell'Apprendimento (DSA), in *DSA e didattica inclusiva: dalle neuroscienze agli interventi in classe. L'innovazione didattica a partire dal post Covid 19,* ed. Maria

Vittoria Isidori (Rome: Editoriale Anicia, 2020); Loredana Giani, Ruggiero Dipace, Marina D'Orsogna and Annarita Iacopino, "Coesione e sviluppo territoriale: valorizzazione delle aree interne e prospettiva macroregionale," in Diritto e processo amministrativo. Giornate di studio in onore di Enrico Follieri, vol. I (Naples: Edizioni Scientifiche Italiane, 2019, 343–359; Loredana Giani, I diritti sociali e le sfide della globalizzazione. Intersystemic competition and regulatory capitalism. Spunti di riflessione sul "nuovo" ruolo dello Stato, in Discorsi interrotti. Il pensiero di Giovanni Marongiu venti anni dopo ed. Pierciro Galeone P and Donatella Morana D, (Rome: Luiss Academy, 2014); Loredana Giani, "Effettività del diritto all'istruzione per gli alunni con Disturbi Specifici dell'Apprendimento (DSA)," in *I Disturbi Specifici dell'Apprendimento a scuola* (Rome:Anicia, 2014): 37–55; Loredana Giani, "Il ruolo delle carte di servizi e dell'azione per l'efficienza nella garanzia della effettività dei diritti degli individui-utenti nel settore socio-assistenziale. Il caso dei disturbi specifici dell'apprendimento," in *I servizi pubblici in Italia e in Argentina*, (Naples: Editoriale Scientifica, 2013); Loredana Giani, "I diritti sociali e la sfida della crisi economica. Equità ed uguaglianza nel diritto all'istruzione dei soggetti diversamente abili," in *Studi in Onore di Claudio Rossano*, (Naples: Jovene, 2013); Loredana Giani, "Diritti fondamentali, disabilità e prestazioni amministrative. Effettività dei diritti delle persone con problemi cognitivo-comportamentali," paper at the Conference "Building Design for Autism" organised by the ITACA Department, Sapienza University of Rome, in Autismo, Protezione sociale e architettura, Alinea, Florence, 2010.
11. On this point we refer to the theoretical approach of Amartya Sen and Martge Nussbaum, *The quality of life*, (Oxford: Clarendon Press, 1993); Amartya Sen, "The idea of justice," *Journal of Human Development*, no. 4 (2009): 331-349; Martha Nussbaum, *Creating capabilities: the human development approach*, (Harvard: Harvard Un. Press, 2011).
12. Jürgen Habermas, *L'inclusione dell'altro*, trans. Leonardo Ceppa (Milan:Feltrinelli, 1998) 153.
13. See Anna Simonati, "Dal "piano nazionale per l'educazione al rispetto" all'autonomia scolastica: il metodo "reticolare" per l'inclusione e l'integrazione," *Federalismi*, no. 32 (2022): 35–48.
14. Paolo Calidoni, "Immagini dalle aule. La perdurante predominanza del modello didattico 'uno-tanti'," *Scuola democratica*, no. 1 (2016): 23–46.
15. Cf. Ferdinando G. Menga, "Il futuro di cui dobbiamo rispondere. Ciò che la rappresentanza politica può ancora insegnarci sulla giustizia intergenerazionale," *Rivista filosofia del diritto,* no. 3 (2022): 301–306.
16. The survey by Denis Meuret and Agathe Dirani, *La nozione di equità nelle ricerche sull'educazione, Scuola Democratica*, no. 2 (2014): 297–302, 320.
17. Paolo Benanti and Sebastiano Maffettone, "Sostenibilità D, Le conseguenze della rivoluzione digitale nelle nostre vite," *Il Mulino*, no. 2 (2021): 191-207.
18. See Alessandro Bianchi, *Infrastrutture per la connettività territoriale, Rivista giuridica del mezzogiorno*, no .1 (2018): 59-74.
19. www.openopolis.it
20. See Orazio Giancola and Luca Salmieri, "L'education e l'andamento delle inequaglianze. Interview with Walter Müller," *Scuola Democratica*, no. 2 (2014):

287–296; Nicola Novacco, "Quantità e qualità di infrastrutture e sviluppo concorrenziale delle aree deboli," *Rivista economica del mezzogiorno*, no. 4 (2006): 445-451.
21. Reasoning to the contrary, cf. Simona Bodo, "Europa: politiche culturali e sociali a confronto nella lotta all'esclusione," *Economia della Cultura*, no. 1 (2004): 153–158.
22. OECD, *The OECD handbook for innovative learning environments*, OECD Publishing, Paris, 2017.
23. On the need to coordinate European and local actions, cf. Maddalena Colombo, "Il contrastare la dispersione scolastica attraverso le politiche locali: dalla ricerca all'azione di rete," *Autonomie locali e servizi sociali*, no. 2 (2011): 169–184.
24. Cf. Alessia Forciniti, Emanuela Spanò and Danilo Taglietti, "La digitalizzazione della scuola. Reti, soggetti e idee per una nuova politics dell'educazione," *Scuola Democratica*, no. 3 (2019): 503–528.
25. See Ida Cortoni, "Il capitale digitale scolastico. Un'indagine sociologica sulle competenze digitali degli insegnanti," *Scuola Democratica*, no. 1 (2021): 65–85.
26. COM (2020) 624 final of 30 September 2020.
27. On the recent difficulties, Andrea Gavosto, "Scuola, fondi sempre più lontani," *La Repubblica*, 17 February 2023; Marco Frojo, "Nuovi edifici e classi digitalizzate così la scuola punta forte sul PNRR," *La Repubblica—Affari & Finanza*, 5 September 2022.
28. COM(2020) 625 final of 30 September 2020.
29. Alejandro Paniagua and David Istance, 9 April 2019; Francesca Di Lascio and Livia Lorenzoni, "Obiettivi e governance dei piani di rilancio nei sistemi europei: un confronto fra cinque Paesi," *Istituzioni del federalismo*, no. 2 (2022): 325–331.
30. Paolo Bianchi, "Via al Piano Scuola 4.0, aule attrezzate per didattica integrativa," *Il Sole 24 ore*, 17 June 2022.
31. Themes that have already emerged in recent years, as noted by Caterina Manco, "Qualcosa di nuovo: innovazione e comunità di pratica," *Scuola Democratica*, no. 3 (2014): 675-680.
32. Vv. Aa., Facciamo un patto!: i patti educativi di comunità e la partecipazione delle ragazze e dei ragazzi, ed. V. Meo (Milan:Franco Angeli, 2022)
33. In these terms, already Daniela Luisi, "Imparare dai territori. La pratica dell'educazione tra scuola pubblica e progetti locali," *Il Mulino*, no. 4 (2020): 902–905.
34. Jürgen Habermas, "Osservazioni su Dieter Grimm," in *Il futuro della costituzione* (Turin: Einaudi, 1996), 373-378; Habermas, "L'inclusione," 75.

REFERENCES

Aa. Vv., Facciamo un patto!: i patti educativi di comunità e la partecipazione delle ragazze e dei ragazzi, ed. V. Meo (Milan:Franco Angeli, 2022)

Baroncelli S., "Diritto alle diversità e inclusione nelle scuole. Disabilità, condizioni economico-sociali, background migratorio, genere, e minoranza linguistiche," *Federalismi*, no. 32 (September 2022): 1–11.

Benanti P., Maffettone S., "Sostenibilità D, Le conseguenze della rivoluzione digitale nelle nostre vite," *Il Mulino*, no. 2 (2021): 191–207.

Bianchi A., *Infrastrutture per la connettività territoriale*, *Rivista giuridica del mezzogiorno*, no .1 (2018): 59–74.

Bianchi P., "Via al Piano Scuola 4.0, aule attrezzate per didattica integrativa," *Il Sole 24 ore*, 17 June 2022.

Bodo S., "Europa: politiche culturali e sociali a confronto nella lotta all'esclusione," *Economia della Cultura*, no. 1 (2004): 153–158.

Calidoni P., "Immagini dalle aule. La perdurante predominanza del modello didattico 'uno-tanti' ", *Scuola democratica*, no.1 (2016): 23–46.

Colombo M., "Il contrastare la dispersione scolastica attraverso le politiche locali: dalla ricerca all'azione di rete," *Autonomie locali e servizi sociali*, no. 2 (2011): 169–184.

Cortoni I., "*Il capitale digitale scolastico. Un'indagine sociologica sulle competenze digitali degli insegnanti*," *Scuola Democratica*, no. 1 (2021): 65–85.

Decarli G., Franchin L., Bozzetto B., Surian L., "Un'indagine sulle buone prassi per la didattica online e per l'insegnamento della matematica indicate dagli insegnanti in epoca di COVID-19," *Psicologia clinica dello sviluppo*, no. 2 (2021): 347–354.

Forciniti A., Spanò E., Taglietti D., "La digitalizzazione della scuola. Reti, soggetti e idee per una nuova politics dell'educazione," *Scuola Democratica*, no. 3 (2019): 503–528.

Franchini C., *L'intervento pubblico di contrasto alla povertà* (Naples: Editoriale scientifica, 2021), Minzyuk L., Russo F., "La misurazione multidimensionale della povertà in istruzione in Italia. Multidimensional Measurement of Educational Poverty in Italy," *Politica economica*, no. 1 (2016): 65–122.

Gavosto A., "Scuola, fondi sempre più lontani," *La Repubblica*, 17 February 2023; Marco Frojo, "Nuovi edifici e classi digitalizzate così la scuola punta forte sul PNRR," *La Repubblica—Affari & Finanza*, 5 September 2022.

Giancola O., Salmieri L., "L'education e l'andamento delle inequaglianze. Interview with Walter Müller," *Scuola Democratica*, no. 2 (2014): 287–296; Nicola Novacco, "Quantità e qualità di infrastrutture e sviluppo concorrenziale delle aree deboli," *Rivista economica del mezzogiorno*, no. 4 (2006): 445–451.

Giani L., "Dalla multilevel governance alla governance reticolare. Esigenze dei territori, capability e appropriatezza degli interventi," in *Scritti in onore di Aldo Carosi* (Naples: Editoriale Scientifica, 2021): 463–490

Giani L., "Diritti fondamentali, disabilità e prestazioni amministrative. Effettività dei diritti delle persone con problemi cognitivo-comportamentali," paper at the Conference "Building Design for Autism" organised by the ITACA Department, Sapienza University of Rome, in Autismo, Protezione sociale e architettura, Alinea, Florence, 2010.

Giani L., "Disabilità e diritto all'istruzione: alla ricerca di un difficile equilibrio tra persona e valore economico della prestazione (pubblica)," in *Funzione amministrativa e diritti delle persone con disabilità*, ed. Margherita Interlandi (Naples:Editoriale scientifica, 2022) 139–155.

Giani L., "Effettività del diritto all'istruzione per gli alunni con Disturbi Specifici dell'Apprendimento (DSA)," in *I Disturbi Specifici dell'Apprendimento a scuola* (Rome: Anicia, 2014): 37–55.

Giani L., "I diritti sociali e la sfida della crisi economica. Equità ed uguaglianza nel diritto all'istruzione dei soggetti diversamente abili," in *Studi in Onore di Claudio Rossano*, (Naples: Jovene, 2013).

Giani L., "Il ruolo delle carte di servizi e dell'azione per l'efficienza nella garanzia della effettività dei diritti degli individui-utenti nel settore socio-assistenziale. Il caso dei disturbi specifici dell'apprendimento," in *I servizi pubblici in Italia e in Argentina*, (Naples: Editoriale Scientifica, 2013).

Giani L., Dipace R., D'Orsogna M., Iacopino A., "Coesione e sviluppo territoriale: valorizzazione delle aree interne e prospettiva macroregionale," in Diritto e processo amministrativo. Giornate di studio in onore di Enrico Follieri, vol. I (Naples: Edizioni Scientifiche Italiane, 2019, 343–359.

Giani L., I diritti sociali e le sfide della globalizzazione. Intersystemic competition and regulatory capitalism. Spunti di riflessione sul "nuovo" ruolo dello Stato, in Discorsi interrotti. Il pensiero di Giovanni Marongiu venti anni dopo ed. Pierciro Galeone P and Donatella Morana D, (Rome: Luiss Academy, 2014).

Giani L., La normativa in materia di Disturbi Specifici dell'Apprendimento (DSA), in *DSA e didattica inclusiva: dalle neuroscienze agli interventi in classe. L'innovazione didattica a partire dal post Covid 19*, ed. Maria Vittoria Isidori (Rome: Editoriale Anicia, 2020).

Habermas J., "Osservazioni su Dieter Grimm," in *Il futuro della costituzione* (Turin: Einaudi, 1996), 373–378.

Habermas J., *L'inclusione dell'altro*, trans. Leonardo Ceppa (Milan:Feltrinelli, 1998) 153.

Luisi D., "Imparare dai territori. La pratica dell'educazione tra scuola pubblica e progetti locali," *Il Mulino*, no. 4 (2020): 902–905.

Manco C., "Qualcosa di nuovo: innovazione e comunità di pratica," *Scuola Democratica*, no. 3 (2014): 675–680.

Menga F.G., "Il futuro di cui dobbiamo rispondere. Ciò che la rappresentanza politica può ancora insegnarci sulla giustizia intergenerazionale," *Rivista filosofia del diritto*, no. 3 (2022): 301–306.

Meuret D., Dirani A., *La nozione di equità nelle ricerche sull'educazione, Scuola Democratica*, no. 2 (2014): 297–302, 320.

Paniagua A., Istance D., 9 April 2019; Francesca Di Lascio and Livia Lorenzoni, "Obiettivi e governance dei piani di rilancio nei sistemi europei: un confronto fra cinque Paesi," *Istituzioni del federalismo*, no. 2 (2022): 325–331.

Panichella N., "Diseguaglianze territoriali e stratificazione sociale," *Il Mulino*, no. 1 (2022): 61–65.

Sabatinelli S., "Le disparità nell'accesso ai servizi per l'infanzia," *Il Mulino*, no. 1 (2022): 78–86.

Sen A., *La diseguaglianza. Un riesame critico* (Bologna: Il Mulino, 1994), 64.

Sen A., Nussbaum M., *The quality of life*, (Oxford: Clarendon Press, 1993); Amartya Sen, "The idea of justice," *Journal of Human Development*, no. 4 (2009):

331–349; Martha Nussbaum, *Creating capabilities: the human development approach*, (Harvard: Harvard Un. Press, 2011).

Simonati A., "Dal "piano nazionale per l'educazione al rispetto" all'autonomia scolastica: il metodo "reticolare" per l'inclusione e l'integrazione," *Federalismi*, no. 32 (2022): 35–48.

CHAPTER 13

STUDENTS WITH MIGRANT BACKGROUND

Diversity and Equal Treatment in Italian Schools

Orsolya Farkas
Free University of Bolzano

ABSTRACT

The chapter examines if Italian schools are fully equipped with the necessary legal instruments and policy tools not only to protect from discrimination, but also to promote substantial equality of students who might face disadvantages because of their migrant background. The EU Commission's Action Plan on integration and inclusion is used as a framework to trace the protection of students with migrant background in the Italian legal order. Whereas the norms and policies generally prove to be accommodating towards vulnerabilities and are built on the principle of inclusion, various areas can be identified where the recognition of the need for supportive measures is not accompanied by adequate guarantees to render effective the exercise of the right to education. Legal interventions in the proposed directions would not only strengthen the process of integration and inclusion in schools, but they would contribute to a better performance also in terms of the goals laid down in the Commission's Action Plan.

Migration in general, without further distinction between refugees and economic migrants, receives much public attention when it is linked to emotionally captive events, like huge flows of refugees landing after perilous journeys to cross the Mediterranean or the precarious conditions of migrants massed in temporary shelters waiting for the opportunity to proceed towards their desired destinations. It is much less reported though what happens after migrants reach European shores, what pathways of integration are available for them and which major challenges they have to face in the host country. This process, built on daily, step-by-step efforts of migrants and those involved in their reception, is less spectacular, but not less important. If the generalized experience of integration of migrants is positive, then the public attitude is more accommodating towards new arrivals, whereas in the opposite case less tolerance is shown and even hostility can arise. Going beyond the conquest of public opinion and turning towards more substantial aspects, integration of migrants is necessary to build cohesive and sustainable societies. The process is long by its nature and it requires a complex set of policy measures reaching out all aspects of social, economic and political life. This chapter focuses on one specific aspect of integration and inclusion, namely on the role of schools in this process and the opportunities of pupils with migrant background enrolled in Italian schools. For them, the principal place of interaction with the host society is in schools. Schools constitute the main context of their integration as well, since educational institutions have the task to prepare young people for their adulthood, in terms of conveying scientific knowledge and, throughout the transmission of soft skills, to enable them to become active citizens and to fully participate in the social, economic and political life of the country. Therefore, the question what arises is if Italian schools are fully equipped with the necessary legal instruments and policy tools not only to protect from discrimination, but also to promote substantial equality of students who might face disadvantages because of their migrant background.

Before turning into the detailed examination of the Italian legal and policy measures, it seems to be useful to place Italian policies in a wider context, as this can serve as a reference in a comparative perspective as well. The Migrant Integration Policy Index[1] judged Italy as performing fairly well, with a score slightly above the average of 56 countries examined. Its integration policies have been assessed overall as "slightly favourable," though in the field of education the outcome was "halfway favourable." This indicator comprises factors such as access to education, targeting policies to specific needs and intercultural aspects of national education policies. The Index noted that migrant students receive little help in accessing all types of schools, but in particular tertiary education, more investment is needed to make equal access and intercultural education a reality and that teachers also receive little support to handle challenges arising in more heterogeneous classes, which amounts as an additional barrier for immigrant students.

Other indicators measure in quantitative terms educational achievements in Italian schools: taking into account all young people in the relative age brackets, the percentage of those (18–24) dropping out or leaving early from education and training (ELET) amounts to 13.10% against an average of 9.90% in the EU(27). As far as young adults (15–19) who are not in education, employment or training (NEET) are concerned, their share amounts to 23.30% in Italy compared to 13.70% in the EU(27).[2] If this already alarm raising data is broken down between Italian and non-Italian citizens, one can see that in relation to early school leavers (ELET), 32.1% of students with non-Italian citizenship are concerned, compared to 11% of native students. Similarly, though to a smaller degree, a higher share of non-Italian young people are among NEETs than natives: 36% against 21.80%.[3] There are multiple factors behind this phenomenon, but it is worthwhile to scrutinize what is the role schools play, more precisely how the normative framework and the policy initiatives are able to address the situation, which are the positive features and critical areas; and what kind of developments should take place.

Italy is certainly not the only country facing difficulties in the integration and inclusion of migrants. The European Commission also acknowledged the importance of the issue and recently published an Action Plan to support the efforts of the EU Member States. The document, which will be recalled in the next section describes the promotion of integration and inclusion not only as a moral duty in line with the EU's fundamental values, but also an economic imperative of social and economic investment which makes European societies more cohesive, resilient and prosperous. The Action Plan pays a particular attention to the education of young people with migrant background as it considers schools as the foundation of a successful participation in economic, social and cultural life, and as one of the most powerful instruments for the construction of more inclusive societies. The Action Plan constitutes the starting point for the reflections collected in this chapter, as it links domestic policies to EU-wide goals.

The successive section of the chapter will map the Italian legal environment in which the Action Plan must be applied and implemented with due attention to the protection of students with learning difficulties. Today Italian legal measures offer protection to a wide category of Students with Special Needs in Education. This includes different types of vulnerabilities, but the most sophisticated tools are available for students with disabilities. This category was the first to obtain legal protection and much experience has been consolidated since then. Therefore, the question arises if the tools elaborated for this category can be used as a pattern and adapted to the needs of students with different types of vulnerabilities.

Before examining this opportunity, it is indispensable to explore the content of some underlying concepts which determine the choice of the tools. In particular, it is necessary to do so with the concepts of integration and inclusion as they are applied in the specific context of education. It is equally important to understand, if the nature of difficulties faced by students with disabilities and migrant background are similar. At first sight one would say that students with migrant background face temporary difficulties due mainly to the lack of linguistic knowledge, but such conclusions often prove to be hasty and misleading. Many students experience not only long-lasting linguistic difficulties, but also disadvantages of socio-economic nature.

What emerges from the legal analysis is that Italian norms provide for differentiated tools according to the type of vulnerability of students, but in the case of students with linguistic-cultural difficulties affirmative actions based on the initiatives of schools prevail. Albeit these actions aim to remove obstacles hampering substantial equality, they are not accompanied by guarantees ensuring the effective exercise of the right to education. Problematic elements can be identified with regard to learning opportunities of Italian language, availability of tutoring and guidance for students in need and the activation of Personalized Study Plans. Policy changes in the indicated areas would strengthen the process of integration and inclusion. The results would become tangible not only in the form of more cohesive schools, but in a wider context as well, measurable in higher educational attainment, lower drop-out and lower risk of social exclusion of students with migrant background. And this becomes again the connecting point with the Action Plan: schools play a fundamental role in forming the societies of tomorrow through education and inclusion. Therefore, if the goal is to improve social inclusion in all segments of society, this should start with a substantial upgrading of the already existing *integration process in inclusive schools*.

THE EUROPEAN CONTEXT AND INITIATIVES FOR MIGRANTS' INTEGRATION

In 2020 the Commission published an Action Plan on Integration and Inclusion 2021–2027[4] to support the Member States in their efforts for a better integration and inclusion of migrants. This document can be considered as a reference point for legislative and policy choices carried out at national level since it indicates the main directions and goals to be achieved throughout implementation. Along the same logic, the Action Plan constitutes a starting point for the reflections of this chapter, and it serves as a compass for the evaluation of national policy choices.

The approach of the Action Program in relation to education and training[5] is founded on the consideration, that schools are placed in a privileged position in view of integration and inclusion of young people with migrant background.[6] They constitute the main access to social relations, they offer the principal opportunity to learn the language and get familiar with the habits of the country of their settlement. Schools provide young people with skills necessary for a full participation in social, economic and political life of their new country.

The Action Plan is not an isolated initiative, it is inserted in the wider framework of the European Pillar of Social Rights,[7] and it makes part of interconnected programmes, like the EU Comprehensive Strategy on the Rights of the Child,[8] the new Pact on Migration and Asylum,[9] the EU's anti-racism action plan.[10] All these initiatives are inspired by similar values, principles and goals, as spelled out in the Action Plan: Ensuring effective integration and inclusion is a social and economic investment that makes European societies more cohesive, resilient and prosperous. It is therefore not only a moral duty in line with the EU's fundamental values, but also an economic imperative to step up action in promoting integration and inclusion.[11] It should be immediately added that the Commission strongly emphasizes that if integration is to be successful, it has to be a two-way process: migrants and EU citizens with migrant background are offered help to integrate, and they in turn make an active effort to be integrated.[12]

As it emerges from the above statements, the goals of the Action Plan are inspired primarily by economic targets in favour of a better labour market performance, accompanied by policies promoting cohesion and backed by solidarity. The contribution of immigrants has an economic value and their skills play a crucial role. And indeed, progress is measured by indicators showing the level of education and school attainment, employment rate and the risk of poverty and social exclusion.

However, the Action Plan does not suggest any model of integration or inclusion, it limits itself to support economically the initiatives of the Member States,[13] and facilitate the dissemination and exchange of best practices, not least because the EU has only a limited competence in the subject matter. Nevertheless, it is easy to find precious hints about critical issues and aspects where policy or legal intervention can promote integration and inclusion.

As it was said earlier, the Action Plan pays much attention to education and training as they are recognised among the most powerful instruments to lay the foundations of a successful adult life. However, the document identifies various situations where students with migrant background experience disadvantage: they face a major risk of drop-out from the school system, many of them obtain lower level of qualifications and they are more exposed to poverty and social exclusion than their native peers. The

Commission claims that schools have the potential to provide students with adequate instruments to improve their social position. Schools can become real hubs of integration for children and their families, as they can connect communities, support services and institutions that can promote integration and inclusion.[14] In fact, if schools aim to obtain success in constructing cohesive communities, they cannot act in isolation, they have to open their gates and involve others, like local communities, associations and civil society organisations.

All together, the indications listed in the Action Plan do not constitute an absolute novelty. The fact that the Action Plan is embedded in the wider context of the European Pillar of Social Rights is only one of the reasons. Several documents published by international organizations or by the European Commission itself have collected similar considerations. Some of these concentrate on the process of integration, whereas others put under the spotlight economic aspects and analyse how immigrants can be put in the position to contribute to economic growth. In both cases schools enjoy a central role. To give some examples, the Migrant integration policy index (MIPEX, as recalled already in the introduction) and its chapter on education measures with specific indicators developed to assess the progress of single countries in fields such as academic guidance and financial resources provided for schools with immigrant pupils; teachers' training in cultural diversity and intercultural education; language support up to academic fluency to migrant pupils.[15] Similarly, the Zaragoza indicators cover education too, they measure the highest educational achievements, access to tertiary education, drop-out from school system and early leavers from education as well as the language proficiency of students with migrant background.[16] Both the EU and the OECD have developed various indicators to analyse the situation, to measure the impact of policies targeting integration, to identify goals, to evaluate the results and to explore gaps and spaces for improvement.[17]

Many studies go beyond quantitative analysis and spell out advise, asking to pay more attention to the educational attainment of immigrants, not only because it is decisive for the individual in terms of access to the labour market, but because investments in training and integration are seen as necessary to obtain a positive overall economic impact of immigration.[18] Other documents are more precise in relation to the role of education. Both the Action Plan on the European Pillar of Social Rights and the European Strategy on the Rights of the Child underline that for children exposed to the risk of social exclusion, schools represent an opportunity to break the intergenerational chain of poverty and that schools play a fundamental role in separating school success from social, economic and cultural status, where this often results decisive for the first.[19] In addition, other sources advocate that support and social assistance given to parents produce a spill-over effect for subsequent generations: children will benefit the most of such support in terms of opportunities of higher educational attainment and consequently of an outlook for a better quality of life.[20]

The fact that multiple documents and organisations dedicate attention to the role of education in the successful integration of migrants makes evident not only the importance of the issue, but it also indicates that considerable space for the improvement of national actions remains before the tasks can be successfully accomplished.

THE ITALIAN LEGAL FRAMEWORK FOR THE INCLUSION OF VULNERABLE STUDENTS

In this section the reflections turn towards the national legal construct in which the goals set out in the Commission's Action Plan are to be implemented. The analysis must not disregard the Constitution as its relevant principles and provisions form the underlying edifice of more specific norms.

In the Italian Constitution[21] the right to education is connected to some of the general principles laid down therein. Art. 2 announces that: "The Republic recognizes and guarantees the inviolable rights of the person, both as an individual and in the social groups where human personality is expressed." Art. 3 defines both formal and substantial equality, and it subscribes as "the duty of the Republic to remove those obstacles of an economic or social nature which constrain the freedom of equality of citizens thereby impeding the full development of the human person and the effective participation of all workers in the political, economic and social organization of the country." Reading these principles Matucci argues that the model of society prefigured by the Constitution is an open society, which is able to accommodate all the different types of diversities by being directly committed to promote the full development of every single person and to ensure their effective participation in the political, economic and social life.[22]

Public education is organized by the Republic, which "lays down general rules for education and establishes state schools of all branches and grades. Entities and private persons have the right to establish schools and institutions of education at no costs to the State."[23] The universal right to access to education is declared by Art. 34: "Schools are open to everyone." Everyone, meaning all members of the community, going beyond categories explicitly mentioned by the fundamental law. Indeed, the inclusiveness of schools is expressly enhanced by further principles of the Constitution. In relation to the economic conditions of students the same Art. 34 expresses that "primary education given at least for 8 years is compulsory and free of tuition." Moreover, with regard to the effective exercise of the right to education the Constitution recalls the Republic to guarantee for capable and deserving pupils, including those lacking adequate financial resources to attain the highest levels of education by providing scholarships, allowances and other benefits. Inclusiveness is specified also as far as health conditions are concerned: Disabled and handicapped people are protected by the Constitution, which announces their entitlement to receive education and vocational training (Art. 38(3)). Thus, the universal nature of the access to education is expressed in a more specific form by the nomination and inclusion of those with social and economic disadvantages and psychophysical hardship.[24]

The long process of inclusion in Italian schools started with the opening up of regular schools for disabled pupils. A series of legal interventions indicate the milestones of this process and the first ones to be mentioned are the laws 118/1971 and 517/1977. These laws meant the end of segregation of pupils with disabilities in special schools. Since then, vulnerable pupils have been enrolled in classes together with their "normal" peers.[25] The specific position of Support Teachers was created with the aim to facilitate the participation and learning of disabled pupils.[26] In 1992 the framework law n. 104 on the rights and protection of disabled people was approved. Still today this norm constitutes the most important legal source for social and school integration of people with disability.

The next milestone to be reminded is the so-called "Moratti Reform" (Law 53/2003) which set out the goal to guarantee the right to education to every student throughout personalized study plans. The recognition of personal needs and difficulties in learning abilities opened up the way towards the enactment of measures for other categories of vulnerable pupils beyond those with medically certified disabilities. Some years later, the Law 170/2010 and in 2011 the Guidelines on "Specific Learning Disorders" (Disturbi Specifici di Apprendimento—DSA) recognized the needs of students with reading, writing and computing difficulties and introduced specific measures to assist in their learning achievements. Subsequently, in 2012–13, further measures were introduced for students with Special Needs in Education (Bisogni Educativi Speciali—BES) including those with cultural, linguistic and socio-economic disadvantages. These students became recognized as vulnerable students and obtained entitlement to Personalized Study Plans according to their needs.[27]

The Ministry of Education justified the establishment of the new category -Students with Special Needs in Education, by stating that the distinction between students with disabilities and without became insufficient in a reality of an ever-increasing complexity and heterogeneity of the students in classes. It was also recognized, that "every pupil, in a continuous way or for a specific period of time, might manifest Special Needs in Education: either for physical, biological, physiological reasons, but also for psychological, social reasons, in front of which the schools must offer and adequate and personalized answer."[28]

The category of students with Special Needs in Education is the one which lays at the foundations of today's legal protection. It is a kind of umbrella category, it pulls together different types of vulnerabilities, and consequently, differentiated sets of measures according to the specific needs. There are three distinct sub-categories: the first one refers to students with disabilities certified according to the Law 104/1992,[29] the second one includes various types of learning and developmental disturbances (Specific Developmental Disorders—Disturbi Evolutivi Specifici) which are clinically identified but which cannot be categorized as disability.[30] The third one relates to students with socio-economic, linguistic or cultural disadvantage, which constitute difficulties beyond the ordinary ones and are associated with learning activities. Students with migrant background make part of this category.

The most recent legislative developments are characterized by a different pattern: they do not focus any more on the widening of the platea of vulnerable students, instead they introduce a shift in concept. The Law 107/2015 (called also as "La Buona Scuola"—"The Good School") uses the term "inclusion" and signals its ambition to extend it to all learners.[31] The two innovations, that is going beyond "integration" and extending inclusion to each and every student were inspired mainly by the UN Convention on the Rights of Persons with Disabilities (CRPD) and by its Art. 24, which constitutes the baseline for the right to education.[32] Italy ratified the Convention with Law 18/2009. As it was mentioned above, Law 105/2017 declares the universality of school inclusion, but the specific norms adopted for the implementation of the Law seem to refocus their attention to the inclusion of students with disabilities and to forget about the other categories of vulnerable students.[33] This direction was confirmed by the legislative decree on the Promotion of Inclusion of Students with Disabilities[34] and by the norm on the new Individualized Study Plan designed for students with disabilities.[35] Along the same lines, the legislative decree on Professional Training of Teachers in Secondary Schools reserves courses on Special Teaching Methods to Support Teachers and does not prescribes them to the entire staff of schools.[36]

Domestic legal developments certainly have been deeply influenced by international sources: not only by UN Conventions, but also by "soft law" initiatives. These initiatives, albeit they have no binding force, nevertheless constitute a source of inspiration for new norms or guidelines. It is easy to follow how the focus of international sources evolved from the protection and support of students with disabilities towards the recognition of all types of vulnerabilities. Among the many documents some should be recalled here: UN Convention on the Rights of the Child (1989), UNESCO

Declaration: Education for All (1990), Salamanca Statement and Framework for Action on Special Needs Education (1994). In the chronological order the next source is the UN Convention on the Rights of Persons with Disabilities (2006), which was already mentioned. Last but not least, the list should include the UNESCO Policy Guidelines on Inclusion in Education (2009), which contains indications that inclusive measures should be expanded to all kinds of vulnerabilities present among students.

From the historical development of the legal framework for the protection of vulnerable students one can see a gradual opening towards various types of vulnerabilities and the recognition of multiple forms of special needs in education. However, only an in-depth analysis of the various measures would reveal what kind of protection is effectively ensured, what is its actual impact on the exercise of the right to education and if appropriate guarantees are available to enforce rights and support measures. Such an analysis would require lengthy and detailed investigations which would go beyond the scope of this chapter. Therefore, a different approach is suggested, which does not alter the essence of the previously raised issues. The protection of students with disabilities can be used as a reference point. This category of vulnerable students was the first one to obtain protection; concepts, norms and measures have evolved since then, they have become fine-tuned and could consolidate over the time. On many occasions the experience gained in this field was applied for the elaboration of measures for new categories of vulnerable students. Against this background we can scrutinize whether the protection of students with disabilities can serve as a pattern: To what extent the concepts and instruments elaborated for students with disabilities might be applicable for students with migrant background and to what extent the available tools are efficient in ensuring the effective exercise of the right to education?

DIFFERENTIATION AMONG THE TYPES OF VULNERABILITIES AND THEIR SUPPORT MEASURES

In order to answer the above questions, first the underlying concepts for the protection of students with disabilities must be recalled. The next step then is to explore if and how these concepts can be applied to students with migrant background and how these concepts appear in legal norms. Afterwards, it is equally important to verify if the difficulties faced by the two groups of vulnerable students are comparable. These questions will delineate what the legislator expects from students with migrant background and what are the main difficulties these pupils have to face in Italian schools. The answers given to these questions will also determine the extent to which the measures elaborated for students with disabilities can serve as a reference point.

The conceptual framework describing the position of disabled students has changed over the time and evolved substantially: first disabled students were excluded from education just as from many other segments of social life. Later they gained access to education, but remained segregated in closed groups, deprived of contacts with the community of "normal" students. The next phase was characterized by the promotion of the integration of disabled students to mainstream schools, which was then overstepped by the notion of inclusion due to the already mentioned UN Convention on the Rights of People with Disabilities. Inclusion became the underlying concept and the CRPD Committee took the opportunity to explain the difference between integration and inclusion in relation to the right to education through the elaboration of two definitions:[37]

> *Integration:* "a process of placing persons with disabilities in existing mainstream educational institutions, as long as the former can adjust to the standardized requirements of such institutions."
> *Inclusion:* "it involves a process of systemic reform embodying changes and modifications in content, teaching methods, approaches, structures and strategies in education to overcome barriers with a vision serving to provide all students of the relevant age range with an equitable and participatory learning experience and environment that best corresponds to their requirements and preferences."

The most striking difference between the two concepts lays within the term of adaptation: who has to adapt to what or what has to be adapted to whom. While in the case of integration a student with disabilities has to adapt to existing and standardized conditions, in the case of inclusion it is the educational environment which has to adapt and create the conditions capable to ensure equal access and full participation for all students. For today the concept of inclusion prevails over the concept of integration and this view is confirmed by the directions and terminology used in the recent legislative developments in Italy, in particular by the reforms announced in the Law "The Good School" ("La Buona Scuola," Law 105/2017) as it was already mentioned above.

Turning towards students with migrant background, the question arises how the abovementioned categories are applied and if their significance remains identical in the context of students with a different type of vulnerability.

In Italy, the access to education for foreigners[38] is regulated by the norms on immigration as described in Art. 38 of the Legislative Decree 286/1998:

"foreign minors are subject of school attendance and all measures in force in relation to the right to education are applicable to them."[39]

The same Legislative Decree gives further elements and indicates the characteristics of the introduction of foreign people to the Italian society. The keyword is integration and Art. 4bis offers a definition inasmuch "a process finalized to promote the coexistence of Italian citizens and foreigners by respecting the values laid down in the Constitution, with mutual commitment to participate in the economic, social and cultural life of the society." An instrument to implement this commitment is the so-called "Integration Agreement" (Accordo di Integrazione), concluded by the State and the foreign individual, where this latter subscribes to specific duties of integration. One of these duties is to "guarantee the fulfillment of the education obligation by minor children."[40]

Another document describes more in details the government's strategy on integration.[41] It identifies schools as the main players during the integration process since these are the places where Italian language is taught, and civic education takes place. This latter includes classes where students become familiar with the Italian Constitution.[42] The choice to focus on schools as hubs of integration means that the process is channeled and directed towards specific goals throughout specific value choices in the educational context.[43]

Therefore, integration seems to have a different meaning for students with migrant background than for students with disabilities at their admission to mainstream classes. While adaptation to the standardized conditions is envisaged for students with disabilities, students with migrant background have to acquire linguistic competences and obtain certain knowledge as part of the commitments described in the legal norms.

What students have to learn relates to the fundamental principles of the Italian culture, the values laid down in the Constitution and, in particular to Italian language.[44] They all together constitute the foundations but also the conditions of a full participation at school and, more generally, in social life. At this point it is important to underline that no document enshrines assimilation, the suggested concept does not cancel differences, instead it asks for the mutual respect of identity both from the part of immigrant and the local communities through a positive interaction and peaceful cohabitation.[45] The goal of integration policies is to establish a common base line of values shared by all, where newcomers inevitably must adjust to the civic and linguistic characteristics of the welcoming community.[46]

The formal fulfilment of the conditions prescribed by the norms on immigration are yet insufficient to create a favourable environment for learning and participation. Reality in schools has become far more complex in the last decades, today students with migrant background amount to 10,3% of all students.[47] It would be also difficult to say that the remaining 90%

constitute a homogenous group, instead every student can be described as having multiple identities,[48] throughout his/her participation in different forms of socialization. In schools this can be translated as diversity, or as the unicity of every individual which asks for differentiated solutions in the challenges of learning.

Thus, in order to respond to the differentiated needs of individuals or groups, it seems to be appropriate to recall the concept of inclusion inasmuch it requires the adaptation of the environment according to the learning needs of the individual. Otherwise, without adaptation, the standardized forms and methods easily leave gaps in accessibility and efficiency and might not function for everyone.[49] These considerations seem to coincide with the guidelines of the Ministry for Education in relation to the welcome and integration of foreign students, as it speaks about a model of *integration in an inclusive school*.[50] This concept captures both notions so far discussed, where integration refers to the necessity to acquire certain knowledge and competencies, whereas inclusion foresees the adaptation of the learning environment to ensure full participation and the development of the potential of everyone according to specific needs.

At this point one can see that the concepts underlying the protection of students with disabilities are not entirely ready-made for the protection of students with migrant background. In the case of this latter group the concept of integration designed in a more complex way: students do not only have to adapt to the standardized conditions, but they must fulfill educational requirements as well. In addition, the concept of integration seems to prevail over the one of inclusion, whereas in the case of students with disabilities it is often described as an obsolete one. Therefore, the differences suggest cautiousness in applying the instruments developed for students with disabilities for another category of vulnerable students.

This suggestion seems to be supported also by the nature of difficulties the two groups face in schools. In the case of students with disabilities, a medical certificate confirms learning difficulties on objective grounds. The disadvantage attributed to students with migrant background is of cultural-linguistic, and often socio-economic as well. Linguistic disadvantage is habitually seen as a temporary one with the expectation of a swift fix: the acquisition of linguistic competencies is just a question of relatively short time. Such conclusions can easily miss the point. As a matter of fact, language knowledge has various levels. Young pupils quickly assimilate the vocabulary of everyday communication, but to be able to study in an appropriate way school materials and to reach proficiency more time is needed.[51] In addition, another element might also hamper the learning process: these young people frequently carry with themselves complex problems which often remain hidden. What comes to one's mind first are the traumatic experiences linked to the migration process itself, but less tragic moments can take their psychological toll too, such as settling down in a completely new and profoundly diverse environment, difficulties to preserve the original cultural belongingness while living in another country, or the typical socio-economic problems of low-income families[52] affecting many immigrants. Such factors do impact the learning abilities of pupils and they require attention, support and adequate accompanying measures in schools.

Contrary to what has just been said, indications from the Ministry of Education seem to pay attention exclusively to linguistic issues: it is possible to establish Personalized Study Plans whenever students face difficulties because of the lack of knowledge of Italian language with the condition that these measures are activated for a strictly necessary period of time.[53] There are no further indications in the document about the goals to be achieved which might quantify a "strictly necessary period of time."[54]

The insufficient outcome produced by such policy choice has indeed reached the ears of the legislator and the Law 107/2015 introduced Italian as second language (L2) in the additional educational offer that single schools set up with the possibility to involve local communities, families and cultural mediators.[55] However, the realization of such a goal seems to be far away as currently teachers qualified to teach Italian as L2 are employed only in Provincial Centers of Adult Education (Centro Provinciale per l'Istruzione degli Adulti–CPIA), and not in schools attended by the overwhelming part of students with migrant background.[56] This fact was underlined by the Observatory for the Integration of Foreign Pupils and for Interculture (Osservatorio per l'integrazione degli alunni stranieri e per l'intercultura)[57] in a document which suggested to launch a nationwide plan of Italian as a second language in schools and outside of them, comprising the national public broadcaster (RAI), associations, local communities and schools.[58] As a matter of fact, various earlier documents of the Observatory already underlined the importance of teaching and learning Italian language,[59] but despite the repetitive calls of the Observatory and the evidence on the ground, institutional changes are yet to be seen.

BEYOND THE LANGUAGE: OTHER QUESTIONS AROUND THE PROTECTION OF STUDENTS WITH MIGRANT BACKGROUND

The question around language knowledge identified a critical point: on the one hand, the norms recalled in the previous paragraphs attribute a fundamental importance to this issue, but on the other, the instruments offered do not seem to be sufficient and adequate to achieve this goal. Today the Law 107/2015 goes beyond the basic need of filling the knowledge gap by a Personalized Study Plan adjusted to the needs of a specific student and it opens towards a structured system of teaching Italian as a second language, but this aspect of the norm has not yet found a large scale and generalized implementation, as indicated by the multiple reminders of the Observatory.

The above paragraphs made clear that albeit the overall aim of the legislator is to realize inclusion for all students with special needs in education, the paths and the instruments to achieve this goal should be diversified according to the type of vulnerability and the specific need emerging from it. Accordingly, students with disabilities, certified by the Law 104/1992 have the right to be accompanied by a Support Teacher, whereas the protection and promotion of students with migrant background are placed within the responsibility of *each and every* teacher of the class.[60] While a coordinated action by all teachers have the potential to produce the planned outcome, there are situations where a single reference person available for the student to discuss both educational issues and questions around his/her wellbeing seems to be more appropriate than a group of teachers. For example, this might be the case of students just arrived from abroad or those who run the risk of dropping out from the school system: a tutor can facilitate the familiarization with the new environment in the first case and alleviate the risk of school failure in the second. The task of a tutor is different from the one of Support Teachers. His role often goes beyond the school as he tries to reach out the family and looks for interaction with a wider social network of the students.

There are many successful initiatives which bear testimony of the importance of tutoring and among these the "*Almeno una stella*" (At least one star) can be recalled. The project was implemented in various Italian cities and aimed at helping young, recently arrived immigrants in their efforts in various segments of their new life: to learn the language, to choose a high school or a vocational training institution and to enter the world of school. Support was provided also by accompanying them in knowing their neighborhood and finding places of aggregation with their peers. Many of the tutors had immigrant background themselves thus their own experience boosted the support they could convey to the young people involved in the project.[61] The conclusions reached by another project were even more explicit about the strategic role of tutoring and of highly individualized projects. This one related to unaccompanied minors and their placement in the educational system: despite the right to education and vocational training guaranteed by the law, what really made a difference in many cases was being accompanied by adults playing significant role and met in the welcoming system. These adults are educators capable to protect the vulnerability and valorize the potential of these minors; teachers and trainers with a crucial role in the orientation and encouragement of these young people to undertake and continue studying; and others, like operators able to negotiate with the educational institutions the acceptance and opportunities of the unaccompanied minors.[62]

However, in the current legislative and institutional framework such opportunities are not guaranteed, they are available under affirmative actions proposed and designed by educational or other institutions participating in the integration and inclusion of immigrants. In practice, vulnerable students can be put in contact with tutors either through specific projects of external associations cooperating with schools and financed typically by EU funds, or these students can count on single individuals guided by personal motivations and altruism.

Within the context of accompanying vulnerable students and promoting their inclusion one more critical aspect is to be mentioned. It would be important to offer training sessions on inclusion to all teachers since they are all responsible for vulnerable students in their class. However, the norms implementing the Law 107/2015 limit the novelties around inclusion to students with disabilities and limit training opportunities in special teaching methods nearly exclusively to Support Teachers.[63] This critical aspect is further exacerbated by the fact that all teachers have knowledge about vulnerabilities present in their school since it is described in the Annual Plan of Inclusion (Piano Annuale di Inclusione–PAI). Every school has to draw up such a Plan and it constitutes the basis for the development of inclusive teaching practices across the entire school. It is designed after a careful observation of the level of inclusivity already achieved and by setting out goals to be achieved. At the same time, the norm which prescribes the enactment of the Plan does not foresee any instrument for the specific training of teachers which would make them capable to obtain the necessary competences to improve the inclusion of vulnerable pupils.[64]

Bearing mind the problems presented above, inclusion in Italian schools presents both positive and negative aspects. In general terms, the complex normative framework is open towards the various types of vulnerabilities and it offers some kind of protection defined along the various groups within the heterogenous category of students with Special Needs in Education.[65] The legislator recognizes the problems and remedies are indicated, but often only general declarations are made without taking further steps to establish enforceable rights and make available guarantees. In the case of students with socio-economic, linguistic and cultural disadvantages, including students with migrant background, the protection is implemented mainly through affirmative actions promoted by single schools and with very few guarantees. As it was recalled, linguistic support is foreseen, but there are hardly any indications about its quality and the standard to be achieved. Similar thoughts can be expressed in relation to the solution that vulnerable students not falling into the category of students with disabilities are supported by all teachers of the class. The choice to leave a considerable space for affirmative actions offers the opportunity to elaborate innovative solutions, but it contains important limits as well: teachers enjoy huge discretion in how, if at all, launch a plan for inclusion designed according to the specific needs of the student. Indeed, a Ministerial Note gives exclusive discretional power to teachers as far as teaching methods, design of development path and the choice of the evaluation are concerned.[66]

And this power raises another question (the last one of this contribution): what happens if despite of obvious difficulties, the Class Council (in primary schools) or the Team of Teachers does not take the step to activate Personalized Study Plans?[67] Who can move to urge an intervention and what can be achieved? Parents can present requests accompanied by a clinical diagnosis, staff from social services can indicate situations causing difficulties which go beyond of what can be considered as acceptable and which can impact in a negative way learning outcomes: these communications are certainly taken into consideration by the school. But there might be situations when nobody raises his/her voice in the interest of the vulnerable student. This can easily happen in the case when the parents of a student with migrant background do not speak Italian, or they do not communicate with the school and nobody makes efforts for reach-out. At this point it seems to be instructive to recall the already mentioned crucial role of operators in welcoming services in the success of inclusion of unaccompanied minors. As it was said, their capacity of negotiation with school principals is often indispensable for a successful enrollment of these particularly vulnerable minors. Following this line of ideas, it looks advisable to involve in the process of inclusion of students with migrant background in a more active and systematic way those who have already gained experience in this field: cultural mediators,[68] welcoming services or immigrants' associations. These actors are able to provide substantial support which can make the difference: they represent the interests of the students, but at the same time they can be of help for the school as well in the delicate process of reach-out and communication with the families of origin.[69]

Such a cooperation is not hampered by the legislation, Law 107/2015 aims at ensuring a favourable learning environment to everyone according to his/her special needs, and indeed many schools have launched projects and activities with external actors. However, the choice is up to the schools and the decision is heavily influenced by the ambitions of school principals and by the available economic and human resources. The lack of guarantees to benefit from individualized guidance (with the eventual support of external actors to the schools) or Personalized Study Plans (activated by the Class Council or Team of Teachers) can significantly impact the learning process of students with migrant background and it affects the effective exercise of their right to education.

The previous paragraphs put under the spotlight various critical elements students with migrant background might have to face during their process of integration and inclusion. As it was said, the normative framework is generous towards the recognition of different types of vulnerabilities, but the space left for mere affirmative actions seems to limit, rather than strengthen their efficiency. Only enforceable rights can put these students in the position where they have a real chance to develop their full potential: i.e., where the obstacles hampering the full development of human personality and a full participation are removed as laid down in Art. 3 of the Italian Constitution and where schools are open to everyone according to Art. 34. The analysis shaped various suggestions for legal interventions to further enhance the implementation of the constitutional principles. First, make sure that every student with cultural and linguistic disadvantage has access to a course of Italian as second language until reaching a level of proficiency. Second, make available a reference person or tutor who can support and accompany the student from welcoming him/her until the choice of upper secondary school. And last, it seems to be advisable to counterbalance the exclusive power of teachers to activate a Personalized Study Plan designed for the needs of a specific student in order to address properly his/her disadvantage. Already applied and tested initiatives could be useful sources for legislative changes. The appropriate guarantees would not only strengthen the process of integration and inclusion in schools, but the results would spill over to other areas and would improve the indicators of more far-reaching goals.

CONCLUDING REMARKS

The reflections departed from the Action Plan of the EU Commission on integration and inclusion of immigrants. This document identifies various aspects where schools, directly or indirectly play a fundamental role in preparing young people for their adulthood: their mission is not confined to education and vocational training, but schools are also places of socialization where shared values of co-existence and knowledge for an active citizenship are conveyed every day. For the measurement of the acquisition of hard and soft skills the Commission applies several indicators: school drop-out, level of highest school attainment and the risk of poverty and social exclusion.

This chapter did not want to analyze the data presented by the indicators, rather it used these indicators as reference points, as goals for improvement. The data is a helpful source in the reading of the level of integration and inclusion of students with migrant background and the statistical information clearly indicates the gap between natives and students with migrant background in particular in relation to first generation migrants. The

EU-level data uncover that a considerable space remains for improvement in Italy in comparison with other Member States.

Single indicators include multiple aspects, therefore various actions of different nature are necessary to achieve measurable change. This chapter made a restrictive choice and it pointed on the examination of the Italian legal framework with the aim to better understand in which normative environment the Action Plan is to be implemented and in which aspects further development is needed to address the challenges. The *model of integration in an inclusive school* was identified which has been capable to follow the changes in the societal environment with the adjustment of legal sources. However, the opening towards the various forms of vulnerabilities has not been fully accompanied with the institutionalization of guarantees and the goal to ensure the effective exercise of the right of education for all has, on many occasions, remained wishful thinking. Several aspects were identified where amendments to existing legal sources would bring along improvements not only in the specific area, but the positive outcomes would spill over to other areas covered by the Commission's indicators. Successful integration and inclusion in schools can be translated in practical terms in lower drop-out, higher level of school attainment which in turn provide better opportunities to students with migrant background on the labour market and in society in general.

Currently single schools are in the key position to launch initiatives and promote inclusion in a legal environment characterized by affirmative actions and far-reaching school autonomy. Collection and dissemination of best practices are certainly important, but they are not sufficient to induce a substantial shift. Without a systematic reform of the legal framework inspired by the principle of an inclusive school open to each and every student, it will not be possible to eradicate the inequalities deriving from the initial social and cultural disparities. No doubt that there will always be excellent initiatives thanks to the devotion, passion and talent of single teachers, but the chance to benefit from these opportunities is often only a question of luck and not that of a choice guaranteed by a normative framework thoroughly structured in the perspective of inclusion.

NOTES

1. "Migrant integration policy index—education, 2020," accessed December 4, 2022, https://www.mipex.eu/education. It should be added, that most countries are slow to respond to changes occurring in their societies and to accommodate the needs of vulnerable children. This, however, cannot be an excuse and it should not prevent our shedding light on some critical aspects and to indicate tools for improvement.
2. Save the Children, *Atlante dell'infanzia a rischio, 2021, Il futuro è già qui,* 166–167.

3. Fondazione ISMU, *27° rapporto sulle migrazioni,* (Milano: Franco Angeli, 2022), 127.
4. COM(2020)758
5. The Action Plan is divided into four thematic areas: education and training, employment, health and housing. While all areas are indispensable for successful integration of migrants, this chapter concentrates only on the first area.
6. Young people or students with migrant background is the common denominator for a heterogenous group which includes both EU and third country citizens. EU citizens might be naturalized third-county nationals, they can descend from foreign-born parents, but they can be citizens of a Member State living in a different EU country as well. Third country citizens can be economic migrants, adopted children, non-accompanied minors, refugees, born in the host Member State or arrived there as young children without the citizenship of that State. The common element shared by all members of the group is that they are vulnerable, face difficulties, or might experience disadvantage because of their cultural and/or linguistic background or experiences linked to migration. The author is fully aware of the fact that such a category is not fit for statistical purposes or for the definition of a legal status. However, a methodological compromise seems to be acceptable to use other categories (such as immigrants or non-Italian citizens) as synonyms throughout this chapter, if the recalled sources do so.
7. The European Pillar of Social Rights was proclaimed at the Social Summit of Gothenburg held in 2017 and it was confirmed at the Social Summit in Porto in 2021. It consists of 20 key principles and rights recognised by EU law and policies. They are considered as indispensable for sustainable and fair labour markets and welfare systems. In 2021 the Commission launched an ambitious Action Plan (COM (2021)102) containing various initiatives to achieve the outlined goals. On the European Pillar of Social Rights see, among many others: Sacha Garben, "The European Pillar of Social Rights: An Assessment of its Meaning and Significance," in *Cambridge Yearbook of European Legal Studies,* (Cambridge: Cambridge University Press, 2019), 101–127.; Silvana Sciarra, *Solidarity and Conflict* (Cambridge: Cambridge University Press, 2018), 138ff.; Stefano Giubboni, "Appunti e disappunti sul pilastro europeo dei diritti sociali," *Quaderni costituzionali,* 37, no. 4 (2017): 953–962.; Stefano Giubboni, "L'insostenibile leggerezza del Pilastro Europeo dei Diritti Sociali," *Politica del Diritto,* 49, no. 4 (2018): 557–578.; Giuseppe Bronzini, ed., *Verso un pilastro sociale europeo,* (Roma: Fondazione Lelio e Lisli Basso, 2018); Maurizio Ferrera, "Si può costruire una Unione sociale europea?" *Quaderni costituzionali* 38, no. 3 (2018): 567–590.; Michele Della Morte, "Tendenze e prospettive dei diritti sociali in Europa. Dalla Carta di Nizza al Pilastro di Göteborg" in *Liber Amicorum* per Pasquale Costanzo, *Diritto costituzionale in trasformazione,* IV. *I diritti fondamentali nel prisma del costituzionalista,* (Genova: Consulta Online, 2020), 19–38.; Marco Benvenuti, "La scuola è aperta a tutti? Potenzialità e limiti del diritto all'istruzione tra ordinamento statale e ordinamento sovranazionale," *Federalismi.it,* no. 4 (September 2018): 101 ff.
8. COM(2021)142

9. https://ec.europa.eu/info/strategy/priorities-2019-2024/promoting-our-european-way-life/new-pact-migration-and-asylum_en
10. European Commission, *A Union of Equality: EU Anti-Racism Action Plan 2020–2025*, COM(2020)565.
11. COM(2020)758, 1–2.
12. COM(2020)758, 2.
13. In particular through the Asylum, Migration and Integration Fund, but also with the support of the European Social Fund (ESF) or the European Regional Development Fund (ERDF)
14. COM(2020)758, p. 8.
15. "Migrant integration policy index—education, 2020"
16. EU Zaragoza Integration Indicators, data available for Italy: https://ec.europa.eu/migrant-integration/librarydoc/eu-zaragoza-integration-indicators-italy On the construction of the indicators see further: Thomas Huddleston, Jan Niessen, and Jasper Dag Tjaden, *Using EU Indicators of Immigrant Integration. Final Report for DG for Home Affairs* (Brussels: Publications Office of the European Union, 2013).
17. Eurostat indicators: https://ec.europa.eu/eurostat/web/migration-asylum/migrant-integration/database, OECD and EU, Settling in 2018: Indicators of Immigrant Integration, 2018, https://www.oecd.org/social/indicators-of-immigrant-integration-2018-9789264307216-en.htm
18. See e.g.,: OECD and European Commission, *Matching economic migration with labour market needs in Europe, Policy Brief*, 2014, https://www.oecd.org/els/mig/OECD-EC%20Migration%20Policy%20Brief%2009-2014.pdf 13 ff.; European Commission, *Demographic Scenarios for the EU. Migration, Population and Education* (Luxembourg: Publication Office of the European Union, 2019), 36ff.
19. Respectively: European Commission, *Action Plan on the European Pillar of Social Rights*, COM(2021)102, point 3.3. and European Commission, *EU Comprehensive Strategy on the Rights of the Child*, COM(2021)142; points 2 and 2.3.
20. OECD and European Commission, *Matching economic migration*, 15.; Huddleston, Niessen and Tjaden, *Using EU Indicators of Immigrant Integration*, 5 ff.
21. The English translation of the Italian Constitution can be retrieved in the repository of the Italian Senate. https://www.senato.it/documenti/repository/istituzione/costituzione_inglese.pdf
22. Giuditta Matucci, "Costituzione e inclusione scolastica: origini e prospettive di sviluppo della «scuola aperta a tutti»," in *La scuola inclusiva dalla Costituzione a oggi. Riflessioni tra pedagogia e diritto,* eds. Monica Ferrari, Giuditta Matucci, Matteo Morandi (Milano: Franco Angeli, 2019), 100.
23. Art. 33 of the Italian Constitution
24. On the evolution of the interpretation of arts. 34 and 38 (3) of the Italian Constitution see further: Giuditta Matucci, "Ripensare la scuola inclusiva: una rilettura dei principi costituzionali," *SINAPPSI—Connessioni tra ricerca e politiche pubbliche* 10, no. 3 (2020): 6.
25. In its judgment No 215/1987 the Italian Constitutional Court confirmed the right of disabled students to enroll in mainstream schools and declared unlawful Art. 28(3) of the Law 118/1971 in its part where it foresaw that the

attendance of middle school would be "eased" for disabled students, instead of stating that attendance would be "ensured."
26. Support Teachers are present in class together with the curricular teachers. This solution can create difficulties and problems around the exact role of the Support Teacher. On this point see further: Ianes, Dario, Heidrun Demo, and Francesco Zambotti. "Integration in Italian Schools: Teachers' Perceptions Regarding Day-to-Day Practice and Its Effectiveness," *International Journal of Inclusive Education* 18, no. 6 (2014): 626–653.
27. MIUR, Direttiva ministeriale 27 dicembre 2012, Strumenti d'Intervento per alunni con Bisogni Educativi Speciali e organizzazione territoriale per l'inclusione scolastica (Ministry of Education, Universities and Research, Ministerial Directive of 27 December 2012, Intervention measures for students with special needs in education and territorial organization for school inclusion) and Circolare n. 8 del 6 marzo 2013 (Ministerial Circular of 6 March 2013, No 8).
28. MIUR, Direttiva ministeriale 27 dicembre 2012, translation by the author
29. The subject continues to attract the attention of numerous constitutional law scholars as demonstrated by the vast doctrinal literature that examines the inclusion of disabled people in relation to social dignity and socialization. See among many: Carlo Colapietro, *Diritti dei disabili e Costituzione* (Napoli: Editoriale Scientifica, 2011). Carlo Colapietro, "I principi-valori della "pari dignità sociale" e del "pieno sviluppo della persona umana" quale fondamento costituzionale della tutela delle persone con disabilità," in *Studi in onore di Franco Modugno* (Napoli: Editoriale Scientifica, 2011), 943-994. Carlo Colapietro, "I diritti delle persone con disabilità nella giurisprudenza della Corte costituzionale: il "nuovo" diritto alla socializzazione," *Dirittifondamentali.it*, no. 2 (2020): 121–164. Paolo Addis, "Il diritto all'istruzione delle persone con disabilità: profili sostanziali e giurisprudenziali," in *I Diritti Sociali Nella Pluralità Degli Ordinamenti*, ed. Elisabetta Catalani, Rolando Tarchi (Napoli: Editoriali Scientifica, 2015), 149–171. Silvio Troilo, *Tutti per uno o uno contro tutti? Il diritto all'istruzione e all'integrazione scolastica dei disabili nella crisi dello Stato sociale* (Milano: Giuffrè, 2012). Simone Scagliarini, "L'incessante dinamica della vita moderna. I nuovi diritti sociali nella giurisprudenza costituzionale," in *I diritti sociali: dal riconoscimento alla garanzia. Il ruolo della giurisprudenza*, ed. Elisa Cavasino, Giovanni Scala, and Giuseppe Verde (Napoli: Editoriale Scientifica, 2013), 235-282. Emanuele Rossi, Paolo Addis, and Francesca Biondi Dal Monte, "La libertà di insegnamento e il diritto all'istruzione nella costituzione italiana." *Rivista AIC*, no. 1 (2016). Fabio Masci, "L'inclusione scolastica dei disabili: inclusione sociale di persone," *Costituzionalismo.it*, no. 2 (2017): 133–177. Giuditta Matucci, ed., *Diritto all'istruzione e inclusione sociale* (Milano: Franco Angeli, 2019). Giuseppe Arconzo, *I diritti delle persone con disabilità. Profili costituzionali* (Milano: Franco Angeli, 2020). Carlo Colapietro, and Federico Girelli, *Persone con disabilità e Costituzione* (Napoli: Editoriale Scientifica, 2020).
30. Heterogenous disorders belong to this category, such as disturbance in attention and hyperactivity, speech deficit, movement coordination deficit or

Specific Learning Disorders (Disturbi Specifici di Apprendimento [DSA]) including dyslexia and dyscalculia.

31. The strengthening of inclusion and the right to education of students with special needs in education and the enhancement of individualized learning paths for all learners in general are listed among the goals of the educational institutions (Art. 1(7) l) and p) of the Law n.107 of 13 July 2015). For a detailed analysis see: Giuditta Matucci, "Il diritto/dovere all'inclusione scolastica," *Gruppo di Pisa, Dibattito Aperto sul Diritto e Giustizia Costituzionale*, no. 1 (2019): in particular 44.
32. On this topic see further: Delia Ferri, "The Past, Present and Future of the Right to Inclusive Education in Italy," in *The Right to Inclusive Education in International Human Rights Law*, eds. Gauthier de Beco, Shivaun Quinlivan, and Janet E. Lord (Cambridge: Cambridge University Press, 2019), 547–579.
33. Giuditta Matucci, ""Buona Scuola": l'inclusione scolastica alla prova dei decreti attuativi," *Osservatorio AIC*, no. 3 (September 2017): 19.
34. D. lgs. 13 aprile 2017, n. 66. (Legislative Decree of 13 April 2017, No 66)
35. Decreto interministeriale del 29 dicembre 2020, n. 182 (Inter-ministerial Decree of 29 December 2020, No 182)
36. D. lgs. 13 aprile 2017, n. 59. (Legislative Decree of 13 April 2017, No 59)
37. The CRDP Committee has the duty to monitor the implementation of the Convention by the States which ratified it. The cited definitions were spelled out in the General Comments n. 4 (Art. 24), paras 11., 2016 https://tbinternet.ohchr.org/_layouts/15/treatybodyexternal/Download.aspx?symbolno=CRPD%2fC%2fGC%2f4%20Plain%20English%20version&Lang=en See also: Delia Ferri, "Unveiling the Challenges in the Implementation of Article 24 CRPD on the Right to Inclusive Education. A Case-Study from Italy," *Laws* 7, no. 1 (2018): 1-17.
38. Legal instruments necessarily make a distinction between Italian and non-Italian citizens, that is foreigners. However, the principles which inspired the norms applicable for foreigners, are potentially relevant for everybody with migrant background. Since the focus of this paragraph is not on the legal status of students, but on the underlying principles guiding their integration and inclusion in schools, in this particular context the categories of foreigners and students with migrant background are intended as synonyms.
39. Translated by the author. The right to education is applicable to all foreign minors who are present on the territory of Italy with no regard to their legal status. The Constitutional Court stated that the fundamental and inviolable human rights are applicable to foreigners as well, and if a legal norm differentiates between citizens and foreigners, a minimum core of these rights, including the right to education, must be recognized to all individuals. (See the judgments of 120/1967 and 104/1969.) The right to education of minors who stay in Italy without a regular permit of stay is recognized on the grounds of these principles by the Legislative Decree of 25 July 1998, n.286. See further: Alberta De Fusco, "Sul diritto all'istruzione come veicolo di integrazione delle seconde generazioni di immigrazione in Italia," *Osservatorio AIC*, no. 1, (February 2018): 161.

40. Art. 2. comma 4, punto d) del D.P.R. 14 settembre 2011, n. 179. (Art. 2(4)d of the Decree of the President of the Republic of 14 September 2011, No 179.)
41. Ministero del Lavoro e delle Politiche Sociali, Ministero dell'Interno e MIUR, *Italia 2020. Piano per l'integrazione nella sicurezza. Identità e Incontro*, 2010.
42. Civic education became (again, in renewed form) a specific course in schools with the Law 92/2019. In previous years civic education had an eclectic experience with mixed outcomes. See further: Giorgio Sobrino, "L'insegnamento della Costituzione nella scuola oggi, strumento istituzionale per la promozione di una cittadinanza "piena" e consapevole," *Federalismi.it*, no. 18 (July 2022): 246–277.
43. An additional value of the process is underlined by the Commission's Action Plan on integration, inasmuch: By teaching democracy, citizenship and critical thinking skills, schools play an important role in preventing young people from being attracted to violent extremist ideologies, organisations and movements. COM(2020)758, 9.
44. Several research articles focus on the issue of linguistic integration. See among many: Vincenzo Casamassima, and Giacomo Delledonne, "Integrazione linguistica e multilinguismo nel contesto dell'ordinamento dell'Unione europea. La prospettiva dell'integrazione scolastica dei migranti," *Osservatorio sulle fonti*, no. 3 (2015). Valeria Piergigli, "Integrazione linguistica e immigrazione. Approcci e tendenze nel diritto comparato europeo," *Federalismi.it*, no. 22 (November 2013). Valeria Piergigli, "L'integrazione degli immigrati da Paesi terzi nel diritto sovranazionale: limiti e potenzialità dell'Unione europea," *Rivista AIC*, no. 3 (2018): 63-88. Valeria Piergigli, "Integration of third country nationals and the European Union: an opportunity not to be missed," in *Economics, Policy and Law, Proceedings of the Research Days, Department of Economics*, ed. Pasquale De Muro, Saverio M. Fratini, and Alessia Naccarato (Roma: Roma Tre Press, 2020), 131. Francesca Biondi dal Monte, Vincenzo Casamassima, and Emanuele Rossi, ed., *Lingua, istruzione e integrazione delle nuove minoranze* (Pisa: Pisa University Press, 2017).
45. Giovanna Zincone, ed., *Secondo Rapporto sull'integrazione degli immigrati in Italia*, (Bologna: Il Mulino, 2000), 88.
46. This goal is defined as "civic integration" as well. See further: Giuseppe Sciortino, "È possibile misurare l'integrazione degli immigrati? Lo stato dell'arte," *Quaderni, Dipartimento di Sociologia e Ricerca Sociale, Università di Trento*, no. 63 (2015): 28. More in general, on the various types of policies (assimilation, integration, multiculturalism) host States can opt for in the management of diversity between immigrants and natives see the stimulating analysis of Tariq Modood, *Post-immigration 'difference' and integration: The case of Muslims in Western Europe* (London: The British Academy, 2012); Stephen Castles, Hein De Haas, and Mark J. Miller, *The Age of Migration. International Population Movements in the Modern World*. 5th Ed. (New York, NY: The Guilford Press, 2014), in particular Chapter 12. *New Ethnic Minorities and Society*.
47. This data can be further broken down: 65.4% of the students with non-Italian citizenship were born in Italy, but according to the norms in force they cannot obtain Italian citizenship before reaching the major age. Fondazione ISMU, *27° rapporto sulle migrazioni* (Milano: Franco Angeli, 2022), 129 and 132.

48. The affirmation has a general value, but it is even more evident in regions characterized by a population which varies according to regional origin or belonging to a linguistic group, like e.g., in South Tyrol. See further: Anssi Paasi, "The Resurgence of the "Region" and "Regional Identity": Theoretical Perspectives and Empirical Observations on Regional Dynamics in Europe," *Review of International Studies* 35, no. Special Issue 1 (February 2009): 32.; Marco Antonsich, "Living in diversity: Going beyond the local/national divide," *Political Geography* 63, (March 2018): 1–9.; Simona Di Mare , Lucia Saulle, "Il non cittadino nella costituzione italiana ed il diritto all'istruzione del minore straniero," *Dirittifondamentali.it*, no. 2, (July 2019): 10.
49. For illuminating ethical reflections on the values of difference, equality and inclusion in education see: Ivo De Gennaro, and Ralf Lüfter, "Ethics of Difference: Towards a Phenomenology of Inclusion," *Philosophy Study* 12, no. 8 (August 2022): in particular 439–441. From a pedagogical point of view the outstanding work of Booth and Ainscow should be also recalled: Tony Booth, and Mel Ainscow, *Index for Inclusion. Developing Learning and Participation in Schools* (Bristol: Centre for Studies on Inclusive Education, 2002).
50. MIUR, *Linee guida per l'accoglienza e l'integrazione degli alunni stranieri*, 2014, 3.
51. Learning Italian for schooling does not occur spontaneously. It requires protracted times and specific, targeted interventions by all teachers, who act not only as teachers of the discipline, but also as teachers of the "micro-language" of their discipline. Graziella Favaro, "L'italiano che include: la lingua per non essere stranieri. Attenzioni e proposte per un progetto di formazione linguistica nel tempo della pluralità," *Italiano LinguaDue* 8, no. 1 (2016): 1–12. Similar considerations are expressed in the Ministerial Guidelines. MIUR, *Linee guida per l'accoglienza,* 16 ff.
52. Many families live in poor living conditions, often different generations share the same apartment and most families have many children. As it became evident during the COVID-19 pandemic, school closures heavily influenced the learning outcome of these students: many of them had no or only limited access to internet and computers to follow online classes or their environment did not make possible to pay the necessary attention to learning activities. Fondazione ISMU, *27° rapporto sulle migrazioni*, 127–128.
53. Circolare n. 8 del 6 marzo 2013 (Ministerial Circular of 6 March 2013, No. 8)
54. The Note of the Ministry of 22 November 2013, No. 2563 gives even more restrictive indications in relation to didactic interventions to promote the learning of Italian language. It suggests that Personalised Study Plans should be used only in exceptional cases: in particular, but not exclusively, for students just arrived in Italy, beyond the age of 13, with a country of origin of non-neolatin language.
55. Art. 1 comma 7 lettera r) della legge 13 luglio 2015, n. 107. (Art. 1(7)r of the Law of 13 July 2015, No. 107) Cultural, or intercultural mediators are professionals with the task to bridge cultural and linguistic differences between immigrants and the local community where they live. Their role is not confined to translation, it includes closing the gaps between different cultures, habits, customs and the facilitation of communication and understanding between the parties. Cultural mediators act in reception centers, hospitals, schools,

social services, etc. Cultural mediators are supposed to have language proficiency and deep knowledge of the culture of the home country and of Italy. There is no national level regulation about the professional conditions to become a cultural mediator, but most Regions have their own norms and offer trainings to become cultural mediator.
56. This situation, and the need for change are confirmed by the "*Conoscere per integrarsi*"—"Know to be integrated" project, which offers not only L2 courses for immigrants at the Provincial Centers of Adult Education but also training courses for teachers and school personnel in teaching Italian and civic education to students with migrant background. https://www.ismu.org/progetto-conoscere-per-integrarsi/?utm_source=Nuovi+iscritti+ISMU&utm_campaign=9d2c17d40e-EMAIL_CAMPAIGN_Marzo+2022_COPY_02&utm_medium=email&utm_term=0_76fdb0bf28-9d2c17d40e-%5BLIST_EMAIL_ID%5D&ct=t%28EMAIL_CAMPAIGN_Marzo+2022_COPY_02%29
57. The Observatory is a consultative body established and later re-established by the Ministry of Education. First it was created in 2006 (Decree of the Minister for Public Education of 6 December 2006, No. 319) but until recently it operated intermittently. The Ministerial Decree of 5 September 2014, No. 718 conferred a 3-year long mandate to it, which in 2017 became permanent despite the fact that in 2 years no meeting was organized at all. It was re-established in its actual form by the Ministerial Decree of 4 December 2019. It is composed of school principals and representatives of research institutes, associations and other ministries. The Communication of the Ministry of Education of 9 November 2017 mentions among the members of the Observatory "associations of young people of non-Italian citizenship," but apart from this general statement no other criterium is available.
58. È la lingua che ci fa uguali. Nota per ripartire senza dimenticare gli alunni stranieri https://www.tuttoscuola.com/integrazione-alunni-stranieri-le-proposte-dellosservatorio/ , July 2020.
59. *Diversi da chi? Raccomandazioni per l'integrazione degli alunni stranieri e per l'intercultura*, Nota MIUR 9 settembre 2015, Prot. n. 5535 (Note of the Ministry of 9 September 2015, No. 5535); Osservatorio, Gruppo 1, Insegnamento dell'italiano come lingua seconda e valorizzazione del plurilinguismo, "L'italiano che include: la lingua per non essere stranieri. Attenzioni e proposte per un progetto di formazione linguistica nel tempo della pluralità." *Italiano LinguaDue* 8, no. 1 (2016): 1–12.
60. Matucci, "Il diritto/dovere all'inclusione scolastica," 43.; and Nota MIUR 22 novembre 2013, n. 2563 (Note of the Ministry of 22 November 2013, No. 2563)
61. The Project run for two years in Milan, Arezzo, Turin, Bologna, in the Autonomous Province of Trento and in the Region of Friuli-Venezia Giulia. On the very positive results see: Graziella Favaro, Monica Napoli, eds., *Almeno una stella. Un progetto di tutoraggio per gli adolescenti immigrati* (Milano: Franco Angeli, 2016).
62. Mariagrazia Santagati, Alessandra Barzaghi, Erica Colussi, "Sguardi incrociati sui percorsi educativi dei minori stranieri non accompagnati. Un'indagine esplorativa," in *Alunni con background migratorio in Italia. Le opportunità oltre gli*

ostacoli. Rapporto nazionale, eds. Mariagrazia Santagati, Erica Colussi (Milano: Fondazione ISMU, 2020), 117 ff.; Mariagrazia Santagati, Alessandra Barzaghi, eds., *Explorative Study on Unaccompanied Minors in Italy and Access to Education and Training* (Milan: ISMU Foundation, 2021), in particular 64–66.

63. For a detailed and critical analysis on the reform of teachers' training see: Matucci, " *"Buona Scuola": l'inclusione scolastica alla prova,"* in particular 15 ff.

64. The Annual Plan of Inclusion was established by the Ministerial Circular of 6 March 2013, No 8 and later specified in the Note of 27 June 2013, No 1551. The Note recognizes the necessity to organize training programs to help the educational institutions to take on the new challenge, but it does not foresee any specific measure. In more general terms, but with similar observations see also: Giovanna Malusà, "Il fallimento delle prescritte soluzioni: un approccio critico all'insuccesso scolastico dei minori di origine migrante in Italia," in *Encyclopaideia* 22, no. 51 (2018): 57 ff.

65. Bruschi and Milazzo note that the multiplicity and complexity of the sources themselves constitute a critical aspect. Max Bruschi, and Salvatore Milazzo, "L'inclusività parcellizzata nella scuola italiana tra paradigma inclusivo e scelte normative," *Federalismi.it* no. 2 (January 2018): 2–22. In addition, as Dovigo recalls, the Ministry often issues new rounds of directives and produces policies to bridge the gap between the Ministry's politics deprived of implementation policies and school practices enacted on the basis of the wide autonomy attributed to them. Instead of better coordination, this leads to further fragmentation between the central administration and single schools, as schools are not always able to act according to the new instructions or at times simply ignore them. Fabio Dovigo et al., *None excluded. Transforming schools and learning to develop inclusive education* (Bergamo: University of Bergamo, 2016), 17.

66. Nota MIUR del 22 novembre 2013, n. 2563, 3. (Note of the Ministry of 22 November 2013, No. 2563)

67. Pupils with medical certifications according to the Laws 104/1992 and 170/2010 enjoy a legal entitlement to make use of the measures provided for and governed by these Laws.

68. Cultural mediators are active in many schools, albeit their participation varies between occasional interpreting and real cultural mediations. For a more detailed analysis see: Marwa Mahmoud, "La mediazione, una risorsa fondamentale nei rapporti scuola-famiglia," in *Scuola e famiglie immigrate: un incontro possibile*, ed. Elisabetta Cicciarelli (Milano: Fondazione ISMU, 2019), 63–68.

69. The Ministerial Guidelines expressly invite schools to promote the participation of parents of foreign students in school activities and in parents' associations. MIUR, *Linee guida per l'accoglienza*, 12.

CLOSING REMARKS

Anna Simonati
University of Trento

At the end of this challenging and charming intellectual journey, one may grasp many interesting sides of the issue of diversity through the lens of administrative action.

First, as is quite obvious indeed, diversity still may be a source for undue and illegal discrimination. Hence, administration has the duty to avoid bias and ensure equal treatment. One has to be aware that, especially when multiple discrimination may occur, it can be somehow "hidden." An interesting test bed for this assumption is the area of gender studies, that are focused on one (simply recognizable) characteristic of people, but, at the same time, can be used as an instrument to interpret many different fields of human behaviour.

As Wendy Farrell well clarifies in her research on female leadership in Tyrol, gender issues become more and more difficult to be managed in relation with age, motherhood, geographical provenience from either urban or mountain/rural areas in the same Country. The element lastly mentioned is particularly interesting, since it shows how deeply cultural backgrounds and stereotypes still matter in this field.

Looking at diversity as a complex factor, another important issue arises from the research, which is that the "internal homogeneity" of gender segregated groups must not be taken for granted. In other words, considering

Diversity as Strategic Opportunity, pages 275–283
Copyright © 2024 by Information Age Publishing
www.infoagepub.com
All rights of reproduction in any form reserved.

female needs and aspirations as monolithic would be wrong. Diversity is part of the female universe as well, which means that diversity in leadership is a value and so should be perceived also inside groups made of individuals belonging to the same gender. This element produces relevant consequences on a methodical ground, as the chapter by Marjukka Mikkonen shows very clearly.

One, in fact, may ask whether gender segregation in the administrative and research projects on leadership is positive or negative. On one hand, gender-segregated spaces for discussion may ensure women a chance to freely express themselves, without being influenced by external (male-oriented-value) pressure; this may be particularly useful in fields where the examples of feminine leadership are a recent novelty, such as sport. On the other hand, gender-segregated best practice—despite being useful on the ground of female self-consciousness and capacity pride—can also be counterproductive in the perspective of culling boundaries and barriers between men and women. This is why the administrative action for women empowerment should consist of a multifaced core of initiatives, some of which should be primarily addressed to men, especially in those fields where they are still strong power holders. Therefore, the real challenge is creating real and deep awareness in leaders—both male and female ones—about equal treatment as a universal value (mostly in public environment), and about pluralism in conceiving and using power as a source for enrichment of administrative action, by the elimination of the ancient stereotypes on male and female "styles" in decision-making.

Another interesting result rising up from some chapters in the first section, that has partially to do with stereotypes as well, is that not always women really and strongly support women. Notwithstanding the importance of the "queen bee syndrome" is probably overrated, one should realize that at present unfortunately women—even when they are leaders—normally have not enough power to be able to make a difference in decision-making.

Finally, one may infer that also legislators and policy makers are sometimes victims of stereotypes. Maternity and childhood support are of course at present fundamental as best practices, in order to allow mothers to be leaders at work. However, it is a cultural duty to make clear that such measures are not "gender friendly" in strict sense. They are, instead, aimed at supporting families as a whole, and they can now advantage almost only women because there is not a real balance in the role of parents yet.

On the other side of the coin, some rules are directly and specifically gender-oriented, and they aim at promoting female-empowerment in the fields where women are still strongly vulnerable. An important example is gender quotas in democratic political life. Actually, even gender quotas, in their mature expression, are not provided for in order to advantage women as such, since, more correctly and consistently with the Constitutional principles of equality and equal treatment, they work to ensure a space for expression of people belonging to the under-represented gender. However, at present this is almost always made by women. Giovanna Iacovone, in her chapter, analyses the Italian case, which is very interesting because many elements (statutes, case law and best practices) have combined in a fluctuating pattern of historical ebb and flow, in a progressively gender-sensitive direction.

In this regard, it is necessary to acknowledge that the legislators and policy-makers are not bound only by the principle of equal treatment as a monolithic value; on the contrary, it has to be harmonized with other fundamental criteria, especially on the ground of electoral tools, where the compliance with democracy has to be carefully ensured. Therefore, the legal and ethical purpose, which represents the conceptual basis of gender equality, must be carefully indicated: one should recognize that it does not lay only on the due protection of the rights of women, but also—and primarily—on the sensitivity for diversity as a source for fairness in decision-making. Such approach allows to connect the principle—and all the implementing rules—with the general interest of the entire society.

The strict relationship between the compliance with gender equality issues and the pursue of the public interest, a little paradoxically, becomes even more evident when it is compared with the concrete efficacy of the same principle in private environment.

The chapter by Arianna Pitino offers a good example of how rules and case law issued with reference to private environment (in the case, private employment) may produce significant impact in the public one, offering a stronger legal basis for the limitations to the expression of religion freedom by working women, and especially by migrant Muslim working women. This issue has clearly much to do with intersectionality and multiple discrimination, which (as previously mentioned) is often less evident and consequently more dangerous. Although the existence of supranational institutional levels (such as the European Union) is presumed to play a sort of harmonizing function in the National systems, the desire to ensure a common minimum degree of protection may concretely produce the reduction of the guarantees required in the States. Therefore, it is crucial to point out that, in order to avoid undue discriminations, the restrictions to individual fundamental freedoms and rights must be allowed only if considered consistent with the proportionality scrutiny.

The double nature of diversity, as possible source for discrimination and for richness in administrative action, clearly arises also in fields different than gender issues. One of the main phenomena of recent times involves the use of artificial intelligence by administration, as the latest side of digitalization.

As Anna Maria Chiariello and Rocco Frondizi observe in their chapter, this brings both opportunities and challenges, especially through the lens of equal treatment. On one hand, in fact, artificial intelligence may help in finding personalized solutions for individual problems, by taking seriously in account all of the characteristics of the case. On the other hand, however, a strong risk of bias should not be underrated, because an algorithm may easily reflect dangerous stereotypes.

The overmentioned risk is perhaps the most evident, but it is not the only one: other worries, in fact, may derive from the lack of participation and transparency in decision-making by artificial intelligence. Actually, a proper management of diversity as a source of fair administrative action would suggest encouraging as largely as possible participation by the citizens, in order to project proper tools of intervention, by enhancing all the points of view coming from different kinds of stakeholders and interlocutors. But, to be realistic, this goal may be achieved only if everyone is put in the condition to comprehend and, then, intervene. The real issue, therefore, is transparency, which must be intended not just as openness and disclosure of documents and data, but as comprehensibility of the information used by administration for decision-making. Hence, the solutions chosen in several legal systems, which are essentially based on accessibility of the robotic tools, may be insufficient, because the most vulnerable parts of population—or even the majority of people, in case of peculiar complexity—have not the technical literacy, required to really understand. In other words, diversity in the starting condition may prevent the diversity of viewpoints from producing a plurality of participatory contributions, which could be very useful to enlarge the perspective in public-interest decision-making. The improvement of transparency in broad sense is then a real core topic for good administration nowadays.

Another relevant effect of digitalization is the progressive increase of potentially harmful behaviours by socially and economically strong subjects against weak and vulnerable ones. Consequently, some fundamental rights (such as privacy) add now new sides in their traditional physiognomy, and this element particularly matters when the (tendentially unbalanced) relationship between an authority and a private individual is concerned. Therefore, an inquiry on the efficacy of the protection of individuals can be extremely useful, and it must be focused (at least partially) on case law, since interpretation by the courts may lead the rules in force to further results in terms of efficacy. In order to properly grasp the future possible developments, a comparison between (apparently) far systems may be useful, as well.

As Jyoti Rattan and Vijai Rattan clearly state in their chapter, technology is at present advancing so fast as to make the statutes in force very quickly obsolete. Both the Member States of the European Union and India have to face the new issues, connected with new forms of inequality deriving also from an (excessively) nonchalant use of technologies. Hence, administration should keep watch carefully, so that diversity does not turn into a weapon against whom already is in a weaker position. Such duty can be fulfilled either directly (when administration is directly involved in the case) or indirectly (because in this field the legal systems often provide for the creation of agencies, with a role of guarantee).

Here comes another challenge for contemporary administration, that is finding a good balance between the needs for privatization (which requires the progressive abandonment of direct management by the public entities) and the retention of incisive supervisory powers.

In this complicated scenario, an open question regards the boundaries of the contribution by legislators and rule-makers. On one hand, precise legal coordinates are strongly needed, in order to offer an efficient guide for practitioners; on the other hand, very strict references may become irrational and disproportionate cages for fairly dynamic administrative action. That's why perhaps a good compromise could be a sort of "double-stage intervention": first, a group of strong binding principles should be laid down; second, sectorial guidelines should be produced and periodically updated with the cooperation by the representatives of all the stakeholders. So doing, diversity in decision-making could be used to avoid and prevent its own degeneration in practice.

However, managing diversity in the composition of administrative decision-making equipes may be itself an issue, as Agnes Jenei, Réka Zsuzsánna Máthé, Maliga Reddy and Strinivasan Pillay point out in their chapter. The analysis of the peculiar case-study, that they have examined, substantially confirms, specifies, and deepens the results which may be grasped considering other chapters of the book.

First, an obstacle potentially preventing diversity from being a driver for good governance lays in cultural stereotypes, which can heavily influence the personal relationship of the members of the group; knowing each other and working together may of course help overcoming this problem. However—and this is the second element that deserves to be underlined—a strong cooperation (not only despite, but even through diversity) is more easily possible when the "rules of the game" are clarified in advance by a third subject, whose authority is fully recognized by all the members of the team. The scientific efforts to measure the difficulties of acting in high-diversity-composed groups may offer precious quantitative indicators for the efficient management of the issue.

Notwithstanding principles and rules play an essential role and must be taken extremely seriously by officers and practitioners (since they may be important problem-solving tools), in some fields equal treatment may be pursued by administration even without resting on precise normative reforms. So may happen in sectors where the corollaries of the principle of good and fair administration have become, thanks to their continuous and dynamic implementation, so strong as to be perceived as self-sufficient on a legal ground.

An important example, that has been taken into account by Annalisa Giusti in her chapter focused on the Italian system, is urban regeneration. Urban regeneration, in fact, has been experimented in recent decades, as an instrument to reduce discriminations in the use of anthropic space and to promote the improvement of life quality for all the inhabitants of the various areas in the same town. This experimentation may teach us much, at least from a double perspective. First, policymakers should be aware that their choices can produce indirect (not desired) effects, that should be carefully considered in advance; to that purpose, the cooperation with holders of different expertise is more and more necessary for efficient administrative action. Second, the capacity to grasp all the consequences of decision-making on the citizens' lifestyle and satisfaction requires the establishment of dialogic communicative models involving the interested local communities; therefore, diversity among groups of people participating in transparent procedures may lead the competent authority toward a better understanding of the situation and consequently to a better solution of the case.

The research carried out by the authors in heterogeneous sectors of administrative action (and sometimes beyond administrative action in strict sense) shows that, notwithstanding the duty to avoid bias and discrimination is always clearly perceived and carefully evaluated, not as often diversity is seen as opportunity. However, so normally happens—at least partially—in some National systems in one specific scope of administrative action, where the competent authorities seem to have already achieved the necessary sensitivity and skills: the sphere of education. The papers contained in the third session of the book focus on the Austrian and the Italian systems; all of them show a high degree of awareness by administration about the possible useful contribution of diverse parties to the quality of public intervention.

Esther Happacher, Lamiss Khakzadeh, and Alexandra Weiss describe in their chapter the normative landscape about diversity management in Austria, and examine the administrative action held by the Innsbruck University. It is interesting to note that gender diversity is considered as a sort of prototypic area for experimentation of diversity management in broader sense, here comprised a growing attention to the prevention of multiple discrimination. The engagement by the University works at numerous levels and with the cooperation of several sectors of the organization itself, with the aim at using—and at the same time improving—targeted expertise. However, a gap in the approach that has been followed can be revealed, because, in such a structured action, although also the opinions of students should be considered, inevitably the institutional procedures only indirectly allow their views to emerge.

In a sort of ideal scientific dialogue, the chapter by Marianna Brunetti, Nathalie Colasanti, Annalisa Fabretti, and Mariangela Zoli offers interesting food for thought, since it is instead focused on the results of a research project—which was conducted at the Faculty of Economics of a large Italian University—about the perception by students on gender gaps and stereotypes, in academia and in job market, especially in STEM fields. The existence of gender bias seems to be still underestimated among students, even though women are more careful and sensitive than men.

Since in the Italian rules and practises the attention paid to raising awareness of the gender issues among students is still quite weak, one could perhaps infer that, when the action devoted to un-build discriminatory mechanisms is less formalized, at least in its starting steps it is less efficient than when it is based on clear and binding rules. Moreover, especially because the system still is based on spontaneous initiatives of promotion of diversity management, one may once more wonder whether the creation of a network of sensible subjects should be solely or essentially based on an alliance of women, reasoning on the positive or negative impact of gender segregation in outreach movements, where the contribution by male components may be very important as well.

However, gender is not the only cause of diversity considered in the third section of the book, and academia is not the only educational environment taken into account. The other chapters, in fact, are focused on the management of diversity in Italian schools (in light of the supra-national legal background), but they regard different sources of difference among pupils.

Stefania Baroncelli offers a broad overview of the normative tools for protection of vulnerable students, complying with the principles of non-discrimination and inclusion. The legal paradigm consists of a multifaced series of instruments. The general approach confirms the overmentioned tendency toward formalization, since in cases where an administrative intervention (especially a medical one, in order to certify the existence of relevant diseases) is compulsorily required by the statutes in force, the defense of the vulnerable student's rights is easier and stronger. The reason seems to lay in the relative modernity of the emersion of such issues as problem of general interest. Therefore, one can hope that, in the next future, the intervention by the public institutions becomes more incisive and is able to grasp also the positive impact of the enhancement of diversity as a chance for personal growth, especially of children and young people.

The dilemma about the dual impact of digitalization recurs inside the educational system and, as Loredana Giani points out in her chapter, this may produce relevant consequences in terms of exacerbation of bias and discrimination of socially and economically disadvantaged pupils. In the Italian context—which is of course strictly linked with the supra-national, and especially European, system—in order to overcome the obstacles to a really equal protection of every pupil, regardless of whether he or she is socio-economically disadvantaged, two important steps must be done. The construction of new competences for public officers must combine with new infrastructural endowments and organizational reforms. Otherwise, diversity of personal conditions will persist as an obstacle rather than an opportunity for individual and collective growth, as the recent sad experience of the pandemic has taught us with reference to the severely discriminatory effects of the digital divide in school learning.

Once more, the danger looming, often covertly, is that of multiple discrimination, especially in case of migrant students, regarding which the apparatus of protective mechanisms provided for by the Italian legislator is not fully formalized, as Orsolya Farkas discusses in her chapter. Regarding diversity management, the persisting dilemma is between integration and inclusion, and, despite the existence of numerous Ministerial Guidelines, the problems in implementation have not been solved yet. One may say that, so far, the initiatives to support migrant students beyond language learning have relied primarily on administrative best practices. Actually, several Italian schools may be considered as policymakers, whose action could be source for inspiration, *mutatis mutandis*, also in other fields of diversity management.

In conclusion, one can say that the joint work of the numerous authors, who generously offered their precious contribution, has a high scientific and practical value, for different reasons.

As already pointed out, a very important item is of course multidisciplinarity: the issue of diversity represents particularly fertile ground for an interweaving of knowledge and know-how typical of different sectors. The reader of this book may be able to grasp the result of such a long-distance dialogue; legal scholars, economists in broad sense, social and political scientists can learn from each-other, and this may happen not only by reasoning on data, but also by studying how the relevant data is collected and organized to guide the following action.

The main step to take, in order to obtain fruitful results toward normative, economic, social and political systems able to be fully respectful of diversity among people and to manage diversity as a resource for good administration, is to be aware that no institutional action is truly and fully neutral. All public choices face and manage differences; before that, they take differences into account, measure and evaluate them, in many ways, in many fields, with many technical tools. This book aims at being a contribution for a better and deeper comprehension of how this may dynamically happen.

Awareness about how deliberative processes should be properly managed is the due starting point for further elaboration of new techniques, hopefully able to combine the traditional perception of diversity as dangerous source for mistakes with its new side as source for richness of the inquiry step in the procedures and opportunity for fair administration.

However, one may recognize that this is an ambitious (albeit very stimulating) challenge of modernity, which requires the creation of unprecedented tools. To win the bet, each authority must be engaged in a step-by-step process, whose concrete physiognomy may vary considering the specific needs of the various sectors. Administration as a whole must be able to transform its functional dynamics, by increasingly being a learning organization.

In such a complex work in progress, taxonomies have a pivotal role. As Leo Huberts clearly shows in his Foreword, notwithstanding equal treatment, protection of rights and contrast of discrimination commonly correspond to Constitutional (or at least legal fundamental) principles, their corollaries (integrity, equity, and so on) may be differently perceived and defined. Moreover, the various technical languages not only often differ from each other but are often different than the common use of the same words. However, there is something more, which is the possible dark side of introducing diversity among the values to be pursued for good administration. One of the open issues (indirectly) arising from Leo Huberts's Foreword regards, a little paradoxically, the danger of "new" discrimination inside the growing sensitivity for diversity. Are diversities all the same? Should we be able to distinguish between different kinds of diversity? Are (apparently) homogeneous groups really homogeneous, or may diversity bring to further discrimination between majority and minorities even within them? And may science (in its multifaced expressions) play a decisive role in the development of diversity as a value for fair administration and in the fight against diversity as a source of discrimination? This is food for thought indeed, and all of us (scientists and academics, practitioners, but also citizens as well) may give a contribution to lead the next steps of the continuous development of public action toward the full implementation of diversity as strategic opportunity for good and fair administration.

ABOUT THE CONTRIBUTORS

Stefania Baroncelli is full professor of public law (Italian and European) at the Free University of Bolzano/Bozen, Italy. She graduated from the School of Law of the University of Florence. She consequently specialized in EU Law, constitutional law and comparative law obtaining a LL.M. degree from the School of Law, New York University, and discussing a PhD thesis at the European University Institute (EUI), Florence, Italy. She has published in Italian Constitutional Law and European Union Law, with a focus on governance, institutions, economics and law, sources of law with specific reference to the relationship between the EU and the Italian legal order, the European Monetary Union, the ECB, the rights of minorities and autonomy, the Europe of Regions and languages' rights, and discrimination issues. She is coordinating some projects of research on discrimination in schools and on the relationship between universities and the city, focusing on the third mission of the university and the role of local entities in supporting the academy. She is also part of the project of research PRIN on "Where is Europe going? Paths and perspectives of the European federalising process."

Marianna Brunetti is associate professor in economic statistics at the Department of Economics and Finance, Tor Vergata University of Rome, Italy. She holds a MSc in Economics from the University of Warwick, UK, and a PhD from the University of Bergamo, Italy. She visited Imperial College Business School in London, and the Stockholm School of Economics. She has written contributions on derivatives' market efficiency and on the interactions between financial variables and the business cycle. The most recent contributions have focused on household portfolio choices, on gender difference, migration and on the impact of population ageing on financial markets.

Anna Maria Chiariello, PhD, is qualified as an associate professor in administrative law. Her areas of interest include biodiversity, environment, and artificial intelligence from a legal point of view. She is the author of several articles and one book. She spent a research period at the London School of Economics and Political Science. In relation to the subject of administrative law she has carried out numerous teaching activities, has taken part, as a speaker, in various scientific conferences and seminars, and participates in editorial boards of scientific journals and research groups, including international ones.

Nathalie Colasanti is a research fellow at the University of Rome Unitelma Sapienza, where she lectures in financial statement analysis. She holds a PhD in public management and governance from the University of Rome Tor Vergata, where she lectures in non profit management and social innovation and commons. Her main research interests focus on commons and urban commons, social innovation and gender issues.

Jean-Michel Eymeri-Douzans, PhD, is a French academic and international expert in comparative public administration. He is currently serving his second term as president of the European Group for Public Administration (EGPA/GEAP, IIAS/IISA). He is an exceptional class professor at Sciences Po Toulouse, and its vice-rector for international relations. Since his secondment as French representative at the European Institute of Public Administration (EIPA) in 1999–2001, interacting with the EUPAN Network under several presidencies of the Council of the EU, he has worked extensively for the European Commission as advisor, trainer, evaluator in Brussels, and in candidate and neighbour countries as high-level expert in capacity-building projects (EU Twinning projects) in a dozen of European countries. In France, he served as chairman of the scientific council of DGAFP, Ministry for the Civil Service, and works regularly for ENA (National School of Administration), now INSP. He is also a specialist of the processes of government at the top, the national coordination of EU policymaking as well as HRM (recruitment, training, careers and rewards) in the higher civil service. Some of his recent publications are: with Gildas Tanguy (Eds.), *Prefects, governors & commissioners. Territorial representatives of the State in Europe*, Palgrave Macmillan, 2021); with Emmanuel Aubin, Jean-François Kerléo and Johanne Saison, *Quelle déontologie pour les hauts fonctionnaires? Enjeux, textes et perspectives*, LGDJ, 2021; with Marius Profiroiu and Călin

Hintea, *The disciplines and the study of Public Administration. Transatlantic perspectives*, Editura Curtea Veche, 2021.

Annalisa Fabretti is an associate professor in applied mathematics at the Department of Economics and Finance, Tor Vergata University of Rome, Italy. Her research activity comprises nonlinear dynamical models in economics and finance, agent-based models, random probability theory, and gender studies. Several results of her research have been presented at international conferences and workshops. She is (co-)author of book chapters and papers published in peer-reviewed international journals, including the *European Journal of Finance, Journal of Interaction and Coordination, Operation Research Letters,* and *Electronic Journal of Statistics*.

Orsolya Farkas is research fellow at the Free University of Bolzano/Bozen, Italy. She earned her PhD at the European University Institute in Florence with a thesis on the evolution of social policies of the EU. Her main research interests include European citizenship, free movement of EU citizens, access to the labour market and integration of immigrants. In the last few years she has been working on a research project on legal and policy measures relating to school inclusion of students with special needs in education in Italy. Her research has focused on students with migrant backgrounds. She has also taught several courses of EU law at the Free University of Bolzano/Bozen and she has been instructor at the Verona and Florence Study Abroad Programs of the University of Georgia (USA) for nearly two decades.

Wendy Farrell, PhD, is a professor at MCI, specializing in international business and organizational behavior. She is particularly interested in studying the interface of culture, technology, and business, seeking to understand how these elements intertwine in our increasingly globalized and interconnected world. Through academic research, she delves into the nuanced complexities of cross-cultural communication and explores the societal and organizational implications of gender and diversity. She actively participates in international conferences, workshops, and seminars and contributes as a peer reviewer. Her professional path has taken her across various global settings, where she has assumed diverse roles within the scope of international business management. These experiences have imbued her with an understanding of cross-cultural dynamics and a deep appreciation for diversity within academic and corporate environments.

Rocco Frondizi, PhD, is lecturer in business management and accounting at the University of Rome Tor Vergata, Italy. He holds a PhD in public management and governance, from the same university. He has been one of the promoters, and currently co-chairs, of the study group Social Innovation,

Commons and Administration of the International Institute of Administrative Sciences. He is the author of more than 50 articles and 1 book.

Loredana N. E. Giani Maguire is full professor of administrative law in the Department of Human Sciences at the European University of Rome. She was dean of the degree course in primary education sciences. She is currently dean of the degree course in tourism and territorial enhancement and head of postgraduate training in schools. She is delegate of the Rector for Disability and member of the National University Conference of Delegates for Disability. She is director of the Research Centre 'Generative Welfare, Sustainability and Rights', and editor of the publishing series "Generative welfare, sustainability and rights" and "Contributions to Administrative Law." She is member of the scientific committee of several journals. Principal investigator of numerous national and international research projects, she is chair of the permanent panel at the EGU Conference on "Risk Law." Her areas of interest include administrative organization, in a dimension geared towards ensuring the appropriateness of administrative action, town planning and environmental law, cultural heritage law, educational legislation, with a special focus on inclusion and gender. She is author of 4 books, including a handbook on school law, editor of 6 volumes and author of more than 150 publications, including book chapters and articles.

Annalisa Giusti, PhD, is associate professor of administrative law at the University of Perugia, Italy. In 2018, she was awarded the national scientific qualification for the position of full professor. Her research interests include administrative justice, urban law and public procurement law. She is the author of three books and publishes in the most important Italian law journals. She is also the author of numerous contributions in collective books. She holds one of the chairs of administrative law in the Department of Law and the chair of urban law and public procurement in the Department of Civil and Environmental Engineering. He is also a member of the Board of Lecturers of the doctoral program in legal sciences. He has lectured at national and international conferences and for the Erasmus educational program.

Esther Happacher, PhD, LLM, is full professor of Italian Constitutional Law at the faculty of law, University of Innsbruck. Her areas of interest include Italian Constitutional Law (sources of law; institutional issues; fundamental rights; relations with the EU legal order), regional law with a focus on South-Tyrolean autonomy and linguistic minorities, law of the European Union, comparative public law and gender issues. She is vice-president of the Working Committee on Equal Opportunities Issues of the University of Innsbruck, an independent body responsible for combating gender discrimination as well as discrimination on the basis of ethnicity, religion or conviction, age, or sexual orientation by university governing bodies. Among others, she is co-chair of the Permanent Study Group XXIII—Administration, Diversity and Equal Treatment of EGPA—The European Group For Public Administration, referee for the journal *Ceridap* (*Journal of the Interdisciplinary Research Centre on Public Administration Law for Efficient, Impartial, and Digital First Administrative Action*) and member of the Scientific Committee of the *European Journal of Minorities Questions*—Europäisches Journal für Minderheitenfragen EJM.

Leo (L.W.J.C.) Huberts is emeritus professor of public administration at the Department of Political Science and Public Administration of the Vrije Universiteit Amsterdam. His main areas of research concern systems of governance and power, and the quality, integrity and ethics of governance. He was (co)chair of study groups on Quality and Integrity of Governance in the International Institute of the Administrative Sciences and the European Group of Public Administration, in which he is still involved (as well as in the section on Ethics and Integrity of Governance of the American Society for Public Administration). He is author or editor of more than twenty books and many articles on influence on governmental policy, power theory and measurement, police administration and integrity, public corruption and fraud and on integrity management, including Leo Huberts (2014). *Integrity of Governance. What It Is, What We Know, What Is Done and Where to Go*. Basingstoke: Palgrave Macmillan and L.W.J.C. Huberts (2018). Integrity: What it is and Why it is Important, *Public Integrity* 20(1), 18–32. DOI: 10.1080/10999922.2018.1477404.

Giovanna Iacovone, PhD, is associate professor of administrative law at the University of Basilicata. Her areas of interest include, in particular, the principles of good administration preliminarily identifiable in participation and simplification, territorial government, cultural heritage law, and gender studies from a legal perspective. She is the author of numerous articles and 3 monographs. She is scientifically responsible for national and international projects on ecological transition and quality of living. She is a member of scientific societies, associations and study centers including the Italian Association of Urban Law and Urban@it (National Centre for Urban Policy Studies). She is a member of the teaching board of the PhD program Cities and Landscapes: Architecture, Archaeology, Cultural Heritage, History and Resources at the University of Basilicata and of the National PhD program in Gender studies at the University of Bari Aldo Moro.

Agnes Jenei, PhD, is associate professor at the University of Public Service (UPS), Hungary, former head of department for public ethics and communication (2010–2016). Biofeedback and neurofeedback trainer (2023), solution-focused mediator (2017), intercultural trainer (2013, 2017), action learning coach (2014), trainer and consultant (2002). Her courses and her research interest are related to the fields of management and organizational behaviour. Currently, she focuses on the enhancement of leadership skills trainings with disruptive/emergent technologies: soft skills development with virtual reality; stress management with biofeedback technology; peak performance training with neurofeedback. She is participant of the EU Erasmus Plus Teaching mobility programs, lecturing in European, African, and Asian countries. She is member of the editorial board (2002–) of Médiakutató (Hungarian review on media research); board director at WCCI (2018–), World Council for Curriculum and Instruction (organization in consultative status with the UN), and member (2022–) of the Hungarian NGO *Close to Africa*.

Lamiss Khakzadeh is full professor of public law at Universität Innsbruck/ Austria. Her areas of interest include human rights, questions of legal protection, and administrative procedure law. In 2022 she was appointed Deputy Legal Protection Commissioner of the Minister of the Interior. She is member and co-chair of the Permanent Study Group on Administration, Diversity and Equal Treatment in EGPA (European Group for Public Administration).

Réka Zsuzsánna Máthé, PhD, is research fellow of the European Strategy Research Institute of the National Public Service University (EUSTRAT), Hungary. Additionally she works as an assistant professor at the Sapientia Hungarian University of Transylvania, and as a senior researcher at the Mathias Corvinus Collegium. She obtained her doctorate degree at the University of Public Service, summa cum lauda. During the doctoral educations, she studied with a scholarship at the Charles University in Prague. Concomitantly with the doctoral studies, she gained a scholarship and studied at the College of Europe, Bruges, where she graduated with a Master's degree in European political science and public administration. She completed her higher education in Romanian, German, English and French. She is a member of International Political Science Association and of World Interdisciplinary Network for Institutional Research.

Marjukka Mikkonen, PhD is a postdoctoral researcher at the faculty of management and business, Tampere University. Her research interests include leadership, management, and governance; (sport) organizations and gender. Her work has been published in scholarly journals and edited books including, *Sport in Society*, *International Journal of Sport Policy and Politics*, *Administrative Sciences* and Routledge. At the moment she is co-editing a book about governing future from a Nordic perspective and serves as a board member in the Finnish Association for Administrative Studies.

Strinivasan S. Pillay is the head of department for public management and economics, faculty of management sciences at the Durban University of Technology. His areas of specialization and interests include the following: public sector human resource management, strategic planning, leadership, change management, managing diversity and intercultural relations, local government management, disaster and risk management, community engagement, international education and partnerships, work integrated learning (placement of students in government departments for their training) and COIL. He is an accredited facilitator, assessor, and moderator to undertake training for the three spheres of government. He has worked extensively and continues to be actively involved with the national, provincial and local governments. Dr. Pillay has presented papers at local, national and international conferences and is involved in the supervision of masters and doctoral students. He serves on numerous structures of the university and the public service.

Arianna Pitino, PhD, is associate professor of public law at the University of Genoa, in Italy. Her areas of interest and research include the right to health in Italy and in Canada (protection of the right and organizational profiles), gender equality (political representation, work, and violence), the protection of rights and the integration of third-country nationals. She is the author of more than 70 articles and two books. She is the scientific coordinator of the Genoa research unit on "The pandemic and the constitutional law studies on health rights and healthcare organization" (funded Project of Relevant National Interest–PRIN2020); she teaches public law, equal opportunities law, migration law, and healthcare law; she is a member in the editorial board of the journals *Corti Supreme e Salute e DPCEonline*; moreover, since 2021 she has been the president of the Committee for Equal Opportunities of the Genoa University.

Jyoti Rattan is full professor of law at Panjab University, Chandigarh, India. Did PhD (law) as UGC Senior Research Fellow, is University Gold Medallist in LLM, stood 2nd in University in MSc (Chemistry) and University Merit Position holder in BSc. Published 22 books in diverse legal fields including international law, United Nations and human rights, cyber law and information technology, taxation laws, right to information (RTI), company law, law of contract and women and law. Also published several research articles in reputed national and international journals and chapters in books including in SAGE Open, chapter in book published by Government of South Korea National Computerization Agency, *Indian Law Institute Law Review*, *Indian Journal of Public Administration* (IJPA) in association with Sage Publications and professional article published in the *International Journal for Court Administration* (IJCA). Presented research papers, won awards at national and international conferences organized in India and abroad including the Indian Science Congress organized by the International Institute of Administrative Sciences, Belgium, in Switzerland, South Korea, Abu Dhabi, United Arab Emirates; besides Mexico, Thailand, Greece, South Africa, Turkey, Morocco, Tunisia and Italy; European Group of Public Administration (EGPA) 2020 and 2022 World Conferences; As Nodal Officer In-charge organized G-20 Meet in collaboration with Govt. of India, at PU, March 2023; 2nd Asia CLE Conference, Chiang Mai, Thailand, May 2023.

Vijay Rattan is consultant to the United Nations; member, International Institute of Administrative Sciences (IIAS), Belgium; life member, Indian Society of International Law (ISIL), New Delhi; life member, Indian Institute of Public Administration (IIPA), New Delhi; formerly, professor of public administration, Panjab University, Chandigarh, India. In 2009, as a United Nations consultant (Department of Economic and Social Affairs, New York, Index No. 991772) at the World Civic Forum, in Seoul, South Korea, delivered lecture on e-governance and the role of ICTs for the implementation of the millennium development Goals (MDGs). In 2007, as a consultant to United Nations, New York, contributed to the Workshop on Knowledge Management, at the 7th Global Forum on "Reinventing Government: Building Trust in Government," organized by the United Nations at the UN Headquarters at Vienna, Austria. Also did assignments as a consultant to UNICEF, to government of India and to state government, besides USAID and CARE-INDIA. His two books on sustainable human development were highly acclaimed by United Nations Development Programme (UNDP), New York and UNICEF. Besides on Republic Day in Chandigarh, in 1997, was felicitated by the President of India, at a special function held in the Rashtrapati Bhawan (president's house), New Delhi.

Maliga Reddy is an associate director in the Department of Public Management and Economics at the Durban University of Technology (DUT). She represents DUT on the various national, provincial and local structures both in a professional as well as an academic capacity. She was part of the National Disaster Management Project Team that was instrumental in the development of the National Disaster Management Education and Training Framework for South Africa. Mal served on the USAID/North-West University Steering Committee responsible for the project on the Disaster Risk Reduction Knowledge Shop, creating, sharing and exchange of information and practices in disaster risk reduction. She serves on the Professional Board for Disaster Management: Disaster Management Institute of Southern Africa (DMISA). Her professional achievement was her election as the president of the Disaster Management Institute of Southern Africa (2012–2014). She continues her involvement by serving on the executive committee/council and board of the Institute. Her areas on interest and research includes, public management, leadership, local government management, disaster risk management. She serves on the editorial board of *JAMBA—Journal of Disaster Risk Studies and Reviews* for various journals, including: the *Journal of Human Ecology* (JHE) and *Alternation: Interdisciplinary Journal for the Study of the Arts and Humanities* in Southern Africa.

Anna Simonati, PhD, is full professor of administrative law at Trento University, in Italy. Her areas of interest include the principles of fair administration (with a focus on the modern legal tools for participation and transparency), land planning, cultural heritage law, gender studies from a legal point of view. She is the author of more than 200 articles and 3 books, co-editor of some books on different topics of public law. She is a member of numerous scientific associations, among which the American Society for Public Administration, and in such context she serves in the executive committee of SEIGov as global membership director. She is the co-coordinator of the Permanent Study Group on Social Innovation, Commons and Administration in IIAS (International Institute of Administrative Sciences), and of the Permanent Study Group on Administration, Diversity and Equal Treatment in EGPA (European Group for Public Administration). This is coupled with other international activities in the field of public law, such as the participation in ELI (European Law Institute)—especially in the Administrative Law Study Group and recently as a member in the Consultative Committee of the Project on Artificial Intelligence and Public Administration; moreover, she is also a field editor of the *Central European Public Administration Review* and a member in the editorial board of the *Administrative and Environmental Law Review*.

Alexandra Weiss, Mag. Dr., is a political scientist. She is the coordinator in the Office for Equality and Gender Studies at the University of Innsbruck (part time), freelance scientist, and lecturer. Her main research topics: gender policy; gender and diversity; labour and working conditions; regulation of sexuality.

Mariangela Zoli is associate professor of economic policy at the Department of Economics and Finance, Tor Vergata University of Rome, where she lectures in economic and financial policy and public economics. Her current research interests focus on gender issues and behavioral and experimental economics applied to pro-environmental behaviors. Her research is broadly within the area of environmental economics: environmental policies, emissions trading taxation, financial barriers to eco-innovation, individual waste management and energy behaviors. Research experiences include participation in Italian (PRIN) and European research projects. She is a member of the Tor Vergata Unit at SEEDS Interuniversity Research Centre and a fellow at CEIS Research Centre. She is co-author of papers published in peer-reviewed journals (including *Ecological Economics, Energy Economics, Climate Policy, European Economic Review*) and book chapters.

Printed in the United States
by Baker & Taylor Publisher Services